Open Veins of Latin America

Open Veins of Latin America

FIVE CENTURIES OF THE PILLAGE OF A CONTINENT

Eduardo Galeano

Translated by
Cedric Belfrage

Foreword by
Isabel Allende

Three Essays
COLLECTIVE

First Edition October 2008
Reprinted 2015, 2016, 2025

ISBN 978-81-88789-66-5

Three Essays Collective
B-957 Palam Vihar, GURGAON (Haryana) 122 017 India
Phone: +91 98681 26587, +91 98683 44843
info@threeessays.com Website: www.threeessays.com
Printed at Replika Press Pvt. Ltd., India

"We have maintained a silence closely resembling stupidity."

—*From the Revolutionary Proclamation of the Junta Tuitiva, La Paz, July 16, 1809*

Contents

FOREWORD BY ISABEL ALLENDE . . . ix

FROM IN DEFENSE OF THE WORD . . . xiv

ACKNOWLEDGEMENT . . . xvi

INTRODUCTION: 120 MILLION CHILDREN IN THE EYE OF THE HURRICANE . . . 1

PART I: MANKIND'S POVERTY AS A CONSEQUENCE OF THE WEALTH OF THE LAND

1. LUST FOR GOLD, LUST FOR SILVER . . . 11
2. KING SUGAR AND OTHER AGRICULTURAL MONARCHS . . . 59
3. THE INVISIBLE SOURCES OF POWER . . . 134

PART II: DEVELOPMENT IS A VOYAGE WITH MORE SHIPWRECKS THAN NAVIGATORS

4. TALES OF PREMATURE DEATH . . . 173
5. THE CONTEMPORARY STRUCTURE OF PLUNDER . . . 205

PART III: SEVEN YEARS AFTER . . . 263

REFERENCES . . . 287

INDEX . . . 307

Foreword
Isabel Allende

Many years ago, when I was young and still believed that the world could be shaped according to our best intentions and hopes, someone gave me a book with a yellow cover that I devoured in two days with such emotion that I had to read it again a couple more times to absorb all its meaning: *Open Veins of Latin America*, by Eduardo Galeano.

In the early 1970s, Chile was a small island in the tempestuous sea in which history had plunged Latin America, the continent that appears on the map in the form of an ailing heart. We were in the midst of the Socialist government of Salvador Allende, the first Marxist ever to become president in a democratic election, a man who had a dream of equality and liberty and the passion to make that dream come true. That book with the yellow covers, however, proved that there were no safe islands in our region, we all shared 500 years of exploitation and colonization, we were all linked by a common fate, we all belonged to the same race of the oppressed. If I had been able to read between the lines, I could have concluded that Salvador Allende's government was doomed from the beginning. It was the time of the Cold War, and the United States would not allow a leftist experiment to succeed in what Henry Kissinger called "its backyard." The Cuban Revolution was enough; no other socialist project would be tolerated, even if it was the result of a democratic election. On September 11, 1973, a military coup ended a century of democratic tradition in Chile and started the long reign of General Augusto Pinochet. Similar coups followed in other countries, and soon half the continent's population was living in terror. This was a strategy designed in Washington and imposed upon the Latin American people by the economic and political forces of the right. In every instance the military acted as mercenaries to the privileged groups in power. Repression was organized on a large scale; torture, concentration camps, censorship, imprisonment without trial, and summary executions became common practices. Thousands of people "disappeared," masses of exiles and refugees left their countries running for their lives. New wounds were added to the old and recent scars that the continent had endured. In this political context, *Open Veins of Latin America* was published. This book made Eduardo Galeano famous overnight, although he was already a well-known political journalist in Uruguay.

Like all his countrymen, Eduardo wanted to be a soccer player. He also wanted to be a saint, but as it turned out, he ended up committing most of the deadly sins, as he once confessed. "I have never killed anybody, it is true, but it is because I lacked the courage or the time, not because I lacked the desire." He worked for a weekly political magazine *Marcha,* and at twenty-eight he became the director of the important newspaper *Epoca,* in Uruguay. He wrote *Open Veins of Latin America* in three months, in the last ninety nights of 1970, while he worked during the day in the university, editing books, magazines, and newsletters.

> Those were bad times in Uruguay. Planes and ships left filled with young people who were escaping from poverty and mediocrity in a country that forced them to be old at twenty, and that produced more violence than meat or wool. After an eclipse that had lasted a century, the military invaded the scene with the excuse of fighting the Tupamaro guerrilla. They sacrificed the spaces of liberty and devoured the civil power, which was less and less civil.

By the middle of 1973 there was a military coup, he was imprisoned, and shortly afterward he went into exile in Argentina, where he created the magazine *Crisis.* But by 1976 there was a military coup also in Argentina, and the "dirty war" against intellectuals, leftists, journalists, and artists began. Galeano initiated another exile, this time in Spain, with Helena Villagra, his wife. In Spain he wrote *Days and Nights of*

Love and War, a beautiful book about memory, and soon after he began a sort of conversation with the soul of America: *Memories of Fire* a massive fresco of Latin American history since the pre-Colombian era to modern times. "I imagined that America was a woman and she was telling in my ear her secrets, the acts of love and violations that had created her." He worked on these three volumes for eight years, writing by hand. "I am not particularly interested in saving time: I prefer to enjoy it." Finally, in 1985, after a plebiscite defeated the military dictatorship in Uruguay, Galeano was able to return to his country. His exile had lasted eleven years, but he had not learned to be invisible or silent; as soon as he set foot in Montevideo he was again working to fortify the fragile democracy that replaced the military junta, and he continued to defy the authorities and risk his life to denounce the crimes of the dictatorship.

Eduardo Galeano has also published several works of fiction and poetry; he is the author of innumerable articles, interviews, and lectures; he has obtained many awards, honorary degrees, and recognition for his literary talent and his political activism. He is one of the most interesting authors ever to come out of Latin America, a region known for its great literary names. His work is a mixture of meticulous detail, political conviction, poetic flair, and good storytelling. He has walked up and down Latin America listening to the voices of the poor and the oppressed, as well as those of the leaders and the intellectuals. He has lived with Indians, peasants, guerrillas, soldiers, artists, and outlaws; he has talked to presidents, tyrants, martyrs, priests, heroes, bandits, desperate mothers, and patient prostitutes. He has suffered tropical fevers, walked in the jungle, and survived a massive heart attack; he has been persecuted by repressive regimes as well as by fanatical terrorists. He has opposed military dictatorships and all forms of brutality and exploitation, taking unthinkable risks in defense of human rights. He has more first-hand knowledge of Latin America than anybody else I can think of, and uses it to tell the world of the dreams and disillusions, the hopes and the failures of its people. He is an adventurer with a talent for writing, a compassionate heart, and a soft sense of humor. "We live in a world that treats the dead better than the living. We, the living are askers of questions and givers of answers, and we have other grave defects unpardonable by a system that believes death, like money, improves people."

All these talents were already obvious in his first book, *Open Veins of Latin America,* as was his genius for story-telling. I know Eduardo Galeano personally: he can produce an endless stream of stories with no apparent effort, for an undetermined period of time. Once we were both stranded in a beach hotel in Cuba with no transportation and no air-conditioning. For several days he entertained me with his amazing stories over piña coladas. This almost superhuman talent for storytelling is what makes *Open Veins of Latin America* so easy to read—like a pirate's novel, as he once described it—even for those who are not particularly knowledgeable about political or economic matters. The book flows with the grace of a tale; it is impossible to put it down. His arguments, his rage, and his passion would be overwhelming if they were not expressed with such superb style, with such masterful timing and suspense. Galeano denounces exploitation with uncompromising ferocity, yet this book is almost poetic in its description of solidarity and human capacity for survival in the midst of the worst kind of despoliation. There is a mysterious power in Galeano's story-telling. He uses his craft to invade the privacy of the reader's mind, to persuade him or her to read and to continue reading to the very end, to surrender to the charm of his writing and the power of his idealism.

In his *Book of Embraces,* Eduardo has a story that I love. To me it is a splendid metaphor of writing in general and his writing in particular.

> There was an old and solitary man who spent most of his time in bed. There were rumors that he had a treasure hidden in his house. One day some thieves broke in, they searched everywhere and found a chest in the cellar. They went off with it and when they opened it they found that it was filled with letters. They were the love letters the old man had received all over the course of his long life. The thieves were going to burn the letters, but they talked it over and finally decided to return them. One by one. One a week. Since then, every Monday at noon, the old man would be waiting for the postman to appear. As soon as he saw him, the old man would start running and the postman, who knew all about it, held the letter in his hand. And even St. Peter could hear the beating of that heart, crazed with joy at receiving a message from a woman.

Isn't this the playful substance of literature? An event transformed by poetic truth. Writers are like those thieves, they take something that is real, like the letters, and by a trick of magic they transform it into something totally fresh. In Galeano's tale the letters existed and they belonged to the old man in the first place, but they were kept unread in a dark cellar, they were dead. By the simple trick of mailing them back one by one, those good thieves gave new life to the letters and new illusions to the old man. To me this is admirable in Galeano's work: finding the hidden treasures, giving sparkle to worn-out events, and invigorating the tired soul with his ferocious passion.

Open Veins of Latin America is an invitation to explore beyond the appearance of things. Great literary works like this one wake up consciousness, bring people together, interpret, explain, denounce, keep record, and provoke changes. There is one other aspect of Eduardo Galeano that fascinates me. This man who has so much knowledge and who has—by studying the clues and the signs—developed a sense of foretelling, is an optimist. At the end of *Century of the Wind,* the third volume of *Memory of Fire,* after 600 pages proving the genocide, the cruelty, the abuse, and exploitation exerted upon the people of Latin America, after a patient recount of everything that has been stolen and continues to be stolen from the continent, he writes:

> The tree of life knows that, whatever happens, the warm music spinning around it will never stop. However much death may come, however much blood may flow, the music will dance men and women as long as the air breaths them and the land plows and loves them.

This breath of hope is what moves me the most in Galeano's work. Like thousands of refugees all over the continent, I also had to leave my country after the military coup of 1973. I could not take much with me: some clothes, family pictures, a small bag with dirt from my garden, and two books: an old edition of the *Odes* by Pablo Neruda, and the book with the yellow cover, *Las Venas Abiertas de America Latina.* More than twenty years later I still have that same book with me. That is why I could not miss the opportunity to write this introduction and thank Eduardo Galeano publicly for his stupendous love for freedom, and for his contribution to my awareness as a writer and as a citizen of Latin America. As he said once: "it's worthwhile to die for things without which it's not worthwhile to live."

In Defense of the Word

One writes out of a need to communicate and to commune with others, to denounce that which gives pain and to share that which gives happiness. One writes against one's solitude and against the solitude of others. One assumes that literature transmits knowledge and affects the behavior and language of those who read. . . . One writes, in reality, for the people whose luck or misfortune one identifies with—the hungry, the sleepless, the rebels, and the wretched of this earth—and the majority of them are illiterate.

. . . How can those of us who want to work for a literature that helps to make audible the voice of the voiceless function in the context of this reality? Can we make ourselves heard in the midst of a deaf-mute culture? The small freedom conceded to writers, is it not at times a proof of our failure? How far can we go? Whom can we reach?

. . . To awaken consciousness, to reveal identity—can literature claim a better function in these times? . . . in these lands?

. . . Our own fate as Latin American writers is linked to the need for profound social transformations. To narrate is to give oneself: it seems obvious that literature, as an effort to communicate fully, will continue to be blocked . . . so long as misery and illiteracy exist, and so long as the possessors of power continue to carry on with impunity their policy of collective imbecilization through . . . the mass media.

. . . Great changes, deep structural changes, will be necessary in our countries if we writers are to go beyond . . . the elites, if we are to express ourselves. . . . In an incarcerated society, free literature can exist only as denunciation and hope.

. . . We are what we do, especially what we do to change what we are. . . .

In this respect a "revolutionary" literature written for the convinced is just as much an abandonment as is a conservative literature devoted to the . . . contemplation of one's own navel. . . .

Our effectiveness depends on our capacity to be audacious and astute, clear and appealing. I would hope that we can create a language more fearless and beautiful than that used by conformist writers to greet the twilight.

. . . In Latin America a literature is taking shape and acquiring strength, a literature . . . that does not propose to bury our dead, but to immortalize them; that refuses to stir the ashes but rather attempts to light the fire . . . perhaps it may help to preserve for the generations to come . . . "the true name of all things."

Eduardo Galeano, 1978
translation by Bobbye Ortiz
from Days And Nights of Love and War *(1983)*
reprinted by Monthly Review Press to honor Judy Ruben

Acknowledgement

This book would not have been possible without the collaboration, in one form or another, of Sergio Bagú, Luis Carlos Benvenuto, Fernando Carmona, Adicea Castillo, Alberto Couriel, Andre Gunder Frank, Rogelio García Lupo, Miguel Labarca, Carlos Lessa, Samuel Lichtensztejn, Juan A. Oddone, Adolfo Perelman, Artur Poerner, Carlos Quijano, Germán Rama, Darcy Ribeiro, Orlando Rojas, Julio Rossiello, Paulo Schilling, Karl-Heinz Stanzick, Vivian Trías, and Daniel Vidart. To them, and to the many friends who have encouraged me in the task of these recent years, I dedicate the result, of which they are of course innocent.

Montevideo, 1970

Introduction: 120 Million Children in the Eye of the Hurricane

The division of labor among nations is that some specialize in winning and others in losing. Our part of the world, known today as Latin America, was precocious: it has specialized in losing ever since those remote times when Renaissance Europeans ventured across the ocean and buried their teeth in the throats of the Indian civilizations. Centuries passed, and Latin America perfected its role. We are no longer in the era of marvels when fact surpassed fable and imagination was shamed by the trophies of conquest—the lodes of gold, the mountains of silver. But our region still works as a menial. It continues to exist at the service of others' needs, as a source and reserve of oil and iron, of copper and meat, of fruit and coffee, the raw materials and foods destined for rich countries which profit more from consuming them than Latin America does from producing them. The taxes collected by the buyers are much higher than the prices received by the sellers; and after all, as Alliance for Progress coordinator Covey T. Oliver said in July 1968, to speak of fair prices is a "medieval" concept, for we are in the era of free trade.

The more freedom is extended to business, the more prisons have to be built for those who suffer from that business. Our inquisitor-hangman systems function not only for the dominating external markets; they also provide gushers of profit from foreign loans and investments in the dominated internal markets. Back in 1913, President Woodrow Wilson observed: "You hear of 'concessions' to foreign capitalists in Latin America. You do not hear of concessions to foreign capitalists in the United States. They are not granted concessions." He was confident: "States that are obliged . . . to grant concessions are in this condition, that foreign interests are apt to dominate their domestic affairs. . . . ," he said, and he was right.[1] Along the way we have even lost the right to call ourselves Americans, although the Haitians and the Cubans appeared in history as new people a century before the *Mayflower* pilgrims settled on the Plymouth coast. For the world today, America is just the United States; the region we inhabit is a sub-America, a second-class America of nebulous identity.

Latin America is the region of open veins. Everything, from the discovery until our times, has always been transmuted into European—or later United States—capital, and as such has accumulated in distant centers of power. Everything: the soil, its fruits and its mineral-rich depths, the people and their capacity to work and to consume, natural resources and human resources. Production methods and class structure have been successively determined from outside for each area by meshing it into the universal gearbox of capitalism. To each area has been assigned a function, always for the benefit of the foreign metropolis of the moment, and the endless chain of dependency has been endlessly extended. The chain has many more than two links. In Latin America it also includes the oppression of small countries by their larger neighbors and, within each country's frontiers, the exploitation by big cities and ports of their internal sources of food and labor. (Four centuries ago sixteen of today's twenty biggest Latin American cities already existed.)

For those who see history as a competition, Latin America's backwardness and poverty are merely the result of its failure. We lost; others won. But the winners happen to have won thanks to our losing: the history of Latin America's underdevelopment is, as someone has said, an integral part of the history of world capitalism's development. *Our defeat was always implicit in the victory of others; our wealth has always generated our poverty by nourishing the prosperity of others—the empires and their native overseers. In the colonial and neocolonial alchemy, gold changes into scrap metal and food into poison.* Potosí, Zacatecas, and Ouro Prêto became desolate warrens of deep, empty tunnels from which the precious metals had been taken; ruin was the fate of Chile's nitrate pampas and of Amazonia's rubber forests. Northeast Brazil's sugar and Argentina's quebracho belts, and communities around oil-rich Lake Maracaibo, have become painfully aware of the mortality of wealth which nature bestows and imperialism appropriates. The rain that irrigates the centers of imperialist power drowns the vast suburbs of the system. In the same way, and symmetrically, the well-being of our dominating classes—dominating inwardly, dominated from outside—is the curse of our multitudes condemned to exist as beasts of burden.

The gap widens. Around the middle of the last century the world's rich countries enjoyed a 50 percent higher living standard than the poor countries. Development develops inequality: in April 1969 Richard Nixon told the Organization of American States (OAS) that by the end of the twentieth century the United States' per capita income would be fifteen times higher than Latin America's. The strength of the imperialist system as a whole rests on the necessary inequality of its parts, and this inequality assumes ever more dramatic dimensions. The oppressor countries get steadily richer in absolute terms—and much more so in relative terms—through the dynamic of growing disparity. The capitalist "head office" can allow itself the luxury of creating and believing its own myths of opulence, but the poor countries on the capitalist periphery know that myths cannot be eaten. The United States citizen's average income is seven times that of a Latin American and grows ten times faster. And averages are deceptive in view of the abyss that yawns between the many poor and the rich few south of the Rio Grande. According to the United Nations, the amount shared by 6 million Latin Americans at the top of the social pyramid is the same as the amount shared by 140 million at the bottom. There are 60 million *campesinos* whose fortune amounts to $.25 a day. At the other extreme, the pimps of misery accumulate $5 billion in their private Swiss or U.S. bank accounts. Adding insult to injury, they squander in sterile ostentation and luxury, and in unproductive investments constituting no less than half the total investment, the capital that Latin America could devote to the replacement, extension, and generation of job-creating means of production. Harnessed as they have always been to the constellation of imperialist power, our ruling classes have no interest whatsoever in determining whether patriotism might not prove more profitable than treason, and whether begging is really the only formula for international politics. Sovereignty is mortgaged because "there's no other way." The oligarchies' cynical alibis confuse the impotence of a social class with the presumed empty destinies of their countries.

Says Josué de Castro: "I, who have received an international peace prize, think that, unhappily, there is no other solution than violence for Latin America." In the eye of this hurricane 120 million children are stirring. Latin America's population grows as does no other: it has more than tripled in half a century. One child dies of disease or hunger every minute, but in the year 2000 there will be 650 million Latin Americans, half of whom will be under fifteen: a time bomb. Among the 280 million Latin Americans of today, 50 million are unemployed or underemployed and about 100 million are illiterate; half of them live in crowded, unhealthy slums. Latin America's three largest markets—Argentina, Brazil, and Mexico—together consume less than France or West Germany, although their combined population considerably exceeds that of any European country. In proportion to population, Latin America today produces less food than it did before World War II, and at constant prices there has been a threefold decline in its per capita exports since the eve of the 1929 crisis.

For its foreign masters and for our commission-agent bourgeoisie, who have sold their souls to the devil at a price that would have shamed Faust, the system is perfectly rational; but for no one else, since the more it develops, the greater its disequilibrium, its tensions, and its contradictions. Even industrialization—coming late and in dependent form, and comfortably coexisting with the latifundia and the structures of inequality—helps to spread unemployment rather than to relieve it; poverty is extended, wealth concentrated in the area where an ever multiplying army of idle hands is available. New factories are built in the privileged poles of development—São Paulo, Buenos Aires, Mexico City—but less and less labor is needed. The system did not foresee this small headache, this surplus of people. And the people keep reproducing. They make love with enthusiasm and without precaution. Ever more people are left beside the road, without work in the countryside, where the latifundios reign with their vast extensions of idle land, without work in the city where the machine is king. The system vomits people. North American missionaries sow pills, diaphragms, intrauterine devices, condoms, and marked calendars, but reap children. Latin American children obstinately continue getting born, claiming their natural right to a place in the sun in these magnificent lands which could give to all what is now denied to almost all.

At the beginning of November 1968 Richard Nixon loudly confirmed that the Alliance for Progress was seven years old and that malnutrition and food shortages had nevertheless intensified in Latin America. A few months earlier, in April, George W. Ball wrote in *Life:* "But at least for the next several decades, the discontent of poorer nations does not threaten world destruction. Shameful as it undoubtedly may be, the world has lived at least two-thirds poor and one-third rich for generations. Unjust as it may be, the power of poor countries is limited."[2] Ball had headed the U.S. delegation to the First Conference on Trade and Development in Geneva, and had voted against nine of the twelve general principles approved by the conference for removing some of the handicaps of the underdeveloped countries in international trade.

The human murder by poverty in Latin America is secret; every year, without making a sound, three Hiroshima bombs explode over communities that have become accustomed to suffering with clenched teeth. This systematic violence is not apparent but is real and constantly increasing: its holocausts are not made known in the sensational press but in Food and Agricultural Organization statistics. Ball says that it is still possible to act with impunity because the poor cannot set off a world war, but the Imperium is worried: unable to multiply the dinner, it does what it can to suppress the diners. "Fight poverty, kill a beggar!" some genius of black humor scrawled on a wall in La Paz. What do the heirs to Malthus propose but to kill all the beggars-to-be before they are born? Robert McNamara, the World Bank president who was chairman of Ford and then secretary of defense, has called the population explosion the greatest obstacle to progress in Latin America; the World Bank, he says, will give priority in its loans to countries that implement birth control plans. McNamara notes with regret that the brains of the poor do 25 percent less thinking, and the World Bank technocrats (who have already been born) set computers humming to produce labyrinthine abracadabras on the advantages of not being born: "If," one of the Bank's documents assures us, "a developing country with an average per capita income of $150 to $200 a year succeeds in reducing its fertility by 50 percent in a period of twenty-five years, at the end of thirty years its per capita income will be higher by at least 40 percent than the level it would otherwise have achieved, and twice as high after sixty years." Lyndon B. Johnson's remark has become famous: "Let us act on the fact that less than $5 invested in population control is worth $100 invested in economic growth."[3] Dwight D. Eisenhower prophesied that if the world's inhabitants continued multiplying at the same rate, not only would the danger of revolution be increased, but there would also be a lowering of living standards for all peoples, including his own.

The United States is more concerned than any other country with spreading and imposing family planning in the farthest outposts. Not only the government, but the Rockefeller and the Ford foundations as well, have nightmares about millions of children advancing like locusts over the horizon from the third world. Plato and Aristotle considered the question before Malthus and McNamara; in our day this global offensive plays a well-defined role. Its aim is to justify the very unequal income distribution between countries and social classes, to convince the poor that poverty is the result of the children they don't avoid having, and to dam the rebellious advance of the masses. While intrauterine devices compete with bombs and machine-gun salvos to arrest the growth of the Vietnamese population, in Latin America it is more hygienic and effective to kill *guerrilleros* in the womb than in the mountains or the streets. Various U.S. missions have sterilized thousands of women in Amazonia, although this is the least populated habitable zone on our planet. Most Latin American countries have no real surplus of people; on the contrary, they have too few. Brazil has thirty-eight times fewer inhabitants per square mile than Belgium, Paraguay has forty-nine times fewer than England, Peru has thirty-two times fewer than Japan. Haiti and El Salvador, the human antheaps of Latin America, have lower population densities than Italy. The pretexts invoked are an insult to the intelligence; the real intentions anger us. No less than half the territory of Bolivia, Brazil, Chile, Ecuador, Paraguay, and Venezuela has no inhabitants at all. No Latin American population grows less than Uruguay's—a country of old folk—yet no nation has taken such a beating in recent years, with a crisis that would seem to drag it into the last circle of hell. Uruguay is empty, and its fertile lands could provide food for infinitely more people than those who now suffer in such penury.

Over a century ago a Guatemalan foreign minister said prophetically: "It would be strange if the remedy should come from the United States, the same place which brings us the disease." Now that the Alliance for Progress is dead and buried the Imperium proposes, more in panic than in generosity, to solve Latin America's problems by eliminating Latin Americans; Washington has reason to suspect that the poor peoples don't *prefer* to be poor. But it is impossible to desire the end without desiring the means. Those who deny liberation to Latin America also deny our only possible rebirth, and incidentally absolve the existing structures from blame. Our youth multiplies, rises, listens: what does the voice of the system offer? The system speaks a surrealist language. In lands that are empty it proposes to avoid births; in countries where capital is plentiful but wasted it suggests that capital is lacking; it describes as "aid" the deforming orthopedics of loans and the draining of wealth that results from foreign investment; it calls upon big landowners to carry out agrarian reforms and upon the oligarchy to practice social justice. The class struggle only exists, we are told, because foreign agents stir it up; but social classes do exist and the oppression of one by the other is known as the Western way of life. The Marines undertake their criminal expeditions only to restore order and social peace; the dictatorships linked to Washington lay foundations in their jails for the law-abiding state, and ban strikes and smash trade unions to protect the freedom to work.

Is everything forbidden us except to fold our arms? Poverty is not written in the stars; underdevelopment is not one of God's mysterious designs. Redemptive years of revolution pass; the ruling classes wait and meanwhile pronounce hellfire anathema on everybody. In a sense the right wing is correct in identifying itself with tranquillity and order: it is an order of daily humiliation for the majority, but an order nonetheless; it is a tranquillity in which injustice continues to be unjust and hunger to be hungry. If the future turns out to be a Pandora's box, the conservative has reason to shout, "I have been betrayed." And the ideologists of impotence, the slaves who look at themselves with the master's eyes, are not slow to join in the outcry. The bronze eagle of the *Maine,* thrown down on the day the Cuban Revolution triumphed, now lies abandoned, its wings broken, in a doorway in the old town in Havana. Since that day in Cuba, other countries have set off on different roads on the experiment of change: perpetuation of the existing order of things is perpetuation of the crime. Recovery of the resources that have always been usurped is recovery of our destiny.

The ghosts of all the revolutions that have been strangled or betrayed through Latin America's tortured history emerge in the new experiments, as if the present had been foreseen and begotten by the contradictions of the past. History is a prophet who looks back: because of what was, and against what was, it announces what will be. And so this book, which seeks to chronicle our despoliation and at the same time explain how the current mechanisms of plunder operate, will present in close proximity the caravelled conquistadors and the jet-propelled technocrats; Hernán Cortés and the Marines; the agents of the Spanish Crown and the International Monetary Fund missions; the dividends from the slave trade and the profits of General Motors. And, too, the defeated heroes and revolutions of our time, the infamies and the dead and resurrected hopes: the fertile sacrifices. When Alexander von Humboldt investigated the customs of the ancient inhabitants of the Bogotá plateau, he found that the Indians called the victims of ritual ceremonies *quihica. Quihica* meant "door"; the death of each chosen victim opened the door to a new cycle of 185 moons.

Part I

Mankind's Poverty as a Consequence of the Wealth of the Land

1. Lust for Gold, Lust for Silver

The Sign of the Cross on the Hilt of the Sword

When Christopher Columbus headed across the great emptiness west of Christendom, he had accepted the challenge of legend. Terrible storms would play with his ships as if they were nutshells and hurl them into the jaws of monsters; the sea serpent, hungry for human flesh, would be lying in wait in the murky depths. According to fifteenth-century man, only 1,000 years remained before the purifying flames of the Last Judgment would destroy the world, and the world was then the Mediterranean Sea with its uncertain horizons: Europe, Africa, Asia. Portuguese navigators spoke of strange corpses and curiously carved pieces of wood that floated in on the west wind, but no one suspected that the world was about to be startlingly extended by a great new land.

America not only lacked a name. The Norwegians did not know they had discovered it long ago, and Columbus himself died convinced that he had reached Asia by the western route. In 1492, when Spanish boats first trod the beaches of the Bahamas, the Admiral thought these islands were an outpost of the fabulous isle of Zipango—Japan. Columbus took along a copy of Marco Polo's book, and covered its margins with notes. The inhabitants of Zipango, said Marco Polo, "have gold in the greatest abundance, its sources being inexhaustible. . . . In this island there are pearls also, in large quantities, of a red color, round in shape, and of great size, equal in value to, or even exceeding that of white pearls."[1] The wealth of Zipango had become known to the Great Kubla Khan, stirring a desire to conquer it, but he had failed. Out of Marco Polo's sparkling pages leaped all the good things of creation: there were nearly 13,000 islands in the Indian seas, with mountains of gold and pearls and twelve kinds of spices in enormous quantities, in addition to an abundance of white and black pepper.

Pepper, ginger, cloves, nutmeg, and cinnamon were as prized as salt in preserving meat against putrefaction and loss of flavor in winter. Spain's Catholic rulers decided to finance the adventure to get direct access to the sources and to free themselves from the burdensome chain of intermediaries and speculators who monopolized the trade in spices and tropical plants, muslins and sidearms, from the mysterious East. The desire for precious metals, the medium of payment in commercial dealings, also sparked the crossing of the sinister seas. All of Europe needed silver; the seams in Bohemia, Saxony, and the Tyrol were almost exhausted.

For Spain it was an era of reconquest: 1492 was not only the year of the discovery of America, the new world born of that error which had such momentous consequences, but also of the recovery of Granada. Early that year Ferdinand of Aragón and Isabella of Castile, whose marriage had linked their dominions, stormed the last Arab redoubt on Spanish soil. It had taken nearly eight centuries to win back what was lost in seven years, and the war of reconquest had drained the royal treasury. But this was a holy war, a Christian war against Islam; and it was no accident that, in that same year of 1492, 150,000 Jews were expelled from the country. Spain achieved unity and reality as a nation wielding swords with the Sign of the Cross on their hilts. Queen Isabella became the patroness of the Holy Inquisition. The feat of discovering America can only be understood in the context of the tradition of crusading wars that prevailed in medieval Castile; the Church needed no prompting to provide a halo for the conquest of unknown lands across the ocean. Pope Alexander VI, who was Spanish, ordained Queen Isabella as proprietor and master of the New World. The expansion of the kingdom of Castile extended God's reign over the earth.

Three years after the discovery Columbus personally directed the military campaign against the natives of Haiti, which he called Española.

A handful of cavalry, 200 foot soldiers, and a few specially trained dogs decimated the Indians. More than 500, shipped to Spain, were sold as slaves in Seville and died miserably. Some theologians protested and the enslavement of Indians was formally banned at the beginning of the sixteenth century. Actually it was not banned but blessed: before each military action the captains of the conquest were required to read to the Indians, without an interpreter but before a notary public, a long and rhetorical *Requerimiento* exhorting them to adopt the holy Catholic faith:

> If you do not, or if you maliciously delay in so doing, I certify that with God's help I will advance powerfully against you and make war on you wherever and however I am able, and will subject you to the yoke and obedience of the Church and of their majesties and take your women and children to be slaves, and as such I will sell and dispose of them as their majesties may order, and I will take your possessions and do you all the harm and damage that I can.[2]

America was the vast kingdom of the Devil, its redemption impossible or doubtful; but the fanatical mission against the natives' heresy was mixed with the fever that New World treasures stirred in the conquering hosts. Bernal Díaz del Castillo, faithful comrade of Hernán Cortés in the conquest of Mexico, wrote that they had arrived in America "to serve God and His Majesty and also to get riches."

At his first landing on San Salvador atoll, Columbus was dazzled by the transparent hues of the Caribbean, the green landscape, the soft clean air, the magnificent birds, and the youths "with size and with good faces and well made" who lived there. He gave the natives "some red caps and strings of beads, and many other trifles of small value, which gave them great pleasure. Wherewith they were much delighted, and this made them so much our friends that it was a marvel to see." They knew nothing of swords, and when these were shown to them they grasped the sharp edges and cut themselves. Meanwhile, as the Admiral relates in his logbook, "I was very attentive to them, and strove to learn if they had any gold. Seeing some of them with little bits of metal hanging at their noses, I gathered from them by signs that by going southward or steering round the island in that direction, there would be found a king who possessed great cups full of gold, and in large quantities."[3] For "of gold is treasure made, and with it he who has it does as he wills in the world and it even sends souls to Paradise."

On his third voyage, Columbus still believed he was in the China Sea when he was off the coast of Venezuela. This did not prevent him from reporting that an endless land which was earthly paradise extended from there. Later Amerigo Vespucci, an early sixteenth-century explorer of the Brazilian coast, reported to Lorenzo de Médicis: "The trees are of such beauty and sweetness that we felt we were in earthly Paradise."[4] * In 1503 Columbus wrote to his monarchs from Jamaica: "When I discovered the Indies, I said they were the greatest rich domain in the world. I spoke of the gold, pearls, precious stones, spices. . . ."

In the Middle Ages a small bag of pepper was worth more than a man's life, but gold and silver were the keys used by the Renaissance to open the doors of paradise in heaven and of capitalist mercantilism on earth. The epic of the Spaniards and Portuguese in America combined propagation of the Christian faith with usurpation and plunder of native wealth. European power stretched out to embrace the world. The virgin lands, bristling with jungles and dangers, fanned the flames of avarice among the captains, the *hidalgos* on horseback, and the ragged soldiers who went out after the spectacular booty of war: they believed in glory, in "the sun of the dead," and in the key to achieving it, which Cortés defined thus: "Fortune favors the daring." Cortés himself had mortgaged everything he owned to equip his Mexican expedition. With a few exceptions—Columbus, Pedrarias Dávila, Magellan—the expeditions of conquest were not financed by the state but by the conquistadors themselves, or by businessmen who put up money for their ventures.

The myth of El Dorado, the golden king, was born: golden were the streets and houses of his kingdom's cities. In search of El Dorado a century after Columbus, Sir Walter Raleigh sailed up the Orinoco and was defeated by its cataracts. The will-o'-the-wisp of the "mountain that gushed silver" became a reality in 1545 with the discovery of Potosí, but before this many adventurers who sailed up the Río Paraná in a vain

* The lawyer Antonio de Léon Pinelo devoted two entire volumes to demonstrating that the Garden of Eden was in America. In *El Paraíso en el Nuevo Mundo* (1656) he had a map of South America showing, in the center, the Garden of Eden watered by the Amazon, the Río de la Plata, the Orinoco, and the Magdalena. The forbidden fruit was the banana. The map showed the exact spot from which Noah's Ark took off at the time of the Flood.

search for the silver spring had died of hunger or disease or pierced by native arrows.

There was indeed gold and silver in large quantities, accumulated in the Mexican plateau and the Andean *altiplano*. In 1519 Cortés told Spain of the fabulous magnitude of Montezuma's Aztec treasure, and fifteen years later there arrived in Seville the gigantic ransom—a roomful of gold and two of silver—which Francisco Pizarro had made the Inca Atahualpa pay before strangling him. Years earlier the Crown had paid the sailors on Columbus's first voyage with gold carried off from the Antilles. The Caribbean island populations finally stopped paying tribute because they had disappeared: they were totally exterminated in the gold mines, in the deadly task of sifting auriferous sands with their bodies half submerged in water, or in breaking up the ground beyond the point of exhaustion, doubled up over the heavy cultivating tools brought from Spain. Many natives of Haiti anticipated the fate imposed by their white oppressors: they killed their children and committed mass suicide. The mid-sixteenth-century historian Fernández de Oviedo interpreted the Antillean holocaust thus: "Many of them, by way of diversion, took poison rather than work, and others hanged themselves with their own hands."[5] *

The Gods Return with Secret Weapons

While passing Tenerife on his first voyage, Columbus had witnessed a great volcanic eruption. It seemed an omen of all that would come later in the immense new lands which, surprisingly, stood athwart the western route to Asia. America was there—at first the subject of conjecture from its endless coasts, then conquered in successive waves like a furious tide beating in. Admirals gave place to governors, ships' crews were converted into invading hosts. Papal bulls had apostolically granted Africa to the Portuguese Crown, and the lands "unknown like those already discovered by your envoys and those to be discovered in the

* His interpretation founded a school. I am amazed to read, in the latest (1970) book by the French technician René Dumont, *Cuba: Is It Socialist?*: "The Indians were not totally exterminated. Their genes subsist in Cuban chromosomes. They felt such an aversion for the tension which continuous work demands that some killed themselves rather than accept forced labor. . . ."

future" to the Crown of Castile. America had been given to Queen Isabella. In 1508 another bull granted the Spanish Crown, in perpetuity, all tithes collected in America. The coveted patronage of the New World Church included a royal prerogative over all ecclesiastical benefices.

The Treaty of Tordesillas, signed in 1494, allowed Portugal to occupy Latin American territories below a dividing line traced by the Pope, and in 1530 Martim Affonso de Sousa founded the first Portuguese communities in Brazil, expelling French intruders. By then the Spaniards, crossing an infinity of hellish jungles and hostile deserts, had advanced far in the process of exploration and conquest. In 1513 the South Pacific glittered before the eyes of Vasco Núñez de Balboa. In the fall of 1522 the eighteen survivors of Ferdinand Magellan's expedition returned to Spain: they had for the first time united both oceans and confirmed that the world was round by circling it. Three years earlier Hernán Cortés's ten ships had sailed from Cuba toward Mexico, and in 1523 Pedro de Alvarado launched the conquest of Central America. Francisco Pizarro, an illiterate pig-breeder, triumphantly entered Cuzco in 1533 and seized the heart of the Inca empire. In 1540 Pedro de Valdivia crossed the Atacama desert and founded Santiago de Chile. The conquistadors penetrated the Chaco and laid bare the New World from Peru to the mouth of the mightiest river on our planet.

There was something of everything among the natives of Latin America: astronomers and cannibals, engineers and Stone Age savages. But none of the native cultures knew iron or the plow, or glass, or gunpowder, or used the wheel except on their votive carts. The civilization from across the ocean that descended upon these lands was undergoing the creative explosion of the Renaissance: Latin America seemed like another invention to be incorporated, along with gunpowder, printing, paper, and the compass, in the bubbling birth of the Modern Age. The unequal development of the two worlds explains the relative ease with which native civilizations succumbed. Cortés landed at Veracruz with no more than 100 sailors and 508 soldiers; he had 16 horses, 32 crossbows, 10 bronze cannon, and a few harquebuses, muskets, and pistols. Pizarro entered Cajamarca with 180 soldiers and 37 horses. That was enough. Yet the Aztec capital, Tenochtitlán, was then five times larger than Madrid and had double the population of Seville, Spain's largest city, and in Peru Pizarro met an army of 100,000 Indians.

The Indians were also defeated by terror. The emperor Montezuma received the first news in his palace: a large hill was moving over the sea. More messengers arrived: "He was very alarmed by the report of how the cannon exploded, how its thunder reverberated, and how it filled one with awe and stunned one's ears. And when it went off, a sort of stone ball came from its entrails and it rained fire." The strangers sat on "deer as high as the rooftops." Their bodies were completely covered, "only their faces can be seen. They are white, as if made of lime. They have yellow hair, although some have black. Long are their beards."[6] Montezuma thought it was the god Quetzalcoatl returning: there had been eight prophesies of this not long before. Hunters had brought him a bird with a round mirror-like crest on its head in which the sunset was reflected; in this mirror Montezuma saw squadrons of warriors marching on Mexico. Quetzalcoatl had come from the east and gone to the east: he was white and bearded. Also white and bearded was Viracocha, the bisexual god of the Incas. And the east was the cradle of the Mayas' hero-ancestors.*

The avenging gods who were now returning to settle accounts with their peoples had armor and coats of mail, lustrous caparisons that deflected arrows and stones; their weapons emitted deadly rays and darkened the air with suffocating smoke. The conquistadors also practiced the arts of treachery and intrigue with refined expertise. They sagely allied themselves with the Tlaxcalans against Montezuma and effectively exploited the split in the Inca empire between the brothers Huáscar and Atahualpa. They knew how to win accomplices for their crimes among the intermediate ruling classes, priests, officials, and defeated soldiers and high Indian chiefs. But they also used other weapons—or, if you prefer, other factors operated objectively for the victory of the invaders. Horses and bacteria, for example.

Horses, like camels, had once been indigenous to Latin America but had become extinct. In Europe, where they were introduced by Arab horsemen, they had proved to be of enormous military and economic value. When they reappeared in Latin America during the conquest, they lent magic powers to the invaders in the natives' astonished eyes.

* These remarkable coincidences have given rise to the hypothesis that the gods of the native religions were really Europeans who reached our shores long before Columbus.[7]

Atahualpa saw the first Spanish soldiers arriving on spirited steeds adorned with plumes and little bells, making thunder and clouds of dust with their swift hooves: panic-stricken, the Inca fell down on his back. The chief Tecum, leading the descendants of the Mayas, beheaded the horse of Pedro de Alvarado with his lance, convinced that it was part of the *conquistador:* Alvarado stood up and killed him. A few horses in medieval war trappings scattered the mass of Indians, sowing terror and death. During the colonizing process, priests and missionaries spread for the superstitious Indians' benefit the tale that horses were of sacred origin, for Santiago, Spain's patron saint, rode a white horse which had won valiant victories against the Moors and the Jews with the aid of Divine Providence.

Bacteria and viruses were the most effective allies. The Europeans brought with them, like biblical plagues, smallpox and tetanus, various lung, intestinal, and venereal diseases, trachoma, typhus, leprosy, yellow fever, and teeth-rotting caries. Smallpox was the first to appear. Must not this unknown and horrible epidemic, which produced burning fever and decomposed the flesh, be a chastisement from the gods? The invaders "moved into Tlaxcala," one native eyewitness reported, "and then the epidemic spread: cough, burning hot pustules." Reported another: "The contagious, oppressive, cruel pustule sickness brought death to many."[8] The Indians died like flies; their organisms had no defense against the new diseases. Those who survived were feeble and useless. The Brazilian anthropologist Darcy Ribeiro estimates that more than half the aboriginal population of America, Australia, and Oceania died from the contamination of first contact with white men.

"They Crave Gold Like Hungry Swine"

Firing their harquebuses, hacking with their swords, and breathing pestilence, the little band of implacable conquistadors advanced into America. The conquered tell us what it was like. After the Cholula massacre Montezuma sent new envoys to Cortés, who was advancing on the Valley of México. They brought gifts of golden collars and quetzal-bird feather banners. The Spaniards "were in seventh heaven," says the Nahuatl text preserved in the Florentine Codex. "They lifted up the gold as if they were monkeys, with expressions of joy, as if it put new life into them and lit up their hearts. As if it were certainly something for which they yearn with a great thirst. Their bodies fatten on it and they hunger violently for it. They crave gold like hungry swine." Later, when Cortés reached Tenochtitlán, the resplendent Aztec capital with 300,000 inhabitants, the Spaniards entered the treasure house, "and then they made a great ball of the gold and set a fire, putting to the flames all that remained no matter how valuable, so that everything burned. As for the gold, the Spaniards reduced it and made bars."

War followed. Finally Cortés, who had lost Tenochtitlán, reconquered it in 1521: "And by then we had no shields left, no clubs, and nothing to eat, we weren't eating anymore." Montezuma, harried by the priests who accused him of treason, had killed himself. Devastated, burned, and littered with corpses, the city fell: "Shields were its defense, but they were not enough. . . ." Cortés had expressed horror at the sacrifices of the Veracruz Indians, who burned children's entrails for a smoke offering to the gods, but there were no limits to his own cruelty in the reconquered city: "And all night long it rained on us." The gallows and torture were not enough, however: the captured treasure never measured up to the Spaniards' imagination, and for years they dug in the lake bottom searching for gold and precious objects presumably hidden by the Indians.

Pedro de Alvarado and his men fell upon Guatemala and "killed so many Indians that it made a river of blood which is called the Olimtepeque," and "the day became red because of all the blood there was on that day." Before the decisive battle, "and seeing Indians tortured, they told the Spaniards not to torture them anymore, that the captains Nehaib and Ixquín—Nehaib in the guise of an eagle and of a lion—had much gold, silver, diamonds, and emeralds for them. Then they gave them to the Spaniards and the Spaniards kept them."[9]

Before Pizarro strangled and decapitated Atahualpa, he got from him a ransom of "gold and silver weighing more than 20,000 marks in fine silver and 1,326,000 escudos in the finest gold." Then Pizarro advanced on Cuzco. His soldiers thought they were entering the city of the Caesars, so dazzling was the capital of the empire, but they proceeded without delay to sack the Temple of the Sun. "Struggling and fighting among each other, each trying to get his hands on the lion's share, the soldiers in their coats of mail trampled on jewels and images and pounded the gold utensils with hammers to reduce them to a more portable size. . . . They tossed all the temple's gold into a melting pot to turn it into bars: the laminae that covered the walls, the marvelous representations of trees, birds, and other objects in the garden."[10]

Today in the enormous bare plaza at the center of Mexico City the Catholic cathedral rises on the ruins of Tenochtitlán's greatest temple and the government palace occupies the site where Cuauhtémoc, the Aztec chief martyred by Cortés, had his residence. Tenochtitlán was razed. In Peru, Cuzco suffered the same fate, but the conquistadors could not completely destroy its massive walls and this testimony in stone to the Inca's colossal architecture can still be seen in the bases of the colonial buildings.

The Silver Cycle: The Splendors of Potosí

They say that even the horses were shod with silver in the great days of the city of Potosí. The church altars and the wings of cherubim in processions for the Corpus Christi celebration in 1658, were made of silver: the streets from the cathedral to the church of Recoletos were completely resurfaced with silver bars. In Potosí, silver built temples and palaces, monasteries and gambling dens; it prompted tragedies and fiestas, led to the spilling of blood and wine, fired avarice, and unleashed extravagance and adventure. The sword and the cross marched together in the conquest and plunder of Latin America, and captains and ascetics, knights and evangelists, soldiers and monks came together in Potosí to help themselves to its silver. Molded into cones and ingots, the viscera of the Cerro Rico—the rich hill—substantially fed the development of Europe. "Worth a Peru" was the highest possible praise of a person or a thing after Pizarro took Cuzco, but once the Cerro had been discovered Don Quixote de la Mancha changed the words: "Worth a Potosí," he says to Sancho. This jugular vein of the viceroyalty, America's fountain of silver, had 120,000 inhabitants by the census of 1573. Only twenty-eight years had passed since the city sprouted out of the Andean wilderness and already, as if by magic, it had the same population as London and more than Seville, Madrid, Rome, or Paris. A new census in 1650 gave Potosí a population of 160,000. It was one of the world's biggest and richest cities, ten times bigger than Boston—at a time when New York had not even begun to call itself by that name.

Potosí's history did not begin with the Spaniards. Before the conquest the Inca Huayna Cápaj had heard his vassals talk of the Sumaj Orko, the beautiful hill, and he was finally able to see it when, having fallen ill, he had himself taken to the thermal springs of Tarapaya. From the straw-hut village of Cantumarca the Inca's eyes contemplated for the first time that perfect cone which rises proudly between the mountain peaks. He was awestruck by its reddish hues, slender form, and giant size, as people have continued to be through ensuing centuries. But the Inca suspected that it must conceal precious stones and rich metals in its bowels, and he wanted to add new decorations to the Temple of the Sun in Cuzco. The gold and silver that the Incas took from the mines of Colque Porco and Andacaba did not leave the kingdom: they were not used commercially but for the adoration of the gods. Indian miners had hardly dug their flints into the beautiful Cerro's veins of silver when a deep, hollow voice struck them to the ground. Emerging as loud as thunder from the depths of the wilderness, the voice said in Quechua: "This is not for you; God is keeping these riches for those who come from afar." The Indians fled in terror and the Inca, before departing from the Cerro, changed its name. It became "Potojsi," which means to thunder, burst, explode.

"Those who come from afar" took little time in coming, although Huayna Cápaj was dead by the time the captains of the conquest made their way in. In 1545 the Indian Huallpa, running in pursuit of an escaped llama, had to pass the night on the Cerro. It was intensely cold and he lit a fire. By its light he saw a white and shining vein—pure silver. The Spanish avalanche was unleashed.

Wealth flowed like water. The Holy Roman Emperor, Charles V, showed his gratitude by bestowing on Potosí the title of Imperial City and a shield with the inscription: "I am rich Potosí, treasure of the world, king of the mountains, envy of kings." Only eleven years after Huallpa's discovery the new-born Imperial City celebrated the coronation of Philip II with twenty-four days of festivities costing 8 million *pesos duros*. The Cerro was the most potent of magnets. Hard as life was at its base, at an altitude of nearly 14,000 feet the place was flooded with treasure hunters who took the bitter cold as if it were a tax on living there. Suddenly a rich and disorderly society burst forth beside the silver, and Potosí became "the nerve center of the kingdom," in the words of Viceroy Antonio de Mendoza. By the beginning of the seventeenth century it had thirty-six magnificently decorated churches, thirty-six gambling houses, and fourteen dance academies. Salons, theaters, and fiesta stage-settings had the finest tapestries, curtains, heraldic emblazonry, and wrought gold and silver; multicolored damasks and cloths of gold and silver hung from the balconies of houses. Silks and fabrics came from Granada, Flanders, and Calabria; hats from Paris and London; diamonds from Ceylon; precious stones from India; pearls from Panama; stockings from Naples; crystal from Venice; carpets from Persia; perfumes from Arabia; porcelain from China. The ladies sparkled with diamonds, rubies, and pearls; the gentlemen sported the finest embroidered fabrics from Holland. Bullfights were followed by tilting contests, and love and pride inspired frequent medieval-style duels with emerald-studded, gaudily plumed helmets, gold filigree saddles and stirrups, Toledo swords, and richly caparisoned Chilean ponies.

In 1579 the royal judge Matienzo complained: "There is never a shortage of novelty, scandal, and wantonness." Potosí had at the time 800 professional gamblers and 120 famous prostitutes, whose resplendent salons were thronged with wealthy miners. In 1608 Potosí celebrated the feast of the Holy Sacrament with six days of plays and six nights of masked balls, eight days of bullfights and three of fiestas, two of tournaments and other dissipations.

Spain Owned the Cow, Others Drank the Milk

Between 1545 and 1558 the prolific silver mines of Potosí, in what is now Bolivia, and of Zacatecas and Guanajuato in Mexico, were discovered, and the mercury amalgam process, which made possible the exploitation of the lowest-grade silver, began to be used. The "silver rush" quickly eclipsed gold mining. In the mid-seventeenth century silver constituted more than 99 percent of mineral exports from Spanish America. Latin America was a huge mine, with Potosí as its chief center. Some excessively enthusiastic Bolivian writers insist that in three centuries Spain got enough metal from Potosí to make a silver bridge from the tip of the Cerro to the door of the royal palace across the ocean. This is certainly fanciful, but even the reality stretches one's imagination to the limit: the flow of silver achieved gigantic dimensions. The large-scale clandestine export of Latin American silver as contraband to the Philippines, to China, and to Spain itself is not taken into account by Earl Hamilton, who nevertheless cites, in his well-known work on the subject, astounding figures based on data from the Casa de Contratación in Seville.[11] Between 1503 and 1660, 185,000 kilograms of gold and 16,000,000 of silver arrived at the Spanish port of Sanlúcar de Barrameda. Silver shipped to Spain in little more than a century and a half exceeded three times the total European reserves—and it must be remembered that these official figures are not complete.

The metals taken from the new colonial dominions not only stimulated Europe's economic development; one may say that they made it possible. Even the effect of the Persian treasure seized and poured into the Hellenic world by Alexander the Great cannot be compared with Latin America's formidable contribution to the progress of other regions. Not, however, to that of Spain, although Spain owned the sources of Latin American silver. As it used to be said in the seventeenth century, "Spain is like a mouth that receives the food, chews it, and passes it on to the other organs, retaining no more than a fleeting taste of the particles that happen to stick in its teeth."[12] The Spaniards owned the cow, but others drank the milk. The kingdom's creditors, mostly foreigners, systematically emptied the "Green Strongroom" of Seville's Casa de Contratación, which was supposed to guard, under three keys in three different hands, the treasure flowing from Latin America.

The Crown was mortgaged. It owed nearly all of the silver shipments, before they arrived, to German, Genoese, Flemish, and Spanish bankers. The same fate befell most of the duty collected in Spain itself: in 1543, 65 percent of all the royal revenues went to paying annuities on debts. Only in a minimal way did Latin American silver enter the Spanish economy; although formally registered in Seville, it ended in the hands of the Fuggers, the powerful bankers who had advanced to the Pope the funds needed to finish St. Peter's, and of other big moneylenders of the period, such as the Welsers, the Shetzes, and the Grimaldis. The silver also went to paying for the export of *non-Spanish* merchandise to the New World.

The rich empire had a poor metropolis, although the illusion of prosperity blew increasingly large bubbles into the air. The Crown kept opening up new war fronts, while on Spanish soil the aristocracy devoted itself to extravagance, and priests and warriors, nobles and beggars, multiplied as dizzily as living costs and interest rates. Industry died with the birth of great sterile latifundia, and Spain's sick economy could not stand up to the impact of the rising demand for food and merchandise that was the inevitable result of colonial expansion. The big rise in public expenditures and the choking pressure of the overseas possessions' consumer needs accelerated trade deficits and set off galloping inflation. Jean-Baptiste Colbert, French minister of marine under Louis XIV, wrote, "The more business a state does with the Spaniards, the more silver it has." There was a sharp European struggle for the Spanish trade, which brought with it the market and the silver of Latin America. A late-seventeenth-century French document tells us that Spain controlled only 5 percent of the trade with "its" overseas colonial possessions, despite the juridical mirage of its monopoly: almost a third of the total was in Dutch and Flemish hands, a quarter belonged to the French, the Genoese controlled over one-fifth, the English one-tenth, and the Germans somewhat less. *Latin America was a European business.*

Charles V, heir to the Holy Roman emperors by purchased election, man of jutting chin and idiot gaze, spent only sixteen of his reign's forty years in Spain. Having occupied the throne without knowing a word of Spanish, he governed with a retinue of rapacious Flemings whom he authorized to take out of Spain muletrain-loads of gold and jewels, and whom he showered with bishoprics, bureaucratic titles, and even the first license to ship slaves to the Latin American colonies. Intent on hounding Satan all across Europe, he drained Latin America of its treasure for his religious wars. The Hapsburg dynasty did not collapse with his death; Spain had to suffer them for nearly two centuries. The great leader of the Counter-Reformation was his son, Philip II. From his huge palace-monastery, Escorial, on the slopes of the Sierra de Guadarrama, Philip spread the grim operations of the Inquisition across the world and launched his armies against the centers of heresy. Calvinism had taken hold in Holland, England, and France, and the Turks embodied the peril of a return to the faith of Allah. Spreading the true faith was a costly business: the few gold and silver objects, marvels of Latin American art, that arrived unmelted-down from Mexico and Peru were quickly taken from the Casa de Contratación in Seville and thrown into the crucibles.

At the same time heretics, or those suspected of heresy, were roasted in the Inquisition's purifying flames, Torquemada burned books, and the Devil's tail peeped out from every crevice. The war against Protestantism was also the war against ascendant capitalism in Europe. The "perpetuation of the Crusades," writes J.H. Elliott, "meant the perpetuation of the archaic social organization of a nation of Crusaders." The metals of Latin America—the delirium and downfall of Spain—provided a means to fight against the nascent forces of the modern economy. Charles V had already defeated the Castilian bourgeoisie in the uprisings of the Comuneros, which had become a social revolution against the nobility, its property and privileges. The uprisings were crushed following the betrayal of the city of Burgos, which would be Francisco Franco's capital four centuries later. With the last rebel fires extinguished, Charles returned to Spain accompanied by 4,000 German soldiers. At the same time, the highly radical insurrection of weavers, spinners, and artisans, who had taken power in the city of Valencia and had extended it through the whole district, was drowned in blood.

Defense of the Catholic faith turned out to be a mask for the struggle against history. The expulsion of the Jews in the time of Ferdinand and Isabella had deprived Spain of many able artisans and of indispensable capital. The expulsion of the Arabs in 1609 is considered less important, although no fewer than 275,000 Moors were put over the border, disastrously effecting the economy of Valencia and ruining the fertile Aragonese lands south of the Ebro. Previously, Philip II had thrown out thousands of Flemish artisans guilty or suspected of Protestantism. England welcomed them and they made a solid contribution to that country's manufactures.

It is clear that the enormous distances and the difficulty of communication were not the main obstacles to Spain's industrial progress. Spanish capitalists became no more than rentiers through the purchase of titles to Crown debts, and did not invest their capital in industrial development. The economic surplus went into unproductive channels:

the old wealthy class, the *señores* of gallows and knife, the owners of land and titles of nobility, built palaces and accumulated jewels; the new rich, speculators and merchants, bought land and titles. Neither the one nor the other paid taxes worth mentioning, nor could they be imprisoned for debt. Anyone devoting himself to industrial activity automatically lost his membership in the gentleman's club.

Successive commercial treaties, signed after Spain's military defeats in Europe, gave concessions that stimulated maritime trade between the port of Cádiz, where Latin America's metals were landed, and French, English, Dutch, and Hanseatic ports. Every year from 800 to 1,000 ships unloaded in Spain the products of other countries' industries. They reloaded with Latin American silver and Spanish wool that went to foreign looms, whence it would be returned already woven by the expanding European industry. The Cádiz monopolists merely forwarded foreign industrial products, which were then shipped to the New World: if Spanish manufactures could not even supply the home market, how could they satisfy the needs of the colonies?

The laces of Lille and Arras, Dutch fabrics, Brussels tapestries, Florentine brocades, Venetian crystal, Milanese arms, and French wines and cloths swamped the Spanish market, at the expense of local production, to satisfy the ostentation and consumer demands of ever more numerous and powerful parasites in ever poorer countries. Industry died in the egg, and the Hapsburgs did their best to speed its demise. The process reached its height in the mid-sixteenth century when importation of foreign textiles was authorized and all export of Castilian fabrics was banned except to Latin America. In contrast, as Jorge Abelardo Ramos has noted, were the policies of Henry VIII and Elizabeth I in England, when in that ascendant nation they banned the export of gold and silver, monopolized letters of credit, stopped wool exports, and ousted the North Sea merchants of the Hanseatic League from British ports. Meanwhile, the Italian republics were protecting their industry and external commerce through tariffs, privileges, and rigorous prohibitions: craftsmen could not leave the country under pain of death.

Everything went to rack and ruin. Of 16,000 looms in Seville on Charles V's death in 1558, only 400 remained when Philip II died forty years later. The 7 million sheep in Andalusian flocks were reduced to 2 million. In *Don Quixote de la Mancha*—which was banned for a long time in Latin America—Cervantes drew a portrait of the society of his time. A mid-sixteenth-century decree stopped the importation of foreign books and barred students from taking courses outside Spain; the Salamanca student body was reduced by half in a few decades; there were 9,000 convents and the clergy multiplied almost as fast as the cloak-and-sword nobility; 160,000 foreigners monopolized foreign trade; and the squanderings of the aristocracy condemned Spain to economic impotence. Around 1630, 150-odd dukes, marquises, counts, and viscounts garnered 5 million ducats in annual rents, adding ever more frills to their fancy titles. The Duke of Medinaceli had 700 servants and the Duke of Osuna, to score off the Tsar of Russia, dressed his 300 in leather cloaks.* The seventeenth century was the time of the *pícaro,* the rogue, and of hunger and epidemics. Spain had countless beggars, but this did not discourage an influx of foreign beggars from every corner of Europe. By 1700 there were 625,000 *hidalgos,* knights of the battlefield, although the country was emptying: its population had dwindled by half in somewhat more than two centuries, and was equal to that of England, which had doubled in the same period. The Hapsburg regime finally ended in 1700 amid total bankruptcy. Chronic unemployment, idle latifundios, chaotic currency, ruined industry, lost wars, empty coffers, central authority ignored in the provinces: the Spain that Philip V faced was "hardly less defunct than its dead master."[13]

The Bourbons gave Spain a more modern look, but at the end of the eighteenth century there were 200,000 clergymen and the unproductive population continued to proliferate at the expense of the country's underdevelopment. More than 10,000 towns and cities were still subject to the seignorial jurisdiction of the nobility and thus outside the king's direct control. The latifundia and the institution of entailed estates remained intact, along with obscurantism and fatalism. Nothing had improved since the era of Philip IV when a group of theologians,

* The species is not yet extinct. I opened a Madrid magazine at the end of 1969 and read of the death of Doña Teresa Beltrán de Lis y Pidal Gorouski y Chico de Guzmán, Duchess of Albuquerque and Marchioness of the Atcañices and Balbases. She is mourned by the widower Duke of Albuquerque, Don Beltrán Alonso Osorio y Diez de Rivera Martos y Figueroa, Marquis of the Alcañices, of the Balbases, of Cadreita, of Cuéllar, of Cullera, of Montaos, Count of Fuensaldaña, of Grajal, of Huelma, of Ledesma, of La Torre, of Villanueva de Cañedo, of Villahumbrosa, thrice Grandee of Spain.

examining a project for a canal between the Manzanares and the Tagus, had ended their deliberations by declaring that if God had wanted the rivers to be navigable, He himself would have so arranged it.

The Distribution of Functions Between Horseman and Horse

Marx wrote in Chapter 3 of the first volume of *Capital:* "The discovery of gold and silver in America, the extirpation, enslavement and entombment in mines of the aboriginal population, the beginning of the conquest and looting of the East Indies, the turning of Africa into a warren for the commercial hunting of black-skins, signalized the rosy dawn of the era of capitalist production. These idyllic proceedings are the chief momenta of primitive accumulation."

Plunder, internal and external, was the most important means of primitive accumulation of capital, an accumulation which, after the Middle Ages, made possible a new historical stage in world economic evolution. As the money economy extended, more and more social strata and regions of the world became involved in unequal exchange. Ernest Mandel has added up the value of the gold and silver torn from Latin America up to 1660, the booty extracted from Indonesia by the Dutch East India Company from 1650 to 1780, the harvest reaped by French capital in the eighteenth-century slave trade, the profits from slave labor in the British Antilles and from a half-century of British looting in India. The total exceeds the capital invested in all European industrial enterprises operated by steam in about 1800.[14] This enormous mass of capital, Mandel notes, created a favorable climate for investment in Europe, stimulated the "spirit of enterprise," and directly financed the establishment of manufactures, which in turn gave a strong thrust to the Industrial Revolution. But at the same time the formidable international concentration of wealth for Europe's benefit prevented the jump into the accumulation of industrial capital in the plundered areas: "The double tragedy of the developing countries consists in the fact that they were not only victims of that process of international concentration, but that subsequently they have had to try and compensate for their industrial backwardness—that is, realize the primitive accumulation of industrial capital—in a world flooded with articles manufactured by an already mature industry, that of the West."[15]

The Latin American colonies were discovered, conquered, and colonized within the process of the expansion of commercial capital. Europe stretched out its arms to clasp the whole world. Neither Spain nor Portugal received the benefits of the sweeping advance of capitalist mercantilism, although it was their colonies that substantially supplied the gold and silver feeding this expansion. As we have seen, while Latin America's precious metals made deceptive fortunes for a Spanish nobility living in a belated and contra-historical Middle Age, they simultaneously sealed the ruin of Spain in centuries to come. It was in other parts of Europe that modern capitalism could be incubated, taking decisive advantage of the expropriation of primitive American peoples. The rape of accumulated treasure was followed by the systematic exploitation of the forced labor of Indians and abducted Africans in the mines.

Europe needed gold and silver. The money in circulation kept multiplying and it was necessary to stimulate the movement of capitalism in the hour of birth: the bourgeoisie took control of the cities and founded banks, produced and exchanged merchandise, conquered new markets. Gold, silver, sugar: the colonial economy, supplying rather than consuming, was built in terms of—and at the service of—the European market. During long periods of the sixteenth century the value of Latin American precious metal exports was four times greater than the value of the slaves, salt, and luxury goods it imported. The resources flowed out so that emergent European nations across the ocean could accumulate them. This was the basic mission of the pioneers, although they applied the Bible almost as often as the whip to the dying Indians. The Spanish colonies' economic structure was born subordinated to the external market and was thus centralized around the export sector, where profit and power were concentrated.

During the process, from the metals stage to that of supplying foodstuffs, each region became identified with what it produced, and each produced what Europe wanted of it: *each product, loaded in the holds of galleons plowing the ocean, became a vocation and a destiny.* The international division of labor, as it emerged along with capitalism, resembled the distribution of function between a horseman and a horse, as Paul Baran put it. The markets of the colonial world grew as mere appendices to the internal market of invading capitalism.

Celso Furtado notes that while most of Europe's feudal seigneurs obtained an economic surplus from the people they dominated and used it in one way or another in the same areas, the chief aim of those Spaniards who received Latin American mines, lands, and Indians from the king was to extract a surplus to send to Europe.[16] This observation helps explain the ultimate goal of the Latin American colonial economy from its inception: although it showed some feudal characteristics, it functioned at the service of capitalism developing elsewhere. Nor, indeed, can the existence of wealthy capitalist centers in our own time be explained without the existence of poor and subjected outskirts: the one and the other make up the same system.

But not all of the surplus went to Europe. The colonial economy was run by merchants, by owners of mines and of big estates, who divided up the usufruct of Indian and black labor under the jealous and omnipotent eye of the Crown and its chief associate, the Church. Power was concentrated in the hands of a few, who sent metals and foodstuffs to Europe and received back the luxury goods to the enjoyment of which they dedicated their mushrooming fortunes. The dominant classes took no interest whatever in diversifying the internal economies or in raising technical and cultural levels in the population: they had a different function within the international complex they were acting for, and the grinding poverty of the people—so profitable from the standpoint of the reigning interests—prevented the development of an internal consumer market.

One French economist argues that Latin America's worst colonial legacy, which explains its backwardness today, is lack of capital.[17] But all the historical evidence shows that the colonial economy produced bountiful wealth for the classes connected internally with the colonial system of domination. The labor that was abundantly available for nothing or practically nothing, and the great European demand for Latin American products, made possible "a precocious and abundant accumulation of capital in the Iberian colonies. The hard core of beneficiaries, far from growing, became smaller in proportion to the mass of the population, as may be seen from the well-known fact that unemployed Europeans and Creoles constantly increased."[18] The capital that stayed in Latin America, after the lion's share went into the primitive accumulation process of European capitalism, did not generate a process similar to that which took place in Europe, where the foundations of industrial development were laid. It was diverted instead into the construction of great palaces and showy churches, into the purchase of jewels and luxurious clothing and furniture, into the maintenance of flocks of servants, and into the extravagance of fiestas. To an important extent this surplus was also immobilized in the purchase of new lands, or continued to revolve around speculative commercial activities.

In the twilight of the colonial era Alexander von Humboldt found in Mexico an enormous amount of capital in the hands of mine owners and merchants, while no less than half of Mexican real estate and capital belonged to the Church, which also controlled much of the remaining land through mortgages.[19] Mexican mine operators invested their surpluses in the purchase of great latifundia and in mortgage loans, as did the big exporters of Veracruz and Acapulco; the Church hierarchy multiplied its possessions in similar fashion. Palatial residences sprang up in the capital, and sumptuous churches appeared like mushrooms after rain; Indian servants catered to the golden luxuries of the powerful.

In mid-seventeenth-century Peru, capital amassed by *encomenderos,** mine operators, inquisitors, and officials of the imperial government was poured into commercial projects. The fortunes made in Venezuela from growing cacao—begun at the end of the sixteenth century and produced by applying whips to the backs of black slaves—were invested in new plantations, other commercial crops, in mines, urban real estate, slaves, and herds of cattle.

The Silver Cycle: The Ruin of Potosí

Andre Gunder Frank, in analyzing "metropolis-satellite" relations through Latin American history as a chain of successive subjections, has highlighted the fact that the regions now most underdeveloped and

---

* An *encomienda* was an estate granted by the Crown to the Spanish conquistadors and colonists for their services to Spain. It included the services of the Indians living on it. The *encomendero* was thus the owner. (Trans.)

poverty-stricken are those which in the past had had the closest links with the metropolis and had enjoyed periods of boom.[20] Having once been the biggest producers of goods exported to Europe, or later to the United States, and the richest sources of capital, they were abandoned by the metropolis when for this or that reason business sagged. Potosí is the outstanding example of this descent into the vacuum.

In the sixteenth and seventeenth centuries the Cerro Rico of Potosí (Mexico's Guanajuato and Zacatecas silver mines had their boom much later) was the hub of Latin American colonial life: around it, in one way or another, revolved the Chilean economy, which sent it wheat, dried meat, hides, and wines; the cattle-raising and crafts of Córdoba and Tucumán in Argentina, which supplied it with draft animals and textiles; the mercury mines of Huancavélica; and the Arica region whence the silver was shipped to Lima, chief administrative center of the period. In the independence period the area, now a part of Bolivia, still had a larger population than what is now Argentina. A century and a half later Bolivia's population is almost six times smaller than Argentina's.

Potosían society, sick with ostentation and extravagance, left Bolivia with only a vague memory of its splendors, of the ruins of its churches and palaces, and of 8 million Indian corpses. Any one of the diamonds encrusted in a rich *caballero's* shield was worth more than what an Indian could earn in his whole life under the *mitayo,** but the *caballero* took off with the diamonds. If it were not a futile exercise, Bolivia—now one of the world's most poverty-stricken countries—could boast of having nourished the wealth of the wealthiest. In our time Potosí is a poor city in a poor Bolivia: "The city which has given most to the world and has the least," as an old Potosían lady, enveloped in a mile of alpaca shawl, told me when we talked on the Andalusian patio of her two-century-old house. Condemned to nostalgia, tortured by poverty and cold, Potosí remains an open wound of the colonial system in America: a still audible "J'accuse."

The people live off the refuse. In 1640 the priest Alvaro Alonso-Barba published in Madrid's royal printshop his excellent work on the art of

---

* A *mitayo* is an Indian who pays a *mita,* or tribute, usually in the form of forced labor in public works, especially the mines. (Trans.)

metals.[21] Tin, he wrote, "is poison." He mentioned the Cerro, where "there is much tin, although few recognize it, and people throw it aside looking for the silver everyone seeks." Today the tin the Spaniards discarded like garbage is exploited in Potosí. Walls of ancient houses are sold as high-grade tin. Through the centuries the wealth has been drained from the 5,000 tunnels the Spaniards bored into the Cerro Rico. As dynamite charges have hollowed it out, its color has changed and the height of its summit has been lowered. The mountains of rock heaped around the many tunnel openings are of all colors: pink, lilac, purple, ochre, gray, gold, brown. A crazy quilt of garbage. *Llamperos* break the rocks and Indian *palliris* in search of tin pick like birds, with hands skilled in weighing and separating, at the mineral debris. Miners still enter old mines that are not flooded, carbide lamps in hand, bodies crouching, to bring out whatever there is. Of silver there is none. Not a glint of it: the Spaniards even swept out the seams with brooms. The *pallacos* use pick and shovel to dig any metal out of the leavings. "The Cerro is still rich," I was blandly told by an unemployed man who was scratching through the dirt with his hands. "There must be a God, you know: the metal grows just like a plant." Opposite the Cerro Rico rises a witness to the devastation: a mountain called Huakajchi, meaning in Quechua "the *cerro* that has wept." From its sides gush many springs of pure water, the "water eyes" that quench the miners' thirst.

In its mid-seventeenth-century days of glory the city attracted many painters and artisans, Spanish and Indian, European and Creole masters and Indian image-carvers who left their mark on Latin American colonial art. Melchor Pérez de Holguín, Latin America's El Greco, left an enormous religious work which betrays both its creator's talent and the pagan breath of these lands: his splendid Virgin, arms open, gives one breast to the infant Jesus and the other to Saint Joseph; she is hauntingly memorable. Goldsmiths, silversmiths, and engravers, cabinetmakers and masters of repoussé, craftsmen in metals, fine woods, plaster, and noble ivory adorned Potosí's many churches and monasteries with works of the imaginative colonial school, altars sparkling with silver filigree, and priceless pulpits and reredoses. The baroque church façades carved in stone have resisted the ravages of time, but not so the paintings, many of them irreparably damaged by damp, or the smaller figures and objects. Tourists and parishioners have emptied the churches of whatever they could carry, from chalices and bells to carvings in beech and ash of Saint Francis and Christ.

These untended churches, now mostly closed, are collapsing under the weight of years. It is a pity, for pillaged as they have been they are still formidable treasures of a colonial art that fuses all styles and glows with heretical imagination: the *escalonado* emblem of the ancient civilization of Tiahuanacu instead of the cross of Christ, the cross joined with the sacred sun and moon, virgins and saints with "natural" hair, grapes and ears of corn twining to the tops of columns along with the *kantuta,* the imperial flower of the Incas; sirens, Bacchus, and the festival of life alternating with romantic asceticism, the dark faces of some divinities, caryatids with Indian features. Some churches have been renovated to perform other services now that they lack congregations. San Ambrosio is the Cine Omiste; in February 1970 the forthcoming attraction was advertised across the baroque bas-reliefs of the façade: *It's a Mad, Mad, Mad, Mad World.* The Jesuit church became a movie house, then a Grace Company warehouse, and finally a storehouse for public charity food.

A few other churches still function as best they can: it is at least a century and a half since Potosíans had the money to burn candles. It is said of the San Francisco church, for example, that its cross grows several centimeters every year, as does the beard of the Señor de la Vera Cruz, an imposing silver-and-silk Christ who appeared in Potosí, brought by nobody, four centuries ago. The priests do not deny that they shave him every so often, and they attribute to him—even in writing—every kind of miracle: incantations, down the centuries, against droughts, plagues, and wars in defense of the beleaguered city.

The Señor de la Vera Cruz was powerless to stop the decline of Potosí. The depletion of the silver was interpreted as divine judgment on the miners' wickedness and sin. Spectacular masses became a thing of the past: like the banquets, bullfights, balls, and fireworks, luxury religion had, after all, been a subproduct of Indian slave labor. In the era of splendor the miners made princely donations to churches and monasteries and sponsored sumptuous funerals, all solid silver keys to the gates of heaven. In 1559 the merchant Alvaro Bejarano directed in his will that "all the priests in Potosí" accompany his corpse. Quack medicine and witchcraft were mixed with authorized religion in the delirious fervors and panics of colonial society. Extreme unction with bell and canopy could, like Communion, succor the dying; but a juicy will that provided for building a church or for a silver altar could prove much more effective. Fevers were combated with the gospels. In certain convents prayers cooled the body, in others they warmed it: "The Credo was cool as tamarind or sweet spirit of nitre, the Salve warm as orange blossoms or cornsilk."[22]

In the Calle Chuquisaca one can admire the time-corroded façade of the palace of the counts of Carma y Cayara, but it is now a dentist's office; the coat-of-arms of Maestro de Campo Don Antonio López de Quiroga, in the Calle Lanza, now adorns a little school; that of the Marqués de Otavi, with its rampant lions, tops the doorway of the Banco Nacional. "Where can they be living now? They must have gone far. . . ." The Potosían old lady, attached to her city, tells me that the rich left first and then the poor: in four centuries the population has decreased threefold. I gaze at the Cerro from a roof in the Calle Uyuni, a narrow, twisting colonial lane with wooden-balconied houses so close together that residents can kiss or hit each other without having to go down to the street. Here, as in all of the city, survive the old street lamps under whose feeble light, as Jaime Molins relates, "lovers' quarrels were resolved, and muffled *caballeros,* elegant ladies, and gamblers flitted by like ghosts." The city now has electric light but one barely notices it. In the dim plazas raffle parties are conducted at night under the ancient lamps: I saw a piece of cake being raffled in the middle of a crowd.

Sucre decayed along with Potosí. This valley city of pleasant climate, successively known as Charcas, La Plata, and Chuquisaca, enjoyed a good share of the wealth flowing from Potosí's Cerro Rico. Here Francisco Pizarro's brother Gonzalo installed his court, as sumptuous as any king's; churches and spacious residences, parks and recreation centers sprouted continuously, together with the lawyers, mystics, and pretentious poets who put their stamp on the city from century to century. "Silence, that is Sucre—just silence. But before. . . ." Before, this was the cultural capital of two viceroyalties, seat of Latin America's chief archdiocese and of the colony's highest court of justice—the most magnificent and cultured city in South America. Doña Cecilia Contreras de Torres and Doña María de las Mercedes Torralba de Gramajo, *señoras* of Ubina and Colquechaca, gave Lucullan banquets in a contest to squander the income from their Potosí mines. When their lavish fiestas ended they threw the silver service and even golden vessels from their balconies to be picked up by lucky passersby.

Sucre still has an Eiffel Tower and its own Arcs de Triomphe, and they say that the jewels of its Virgin would pay off the whole of Bolivia's huge external debt. But the famous church bells, which in 1809 rang out joyfully for Latin America's emancipation, play a funereal tune today. The harsh chimes of San Francisco, which so often announced uprisings and rebellions, toll a death knell over torpid Sucre. It matters little that Sucre is Bolivia's legal capital, still the seat of its highest court. Through its streets pass countless pettifogging lawyers, shriveled and yellow of skin, surviving testimonies to its decadence: learned doctors of the type who wear pince-nez complete with black ribbon. From the great empty palaces Sucre's illustrious patriarchs send out their servants to sell baked tidbits down at the railroad station. In happier times there were people here who could buy anything up to the title of prince.

Only ghosts of the old wealth haunt Potosí and Sucre. In Huanchaca, another Bolivian tragedy, Anglo-Chilean capitalists in the past century stripped veins of highest-grade silver more than two yards wide; all that remains is dusty ruin. Huanchaca is still on the map as if it continued to exist—identified by crossed pick and shovel as a live mining center. Did the Mexican mines of Guanajuato and Zacatecas enjoy a better fate? On the basis of Alexander von Humboldt's figures in his already cited *Political Essay on the Kingdom of New Spain,* the economic surplus drained from Mexico between 1760 and 1809—barely half a century—through silver and gold exports has been estimated at some 5 billion present-day dollars.[23] In Humboldt's time there were no more important mines in Latin America. The great German scholar compared Guanajuato's Valenciana mine with the Himmelsfürst in Saxony, then the richest in Europe; the Valenciana was producing thirty-six times more silver at the turn of the century and its profits were thirty-three times as great for its investors. Count Santiago de la Laguna trembled with emotion in describing, in 1732, the Zacatecas mining district and "the precious treasures concealed in its deep womb," in mountains "graced with more than 4,000 shafts, the better to serve both of Their Majesties," God and the King, "with the fruit of its entrails," and that "all might come to drink and participate of the great, the rich, the learned, the urban and the noble" because it was a "fount of wisdom, order, arms, and nobility."[24] The priest Marmolejo would later describe the city of Guanajuato, crisscrossed by rivers and bridges, with its gardens recalling those of Semiramis in Babylon and its ornate churches, theater, bullring, cockfight arenas, and towers and cupolas rising against the green mountainsides. But this was "the country of inequality," about which Humboldt could write: "Perhaps nowhere is inequality more shocking. . . . The architecture of public and private buildings, the women's elegant wardrobes, the high-society atmosphere: all testify to an extreme social polish which is in extraordinary contrast to the nakedness, ignorance, and coarseness of the populace." The new veins of silver gobbled up men and mules in the *cordillera* foothills; the Indians, who "lived from day to day," suffered chronic hunger and epidemics killed them off like flies. In only one year, 1784, more than 8,000 died in Guanajuato when a lack of food, the result of a bad cold spell, set off a wave of disease.

Capital, far from accumulating, was squandered. There was a saying: "Father a merchant, son a gentleman, grandson a beggar." In a plea to the government in 1843 Mexican politician Lucas Alamán gave a somber warning and insisted on the need to defend national industry by banning or imposing heavy duties on foreign imports. "We must proceed to develop industry as the only source of general prosperity," he wrote. "The riches of Zacatecas would bring no benefits to Puebla but for the former's consumption of the latter's manufactures, and if these decline again, as has happened before, that presently flourishing area will be ruined and the riches of the mines will not be able to save it from poverty." The prophesy proved true. In our time Zacatecas and Guanajuato are not even the most important cities in their own regions. Both languish amid the skeletons of the camps of the mining boom. Zacatecas, high and arid, lives from agriculture and exports labor to other states; its gold and silver are low in quality compared to former days. Of the fifty mines once exploited in the Guanajuato district, only two remain today. The population of the beautiful city does not grow, but tourists flock there to view the exuberant splendor of olden times. San Diego, La Valenciana, La Compañía, the cemetery in whose catacombs more than a hundred mummies, preserved intact by the salinity of the soil, are on show. Half the families in Guanajuato state average more than five members and live today in one-room hovels.

A Flood of Tears and Blood: And Yet the Pope Said Indians Had Souls

In 1581 Philip II told the *audiencia** of Guadalajara that a third of Latin America's Indians had already been wiped out, and that those who survived were compelled to pay the tributes for the dead. The monarch added that Indians were bought and sold; that they slept in the open air; and that mothers killed their children to save them from the torture of the mines.[25] Yet the Crown's hypocrisy had smaller limits than the empire: it received a fifth of the value of the metals extracted by its subjects in all of the Spanish New World, as well as other taxes, and the Portuguese Crown was to have the same arrangement in eighteenth-century Brazil. Latin American silver and gold—as Engels put it—penetrated like a corrosive acid through all the pores of Europe's moribund feudal society, and, for the benefit of nascent mercantilist capitalism, the mining entrepreneurs turned Indians and black slaves into a teeming "external proletariat" of the European economy. Greco-Roman slavery was revived in a different world; to the plight of the Indians of the exterminated Latin American civilizations was added the ghastly fate of the blacks seized from African villages to toil in Brazil and the Antilles. The colonial Latin American economy enjoyed the most highly concentrated labor force known until that time, making possible the greatest concentration of wealth ever enjoyed by any civilization in world history.

The price of the tide of avarice, terror, and ferocity bearing down on these regions was Indian genocide: the best recent investigations credit pre-Columbian Mexico with a population between 30 and 37.5 million, and the Andean region is estimated to have possessed a similar number; Central America had between 10 and 13 million. The Indians of the Americas totaled no less than 70 million when the foreign conquerors appeared on the horizon; a century and a half later they had been reduced to 3.5 million. In 1685 only 4,000 Indian families remained of the more than 2 million that had once lived between Lima and Paita, according to the Marquis of Barinas. Archbishop Liñán y Cisneros

* An *audiencia* was a judicial district as well as a judicial, administrative, and advisory body. In Mexico, it was the supreme court of administration and judgment. (Trans.)

denied that the Indians had been annihilated: "The truth is that they are hiding out," he said, "to avoid paying tribute, abusing the liberty which they enjoy and which they never had under the Incas."[26]

While metals flowed unceasingly from Latin American mines, equally unceasing were the orders from the Spanish Court granting paper protection and dignity to the Indians whose killing labor sustained the kingdom. The fiction of legality protected the Indian; the reality of exploitation drained the blood from his body. From slavery to the *encomienda* of service, and from this to the encomienda of tribute and the regime of wages, variants in the Indian labor force's juridical condition made only superficial changes in the real situation. The Crown regarded the inhuman exploitation of Indian labor as so necessary that in 1601 Philip III, banning forced labor in the mines by decree, at the same time sent secret instructions ordering its continuation "in case that measure should reduce production."[27] Similarly, between 1616 and 1619, Governor Juan de Solórzano carried out a survey of work conditions in the Huancavelica mercury mines (directly exploited by the Crown, in distinction to the silver mines, which were in private hands): "The poison penetrated to the very marrow, debilitating all the members and causing a constant shaking, and the workers usually died within four years," he reported to the Council of the Indies and to the king. But in 1631 Philip IV ordered that the same system be continued, and his successor Charles II later reaffirmed the decree.

In three centuries Potosí's Cerro Rico consumed 8 million lives. The Indians, including women and children, were torn from their agricultural communities and driven to the Cerro. Of every ten who went up into the freezing wilderness, seven never returned. Luis Capoche, an owner of mines and mills, wrote that "the roads were so covered with people that the whole kingdom seemed on the move." In their communities the Indians saw "many afflicted women returning without husbands and with many orphaned children" and they knew that "a thousand deaths and disasters" awaited them in the mines. The Spaniards scoured the countryside for hundreds of miles for labor. Many died on the way, before reaching Potosí, but it was the terrible work conditions in the mine that killed the most people. Soon after the mine began operating, in 1550, the Dominican monk Domingo de Santo Tomás told the Council of the Indies that Potosí was a "mouth of hell" which swallowed Indians by the thousands every year, and that rapacious mine owners treated them "like stray animals." Later Fray Rodrigo de Loaysa said: "These poor Indians are like sardines in the sea. Just as other fish pursue the sardines to seize and devour them, so everyone in these lands pursues the wretched Indians." Chiefs of Indian communities had to replace the constantly dying *mitayos* with new men between eighteen and fifty years old. The huge stone-walled corral where Indians were assigned to mine and mill owners is now used by workers as a football ground. The *mitayos'* jail—a shapeless mass of ruins—can still be seen at the entrance to Potosí.

The Compilation of the Laws of the Indies abounds with decrees establishing the equal right of Indians and Spaniards to exploit the mines, and expressly forbidding any infringement of Indian rights. Thus formal history—the dead letter of today which perpetuates the dead letter of the past—has nothing to complain about, but while Indian labor legislation was debated in endless documents and Spanish jurists displayed their talents in an explosion of ink, in Latin America the law "was respected but not carried out." In practice "the poor Indian is a coin with which one can get whatever one needs, as with gold and silver, and get it better," as Luis Capoche put it. Many people claimed mestizo status before the courts to avoid being sent to the mines and sold and resold in the market.

At the end of the eighteenth century, Concolorcorvo, who had Indian blood, denied his own people: "We do not dispute that the mines consume a considerable number of Indians, but this is not due to the work they do in the silver and mercury mines but to their dissolute way of life." The testimony of Capoche, who had many Indians in his service, is more enlightening. Freezing outdoor temperatures alternated with the infernal heat inside the Cerro. The Indians went into the depths "and it is common to bring them out dead or with broken heads and legs, and in the mills they are injured every day." The *mitayos* hacked out the metal with picks and then carried it up on their shoulders by the light of a candle. Outside the mine they propelled the heavy wooden shafts in the mill or melted the silver on a fire after grinding and washing it.

The *mita* labor system was a machine for crushing Indians. The process of using mercury to extract silver poisoned as many or more than did the toxic gases in the bowels of the earth. It made hair and teeth fall out and brought on uncontrollable trembling. The victims ended up dragging themselves through the streets pleading for alms. At night 6,000 fires burned on the slopes of the Cerro and in these the silver was worked, taking advantage of the wind that the "glorious Saint Augustine" sent from the sky. Because of the smoke from the ovens there were no pastures or crops for a radius of twenty miles around Potosí and the fumes attacked men's bodies no less relentlessly.

Ideological justifications were never in short supply. The bleeding of the New World became an act of charity, an argument for the faith. With the guilt, a whole system of rationalizations for guilty consciences was devised. The Indians were used as beasts of burden because they could carry a greater weight than the delicate llama, and this proved that they were in fact beasts of burden. The viceroy of Mexico felt that there was no better remedy for their "natural wickedness" than work in the mines. Juan Ginés de Sepúlveda, a renowned Spanish theologian, argued that they deserved the treatment they got because their sins and idolatries were an offense to God. The Count de Buffon, a French naturalist, noted that Indians were cold and weak creatures in whom "no activity of the soul" could be observed. The Abbé De Paw invented a Latin America where degenerate Indians lived side by side with dogs that couldn't bark, cows that couldn't be eaten, and impotent camels. Voltaire's Latin America was inhabited by Indians who were lazy and stupid, pigs with navels on their backs, and bald and cowardly lions. Bacon, De Maistre, Montesquieu, Hume, and Bodin declined to recognize the "degraded men" of the New World as fellow humans. Hegel spoke of Latin America's physical and spiritual impotence and said the Indians died when Europe merely breathed on them.

In the seventeenth century Father Gregorio García detected Semitic blood in the Indians because, like the Jews, "they are lazy, they do not believe in the miracles of Jesus Christ, and they are ungrateful to the Spaniards for all the good they have done them." At least this holy man did not deny that the Indians were descended from Adam and Eve: many theologians and thinkers had never been convinced by Pope Paul III's bull of 1537 declaring the Indians to be "true men." When Bartolomé de las Casas upset the Spanish Court with his heated denunciations of the conquistadors' cruelty in 1557, a member of the Royal

Council replied that Indians were too low in the human scale to be capable of receiving the faith. Las Casas dedicated his zealous life to defending the Indians against the excesses of the mine owners and *encomenderos.* He once remarked that the Indians preferred to go to hell to avoid meeting Christians.

Indians were assigned or given in *encomienda* to conquistadors and colonizers so that they could teach them the gospel. But since the Indians owed personal services and economic tribute to the *encomenderos,* there was little time for setting them on the Christian path to salvation.

Indians were divided up along with lands given as royal grants, or were obtained by direct plunder: in reward for his services, Cortés received 23,000 vassals. After 1536 Indians were given in *encomienda* along with their descendants for the span of two lifetimes, those of the *encomendero* and of his immediate heir; after 1629 this was extended to three lifetimes and, after 1704, to four. In the eighteenth century the surviving Indians still assured many generations to come of a cozy life. Since their defeated gods persisted in Spanish memory, there were saintly rationalizations aplenty for the victors' profits from their toil; the Indians were pagans and deserved nothing better.

The past? Four hundred years after the papal bull, in September 1957, the highest court in Paraguay published a notice informing all the judges of the country that "the Indians, like other inhabitants of the republic, are human beings." And the Center for Anthropological Studies of the Catholic University of Asunción later carried out a revealing survey, both in the capital and in the countryside: eight out of ten Paraguayans think that "Indians are animals." In Caaguazú, Alta Paraná, and the Chaco, Indians are hunted down like wild beasts, sold at bargain prices, and exploited by a system of virtual slavery—yet almost all Paraguayans have Indian blood, and Paraguayans tirelessly compose poems, songs, and speeches in homage to the "Guaraní soul."

The Militant Memory of Tupac Amaru

When the Spaniards invaded Latin America, the theocratic Inca empire was at its height, spreading over what we now call Peru, Bolivia, and Ecuador, taking in part of Colombia and Chile, and reaching northern Argentina and the Brazilian jungle. The Aztec confederation had achieved a high level of efficiency in the Valley of Mexico, and in Yucatán and Central America the remarkable civilization of the Mayas, organized for work and war, persisted among the peoples who succeeded them.

These societies have left many testimonies to their greatness despite the long period of devastation: religious monuments built with more skill than the Egyptian pyramids, technically efficient constructions for the battle against nature, art works showing indomitable talent. In the Lima museum there are hundreds of skulls which have undergone trepanning and the insertion of gold and silver plates by Inca surgeons. The Mayas were great astronomers, measuring time and space with astonishing precision, and discovered the value of the figure zero before any other people in history. The Aztecs' irrigation works and artificial islands dazzled Cortés—even though they were not made of gold.

The conquest shattered the foundations of these civilizations. The installation of a mining economy had direr consequences than the fire and sword of war. The mines required a great displacement of people and dislocated agricultural communities; they not only took countless lives through forced labor, but also indirectly destroyed the collective farming system. The Indians were taken to the mines, were forced to submit to the service of the *encomenderos*, and were made to surrender for nothing the lands which they had to leave or neglect. On the Pacific coast the Spaniards destroyed or let die out the enormous plantations of corn, yucca, kidney and white beans, peanuts, and sweet potato; the desert quickly devoured great tracts of land which the Inca irrigation network had made abundant. Four and a half centuries after the Conquest only rocks and briars remain where roads had once united an empire. Although the Incas' great public works were for the most part destroyed by time or the usurper's hand, one may still see across the Andean cordillera traces of the endless terraces which permitted, and still permit, cultivation of the mountainsides. A U.S. technician estimated in 1936 that if the Inca terraces had been built by modern methods at 1936 wage rates they would have cost some $30,000 per acre.[28] In that empire which did not know the wheel, the horse, or iron, the terraces and aqueducts were made possible by prodigious organization and technical perfection achieved through wise distribution of labor, as well as by the religious force that ruled man's relation with the soil—which was sacred and thus always alive.

The Aztecs also responded in a remarkable way to nature's challenges. The surviving islands in the dried-up lake where Mexico City now rises on native ruins are known to tourists today as "floating gardens." The Aztecs created these because of the shortage of land in the place chosen for establishing Tenochtitlán. They moved large quantities of mud from the banks and shored up the new mud-islands between narrow walls of reeds until tree roots gave them firmness. Between these exceptionally fertile islands flowed the canals, and on them arose the great Aztec capital, with its broad avenues, its austerely beautiful palaces, and its stepped pyramids: rising magically out of the lake, it was condemned to disappear under the assaults of foreign conquest. Mexico took four centuries to regain the population of those times.

As Darcy Ribeiro puts it, the Indians were the fuel of the colonial productive system. "It is almost certain," writes Sergio Bagú, "that hundreds of Indian sculptors, architects, engineers, and astronomers were sent into the mines along with the mass of slaves for the killing task of getting out the ore. The technical ability of these people was of no interest to the colonial economy. They were treated as so many skilled workers." Yet all traces of those broken cultures were not lost: hope of the rebirth of a lost dignity sparked many Indian risings.

In 1781 Tupac Amaru laid siege to Cuzco. This mestizo chief, a direct descendant of the Inca emperors, headed the broadest of messianic revolutionary movements. The rebellion broke out in Tinta province, which had been almost depopulated by enforced service in the Cerro Rico mines. Mounted on his white horse, Tupac Amaru entered the plaza of Tungasuca and announced to the sound of drums and *pututus* that he had condemned the royal Corregidor Antonio Juan de Arriaga to the gallows and put an end to the Potosí *mita.* A few days later Tupac issued a decree liberating the slaves. He abolished all taxes and forced labor in all forms. The Indians rallied by the thousands to the forces of the "father of all the poor and all the wretched and helpless." He moved against Cuzco at the head of his *guerilleros,* promising them that all who died while under his orders in this war would return to life to enjoy the happiness and wealth the invaders had wrested from them. Victories and defeats followed; in the end, betrayed and captured by one of his own chiefs, Tupac was handed over in chains to the royalists. The Examiner Areche entered his cell to demand, in exchange for promises, the names of his rebel accomplices. Tupac Amaru replied scornfully, "There are no accomplices here other than you and I. You as oppressor, I as liberator, deserve to die."[29]

Tupac was tortured, along with his wife, his children, and his chief aides, in Cuzco's Plaza del Wacaypata. His tongue was cut out; his arms and legs were tied to four horses with the intention of quartering him, but his body would not break; he was finally beheaded at the foot of the gallows. His head was sent to Tinta, one arm to Tungasuca and the other to Carabaya, one leg to Santa Rosa and the other to Livitaca. The torso was burned and the ashes thrown in the Río Watanay. It was proposed that all his descendants be obliterated up to the fourth generation.

In 1802 a chief named Astorpilco, also a descendant of the Incas, was visited by Humboldt in Cajamarca, on the exact spot where his ancestor Atahualpa had first seen the conquistador Pizarro. The chief's son took the German scholar on a tour of the ruins of the town and the rubble of the old Inca palace, and spoke as they walked of the fabulous treasures hidden beneath the dust and ashes. "Don't you sometimes feel like digging for the treasure to satisfy your needs?" Humboldt asked him. The youth replied: "No, we never feel like doing that. My father says it would be sinful. If we were to find the golden branches and fruits, the white people would hate us and do us harm."[30] The chief himself raised wheat in a small field, but that was not enough to save him from white covetousness. The usurpers, hungry for gold and silver and for slaves to work the mines, never hesitated to seize lands when their crops offered a tempting profit.

The plunder continued down the years and in 1969, when agrarian reform was announced in Peru, reports still appeared in the press of Indians from the broken mountain communities coming with flags unfurled to invade lands that had been robbed from them or their ancestors, and of the army driving them away with bullets. Nearly two centuries had to pass after Tupac Amaru's death before the nationalist general Juan Velasco Alvarado would take up and apply Tupac's resounding, never forgotten words: *"Campesino!* Your poverty shall no longer feed the master!"

Other heroes whose defeat was reversed by time were the Mexicans Miguel Hidalgo and José María Morelos. Hidalgo, who till the age of fifty was a peaceable rural priest, pealed the bells of the church of Dolores one fine day to summon the Indians to fight for their freedom: "Will you stir yourselves to the task of recovering from the hated Spaniards the lands robbed from your ancestors 300 years ago?" He raised the standard of the Indian Virgin of Guadalupe and before six weeks were out 80,000 men were following him, armed with machetes, pikes, slings, and bows and arrows. The revolutionary priest put an end to tribute and divided up the lands of Guadalajara; he decreed freedom for the slaves and led his forces toward Mexico City. He was finally executed after a military defeat and is said to have left a testament of passionate repentance. The revolution soon found another leader, however, the priest José María Morelos: "You must regard as enemies all the rich, the nobles, and high-ranking officials. . . ." His movement—combining Indian insurgency and social revolution—came to control a large part of Mexico before he too was defeated and shot. As one U.S. senator wrote, the independence of Mexico, six years later, "turned out to be a typically Hispanic family affair between European and American-born members . . . a political fight within the dominating social class."[31] The *encomienda* serf became a peon and the *encomendero* a hacienda owner.

For the Indians, No Resurrection at the End of Holy Week

Masters of Indian *pongos*—domestic servants—were still offering them for hire in La Paz newspapers at the beginning of our century. Until the revolution of 1952 restored the forgotten right of dignity to Bolivian Indians, the *pongo* slept beside the dog, ate the leftovers of his dinner, and knelt when speaking to anyone with a white skin. Four-legged beasts of burden were scarce in the conquistadors' time and they used Indian backs to transport their baggage; even to this day Aymara and Quechua porters can be seen all over the Andean *altiplano* carrying loads for a crust of bread. Pneumoconiosis was Latin America's first occupational disease, and the lungs of today's Bolivian miner refuse to continue functioning at the age of thirty-five: the implacable silica dust impregnates his skin, cracks his face and hands, destroys his sense of smell and taste, hardens and kills his lungs.

Tourists love to photograph *altiplano* natives in their native costumes, unaware that these were imposed by Charles III at the end of the eighteenth century. The dresses that the Spaniards made Indian females wear were copied from the regional costumes of Estremaduran, Andalusian, and Basque peasant women, and the center-part hair style was imposed by Viceroy Toledo. The same was not true of the consumption of coca, which already existed in Inca times. But coca was then distributed in moderation; the Inca government had a monopoly on it and only permitted its use for ritual purposes or for those who worked in the mines. The Spaniards energetically stimulated its consumption. It was good business. In Potosí in the sixteenth century as much was spent on European clothes for the oppressors as on coca for the oppressed. In Cuzco 400 Spanish merchants lived off the coca traffic; every year 100,000 baskets with a million kilos of coca-leaf entered the Potosí silver mines. The Church took a tax from the drug. The Inca historian Garcilaso de la Vega tells us in his *Comentarios Reales Que Tratan del Origen de los Incas* that the bishop, canons, and other Cuzco church dignitaries got most of their income from tithes on coca, and that the transport and sale of the product enriched many Spaniards. For the few coins they received for their work the Indians bought coca-leaf instead of food: chewing it, they could—at the price of shortening their lives—better endure the deadly tasks imposed on them. In addition to coca the Indians drank potent *aguardiente,* and their owners complained of the propagation of "maleficent vices." In twentieth-century Potosí the Indians still chew coca to kill hunger and themselves, and still burn their guts with pure alcohol—sterile forms of revenge for the condemned. Bolivian miners still call their wages *mita* as in olden days.

Exiled in their own land, condemned to an eternal exodus, Latin America's native peoples were pushed into the poorest areas—arid mountains, the middle of deserts—as the dominant civilization extended its frontiers. *The Indians have suffered, and continue to suffer, the curse of their own wealth; that is the drama of all Latin America.* When placer gold was discovered in Nicaragua's Río Bluefields, the Carca Indians were quickly expelled far from their riparian lands, and the same happened with the Indians in all the fertile valleys and rich-subsoil lands south of the Río Grande. The massacres of Indians that began with Columbus never stopped. In Uruguay and Argentine Patagonia they were exterminated during the last century by troops that hunted them down and penned them in forests or in the desert so that they might not disturb the organized advance of cattle latifundia.* The Yaqui Indians of the Mexican state of Sonora were drowned in blood so that their lands, fertile and rich in minerals, could be sold without any unpleasantness to various U.S. capitalists. Survivors were deported to plantations in Yucatán, and the Yucatán peninsula became not only the cemetery of the Mayas who had been its owners, but also of the Yaquis who came from afar: at the beginning of our century the fifty kings of henequen had more than 100,000 Indian slaves on their plantations. Despite the exceptional physical endurance of the strapping, handsome Yaquis, two-thirds of them died during the first year of slave labor. In our day henequen can compete with synthetic fiber substitutes only because of the workers' abysmally low standard of living. Things have certainly changed, but not as much—at least for the natives of Yucatán—as some believe: "The living conditions of these workers are much like slave labor," says one contemporary authority.[32] On the Andean slopes near Bogotá the Indian peon still must give a day's work without pay to get the *hacendado*'s permission to farm his own plot on moonlit nights. As René Dumont says, "This Indian's ancestors, answering to no man, used once to cultivate the rich soil of the ownerless

---

* The last of the Charruas, who lived by raising bulls in the wild pampas of northern Uruguay, were betrayed in 1832 by President José Fructuoso Rivera. Removed from the bush that gave them protection, deprived of horses and arms by false promises of friendship, they were overwhelmed at a place called Boca del Tigre. "The bugles sounded the attack," wrote Eduardo Acevedo Díaz in *La Época* (August 19, 1890). "The horde churned about desperately, one after the other of its young braves falling like bulls pierced in the neck." Many chiefs were killed. The few Indians who could break through the circle of fire took vengeance soon afterward. Pursued by Rivera's brother, they laid an ambush and riddled him and his soldiers with spears. The chief Sepe "had the tip of his spear adorned with some tendons from the corpse."

In Argentine Patagonia soldiers drew pay for each pair of testicles they brought in. David Viñas's novel *Los dueños de la tierra* (1959) opens with an Indian hunt: "For killing was like raping someone. Something good. And it gave a man pleasure: you had to move fast, you could yell, you sweated and afterward you felt hungry. . . . The intervals got longer between shots. Undoubtedly some straddled body remained in one of these coverts—an Indian body on its back with a blackish stain between its thighs. . . ."

plain. Now he works for nothing to gain the right to cultivate the poor slopes of the mountain."[33]

Not even Indians isolated in the depths of forests are safe in our day. At the beginning of this century 230 tribes survived in Brazil; since then ninety have disappeared, erased from the planet by firearms and microbes. Violence and disease, the advance guard of civilization: for the Indian, contact with the white man continues to be contact with death. Every legal dispensation since 1537 meant to protect Brazil's Indians has been turned against them. Under every Brazilian constitution they are "the original and natural masters" of the land they occupy, but the richer that virgin land proves to be, the greater the threat hanging over their lives. Nature's very generosity makes them targets of plunder and crime. Indian hunting has become ferocious in recent years; the world's greatest forest, a huge tropical zone open to legend and adventure, has inspired a new "American dream." Men and business enterprises from the United States, a new procession of conquistadores, have poured into Amazonia as if it were another Far West. This U.S. invasion has inflamed the avarice of Brazilian adventurers as never before. The Indians die out leaving no trace, and the land is sold for dollars to the new interested parties. Gold and other plentiful minerals, timber and rubber, riches whose commerical value the Indians are not even aware of, recur in the reports of each of the few investigations that have been made. It is known that the Indians have been machine-gunned from helicopters and light airplanes and inoculated with smallpox virus, that dynamite has been tossed into their villages, and that they have been given gifts of sugar mixed with strychnine and salt mixed with arsenic. The director of the Indian Protection Service, named by the Castelo Branco dictatorship to clean up its administration, was himself accused, with proof, of committing forty-two different kinds of crimes against the Indians. That scandal broke in 1968.

Indian society in our time does not exist in a vacuum, outside the general framework of the Latin American economy. There are, it is true, Brazilian tribes still sealed within the jungle, *altiplano* communities totally isolated from the world, redoubts of barbarism on the Venezuelan frontier; but in general the Indians are incorporated into the system of production and the consumer market, even if indirectly. They participate in an economic and social order which assigns them the role of victim—the most exploited of the exploited. They buy and sell a good part of the few things they consume and produce, at the mercy of powerful and voracious intermediaries who charge much and pay little; they are day laborers on plantations, the cheapest work force, and soldiers in the mountains; they spend their days toiling for the world market or fighting for their conquerors. In countries like Guatemala, for example, they are at the center of national economic life: in a continuous annual cycle they leave their "sacred lands"—high lands where each small farm is the size of a corpse—to contribute 200,000 pairs of hands to the harvesting of coffee, cotton, and sugar in the lowlands. They are transported in trucks like cattle, and it is not always need, but sometimes liquor, that makes them decide to go. The contractors provide a marimba band and plenty of *aguardiente* and when the Indian sobers up he is already in debt. He will pay it off laboring on hot and strange lands which—perhaps with a few centavos in his pocket, perhaps with tuberculosis or malaria—he will leave after a few months. The army collaborates efficiently in the task of convincing the reluctant. Expropriation of the Indians—usurpation of their lands and their labor—has gone hand in hand with racist attitudes which are in turn fed by the objective degradation of civilizations broken by the Conquest. The effects of the Conquest and the long ensuing period of humiliation left the cultural and social identity the Indians had achieved in fragments. Yet in Guatemala this pulverized identity is the only one that persists.* It persists in tragedy. During Holy Week, processions of the heirs of the Mayas produce frightful exhibitions of collective masochism. They drag heavy crosses and participate in the flagellation of Jesus step by step along the interminable ascent to Golgotha; with howls of pain they turn His death and His burial into the cult of their own death and their own burial, the annihilation of the beautiful life of long ago. Only there is no Resurrection at the end of their Holy Week.

---

* The Maya-Quichés believed in a single god; practiced fasting, penitence, abstinence, and confession; and believed in the flood at the end of the world. Christianity thus brought them few novelties. Religious disintegration began with colonization. The Catholic religion assimilated a few magical and totemic aspects of the Maya religion in a vain attempt to submit to the Indian faith to the conquistadors' ideology. The crushing of the original culture opened the way for syncretism.[34]

Ouro Prêto, the Potosí of Gold

The gold fever which is still sentencing Amazonian Indians to death or slavery is no novelty in Brazil. For two centuries after Brazil's discovery, the soil stubbornly denied metal to its Portuguese proprietors. In the first period of coastal colonization timber, or brazilwood, was commercially exploited; then sugar plantations were started in the Northeast. In contrast to Spanish Latin America, there seemed to be no gold or silver. Having found no highly developed and organized civilizations, only savage and scattered tribes who had no knowledge of metal, the Portuguese had to discover the gold on their own as they opened up the territory and exterminated its inhabitants.

The *bandeirantes** of the São Paulo region had crossed the great expanse between the Serra da Mantiqueira and the Rio São Francisco headwaters, and had observed small traces of alluvial gold in the beds and banks of several streams. The millennial action of the rains had eaten into the seams in the rocks and deposited gold in river beds, valleys, and mountain ravines. Beneath the layers of sand, dirt, or clay, the stony subsoil revealed nuggets that were easily removed from the quartz *cascalho,* or gravel; methods of extraction became more complex as the more superficial deposits were exhausted. Thus the Minas Gerais region entered history with a rush: the largest amount of gold ever discovered in the world till then was extracted in the shortest space of time.

"Here the gold was a forest," says the beggar one meets today, his eyes scanning the church towers. "There was gold on the sidewalks, it grew like grass." He is seventy-five years old now and considers himself part of the folklore in Mariana, the mining town where, as in nearby Ouro Prêto, the clock has simply stopped. "Death is certain, the hour uncertain—everyone has his time marked in the book," the beggar tells me. He spits on the stone steps and shakes his head: "They had more money than they could count," he says, as if he had seen them. "They didn't know where to put it, so they built churches one next to the other."

---

* A *bandeirante* was a member of a *bandeira,* a band of Portuguese slave- or gold-hunters in the Brazilian interior. The São Paulo *bandeiras* were part of a paramilitary organization whose strength varied. Their expeditions into the jungle played an important role in the interior colonization of Brazil. (Trans.)

Once this was the most important region of Brazil. Now . . . "Well, there's no life at all," says the old man. "No young folk. They all go." His bare feet move slowly beside me under the warm afternoon sun. "See that? On the front of that church, the sun and moon. That means that the slaves worked day and night. This church was built by black men; that one by white men. And that's the house of Monsenhor Alipio who died right on his ninety-ninth birthday."

In the eighteenth century Brazilian production of the coveted metal exceeded the total volume of gold that Spain had taken from its colonies in two previous centuries. Adventurers and fortune hunters poured in. Brazil had 300,000 inhabitants in 1700; a century later, at the end of the gold years, the population had multiplied eleven times. No less than 300,000 Portuguese emigrated to Brazil in the eighteenth century, a larger contingent than Spain contributed to all its Latin American colonies. From the conquest of Brazil until abolition, it is estimated that some 10 million blacks were brought from Africa; there are no precise figures for the eighteenth century, but the gold cycle absorbed slave labor in prodigious quantities.

Salvador de Bahia was the Brazilian capital of the prosperous Northeastern sugar cycle, but the "golden age" in Minas Gerais moved the country's economic and political capital southward and Rio de Janeiro, the region's port, became the new capital in 1763. In the dynamic heart of the new mining economy, camps bloomed abruptly into cities, described by a contemporary colonial authority as "sanctuaries for criminals, vagabonds, and malefactors," in a vertigo of easy riches. The "Vila Rica de Ouro Prêto"* had grown to city size by 1711; born of the miners' avalanche, it was the quintessence of the gold civilization. Simão Ferreira Machado, describing it twenty-three years later, said that the power of Ouro Prêto businessmen surpassed by far that of Lisbon's most flourishing merchants: "Hither, as to a port, are directed and collected in the Royal Mint the grandiose amounts of gold from all the Mines. Here dwell the best educated men, both lay and ecclesiastic. Here is the seat of all the nobility and the strength of the military. It is, by virtue of its natural position, the head of the whole of America; and by the wealth

* The "Rich Town of Black Gold," so called because the mined gold turned black on exposure to the humid air, due to the presence of silver. (Trans.)

of its riches, it is the precious pearl of Brazil."[35] Another writer of the period, Francisco Tavares de Brito, in 1732 defined Ouro Prêto as "the Potosí of gold."

Frequent complaints and protests reached Lisbon about the sinful life in Ouro Prêto, Sabará, São João d'El Rei, Mariana, and the whole turbulent mining district. Fortunes were made and lost overnight. It was commonplace for a miner to pay a fortune for a black who played a good trumpet and twice as much for a mulatto prostitute, "to abandon himself with her to continuous and scandalous sins." Men of the cloth behaved no better: official correspondence of the time contains many complaints against "bad clergymen" infesting the area. They were accused of using their immunity to smuggle gold inside little wooden images of saints. It was said that in 1705 Minas Gerais did not contain one priest who was interested in the Christian faith of the people, and six years later the Crown banned the establishment of any religious order in the mining district.

In any case, there was a proliferation of handsome churches built and decorated in the baroque style characteristic of the region. Minas Gerais attracted the best artisans of the time. Outwardly the churches looked sober and austere, but the interiors, symbolizing the divine soul, glistened with pure gold on their altars, reredoses, pillars, and bas-relief panels. Precious metals were not spared, so that the churches could achieve "the riches of Heaven," as the monk Miguel de São Francisco recommended in 1710. The price of religious services was astronomical, but everything in the mining area was exorbitant. As had happened in Potosí, Ouro Prêto devoted itself to squandering its sudden wealth. Processions and spectacles provided occasions to exhibit splendid robes and adornments. A religious festival in 1733 lasted over a week. There were not only processions on foot, on horseback, and in triumphal mother-of-pearl, silk, and gold chariots, with fantastic costumes and dazzling settings, but there were equestrian tournaments, bullfights, and dancing in the streets to the sound of flutes, flageolets, and guitars.

The slaves spent their strength and their days in the gold-washing installations. "There they work," wrote Luis Gomes Ferreira, a doctor who lived in Minas Gerais during the first half of the eighteenth century, "there they eat, and often there they have to sleep; and since when they work they are bathed in sweat, with their feet always in the cold earth, on stones, or in water, when they rest or eat their pores close and they become so chilled that they are susceptible to many dangerous illnesses, such as very severe pleurisies, apoplectic and paralytic fits, convulsions, pneumonia, and many other diseases."[36] *The capitães do mato* of Minas Gerais collected rewards in gold for the severed heads of slaves who tried to escape. Disease was a blessing from heaven because it meant the approach of death.

The slaves were called the "coins of the Indies" when they were measured, weighed, and embarked in Luanda in the Portuguese colony of Angola; in Brazil those surviving the ocean voyage became "the hands and feet" of the white master. Angola exported Bantu slaves and elephant tusks in exchange for clothing, liquor, and firearms, but Ouro Prêto miners preferred blacks shipped from the little beach of Ouidah on the Gulf of Guinea because they were more vigorous, lasted somewhat longer, and had the magic power to find gold. Every miner also needed a black mistress from Ouidah to bring him luck on his expeditions.[37] * Ouro Prêto's appetite for slaves became insatiable; they expired in short order, only in rare cases enduring the seven years of continuous labor. Yet the Portuguese were meticulous in baptizing them all before they crossed the Atlantic, and once in Brazil they were obliged to attend mass, although they were not allowed to sit in the pews or to enter the chancel.

The gold explosion not only increased the importation of slaves, but absorbed a good part of the black labor from the sugar and tobacco plantations elsewhere in Brazil, leaving them without hands. The miners were contemptuous of farming, and in 1700 and 1713, in the full flush of prosperity, hunger stalked the region: millionaires had to eat cats, dogs, rats, ants, and birds of prey. A royal decree in 1711 banned the sale of slaves occupied in agriculture, with the exception of those who showed "perversity of character."

By the middle of the eighteenth century many miners had gone to look for diamonds in Serra do Frio. The crystalline stones the gold

---

* In Cuba, medicinal powers were attributed to female slaves. According to onetime slave Esteban Montejo, "There was one type of sickness the whites picked up, a sickness of the veins and male organs. It could only be got rid of with black women; if the man who had it slept with a Negress he was cured immediately."[38]

hunters had tossed aside while exploring the riverbeds had turned out to be diamonds; Minas Gerais had both diamonds and gold in equal quantities. The booming camp of Tijuco became the center of the diamond district and there, as in Ouro Prêto, the wealthy sported the latest European fashions, bringing luxurious clothes, weapons, and furniture from across the ocean for their hour of delirium and dissipation. A mulatto slave, Francisca da Silva, or Xica da Silva, won her freedom by entering the bed of millionaire João Fernandes de Oliveira, the uncrowned king of Tijuco; she was ugly and had two children, but became "the *xica* who gives orders."[39] As she had never seen the sea and wanted it near her, her *cavalheiro* made her a large artificial lake on which he floated a ship, complete with crew. In the São Francisco foothills he built her a castle with a garden of exotic plants and artificial waterfalls; in her honor he gave sumptuous banquets with the finest wines, balls that never ended, and theater and concert performances.

In 1818 Tijuco could still manage a large-scale celebration of the prince of Portugal, but ten years earlier the Englishman John Mawe had visited Ouro Prêto and had been startled by its poverty. He found empty and worthless houses with futile "for sale" signs, and ate wretched and meager food. Tijtico did not take long to meet the same fate. The crisis had at first led to rebellion. José Joaquim da Silva Xavier, known as "Tiradentes"—the "toothpuller"—was hanged and quartered after being tortured, and other fighters for independence had disappeared from Ouro Prêto into jail or exile.

What Brazilian Gold Contributed to Progress in England

The gold began to flow just when Portugal signed the Methuen Treaty with England in 1703. The treaty crowned a long series of privileges obtained by British merchants in Portugal. In return for some advantages for its wines in the English market, Portugal opened its own and its colonies' markets to British manufactures. In view of the existing inequality of industrial development, this proved disastrous for local Portuguese manufactures. It was not with wine that English textiles were paid for, but with gold—Brazilian gold—and in the process Portuguese looms were paralyzed. Not content with killing its own industry in the bud, Portugal destroyed the seeds of any kind of manufacturing development in Brazil: until 1715 sugar refineries were banned, in 1729 it was made a criminal offense to open new roads in the mining region, and in 1785 local looms and spinning mills were ordered burned.

England and Holland, the leading gold and slave contrabandists, amassed fortunes in the illegal "black meat" traffic and are said to have illicitly garnered more than half the metal the Portuguese Crown was supposed to get from Brazil in *quinto real* tax. But Brazilian gold was channeled to London by licit as well as illicit methods. The gold boom, which brought a host of Portuguese to Minas Gerais, sharply stimulated colonial demand for industrial products and at the same time provided the means to pay for them. Just as Potosí silver rebounded off Spanish soil, Minas Gerais gold only reached Portugal in transit. The metropolis became an intermediary. In 1755 the Marquis de Pombal, Portugal's prime minister, tried to revive a protectionist policy, but it was too late. He declared that the English had conquered Portugal without the trouble of a conquest, that they were supplying two-thirds of its needs, and that British agents controlled the whole of Portuguese trade. Portugal was producing almost nothing, and the wealth brought by gold was so illusory that even the black slaves who mined it were clothed by the British.

Celso Furtado has noted that Britain, following a farsighted policy with respect to industrial development, used Brazilian gold to pay for essential imports from other countries and could thus concentrate on investments in the manufacturing sector. Thanks to this historical graciousness on the part of the Portuguese, Britain could apply rapid and efficient technical innovations. Europe's financial center moved from Amsterdam to London. According to British sources, the value of Brazilian gold arriving in London reached £50,000 a week in some periods. Without this tremendous accumulation of gold reserves, Britain would not have been able, later on, to confront Napoleon.

No result of the dynamic stimulus of gold remained on Brazilian soil except churches and works of art. By the end of the eighteenth century, although the diamond supply was still not exhausted, the country was prostrate. Furtado calculates that at that time—the low point of the whole colonial period—the per capita income of the 3 million-odd

Brazilians did not exceed $50 a year in today's buying power. Minas Gerais drowned in a long wave of decadence and insolvency. Incredibly, a modern Brazilian author expresses gratitude for the favor and submits that the capital the English derived from Minas Gerais "aided the great banking network that built international trade and made it possible to raise the living standards of peoples capable of progress."* Inexorably condemned to poverty so that foreigners might progress, the "incapable" mining communities moldered in isolation and could only resign themselves to scraping a livelihood from lands already despoiled of metals and precious stones. Subsistence farming replaced mining. Today the Minas Gerais countryside, like the Northeast, is the kingdom of the latifundio and the "hacienda colonels," a dauntless bastion of backwardness. The sale of Minas Gerais workers to haciendas in other states is almost as common as the slave traffic in the Northeast. Recently, Franklin de Oliveira toured Minas Gerais. He found collapsing wooden huts, villages without water or light, prostitutes of an average age of thirteen on the road in the valley of the Jequitinhonha, and crazed and famished people along the roadsides.[41] Minas Gerais was once accurately described as having a heart of gold in a breast of iron, but its fabulous "iron quadrilateral" is being exploited today by a joint Hanna Mining Company-Bethlehem Steel enterprise: the deposits were surrendered in a sinister deal in 1964. The iron, in foreigners' hands, will leave no more behind than did the gold.

Only the explosion of artistic talent remains as a memento of the gold delirium, apart from the holes in the ground and the abandoned cities; nor could Portugal salvage anything creative except for the aesthetic revolution. The convent of Mafra, pride of Dom João V, lifted Portugal from artistic decadence: in its carillons of thirty-seven bells and in its solid gold vessels and candelabra, there still glints the gold of Minas Gerais. The Minas churches have been extensively plundered and few sacred objects of portable size remain in them, but monumental baroque works still rise above the colonial ruins—façades and pulpits, galleries, reredoses, human figures designed, carved, or sculpted by Antônio

* The author, Augusto de Lima Jr., derives great happiness from "the expansion of colonizing imperialism which ignorant people today, inspired by their Moscow masters, describe as a crime."[40]

Francisco Lisboa—"Aleijadinho"—"Little Cripple," genius son of a female slave and a famous artisan. The eighteenth century was coming to a close when "Aleijadinho" began carving in stone a group of large sacred figures in the garden of the Bom Jesus do Matosinhos church in Congonhas do Campo. The work was called "The Prophets," but there was no longer any glory in prophesying. The gold euphoria was a thing of the past; all the pomp and gaiety had vanished and there was no room for hope. This dramatic final testimony, like a grand monument to the fleeting gold civilization that was born to die, was left to succeeding generations by the most talented artist in all Brazil's history. "Aleijadinho," disfigured and crippled by leprosy, created his masterpiece with chisel and hammer tied to fingerless hands, dragging himself on his knees to his workshop every morning.

Legend insists that in the Nossa Senhora das Mercês e Misericordia church in Minas Gerais, dead miners still celebrate mass on cold rainy nights. When the priest turns around, raising his arms from the high altar, one sees the bones of his face.

2. King Sugar and Other Agricultural Monarchs

Plantations, Latifundia, and Fate

Undoubtedly gold and silver were the main motivating force in the Conquest, but Columbus on his second voyage brought the first sugar-cane roots from the Canary Islands and planted them in what is now the Dominican Republic. To the Admiral's joy they took hold rapidly. Grown and refined on a small scale in Sicily, Madeira, and the Cape Verde Islands, and purchased in the Orient at high prices, sugar was so precious to Europeans that it figured in the dowries of queens. It was sold in pharmacies, weighed out by the gram. For almost three centuries after the discovery of America no agricultural product had more importance for European commerce than American sugar. Canefields were planted in the warm, damp littoral of Northeast Brazil; then in the Caribbean islands—Barbados, Jamaica, Haiti, Santo Domingo, Guadeloupe, Cuba, Puerto Rico—and in Veracruz and the Peruvian coast, which proved to be ideal terrain for the "white gold." Legions of slaves came from Africa to provide King Sugar with the prodigal, wageless labor force he required: human fuel for the burning. The land was devastated by this selfish plant which invaded the New World, felling forests, squandering natural fertility, and destroying accumulated soil humus. The long sugar cycle generated a prosperity as mortal as the prosperity generated by the silver and gold of Potosí, Ouro Prêto, Zacatecas, and Guanajuato. At the same time, directly or indirectly but decisively, it spurred the growth of Dutch, French, English, and U.S. industry.

The demand for sugar produced the plantation, an enterprise motivated by its proprietor's desire for profit and placed at the service of the international market Europe was organizing. Internally, however—since it was to a considerable extent self-sufficient—the plantation was feudal in many important aspects, and its labor force consisted mainly of slaves. Thus three distinct historical periods—mercantilism, feudalism, slavery—were combined in a single socioeconomic unit. But in the constellation of power developed by the plantation system, the international market soon took the center of the stage.

Subordinated to foreign needs and often financed from abroad, the colonial plantation evolved directly into the present-day latifundio, one of the bottlenecks that choke economic development and condemn the masses to poverty and a marginal existence in Latin America today. The latifundio as we know it has been sufficiently mechanized to multiply the labor surplus, and thus enjoys an ample reserve of cheap hands. It no longer depends on the importation of African slaves or on the *encomienda* of Indians; it merely needs to pay ridiculously low or in-kind wages, or to obtain labor for nothing in return for the laborer's use of a minute piece of land. It feeds upon the proliferation of minifundios—pocket-sized farms—resulting from its own expansion, and upon the constant internal migration of a legion of workers who, driven by hunger, move around to the rhythm of successive harvests.

The plantation was so structured as to make it, in effect, a sieve for the draining-off of natural wealth, and today the latifundio functions in the same way. Each region, once integrated into the world market, experiences a dynamic cycle; then decay sets in with the competition of substitute products, the exhaustion of the soil, or the development of other areas where conditions are better. The initial productive drive fades with the passing years into a culture of poverty, subsistence economy, and lethargy. The Northeast was Brazil's richest area and is now its poorest; in Barbados and Haiti human antheaps live condemned to penury; in Cuba sugar became the master key for U. S. domination, at the price of monoculture and the relentless impoverishment of the soil.

And this has not been the role of sugar alone: the story has been the same with cacao, which made the fortunes of the Caracas oligarchy; with the spectacular rise and fall of cotton in Maranho; with the Amazonian rubber plantations, which became the cemeteries of Northeastern workers recruited for a few pennies; with the devastated quebracho forests in northern Argentina and Paraguay; with Yucatán's henequen plantations, where Yaqui Indians were sent for extermination. It is also the story of coffee, which advances leaving deserts behind it, and of the fruit plantations in Brazil, Colombia, Ecuador, and the unhappy lands of Central America. Each product has come to embody the fate of countries, regions, and peoples; and mineral-producing communities have, of course, traveled the same melancholy road. The more a product is desired by the world market, the greater the misery it brings to the Latin American peoples whose sacrifice creates it. The area least affected by this iron law has been Río de la Plata, feeding the international market with its hides, meat, and wool; yet even it has been unable to break out of the cage of underdevelopment.

How the Soil Was Ravaged in Northeast Brazil

Because they discovered precious metals first, the Spaniards only began raising sugar in their colonies—initially in Santo Domingo, then in Veracruz, Peru, and Cuba—as a secondary activity. Brazil, on the other hand, became the world's largest sugar producer and remained so until the middle of the seventeenth century. Portugal's Latin American colony was also the chief market for slaves; native workers, always scarce, were rapidly killed off by the forced labor, and sugar needed thousands of hands to clear and prepare the ground, to plant, harvest, transport, grind, and refine the cane. Brazilian colonial society flourished in Bahia and Pernambuco as a sub-product of sugar until the discovery of gold moved its center to Minas Gerais.

The Portuguese Crown granted lands in usufruct to Brazil's first big landlords. The feats of conquest proceeded in tandem with the organization of production. Twelve "captains" received by written grant the whole of the vast unexplored territory, to be exploited in the king's service. However, the business was mostly financed by Dutch capital and thus became more Flemish than Portuguese. Dutch entrepreneurs not only participated in establishing sugar estates and importing slaves; they also picked up the crude sugar in Lisbon, refined it, sold it in Europe, and pocketed a third of its value in profits. In 1630 the Dutch West India Company invaded and conquered the northeast coast of Brazil and took over direct control of sugar production. To multiply their profits, the sources of sugar had to be multiplied, and the company offered the British in Barbados all facilities to start massive production in the Antilles. It brought Caribbean colonists to Brazil to acquire technical and organizational knowledge. When the Dutch were finally thrown out of the Brazilian Northeast in 1654, they had already laid the foundations for intense and ruinous competition by Barbados. They had taken slaves and cane-roots there, had set up sugar estates, and had provided all the implements. Brazilian exports plummeted to half of what they had been, and sugar prices were halved by the end of the seventeenth century. Meanwhile, Barbados's black population increased tenfold in a few decades. The Antilles were nearer to the European market, and Barbados developed superior techniques and offered virgin land—while Brazilian soil was wearing out. The crisis in the sugar-growing Northeast was also precipitated by serious slave revolts and by the gold boom to the south, which robbed the plantations of labor. The crisis was definitive: it has dragged itself painfully down the centuries into our time.

Sugar had destroyed the Northeast. The humid coastal fringe, well watered by rains, had a soil of great fertility, rich in humus and mineral salts and covered by forests from Bahia to Ceará. This region of tropical forests was turned into a region of savannas. Naturally fitted to produce food, it became a place of hunger. Where everything had bloomed exuberantly, the destructive and all-dominating latifundio left sterile rock, washed-out soil, eroded lands. At first there had been orange and mango plantations, but these were left to their fate, or reduced to small orchards surrounding the sugarmill-owner's house, reserved exclusively for the family of the white planter. Fire was used to clear land for canefields, devastating the fauna along with the flora: deer, wild boar, tapir, rabbit, pacas, and armadillo disappeared. All was sacrificed on the altar of sugarcane monoculture.

At the end of the sixteenth century Brazil had no less than 120 sugarmills worth some £2 million, but their masters, owners of the best lands, grew no food. They imported it, just as they imported an array of luxury articles which came from overseas with the slaves and bags of salt. Abundance and prosperity went hand in hand, as usual, with chronic malnutrition and misery for most of the population. Cattle were relegated to deserts far inland from the humid coastal zone to the *sertão* which, with two head of cattle to the square mile, supplied (and still supplies) tough, tasteless, and always scarce meat.

A legacy of those colonial days which continues is the custom of eating dirt. Lack of iron produces anemia, and instinct leads Northeastern children to eat dirt to gain the mineral salts which are absent from their diet of manioc starch, beans, and—with luck—dried meat. In former times this "African vice" was punished by putting muzzles on the children or by hanging them in willow baskets far above the ground.*

The Brazilian Northeast is today the most underdeveloped area in the Western hemisphere.† As a result of sugar monoculture it is a concentration camp for 30 million people—on the same soil that produced the most lucrative business of the colonial agricultural economy in Latin America. Today less than a fifth of Pernambuco's humid zone is used for growing sugar; the rest is not used at all.[1] The big sugarmill owners, who are also the biggest planters of cane, permit themselves this luxury of waste. It is not in the Northeast's arid and semi-arid interior that food conditions are worst, as is erroneously believed. The *sertão,* a desert of stones and sparse vegetation, has periods of hunger when the scorching sun produces drought and the semblance of a lunar landscape, forcing the people to flee and sowing crosses along the roadsides. But in the humid littoral—that coastal fringe still so ironically known as the "forest zone" in tribute to the remote past and to the pitiful remnants of forestation surviving from centuries of sugar—

---

* An English traveler, Henry Koster, attributed this custom to the contact the white children had with little blacks "who infect them with this African vice."

† In various ways the Northeast is the victim of internal colonialism for the benefit of the industrialized south. Within the Northeast, the *sertão* region is subordinated to the sugarbelt which it supplies, and the latifundios in their turn are subordinated to processing plants that industrialize sugar production. The ancient institution of the individually owned sugar estate is in crisis: the central mills have devoured the plantations.

hunger is endemic. Where opulence is most opulent, there—in this land of contradictions—misery is most miserable; the region nature chose to produce all foods, denies all. The sugar latifundio, a structure built on waste, must still import food from other areas, particularly from the center and south, at escalating prices. The cost of living in Recife is the highest in Brazil, well above Rio de Janeiro. Beans cost more in the Northeast than in Ipanema, the capital city's most luxurious beach resort. The price of half a kilo of manioc starch equals the wage an adult sugar-plantation worker receives for working from sunrise to sunset: if he complains, the foreman summons the carpenter to measure the man for the length and width of the boards that will be needed. In large areas the owner's or administrator's "right of the first night" for each girl is still effective. A third of Recife's population lives in miserable hovels; in one district, Casa Amarela, more than half the babies die before they are a year old. Child prostitution—girls of ten or twelve sold by their parents—is common in Northeastern cities. Some plantations pay less for a day's work than the lowest wage in India. A United Nations Food and Agriculture Organization (FAO) report in 1957 said that in the area of Victoria, near Recife, protein deficiency in children produces a weight loss 40 percent worse than is generally found in Africa. Many plantations still operate private prisons, but, as René Dumont notes, "those who are responsible for murder by undernourishment are not locked inside, since they are the keepers of the keys."[2]

Pernambuco now produces less than half as much sugar as the state of São Paulo, and has a far lower per hectare yield; but Pernambuco's inhabitants, densely concentrated in the humid zone, depend on sugar for their livelihood, while São Paulo contains the greatest industrial center in Latin America. In the Northeast not even progress is progressive, for it is in the hands of a few owners. The food of the minority is the hunger of the majority. Beginning in 1870 the sugar industry was substantially modernized as big central mills were installed, and the absorption of land by latifundios progressed alarmingly, sharpening the hunger of the area. In the 1950s, booming industrialization increased the consumption of sugar in Brazil itself. This stimulated Northeastern production, but without causing any rise in the per hectare yield. New lands of inferior quality were planted to cane, and sugar devoured still more of the few food-producing areas. Turned into a wage-worker, the peasant who had previously tilled his small plot experienced no benefit, since he did not earn enough money to buy what he had once produced. As usual, the expansion expanded hunger.

The Devastation of the Caribbean

"You believe perhaps, gentlemen," said Karl Marx in 1848, "that the production of coffee and sugar is the natural destiny of the West Indies. Two centuries ago, nature, which does not trouble herself about commerce, had planted neither sugarcane nor coffee trees there."[3] The international division of labor was not organized by the Holy Ghost but by men—more precisely, as a result of the world development of capitalism.

It was the fate of the "sugar islands"—Barbados, the Leewards, Trinidad-Tobago, Guadeloupe, Puerto Rico, Haiti, and Santo Domingo—to be incorporated one by one into the world market and condemned to sugar until our day. Grown on a grand scale, sugar spreads its blight on a grand scale and today unemployment and poverty are these islands' permanent guests. Cuba also continues to depend on the sale of sugar, although the agrarian reforms of 1959 sparked an intensive diversification of the economy which has ended seasonal unemployment. Cubans no longer work only during the five or so months of the sugar harvest, but for twelve months in the continuous job of building a new society.

Barbados was, starting in 1641, the first Caribbean island where sugar was grown for bulk export, although the Spaniards had planted cane earlier in Santo Domingo and Cuba. It was, as we have seen, the Dutch who introduced sugar into the little British island; by 1666 Barbados had 800 plantations and more than 80,000 slaves. Occupied vertically and horizontally by the developing latifundio, Barbados suffered no better fate than the Brazilian Northeast. It had previously produced a variety of crops on small holdings: cotton and tobacco, oranges, cows and pigs. Canefields devoured all this and devastated the dense forests in the name of a glorious illusion. The island soon found that its soil was exhausted, that it was unable to feed its population, and that it was producing sugar at uncompetitive prices.

By this time sugar cultivation had spread to the Leeward Islands, to Jamaica, and to the Guianas on the South American mainland. Jamaica entered the eighteenth century with ten times more slaves than white colonists. Its soil too was soon exhausted. In the second half of the century the world's best sugar was being raised on the spongy coastal plains of Haiti, a French colony then known as Saint Domingue. Northern and western Haiti became a human antheap: sugar needed hands and more hands. In 1786 the colony brought in 27,000 slaves; in the following year, 40,000. Revolution broke out in the fall of 1791 and in one month, September, 200 sugar plantations went up in flames; fires and battles were continuous as the rebel slaves pushed France's armies to the sea. Ships sailed containing ever more Frenchmen and ever less sugar. The war spilt rivers of blood, wrecked the plantations, and paralyzed the country, and by the end of the century production had fallen to almost nothing. By November 1803 almost all of the once flourishing colony was in ashes and ruins. The Haitian revolution had coincided—and not only in time—with the French Revolution, and Haiti bore its share of the international coalition's blockade against France: England controlled the seas. Later, as its independence became inevitable, Haiti also had to suffer blockade *by* France. The U.S. Congress, yielding to French pressure, banned trade with Haiti in 1806. In 1825 France recognized its former colony's independence, but only in exchange for a huge cash indemnity. General Leclerc had written to his brother-in-law Napoleon in 1802, soon after taking prisoner the slave armies' leader Toussaint L'Ouverture, "Here is my opinion about this country: all the blacks in the mountains, men and women, must be suppressed, keeping only the children under twelve; half the blacks in the plains must be exterminated, and not a single mulatto with epaulets must be left in the colony."[4] The tropics took their revenge on Leclerc: "Gripped by the black vomit," and despite the magical incantations of Pauline Bonaparte, he died without carrying out his plan.* But the cash indemnity was a millstone around the necks of those independent Haitians who survived the bloodbaths of the successive military

* Alejo Carpentier has written a fine novel about this fascinating period of Haitian history, *The Kingdom of This World* (1957). It contains a perfect recreation of the Caribbean adventures of Pauline and her husband.

expeditions against them. The country was born in ruins and never recovered: today it is the poorest in Latin America.

The crisis in Haiti produced the sugar boom in Cuba, which quickly became the world's top producer. Cuban production of coffee, another item in great demand overseas, was also stimulated by the collapse of Haitian production, but sugar won the monocultural race: in 1862 Cuba had to import coffee from abroad. A respected member of the Cuban "sugarocracy" held forth on "the proven advantages that can be obtained from another's misfortune."[5] After the Haitian rebellion, sugar prices in European markets topped all records, and by 1806 Cuba had doubled both its mills and its productivity.

Sugar Castles on Cuba's Scorched Earth

The British had taken Havana briefly in 1762. The island's rural economy was then based on small tobacco plantations and on cattle ranching; Havana, a military bastion, had craftsmen with advanced skills, an important foundry manufacturing cannon, and Latin America's first shipyard for building merchant and war ships on a big scale. Eleven months sufficed for the British occupiers to introduce as many slaves as would otherwise have entered in fifteen years, and from that time on the Cuban economy was shaped by the foreign need for sugar: slaves produced it for the world market and its bounteous surplus value was enjoyed by the local oligarchy and by imperialist interests.

Cuban sugar historian Manuel Moreno Fraginals describes with eloquent data the headlong advance of sugar in the years following the British occupation. Spain's commercial monopoly had in fact been blown apart, and all brakes on the entry of slaves had been removed. The sugarmills absorbed everything, men and land. To the mills went shipyard and foundry workers and the countless small artisans who had contributed decisively to the development of industry. Small peasants growing tobacco in the *vegas* or fruit in the orchards, victims now of the canefields' brutally destructive advance, also turned to sugar production. Extensive planting relentlessly reduced the soil's fertility; sugarmill towers multiplied in the Cuban countryside and each one needed more and more land. Fire devoured tobacco *vegas,* forests, and pasturelands.

Dried meat, a Cuban export a few years earlier, was by 1792 arriving in large quantities from abroad and was an import from then on.* The shipyard and foundry languished, tobacco production plummeted; the slaves of sugar put in a workday of up to twenty hours. On smoking lands the "sugarocracy" consolidated its power. In the late eighteenth-century euphoria of sky-high international prices, speculation ran riot: land prices went up twenty times in Güines; in Havana, eight times the legal rate of interest was paid; and throughout Cuba the fees for baptisms, burials, and masses rose in proportion to the soaring prices of blacks and oxen.

Early chroniclers told of traveling across all of Cuba in the shade of giant palms and through leafy forests abounding in mahogany, cedar, and ebony. Cuba's precious woods may still be admired in the tables and windowframes of the Escorial and in the doors of the royal palace in Madrid, but in Cuba the sugarcane invasion sent the best virgin forests up in smoke. In the same years it was destroying its own timberlands, Cuba became the chief purchaser of U.S. timber. The extensive plunder-culture of sugarcane meant not only the death of the forest but also, in the long run, the death of the island's fabulous fertility.† With forests surrendered to the flames, erosion soon did its work on the defenseless soil and thousands of streams dried up. The present-day per hectare yield from sugar plantations in Cuba is more than three times lower than in Peru and four and one-half times lower than in Hawaii. Irrigation and fertilization of the land are priority tasks for the Cuban Revolution. Large and small hydraulic dams are multiplying,

---

* The Río de la Plata meatpacking plants were already in operation. Argentina and Uruguay (then without separate existence and not so named) had adapted their economies to the massive export of dried and salted meat, hides, fats, and tallows. Brazil and Cuba, the nineteenth century's two great slave centers, were fine markets for dried meat, a very cheap food easily transported and warehoused since it did not go bad in the tropical heat. Cuba was the first market for Uruguayan meat—then shipped in thin, dry slices—at the end of the eighteenth century. Cubans still call dried meat "Montevideo," but Uruguay stopped selling it to Cuba in 1985 when they joined the OAS anti-Cuban bloc, thus idiotically losing their last market for the product.[6]

† Until recently, *palanqueros* operated on the Río Sagua. According to Fraginals, "They carry a long pole with an iron tip. With this they prod the riverbed until they strike a piece of wood. . . . Thus, day after day, they bring up from the river the remains of the trees that sugar felled. They live from the corpses of the forest."

fields are being irrigated, and fertilizer is being scattered over lands weak from centuries of punishment.

The "sugarocracy" piled up their fraudulent fortunes while reinforcing Cuba's dependence. Among those who savagely devastated Cuba's fertile soil were persons of refined European culture who could spot a genuine Brueghel and afford to buy it; they returned from frequent Paris trips with Etruscan vases and Greek amphorae, Gobelin tapestries and Ming screens, landscapes and portraits by the most fashionable British artists. I was startled to find in the kitchen of a Havana mansion an enormous strongbox with a secret combination in which a countess used to protect her table service. Up until 1959 it was not factories, but sugar castles that were built on the island: sugar installed and removed dictators, gave or denied jobs to workers, decided the rhythm of the "dance of the millions"—the 1919–1921 boom period—and of the terrible crises. The city of Trinidad is today a resplendent corpse. It collapsed, never to rise again, with the collapse of sugar prices in 1857.* In the mid-nineteenth century it had forty sugarmills producing 700,000 arrobas of sugar. Poor tobacco-farming peasants had been displaced by force and violence, and meat for the district—which had also raised cattle and had once exported meat—was being bought abroad. There was a flowering of colonial-style palaces with furtively shadowed porticos, chandeliers dripping crystal in high-ceilinged salons, Persian carpets, minuets faintly breaking the velvet silence, ormolu mirrors reflecting the graces of buckle-shod, bewigged caballeros. Great marble and stone skeletons, proud silent bell towers, and Spanish carriages invaded by grass remain today as testimony to all this. Trinidad became known as "the city of the 'hads'" because its white survivors always talked of past days when they "had" power and glory.

When the Sierra Maestra *guerrilleros* took power, Cuba's destiny was still tied to sugar prices. "A people that entrusts its subsistence to one product alone commits suicide," the national hero José Martí had prophesied. When sugar stood at $.22 a pound in 1920, Cuba beat the world record in per capita export—even surpassing England—and had

* Fraginals has perceptively noted that the names of sugar estates started in the nineteenth century reflected the rise and fall of the sugar curve: "Hope," "New Hope," "Audacious," "Gamble"; "Hopeful, "Conquest," "Confidence," "Good Results"; "Wit's End," "Woe," "Disenchantment." There were four estates named—with premonition—"Disenchantment."

Latin America's highest per capita income. But in December of that year the price fell to $.04 and a crisis of hurricane force descended in 1921: many sugarmills went bankrupt—to be bought up by U.S. interests—as did all the Cuban and Spanish banks, including the Banco Nacional itself. Only the branches of U.S. banks survived. The 1921 disaster had been brought on by the fall in sugar prices on the U.S. market, and from the United States came a prompt credit of $50 million. On the heels of the credit came General Enoch Crowder who, under the pretext of controlling the use of the funds, became Cuba's de facto governor. Thanks to his good offices the Machado dictatorship came to power in 1924, but the Great Depression of the 1930s lay ahead for this bloody regime, with Cuba paralyzed by a general strike. The U.S. crisis of 1929 could not but have a fierce impact on so dependent and vulnerable an economy as Cuba's: the price of sugar sank well below $.01 by 1932, and in three years the value of exports fell by 75 percent. At that time the unemployment index would have been hard to match in any other country.

What happened to prices was repeated in volume of exports. The United States lowered import duties on Cuban sugar in exchange for similar privileges for U.S. exports to Cuba, but such "favors" only consolidated Cuba's dependence. By 1948 Cuba had recovered its quota to the point of supplying one-third of the U.S. sugar market, at prices lower than U.S. producers received but higher and more stable than those in the international market. Sugar production was arbitrarily limited by Washington's needs. The 1925 level of some 5 million tons remained the average through the 1950s; dictator Fulgencio Batista took power in 1952 on the heels of the biggest harvest in Cuban history—over 7 million tons—with the mission of tightening the screws, and in the following year production, obedient to the demand in the north, fell to 4 million tons.* When Batista fell in 1959, Cuba was selling almost all its sugar to the United States. As Martí said and Che Guevara quoted at the OAS Punta del Este conference in 1961, "The nation that buys commands, the nation that sells serves; it is necessary to balance trade

* The director of the U.S. Department of Agriculture's sugar program declared soon after the Revolution: "Since Cuba has left the scene, we cannot count on that country, the world's biggest exporter, which always had enough reserves to supply our market when need arose."[7]

in order to ensure freedom; the country that wants to die sells only to one country, and the country that wants to survive sells to more than one."

The Cuban Revolt Against the Structure of Impotence

Geographical proximity and the advent of beet sugar production in France and Germany during the Napoleonic wars made the United States the chief customer for Antillean sugar. By 1850 the United States was absorbing one-third of all Cuban trade, selling it more and buying more from it than Spain, whose colony it was; the Stars and Stripes fluttered from more than half the ships arriving at the island. A Spanish traveler found U.S.-made sewing machines in remote Cuban villages in 1859. The main streets of Havana were paved with New England granite.

At the dawn of the twentieth century one could read in the *Louisiana Planter:* "Little by little the whole island of Cuba is passing into the hands of U.S. citizens, which is the simplest and safest way to obtain annexation to the United States." There was already talk in the Senate of a new star in the flag; with Spain's defeat, General Leonard Wood governed the island. At the same time the Philippines and Puerto Rico dropped into the United States' lap.* "They have been conferred upon

---

* Puerto Rico, another sugar factory, remained a prisoner. From the U.S. standpoint, Puerto Ricans are not good enough to live in a country of their own but are good enough to die in Vietnam for a country which is not theirs. In proportion to population, the "Free Associated State" of Puerto Rico has more soldiers fighting in Southeast Asia than the rest of the United States. Puerto Ricans resisting compulsory military service in Vietnam are sent to U.S. penitentiaries. Other humiliations inherited from the invasion of 1898 and blessed by law (the law of the U.S. Congress) are added to service in the U.S. armed forces. Puerto Rico is symbolically represented in the Congress, being without vote and virtually without voice. In exchange for this right: colonial status for an island that before the U.S. occupation had its own currency and carried on prosperous trade with the principal markets. Today the currency is the dollar and customs duties are fixed in Washington, where everything connected with the island's external and internal trade is decided. The same for foreign relations, transport, communications, wages, and work conditions. U.S. federal courts sit in judgment on Puerto Ricans; the local army is part of the U.S. army. Industry and commerce are in the hands of U.S. private interests. The emigration of Puerto Ricans has threatened to make denationalization complete: poverty has driven more than a million to New York hoping to improve their lot at the cost of losing their national identity. There they form a subproletariat which piles up in the most sordid slums.

us by the war," said President McKinley, including Cuba in his remarks, "and with God's help and in the name of the progress of humanity and civilization, it is our duty to respond to this great trust." In 1902 Tomás Estrada Palma had to renounce the U.S. citizenship he had acquired while living there in exile; the U.S. occupation forces made him the first president of Cuba. In 1960 the former U.S. ambassador to Cuba, Earl Smith, told a Senate subcommittee: "Until Castro came to power, the United States had such an irresistible influence in Cuba that the U.S. ambassador was the country's second personage, sometimes even more important than the Cuban president."

In 1954 a young revolutionary lawyer accurately prophesied, in his testimony to a court trying him for the attack on the Moncada barracks, that history would absolve him: "Cuba," he said in his resounding defense plea, "continues to be a producer of raw materials. We export sugar to import candy, we export hides to import shoes, we export iron to import plows."[8] Cuba bought not only automobiles, machinery, chemical products, paper, and clothing, but also rice and beans, garlic and onions, fats, meat, and cotton, all from the United States. Ice cream came from Miami, bread from Atlanta, and even luxury suppers from Paris. The country of sugar imported nearly half the fruit and vegetables it consumed, although only a third of its population had regular jobs and half of the sugar estate lands were idle acres where nothing was produced. Thirteen U.S. sugar producers owned more than 47 percent of the total area planted to cane and garnered some $180 million from each harvest. The subsoil wealth—nickel, iron, copper, manganese, chrome, tungsten—formed part of the United States' strategic reserves and were exploited in accordance with the varying priorities of U.S. defense and industry. In 1958 Cuba had more registered prostitutes than mine workers and a million and a half Cubans were wholly or partly unemployed.

The country's economy moved in step with its sugar harvests. The purchasing power of Cuban exports between 1952 and 1956 was no greater than it had been thirty years earlier, although foreign currency was much more needed. In the 1930s, when the crisis deepened the economy's dependence instead of helping to break it, newly installed factories were actually dismantled to sell to other countries. When the Revolution triumphed on the first day of 1959, Cuba's industrial development was poor and sluggish, over half the production was concentrated in Havana, and the few technologically modern factories were managed by remote control from the United States. A Cuban economist, Regino Botí, co-author of the Sierra *guerrilleros'* economic theses, cites the example of a Nestle's affiliate producing condensed milk in Bayamo: "When there was a breakdown, the technician simply phoned Connecticut and told them what he thought had gone wrong. He was told at once what to do about it and he simply followed instructions, without having to bother his head about theory. If this did not do the trick, a plane would arrive four hours later with a team of specialists. After nationalization, we could no longer phone for help, and the few technicians who might have been able to deal with minor faults had gone."[9] This illustrates precisely what problems the Revolution faced when it embarked on the adventure of converting the colony into a fatherland.

Cuba was crippled by its dependent status, and walking on its own feet has not been easy. Half of its children did not go to school in 1958, but, as Fidel Castro has said many times, the ignorance was much broader and more serious than mere illiteracy. The big campaign of 1961 mobilized an army of young volunteers to teach all Cubans to read and write, and the results astonished the world: according to UNESCO's Department of Education, Cuba now has the lowest percentage of illiterates and the highest percentage attending primary and secondary school in Latin America. But the inherited curse of ignorance cannot be overcome overnight—or in twelve years. A lack of efficient technicians, administrative incompetence and disorganization of production, and a bureaucratic fear of creative imagination and decision still obstruct the development of socialism. Yet despite the whole structure of impotence forged by four and one-half centuries of oppression, Cuba is being reborn with an enthusiasm that never flags: against obstacles it matches its strength, its gaiety, and its audacity.

In Cuba, Sugar Was the Knife, Imperialism the Assassin

"Is building on sugar better than building on sand?" Jean-Paul Sartre asked himself when he was in Cuba in 1960.

On the pier in the port of Guayabal, which exports sugar in bulk, pelicans wheel over an enormous shed. Entering it, I am astonished to see a golden pyramid of sugar. As hatches open to run the unsacked cargo down into the ships below, more cascades of gold—sugar newly brought from the mills—pour in through openings in the roof. It glints and sparkles in beams of sunlight. This warm mountain, too big for my eyes to take in, is worth some $4 million. Here, I think to myself, is summed up all the euphoria and drama of the record harvest of 1970, a harvest which aspired—but despite superhuman effort, was not able—to reach 10 million tons. Yet the story behind the golden cascade is a much longer one. I think about the Francisco Sugar Company (in which Allen Dulles was a director), where I have passed a week listening to stories of the past and seeing the birth of the future. . . . Josefina, daughter of Caridad Rodríguez, who studies in a classroom that was a barracks cell, the exact place where her father was held and tortured before he died; Antonio Bastidas, the seventy-year-old black who, early one morning this year, seized the lever of the siren with both hands, dancing in the air because the mill had overfilled its quota and yelling, "Shit, man, we done it!"—and no one would take Antonio's clenched hands off the lever while the siren, which had awakened the community, was awakening all Cuba. Stories of evictions, bribery, murder, hunger, of strange occupations which unemployment—obligatory more than six months of every year—engenders: hunting crickets in the fields, for example.

But those who died did not do so in vain: Amancio Rodríguez, for one, riddled with bullets by strikebreakers at a meeting, had angrily refused a blank check from the boss; his comrades, when they went to get his body, found he owned no underwear or socks to be buried in. Or Pedro Plaza, arrested at age twenty, who guided a truckful of soldiers over mines he had himself laid and was blown up with the truck and the soldiers. And so many more, in this area and all over: "Here," an old sugar worker told me, "the people have a great love for martyrs—but only after they're dead. Before, there's nothing but complaints." It wasn't an accident, I think to myself, that Fidel Castro recruited three-quarters of his *guerrilleros* from among the *campesinos,* the sugar workers; nor that Oriente province has throughout Cuba's history been the biggest source of both sugar and rebellion. I understand the accumulated rancor that made the Revolution, after the big harvest of 1961, decide to take revenge on sugar, the living memory of humiliation. Was it also Cuba's fate? Did it then become a penitence? Could it now be a lever, a catapult for economic development?

When a pardonable impatience set in, the Revolution destroyed many canefields and sought to diversify agriculture overnight. It didn't fall into the traditional error of dividing the latifundios into unproductive small farms, but every socialized farm proceeded to make sudden and excessive variations in its crops. Yet there had to be large-scale imports to industrialize the country, raise agricultural production, and satisfy many consumer needs which, in redistributing wealth, the Revolution enormously increased. Without big sugar harvests, where would the currency for these imports come from? The development of mining—particularly nickel—requires large investments, and these are being made; fishery production, also needing enormous investments, has risen eight times thanks to the growth of the fleet; ambitious plans for citrus fruit production are being implemented, but the interval of years between planting and harvesting demands patience. The Revolution, after discovering that it had confused the knife with the assassin, turned sugar, which had been responsible for underdevelopment, into an instrument of development. There was no alternative but to use the fruits of monoculture and dependence, born of Cuba's incorporation into the world market, to break the spine of that monoculture and dependence. No longer was the income earned by sugar to go to consolidate the structure of submission.*

Imports of machinery and industrial installations have risen by 40 percent since 1958; the economic surplus generated by sugar has been mobilized to develop basic industries and to see that neither lands nor workers are condemned to idleness. Cuba had 5,000 tractors and 30,000 automobiles when the Batista dictatorship fell. Today it has 50,000

* The stable sugar price guaranteed by the socialist countries has played a decisive role in this respect, as has the breaking of the U.S.-organized blockade by intensive trading with the West European countries. A third of Cuba's exports earn dollars—that is, convertible currency; the rest is on a barter basis with the Soviet Union and the ruble zone. This system of trading creates certain difficulties: while Soviet turbines for thermoelectric installations are of excellent quality, like all Soviet-made heavy equipment, this is not true of consumer goods produced by its light or medium-sized industry.

tractors—although they are to a large extent wasted because of organizational deficiencies—and nothing remains of that fleet of automobiles, mainly luxury models, except a few specimens fit for scrap-iron. The cement industry and electrical plants are growing with extraordinary speed; big fertilizer factories created by the Revolution have enabled Cuba to use five times more fertilizer than in 1958. Reservoirs built all over the island today contain seventy-three times as much water as was available in 1958, and Cuba has made a seven-league-boot advance in areas under irrigation. New highways throughout Cuba have broken what once seemed to be the eternal isolation of many regions. Holstein bulls, brought in to increase the meager milk production from Cebu cattle, have produced 800,000 cross-bred cows by artificial insemination.

Much progress—but still not enough—has been made in the mechanization of sugarcane cutting and loading, mainly using Cuban inventions. A new work system is being organized, with difficulty, to replace the old one which could not survive the changes brought by the Revolution. Professional *macheteros*, canecutters who are prisoners of sugar, are an extinct species: for them too, the Revolution meant freedom to choose other less grueling work, and for their children the chance of scholarships to study in the cities. Unavoidably, the sugar workers' liberation has resulted in serious upsets in the economy. In the 1970 harvest Cuba had to use three times as many workers as before, mainly volunteers or soldiers or people from different jobs, thereby harming other rural and urban activities—the harvesting of other products, the work-rhythm in the factories. Here one must bear in mind that in a socialist society, unlike in a capitalist one, workers are not motivated by fear of unemployment or by avarice. Other drives—solidarity, collective responsibility, awareness of the duties and rights that move a man beyond selfishness—must be brought into play. And the conscience of a whole people is not changed in a moment. When the Revolution came to power most Cubans, according to Fidel Castro, were not even anti-imperialists.

Cubans became radicalized along with their Revolution as challenges and responses, blows and counter-blows between Havana and Washington followed one upon the other, and as the Revolution proceeded to turn its promises of social justice into solid facts. It built 170 new hospitals and as many polyclinics, and made medical care free. It multiplied by three the number of students enrolled at all levels and also made education free; more than 300,000 children and youths benefit today from scholarships, and boarding schools and kindergartens have proliferated. A large part of the population pays no rent and no one pays for water, light, public telephones, funerals, or sporting events. Spending on social services increased five times in a few years. But now that everyone has education and shoes, necessities multiply geometrically and production can only grow arithmetically. Cuba has been compelled to escalate its exports, and sugar continues to be its major resource. Many products are in short supply: in 1970, fruit and refrigerators and clothing. Queues, part of the daily routine, are not solely due to disorganized distribution. The essential cause of scarcity is the new abundance of consumers: the country now belongs to everyone, consumption is by all, not just a few. Thus it is scarcity of an opposite kind to that in other Latin American countries. The Revolution is indeed living through the hard times of transition and sacrifice. The Cubans themselves have learned that socialism is built with clenched teeth and that revolution is no evening stroll. But after all, if the future came on a platter, it would not be of this world.

The Revolution is forced to sleep with its eyes open, and in economic terms this also costs dearly. Constantly harassed by invasion and sabotage, it does not fall because—strange dictatorship!—it is defended by a people in arms. The expropriated expropriators do not give up. The brigade that landed at the Bay of Pigs in April 1961 was not only made up of former Batista soldiers and policemen, but also of the previous owners of more than 370,000 hectares of land, nearly 10,000 buildings, seventy factories, ten sugarmills, three banks, five mines, and twelve cabarets. Guatemalan dictator Miguel Ydígoras Fuentes provided training camps for the expedition in return, as he later admitted, for U.S. promises of cash (which was never paid) and an increase in the Guatemalan sugar quota in the U.S. market.

In 1965 another sugar country, the Dominican Republic, was invaded, this time—according to their commander, General Bruce Palmer—by 40,000 U.S. Marines ready "to stay indefinitely in this country in view of the reigning confusion." The vertical drop in sugar prices had been a factor in setting off popular indignation; the people rose against the military dictatorship and U.S. troops arrived promptly to restore order. They left 4,000 dead in battles fought by patriots, body to body, in a crowded Santo Domingo slum, between the Río Ozama and the Caribbean.* The Organization of American States—which has the memory of a donkey, never forgetting where it eats—blessed the invasion and supplied it with new forces. The germ of another Cuba had to be exterminated.

From the Sacrifice of the Slaves in the Caribbean Were Born James Watt's Steam Engine and George Washington's Cannon

Che Guevara said that underdevelopment was a dwarf with an enormous head and a bloated stomach: its spindly legs and stubby arms do not fit with the rest of the body. In yesterday's Havana fashionable avenues glittered and purred with Cadillacs, and luscious starlets undulated to the rhythms of Lecuona's famous band in the world's largest cabaret; meanwhile in the Cuban countryside only one in every ten peasants ever drank milk, barely 4 percent ate meat, and the wages of three out of five (according to the National Economic Council) were three to four times lower than the cost of living.

But sugar did not only produce dwarfs. It also produced giants, or at least contributed generously to their growth. The sugar of tropical Latin America gave powerful impetus to the accumulation of capital for English, French, Dutch, and U.S. industrial development, while at the same time mutilating the economy of Northeast Brazil and the Caribbean islands and consummating the historic ruin of Africa. The fulcrum

* After the invasion, President Lyndon Johnson's special envoy to the Dominican Republic was Ellsworth Bunker, the chairman of the National Sugar Refining Company. National Sugar's interests in this small country were safeguarded under Bunker's attentive eye: the occupation troops withdrew, leaving in power, after very democratic elections, Joaquín Balaguer, Trujillo's right arm throughout his brutal dictatorship. The Dominicans had fought in the streets and on rooftops, with sticks, machetes, and guns, against the foreign forces' tanks, bazookas, and helicopters for the return to power of constitutionally elected President Juan Bosch, who had been overthrown by a military coup. History plays derisively prophetic games. On the day when Bosch began his brief presidency, after thirty years of Trujillo tyranny, Lyndon Johnson, then vice-president, brought his government's official gift to Santo Domingo: it was an ambulance.

of the triangular trade—manufactures, slaves, sugar—between Europe, Africa, and America was the traffic in slaves for sugar plantations. As Auguste Cochin wrote: "The story of a grain of sugar is a whole lesson in political economy, in politics, and also in morality."

West African tribes fought among themselves to add prisoners of war to their reserves of slaves. They were in Portugal's colonial orbit, but when the slave trade boomed the Portuguese, lacking ships and industrial articles to offer in exchange, became mere middlemen between African potentates and slaver captains of other nations. The English were the champions in buying and selling human flesh until it ceased to be convenient for them. The Dutch, however, had longer experience in the business—Charles V had given them a monopoly in shipping slaves to the Americas before England obtained the right to introduce slaves into the colonies. As for France, the "Sun King" Louis XIV shared with the king of Spain half the profits of the Guinea Company, formed in 1701 to facilitate the slave trade to the Americas; and his finance minister Jean-Baptiste Colbert, the architect of French industrialization, had good reason to describe the slave traffic as "recommended for the progress of the national merchant marine."[10]

Adam Smith said that one of the principal effects of the discovery of America "has been to raise the mercantile system to a degree of splendour and glory which it could never otherwise have attained to."[11] According to Sergio Bagú, the most potent force for the accumulation of mercantile capital was slavery in the Americas; and this capital in turn became "the foundation stone on which the giant industrial capital of modern times was built." The New World revival of Greco-Roman slavery had miraculous qualities: it multiplied the ships, factories, railroads, and banks of countries that were not originally involved in Africa or—with the exception of the United States—in the fate of the slaves crossing the Atlantic. From the dawn of the sixteenth to the dusk of the nineteenth centuries, many millions of Africans—no one knows how many—crossed the ocean; what is known is that they greatly exceeded the number of white emigrants from Europe, although many fewer survived. From the Potomac to the Río de la Plata, slaves built the houses of their masters, felled the forests, cut and milled the sugarcane, planted the cotton, cultivated the cacao, harvested the coffee and tobacco, and were entombed in the mines. How many Hiroshimas did these successive exterminations add up to? As an English planter in Jamaica remarked, "It's easier to buy niggers than to breed them." Caio Prado estimates that up to the beginning of the nineteenth century between 5 and 6 million Africans arrived in Brazil alone, and that Cuba was then as big a slave market as the whole Western hemisphere had been before.

Back in 1562 Captain John Hawkins had smuggled 300 blacks out of Portuguese Guinea. Queen Elizabeth was furious: "It was detestable and would call down vengeance from heaven upon the undertakers," she cried.[12] But Hawkins told her that in exchange for the slaves he had a cargo of sugar, hides, pearls, and ginger in the Caribbean, and she forgave the pirate and became his business partner. A century later the Duke of York was branding the initials "DY" on the left buttock or breast of each of the 3,000 blacks his concern annually took to the "sugar islands." The Royal African Company, whose shareholders included Charles II, paid 300 percent in dividends, although only 46,000 of the 70,000 slaves it shipped between 1680 and 1688 survived the crossing. On the voyage many Africans died of epidemics or malnutrition; others commited suicide by refusing to eat, hanging themselves by their chains, or throwing themselves into a sea bristling with sharks' fins.

Slowly but surely England broke Holland's slave-trade hegemony. The South Sea Company was the chief beneficiary of the *asiento*, the royal monopoly on the slave trade which Spain had conceded to England, and leading figures in British politics and finance were connected with the company. Its business topped all others, agitated the London stock exchange, and set off reckless speculation. Traffic in slaves raised the shipping center of Bristol to the rank of Britain's second city and made Liverpool the world's greatest port. Ships sailed with cargoes of duly blessed weapons, cloth, gin and rum, baubles and colored glass, the means of payment for Africa's human merchandise and for the sugar, cotton, coffee, and cacao of American colonial plantations. The British established their reign over the seas. At the end of the eighteenth century, Africa and the Caribbean were providing work for 180,000 textile workers in Manchester; Sheffield produced the knives, Birmingham produced 150,000 muskets a year. African chiefs received the products of British industry and delivered the human cargoes to slaver captains. This provided them with new weapons and plenty of liquor to embark on the next manhunts in the villages. They also supplied ivory, wax, and palm oil. Many of the slaves came from forest areas and had never seen the sea; they mistook its roaring for that of some underwater beast waiting to devour them, or (according to a slavetrader of the period) believed, not entirely without reason, that "they are carried like sheep to the slaughter and that Europeans are fond of their flesh. . . ."[13] The cat-o'-nine-tails could do little to contain the Africans' desperate suicides.

The "bundles" who survived the hunger and disease, the weeks of lying crammed together below decks, were exhibited in rags—mere skin and bones—in the public square after being paraded through colonial streets to the sound of bagpipes. Those arriving too exhausted could be fattened up in the slave barracks before showing them to buyers; the sick ones were left to die on the piers. Slaves were sold for cash or on three-year credit. The ships sailed back to Liverpool carrying various tropical products: in the early eighteenth century three-quarters of the cotton used by the British textile industry came from the Antilles, although Georgia and Louisiana later became its chief sources; by mid-century there were 120 sugar refineries in Britain.

At that time an Englishman could live on £6 a year; Liverpool slave merchants garnered more than £1.1 million a year in the Caribbean alone, not including their fat profits from the additional trade. Ten big concerns controlled two-thirds of the traffic. Liverpool installed a new system of docks; more, longer, and heavier ships were constantly being built. Silversmiths offered "silver padlocks and collars for niggers and dogs," elegant ladies paraded about with monkeys in embroidered jackets and child slaves in turbans and ballooning silk trousers. An economist described the slave trade as "the basic and fundamental principle of all the rest, like the mainspring of the machine which sets every cogwheel in motion." Banks proliferated in Liverpool, Manchester, Bristol, London, and Glasgow; Lloyds piled up profits insuring slaves, ships, and plantations. From the beginning, *London Gazette* announcements advised that fugitive slaves should be returned to Lloyds. Slave-trade profits financed the building of Britain's Great Western railway and of industries such as the Welsh slate factories. Capital accumulated in the triangular trade made possible the invention of the steam engine: James Watt was subsidized by businessmen who had made their fortunes in that trade.[14]

Early in the nineteenth century Britain became the leader in the anti-slavery campaign. British industry needed international markets with more purchasing power, which led it to preach the gospel of wages. But the introduction of wages in Britain's Caribbean colonies gave renewed advantage to Brazilian sugar, with its comparatively lower costs from using slave labor.* The British fleet now attacked the slavers, but the traffic to supply Cuba and Brazil continued growing. Before a British ship could reach a pirate ship, the slaves were thrown into the sea; all that remained on board were the smell and the laughing captain on deck. Repression of the traffic raised prices and further pyramided profits. By the middle of the century slavers were selling vigorous slaves, whom they had got for an old rifle, for more than $600 a head in Cuba.

The little Caribbean islands had been far more important to Britain than its colonies to the north: Barbados, Jamaica, and Monserrat were forbidden to make so much as a needle or a horseshoe for themselves. But the situation was quite different in New England, and this facilitated both its economic development and its political independence. In New England the slave trade gave birth to a large part of the capital that produced the U.S. industrial revolution. In the middle of the eighteenth century Northern slave ships carried barrels of rum to Africa from Boston, Newport, and Providence; they exchanged the rum for slaves, sold the slaves in the Caribbean, and from there brought molasses to Massachusetts, where it was distilled and converted into rum, completing the cycle. The best Antillean rum, "West Indian Rum," was not even made in the Antilles. With capital obtained from this trade in slaves, the Brown brothers of Providence installed the foundry that provided George Washington with guns for the American Revolution. Caribbean sugar plantations, condemned as they were to cane monoculture, were not the dynamic center of development for the "thirteen colonies" solely because of the impetus the slave trade gave to naval industry and to the New England distilleries; they also provided a large market for the export of foodstuffs, timber, and sugarmill implements, lending economic viability to the farm and budding factory economy of the North Atlantic. Ships built in the colonists' yards carried to the Caribbean

* The first law expressly banning slavery in Brazil was not Brazilian. It was—and not by accident—English. The British parliament voted it on August 8, 1845.

massive cargoes of fresh and smoked fish, grain, beans, flour, fats, cheese, onions, horses and oxen, candles and soap, textiles, pine, oak, and cedar for sugar boxes (Cuba had the first steam saw in Hispanic America but no timber to cut), and barrel staves, hoops, rings, and nails.

The whole process was a pumping of blood from one set of veins to another: the development of the development of some, the underdevelopment of others.

The Rainbow Is the Road Back to Guinea

From Santo Domingo, a lawyer named Alonso Zuazo reported to Charles V in 1518: "Fears of a possible rising by the blacks are groundless; there are widows living tranquilly with eight hundred slaves in Portuguese islands; it is all a matter of how they are handled. I found on arrival here some cunning niggers, and others who had taken to the woods; I thrashed some, cut off the ears of others, and there has been no more trouble." Four years later the first slave rising in the Americas broke out: the slaves of Diego Columbus, son of the discoverer, started the revolt and ended on gallows lining the sugarmill lanes. Other rebellions followed, in Santo Domingo and then in all the Caribbean sugar islands. A couple of centuries after the Diego Columbus uprising, at the other end of the island, runaway slaves fled to the Haitian mountains and there reconstructed African life, growing their food, worshiping their gods, practicing their ancient customs. For the people of Haiti the rainbow still symbolizes the road back to Guinea—in a ship with a white sail. In Dutch Guiana (Surinam) communities of Djukas, descendants of slaves who fled into the forest, have survived for three centuries across the Courantyne River. In these villages "obeah shrines like those in Guinea can be seen, ceremonial dances are performed that could take place in Ghana, and the people talk with drums, which are made like Ashanti drums."[15] The first big revolt in Guiana occurred one hundred years after the flight of the Djukas: the Dutch recovered the plantations and burned the slave leaders in slow fires. But in Brazil a little before the Djuka exodus, fugitive slaves had organized the black kingdom of Palmares in the Northeast, and throughout the eighteenth century had successfully resisted dozens of military expeditions sent to suppress them, first by the Dutch and then by the Portuguese. Assaults by thousands of soldiers were fruitless against the guerrilla tactics which, until 1693, made the refuge invulnerable. The independent kingdom of Palmares—a call to rebellion, a banner of liberty—was organized as a state, similar to the many that existed in Africa in the seventeenth century. It extended from near Cape Santo Agostinho in Pernambuco to the northern Rio Saõ Francisco zone in Alagoas, an area one-third the size of Portugal and surrounded by dense, wild forests. The ruling chief was elected from among the wisest and most skillful: the man of greatest prestige and success in war or command. When the sugar plantation was at its height of omnipotence, Palmares was the one corner of Brazil where agriculture was being diversified. Guided by their own experience or that of their ancestors in African savannas and forests, the blacks raised corn, sweet potatoes, beans, manioc, bananas, and other foods. The colonial troops, assigned to bring back the men who had crossed the sea in chains and deserted the plantations, believed—and not without reason—that the destruction of these crops was their main purpose.

The abundance of food in Palmares contrasted with its lack in coastal areas at the zenith of the sugar prosperity. The slaves who had won liberty defended it ably and bravely because they shared its fruits: land in the black state was held in common and no money circulated. No slave rebellion in world history lasted as long as that in Palmares: Spartacus's rebellion, which shook the most important slave system of ancient times, lasted eighteen months.[16] For the final onslaught the Portuguese Crown mobilized the biggest army seen in Brazil until the colony became independent much later. No fewer than 10,000 people defended the last bastion of Palmares; the survivors were beheaded, thrown from precipices, or sold to merchants in Rio de Janeiro and Buenos Aires. Two years later the chief Zumbi, whom the slaves believed to be immortal, was betrayed and captured. He was surrounded in the forest and his head cut off. And rebellions continued. Not long afterward Captain Bartolomeu Bueno do Prado returned from the Rio das Mortes with trophies of victory over another slave rising. He brought 3,900 pairs of ears in his horses' saddlebags.

In Cuba, too, there were risings. Some slaves committed mass suicide, mocking their masters, as Fernando Ortiz has put it, "with their eternal strikes, their unending flight to the other world." They thought they would thus be brought back to life, body and soul, in Africa. By mutilating the corpses so they would return to life castrated, maimed, or decapitated, the masters dissuaded many from killing themselves. Around 1870, according to a recent account by a Las Villas 100-year-old slave who took to the woods as a youth, blacks in Cuba no longer chose suicide. A magic chain gave them power and they "flew through the sky and returned to their own land"; or they lost themselves in the mountains because "everyone wearied of life, and the ones who got used to it were broken in spirit. Life in the forest was healthier."[17]

The gods of Africa remained alive for the slaves, as did the nostalgia-nourished legends and myths of their lost fatherlands. In their ceremonies, dances, and incantations the blacks clearly expressed the need to affirm a cultural identity that Christianity denied, but the Church's material stake in the exploitation they suffered must have been a factor also. In the early eighteenth century, while slaves convicted of crimes in British islands were crushed between cane-milling cylinders, and in French islands were burned alive or broken on the wheel, the Jesuit Antonil was offering Brazilian sugarmill owners kindly recommendations for the avoidance of excesses: "Administrators should under no circumstances be permitted to administer kicks in the belly to pregnant women nor beatings to the slaves, since anger may prevail over restraint and an efficient and valuable slave may be injured in the head and lost."[18] In Cuba, overseers applied their thongs of hide or hemp to the backs of pregnant females who had erred, but not before stretching them out with their bellies over a hole to avoid damaging "the little creature"; priests, who received 5 percent of sugar production as a tithe, gave Christian absolution; the overseer administered punishment like Jesus Christ castigating sinners. The apostolic missionary Juan Perpiña y Pibernat published his sermons to the blacks: "My poor little ones! Be not afraid because as slaves you have so many burdens to bear! Your body may be enslaved, but your soul remains free to fly one day to the happy mansions of the chosen."[19] *

The god of the pariahs is not always the same as the god of the system that makes them pariahs. Although the Catholic religion officially embraces 94 percent of the population of Brazil, black Brazilians today maintain their African traditions and keep alive their religious faith, often camouflaged behind Christian saints; cults of African origin are widely practiced by the oppressed, whatever their skin color. The same is true in the Antilles. The voodoo gods in Haiti, Cuba's *bembé,* and Brazil's *umbanda* and *quimbanda* are more or less the same, despite the greater or smaller transfiguration that rites and original gods have undergone through American naturalization. In the Caribbean and in Bahia the ceremonial chants are intoned in Nagô, Yoruba, Congo, and other African languages. In the big city suburbs of southern Brazil, on the other hand, Portuguese predominates. But from the West African coast the gods of good and evil have endured throughout the centuries to become the avenging phantoms of the disinherited, the humiliated poor who chant in the slums of Rio de Janeiro:

> Power of Bahia,
> Power of Africa,
> Divine power,
> Come to us,
> Come and help us.

Peasants for Sale

Brazil abolished slavery in 1888, but it did not abolish the latifundio, and in the same year an eyewitness wrote from Ceará, in the Northeast: "The human cattle market was open as long as there was hunger, and there was no lack of buyers. Rare was the steamer in which large numbers of Ceará people were not shipped out."[20] Half a million Northeasterners emigrated to Amazonia, drawn by the rubber mirage, until the turn of the century; after that the exodus continued as periodic droughts devastated the *sertão* and "forest zone" sugar latifundios expanded in successive waves. In 1900, 40,000 drought victims left Ceará. They took

---

* One Holy Thursday the Count of Casa Bayona decided to humiliate himself before his slaves. Inflamed with Christian fervor, he washed the feet of twelve blacks and invited them to dine with him at his table. It was in truth the last supper. Next day the slaves rebelled and set fire to the sugarmill. Their heads were stuck on twelve lances in the middle of the estate.

the road that everyone took at the time, north to the jungle. Later the direction changed: in our day Northeasterners emigrate to the center and south of Brazil. The drought of 1970 drove hungry multitudes into the cities of the Northeast. They plundered trains and stores, implored the saints to send rain, and clogged the roads. "Pernambuco state police," said a wire service cable in April 1970, "last Sunday arrested in the municipality of Belém do São Francisco 210 peasants who were to be sold for $18 a head to rural landowners in Minas Gerais state."[21] * The peasants came from Paraíba and Rio Grande do Norte, the two states most punished by drought. In June, statements by the federal police chief came over the teletype: no effective means of ending the slave traffic were available to him, and although ten investigations had been launched in recent months, the sale of Northeastern workers to rich landowners in other areas continues.

The Rubber Cycle: Caruso Inaugurates a Jungle Theater

Some authors estimate that in the period of the rise of rubber no less than half a million Northeasterners succumbed to epidemics, malaria, tuberculosis, or beriberi. Says one: "This grim charnel house was the price of the rubber industry."[22] Peasants with no nutritional reserves went from the dry lands to the swampy jungle, where fevers lay in wait for them. Packed into ships' holds for the long journey, many anticipated their fate by dying en route. Others did not even reach the ships. In 1878, 120,000 of Ceará's 800,000 population headed for the Amazon and less than half got there; the rest collapsed from hunger or disease on the *sertão* trails or in the suburbs of Fortaleza. A year earlier one of the Northeast's seven greatest droughts of the past century had begun.

Not only fevers awaited them in the jungle, but a work regime very similar to slavery. *Guardias rurales* posted along the riverbanks shot at fugitives. The pay was in kind—dried meat, manioc flour, lumps of

* In 1938 the pilgrimage of a cowhand over the parched roads of the *sertão* inspired one of the best novels in Brazilian literature. On cattle ranches in the interior, subordinated to coastal sugarmills, there has been no let-up in the scourge of drought and the effects continue the same. The world of Graciliano Ramos's *Barren Lives*—in which the parrot imitates the dog's bark because his masters have almost stopped using the human voice—remains intact.

unrefined sugar, *aguardiente*—until the rubber worker paid off his debts, a miracle that rarely occurred. Employers had an agreement among themselves not to give jobs to workers who were in debt to other employers. Debts piled on debts. To the cost of transport from the Northeast were added the debts for work tools, machetes, knives, and eating bowls; and since the worker consumed food—and above all liquor, never a scarce commodity in the rubber forests—the longer he worked the higher his accumulated debt. The illiterate Northeasterners were at the mercy of the administrators' conjuring tricks with the ledgers.

In 1770 J.B. Priestley had observed that rubber would erase pencil marks on paper, and seventy years later Charles Goodyear and the Englishman Thomas Hancock simultaneously discovered the process of vulcanizing rubber, making it flexible and impervious to temperature changes. By 1850 the wheels of vehicles were being sheathed in rubber. At the end of the century the automobile industry was born in the United States and Europe, and with it the consumption of great quantities of pneumatic tires. World demand for rubber soared. The rubber-tree was bringing Brazil a tenth of its export income in 1890, and by 1910 this had risen to 40 percent, making rubber sales almost equal to those of coffee, although coffee was then at the height of its prosperity. Most of the rubber production came from the Acre area, which Brazil had wrested from Bolivia after a lightning military campaign.*

With Acre in its possession, Brazil had almost all of the world's rubber reserves. Prices were at their peak on the international market and it seemed that good times had come to stay. The rubber workers, of course, did not share in this, although it was they who went out from their huts each dawn, receptacles strapped on their backs, to bleed the giant *Hevea brasiliensis* trees. They made incisions in the trunks and in thick branches and the whitish, sticky latex dripped from the wounds, filling the cups in a couple of hours. At night the flat slabs of rubber which had accumulated in the administration center were cooked. The sour and revolting smell of rubber impregnated the city of Manaus, world capital of the rubber business. Manaus had 5,000 inhabitants in 1849; it had 70,000 in little more than half a century. There rubber magnates

---

* Some 75,000 square miles were lopped off Bolivia. In 1902 it got a £2 million indemnity and a railway line giving it access to the Madeira and Amazon rivers.

built their extravagantly designed and sumptuously decorated mansions with precious Oriental woods, Portuguese majolicas, columns of Carrara marble, and furniture by French master cabinetmakers. The nouveau riche of the jungle had the most costly foods brought from Rio de Janeiro; Europe's top couturiers cut their dresses and outfits; they sent their sons to study at British schools. The Amazonas theater, a baroque monument in triumphantly poor taste, is the chief symbol of that vertigo of wealth at the beginning of our century. Caruso navigated the river through the jungle to sing to Manaus's inhabitants for a kingly fee on opening night; Pavlova, who was supposed to dance there, could not get beyond Belém but sent her apologies.

In 1913 sudden disaster hit Brazilian rubber. The world price fell to a quarter of the two shillings it had been three years earlier. The Far East had only exported four tons of rubber in 1900; in 1914 Ceylonese and Malay plantations poured over 70,000 tons onto the world market, and within five years their exports approached the 400,000-ton mark. By 1919 Brazil, which had had a virtual monopoly, was supplying only one-eighth of world consumption. A half-century later Brazil is buying more than half its rubber from abroad.

What happened? Back in 1873 Henry Wickham, an Englishman who owned rubber forests on the Rio Tapajoz and was known for his botanical manias, had sent sketches and leaves of the rubber tree to the director of Kew Gardens in London. He got an order for a quantity of seeds from the yellow fruit of *Hevea brasiliensis*. Since Brazil severely punished any leakage of seeds, he had to smuggle them out, which was not easy: ships were meticulously searched by the authorities. Then, as if under a magic spell, an Inman Line ship penetrated 1,200 miles further than usual into the interior of Brazil. On its return, Henry Wickham was aboard as a member of the crew. He had selected the best seeds after putting the fruit out to dry in a native village, and had put them in a locked cabin, wrapped in banana leaves and suspended on strings so that the ship's rats could not get at them. The rest of the ship was empty. In the port of Belém, at the river's mouth, Wickham invited the authorities to a grand banquet. The Englishman's eccentricities were notorious—all Amazonia knew that he collected orchids—and he explained that on order from the English king he was carrying a collection of rare orchid bulbs to Kew Gardens. As the plants were very delicate he had them in a hermetically sealed cabin at a special temperature: if it was opened the flowers would be ruined. Thus the seeds reached the Liverpool docks unscathed. Forty years later the British invaded the world market with Malayan rubber. The Asian plantations, skillfully developed from shoots grown at Kew Gardens, easily supplanted Brazilian production.

Amazonian prosperity vanished in a puff of smoke. The jungle closed back upon itself. Fortune hunters left for other parts and the luxurious camp disintegrated. The only people remaining, surviving as best they could, were the workers who had been brought from afar to make fortunes for others—and not even for Brazilians. For Brazil had merely responded to the siren song of world demand for raw materials, without itself participating in the real business of rubber—finance, trade, industrialization, and distribution. The siren fell mute until World War II gave a new but fleeting push to Amazonian rubber. The Allied powers desperately searched for supplies when the Japanese occupied Malaya: the Peruvian jungle was ransacked and the so-called Battle of Rubber once again mobilized Brazil's Northeastern peasants.* This time, according to an accusation made in the Congress when the "battle" ended, the victims of disease and hunger, whose bodies remained to rot among the rubber trees, numbered some 50,000.

The rubber boom and the rise of coffee growing involved big levies of Northeastern workers. But the government also uses its bottomless reserve of cheap labor for public works. The naked men who built the city of Brasilia almost overnight were Northeasterners transported like cattle to the wilderness site. Today this most modern of the world's cities is surrounded by a great belt of poverty: when they finished their work, these people—known as *candangos*—were dumped in outlying hovels. There, always available for any task, 300,000 Northeasterners live off the splendid capital's leavings.

The Northeasterners' slave labor is now constructing the great trans-Amazonia highway that will cut Brazil in two, penetrating the jungle up

---

* Early in our century, rubber-forested mountains in Peru had held out the promise of a new El Dorado. In 1908 Francisco García Calderón wrote in *El Perú contemporáneo* that rubber was the great wealth of the future. In his novel *The Green House,* Mario Vargas Llosa reconstructs the feverish atmosphere in Iquitos and in the jungle, where adventurers robbed the Indians and each other. Nature had leprosy and other weapons with which to take its vengeance.

to the Bolivian border. The "march to the west," as the plan is called, also involves an agricultural colonization project to extend "the frontiers of civilization"; each peasant will get ten hectares of land if he survives the tropical fevers. The Northeast contains 6 million landless peasants while 15,000 people own half of all the land. Agrarian reform is not carried out in the already occupied areas, where the latifundistas' property rights remain sacred, but in the jungle. Thus a road for the latifundio's expansion into new territory is being opened up by its victims, the *flagelado,* or "tormented ones," of the Northeast. Without capital or implements, what is the use of ten hectares one to two thousand miles from consumer centers? One must conclude that the government's real aims are quite different: to provide labor for the U.S. latifundistas who have bought or appropriated half the lands north of the Rio Negro, and also for U.S. Steel, which received Amazonia's rich iron and manganese deposits from General Garrastazú Médici.*

Cacao Planters Lit Their Cigarettes with 500,000-Reis Bills

For a long time Venezuela was identified with cacao, a native South American plant. Venezuelans, as Domingo Rangel says, have been made to sell cacao and distribute foreign trinkets in their own lands.[23] The cacao oligarchs made up a "Holy Trinity of backwardness," along with moneylenders and traders. Cacao coexisted with indigo, sugar, tobacco, and a few mines, and cattle-raising on the plains, but the people correctly baptized as "Gran Cacao" the slave-owning oligarchy in Caracas, which supplied cacao to Mexico's mining oligarchy and to the Spanish metropolis, thus using black labor to enrich itself. A coffee era began in Venezuela in 1873; coffee, like cacao, needs sloping lands or warm valleys. Despite this competition, cacao continued to expand, invading the humid lands of Carúpano. Venezuela remained an agricultural country condemned to the cyclical rise and fall of coffee and cacao prices;

* In October 1970 the Bishop of Pará denounced to the president of Brazil the brutal exploitation of Northeastern workers by contractors for the trans-Amazonia highway. The government calls it "the work of the century."

the two products created the capital that enabled landlords, merchants, and moneylenders to live as wasteful parasites.

Then, in 1922, the country suddenly became a fountain of oil, and oil has reigned without interruption ever since. The black gold finally gushed forth, justifying, four centuries late, the fantasies of the Spanish conquistadors: searching in vain for the king who bathed in gold, they had become mad enough to confuse a little Maracaibo village with Venice and the fetid coast of Pariá with earthly paradise.

The last decades of the nineteenth century marked the rise of European and U.S. gluttony for chocolate. The industry's progress lent great impetus to Brazilian cacao and to production in the old Venezuelan and Ecuadorean plantations. Cacao made its entrance onto the Brazilian economic stage at the same time as rubber, and like rubber it gave work to Northeastern peasants. São Salvador, now Bahia, on Todos os Santos bay, once capital of Brazil and of sugar and one of Latin America's most important cities, revived as the cacao capital. In our time latifundios south of Bahia—from the Recôncavo region to the state of Espírito Santo, between the littoral lowlands and the mountain chain along the coast—still supply raw material for a good part of the world's chocolate consumption. Like sugarcane, cacao means monoculture, the burning of forests, the dictatorship of international prices, and perpetual penury for the workers. The plantation owners, who live on the Rio de Janeiro beaches and are more businessmen than farmers, do not permit a single inch of land to be devoted to other crops. Their managers normally pay wages in kind—jerked beef, flour, beans; when paid in cash, the peasant receives the equivalent of a liter of beer for a whole day's work, and must work a day and a half to buy a can of powdered milk.

For some time Brazil was favored in the international market, but from the outset Africa offered serious competition. By the 1920s the Gold Coast (now Ghana) had won the top position as a world cacao supplier: the British had developed cacao plantations in their colony on a large scale with modern methods. Brazil fell back to second place, and years later to third. But there was more than one period when no one would have believed that the fertile lands of southern Bahia were destined for mediocrity. Unused throughout the colonial period, the soil yielded prodigally: peons split the pods with their knives, collected the beans, and loaded them into donkey-drawn carts to be taken to the grinders; it became necessary to fell ever more forests, to open up new clearings and conquer new territory with machete and gun. The peons knew nothing of prices or markets. They did not even know who ruled Brazil—up until not long ago one could still meet hacienda workers who were convinced that King Pedro II was still on the throne. The cacao masters rubbed their hands together: *they* knew, or thought they knew. Chocolate consumption grew, and with it prices and profits. The port of Ilhéus, from which almost all the cacao was shipped, became known as "Queen of the South," and although it is languishing today, the small but massive palaces which the hacendados furnished with the greatest luxury and the worst taste may still be seen there. Jorge Amado wrote several novels about it. He recreates one of the high-price periods thus: "Ilhéus and the cacao zone swam in gold, bathed in champagne, slept with French ladies from Rio de Janeiro. At the Trianon, the city's most chic cabaret, Colonel Maneca Dantas lit cigarettes with 500,000-reis bills, repeating the gesture of all the country's rich *fazendeiros* during the previous rises in coffee, rubber, cotton, and sugar prices."* With the rise in price, production increased; then prices fell. Conditions became more and more unstable and land kept changing hands. The era of "beggar millionaires" began, as plantation pioneers yielded to exporters, who took over the lands for payment of debts.

In barely three years, from 1959 to 1961—to give but one example—the international price of the Brazilian cacao bean fell by one third. Since then the tendency to rise has opened the door of hope a crack, but the United Nations Economic Commission for Latin America (ECLA) predicts a short life for the upward curve.† To keep their chocolate cheap, the big cacao consumers—the United States, Britain, West Germany,

---

* In Brazil the title of "colonel" is conferred with the greatest ease on old-established latifundistas and, by extension, on all important persons. The quoted passage comes from Jorge Amado's novel *São Jorge dos Ilhéus* (1946). From another novel, *Cacao* (1935): "Not even the children touched the cacao fruit. They were afraid of those yellow berries, so sweet on the inside, which enslaved them to this life of breadfruit and dried meat." For, after all, "cacao was the great *senhor* feared even by the colonel." In still another novel, *Gabriela, Clove and Cinnamon* (1959), a character speaks of Ilhéus in 1925, pointing a categorical finger: "In the north of the country there exists no more rapidly progressing city." Ilhéus today is not even the shadow of what it was.

† Referring to the improvements in cacao and coffee prices, ECLA says they are relatively transitory and result largely from occasional harvest setbacks.[24]

Holland, France—stimulate competition between African cacao and cacao from Brazil and Ecuador. Controlling prices as they do, these nations bring on periods of depression which put cacao workers back on the road. The unemployed look for trees to sleep under and green bananas to fool their stomachs: one product they certainly don't eat is the fine chocolate that Brazil actually imports from France and Switzerland. Chocolate costs more and more; cacao less and less. Between 1950 and 1960 Ecuador's cacao sales rose more than 30 percent in volume but only 15 percent in value. The remaining 15 percent was a gift from Ecuador to those rich countries which, in the same period, sent it their industrial products at escalating prices. Ecuador's economy depends on the sale of bananas, coffee, and cacao, three food products highly subject to price fluctuations. According to official data, seven of every ten Ecuadoreans suffer from basic malnutrition, and the country has one of the highest death rates in the world.

Cheap Hands for Cotton

Brazil is the fourth largest cotton-producing country, Mexico the fifth. More than one-fifth of all cotton consumed by the world's textile industries comes from Latin America. At the end of the eighteenth century, cotton had become the most important industrial raw material in Europe; England multiplied its purchases of the fiber by five in thirty years. The spinning frame invented by Arkwright—at the same time that Watt was patenting his steam engine—and Cartwright's later development of the mechanical loom gave textile manufacturing a decisive push and provided the cotton plant with eager overseas markets. The cotton euphoria brusquely awakened the port of São Luiz do Maranhão from a long tropical siesta previously interrupted only by the arrival of a couple of ships a year. Now black slaves streamed onto the north Brazilian plantations and some 200 ships a year, carrying a million pounds of raw cotton, sailed from São Luiz. The economic crisis in mining at the beginning of the nineteenth century gave cotton an abundance of slave labor; with the exhaustion of the gold and diamond supply in the south, Brazil seemed to revive in the north. The port flourished, producing enough poets to become known as the Athens of

Brazil, but since no one in the Maranhão region bothered to raise food, hunger entered along with prosperity. Sometimes there was only rice to eat. The story ended as it had begun: suddenly. Large-scale cotton production on southern United States plantations, which had better soil and machines for cleaning and baling, lowered prices by two-thirds and Brazil dropped out of the race. Prosperity returned when the Civil War interrupted U.S. supplies, but did not last long. Between 1934 and 1939, Brazilian cotton production grew impressively, from 125,000 to more than 320,000 tons; then the United States flooded the world market with its surpluses and prices slumped again.

The United States' agricultural surpluses are, as we know, the result of fat subsidies to its producers; it spills the surpluses out across the world at dumping prices as part of its foreign aid program. Cotton was Paraguay's chief export until the ruinous competition of U.S. cotton displaced it in the market, and Paraguayan production has fallen by 50 percent since 1952. (In the same way Uruguay lost the Canadian market for its rice, and the wheat of Argentina, once the world's granary, virtually vanished from international markets.) The United States' dumping of cotton has not affected the imperial hold of a U.S. firm, Anderson, Clayton & Co., over this product in Latin America, or interfered with U.S. purchases, through the firm, of Mexican cotton for resale to other countries.

World trade of Latin American cotton nevertheless remains lively thanks to its extremely low production costs. Even reality-concealing official figures betray the wretched standards of pay for actual work. In Brazil it is done either for hunger wages or on a serf basis. In Guatemala, plantation owners boast of paying 19 quetzals (about $10) a month, most of it in kind at prices they themselves determine. Mexican migrant workers, moving from harvest to harvest at $1.50 a day, suffer from underemployment and consequent undernutrition. The lot of Nicaraguan cotton workers is much worse, and Salvadorans, who supply cotton to Japanese textile industries, consume fewer calories and proteins than the hungry peasants of India.

In Peru's economy cotton is the second agricultural source of foreign currency. José Carlos Mariátegui has noted how foreign capitalism, in its constant search for land, labor, and markets, came to control Peru's export crops by foreclosing the mortgages of debt-delinquent landowners.[25] When General Velasco Alvarado's nationalist government came to power in 1968, less than one-sixth of the land suitable for intensive cultivation was being used, per capita income was fifteen times less than in the United States, and consumption of calories was among the world's lowest. But cotton production, like sugar, was still dictated by the same non-Peruvian criteria exposed by Mariátegui. The best lands, those along the coast, belonged to U.S. enterprises or to landlords who, like the Lima bourgeoisie, were only nationals in a geographical sense. Five big concerns (two of which—Anderson, Clayton and Grace—are based in the United States) dominated the export of cotton and sugar and also produced them in their own "agro-industrial complexes." Coastal sugar and cotton plantations—supposedly centers of prosperity and progress in contrast to sierra latifundios—paid hunger wages until the 1969 agrarian reform expropriated them and handed them over to the workers as cooperatives. According to the Inter-American Committee for Agricultural Development, the income for each member of a coastal worker's family amounted to a mere $5 a month.[26]

With thirty affliliates in Latin America, Anderson, Clayton has a monopoly: it not only sells cotton, but its network controls the financing and industrialization of the fiber and its derivatives, and also produces food on a large scale. In Mexico, for example, while the company owns no land, it still dominates cotton production and the 800,000 Mexicans who harvest the crop are in fact at its mercy. It buys the excellent Mexican cotton at a very low price, having previously extended credits to producers on the condition that they sell to it at the price with which it opens the market. In addition to advancing money, it supplies fertilizers, seeds, and insecticides; it reserves the right to supervise the application of fertilizer, the sowing, and the harvesting. It fixes its own price for ginning the cotton, and uses the seeds in its oil, fat, and margarine factories. In recent years the firm, not content with dominating the cotton business, has even broken into the candy and chocolate fields, recently buying the well-known firm Luxus.

Anderson, Clayton is also involved in coffee, and is the chief exporter of Brazilian coffee. It first took an interest in that business in 1950, and three years later it had dethroned the American Coffee Corporation. It is also the top producer of Brazilian foodstuffs and is one of the country's thirty-five most powerful firms.

Cheap Hands for Coffee

Some people rank coffee almost on a par with oil in its importance on the international market. At the beginning of the 1950s Latin America was supplying four-fifths of the coffee the world consumed; since then the competition of "robust" African coffee, lower in quality but also in price, has reduced Latin America's share. Nevertheless, one-sixth of the currency the region obtains abroad now comes from coffee. Its price fluctuations affect fifteen countries south of the Río Grande. Brazil is the world's top producer, getting about half of its export income from coffee. El Salvador, Guatemala, Costa Rica, and Haiti also largely depend on coffee, and it accounts for two-thirds of Colombia's foreign exchange.

Coffee brought inflation to Brazil. Between 1824 and 1854 the price of a man doubled. At that figure, and with their prosperous days a thing of the past, neither the north's cotton producers nor the Northeast's sugar producers could afford slaves. Brazil's center of gravity moved south. In addition to slave labor, the coffee producers used European immigrants, who brought in 50 percent of the harvests in a sharecropping setup that still prevails in Brazil's interior. Today's tourists who drive through the woods for a swim at Tijuca beach are unaware that there, in the mountains surrounding Rio de Janeiro, big coffee plantations existed more than a century ago. Flanking the Sierra, these plantations spread toward the state of São Paulo in their endless pursuit of the humus of virgin lands. Toward the end of the century coffee planters, by then the new Brazilian social elite, sharpened their pencils and totted up their accounts: subsistence wages worked out cheaper than the purchase and maintenance of increasingly scarce slaves. With the abolition of slavery in 1888, the combined forms of feudal serfdom and wage labor that still persist were inaugurated. From then on an army of "free" farmhands would accompany coffee on its travels. The Rio Paraíba became the country's richest area, to be quickly ruined by a plant whose destructive form of cultivation left forests razed, natural reserves exhausted, and general decadence in its wake. Previously virgin lands were pitilessly eroded as the plunder-march of coffee advanced, weakening the plants and making them vulnerable to diseases. The coffee plantation invaded the broad purple plateau west of São Paulo, converting it into a "sea of coffee" with slightly less crude farming methods, and continued advancing westward. It reached the banks of the Paraná where, facing the Mato Grosso savannas, it turned south; in recent years it has again moved west along the Paraguayan border.

Today São Paulo is the most developed state in Brazil, containing the country's industrial center, but its coffee plantations still teem with "vassal inhabitants" who pay rent for their land with their and their children's toil. In the prosperous post-World War I years the coffee growers' voracity virtually ended the system under which plantation workers could grow food crops on their own. Now they can only do it by paying rent in the form of wageless labor. The latifundista also uses contractual sharecroppers who are allowed to raise seasonal crops in return for planting still more coffee trees for his benefit. Four years after planting, when the branches are yellow with beans, the land has multiplied in value and it is time for the sharecropper to move on.

Coffee plantations pay even less in Guatemala than cotton plantations. On the southern slopes the owners claim to pay $15 a month to the thousands of natives who descend southward each year from the *altiplano* to sell their labor during the harvests. The plantations have private police forces: there, as the popular saying has it, "a man is cheaper than a mule," and the repressive apparatus sees that he remains so. In the Alta Verapaz region the situation is even worse. The planters have no trucks or carts: they do not need them since it costs less to use the Indians' backs.

Coffee is basic to the economy of El Salvador, a little country owned by a handful of oligarchical families: monoculture makes it necessary to import the beans—the people's only source of protein—corn, vegetables, and other foods the country traditionally produced. A quarter of all Salvadorans die of avitaminosis, or severe vitamin deficiency. As for Haiti, it has Latin America's highest death rate, and more than half of its children are anemic. The wages Haiti requires by law belong in the department of science fiction: actual wages on coffee plantations vary from $.07 to $.15 a day.

In Colombia, where suitable slopes abound, coffee is king. According to a *Time* magazine report in 1962, only 5 percent of the price yielded by coffee in its journey from tree to U.S. consumer goes into the wages of the workers who produce it.[27] * In contrast to Brazil, most Colombian coffee is produced not by latifundios but by minifundios—small farms which tend to become increasingly smaller and smaller. Between 1955 and 1960, 100,000 new plantations appeared, most of them minute—less than one hectare. Small and very small farmers produce three-quarters of the coffee exported by Colombia, and 96 percent of the plantations are minifundios. "Juan Valdés" smiles in the ads, but in fact atomization of the land is steadily forcing his living standards down and making it easier for the Federación Nacional de Cafeteros, which represents the big landowners and virtually monopolizes trade in the product, to manipulate the situation. Farms of less than a hectare produce starvation incomes—an average of $130 *a year.*

Burn the Crops? Get Married? The Price of Coffee Dictates All

What's this? An electroencephalogram of a lunatic? In 1889 coffee was worth two cents and six years later it had risen to nine; three years later it was down to four, five years after that to two. A typical period. The graph of coffee prices, like those of all tropical products, has always resembled a clinical epilepsy chart—more than ever when it shows the value of coffee in exchange for machinery and industrial products. Colombian President Lleras Restrepo complained that in 1967 his country had to pay fifty-seven sacks of coffee for a jeep that had only cost seventeen sacks in 1950. Figures offered at the same time by Brazilian Minister of Agriculture Herbert Levi were more dramatic: for a tractor, which had cost 70 sacks of coffee fourteen years earlier, Brazil now had to pay 350 sacks. When President Getulio Vargas put a bullet through his heart in 1954, the price of coffee played a role in the tragedy: "The crisis in coffee production came," he wrote in his moving final testament, "and the price of our chief product went up. We tried to defend the price and the answer was such violent pressure on our

---

* The price breakdown is as follows: 40 percent for middlemen, exporters, and importers; 10 percent for taxes imposed by both governments; 10 percent for transport; 5 percent for publicity by the Pan-American Coffee Bureau; 30 percent for plantation owners; and 5 percent for workers' wages.

economy that we had to give in." Vargas hoped that his blood would buy salvation for the Brazilian people.

If the 1964 coffee crop had been sold on the U.S. market at 1955 prices, Brazil would have received $200 million more. A drop of only one cent in the price meant a loss of $65 million to the combined producing countries. With the price falling continually between 1964 and 1968, the consuming country—the United States—helped itself to more and more millions from the producing country, Brazil. But for the benefit of whom? Of the coffee-drinking citizen? In July 1968 Brazilian coffee cost 30 percent less in the United States than in January 1964, but U.S. consumers did not pay less: they paid 13 percent more. Thus in the 1964–1968 period middlemen kept the 13 percent as well as the 30 percent, feathering their nests twice over. In the same period the price Brazilian producers received for each sack of coffee dropped by half.[28] Who are the middlemen? Six U.S. concerns control more than a third of the coffee that leaves Brazil, and another six control more than a third of what enters the United States: these firms dominate the business at both ends.[29] Just as United Fruit monopolizes the sale of bananas from Central America, Colombia, and Ecuador, as well as their importation and distribution in the United States, so U.S. firms run the coffee business and Brazil only participates as supplier and victim. The Brazilian state takes over the stocks when overproduction demands the accumulation of reserves.

But isn't there an International Coffee Agreement to stabilize prices on the market? The World Coffee Information Center published a detailed document in Washington in 1970 to try and convince legislators that the United States should keep the agreement in force after September. The report affirms that the agreement's chief beneficiary has been the United States, which consumes more than half the coffee sold in the world. The purchaser of the coffee beans always gets a bargain. In the U.S. market, the trivial rise in price (for the middleman's benefit, as we have seen) has been much less than the general rise of living costs and internal wage levels; U.S. exports rose in value by one-sixth between 1960 and 1969, and in the same period the value of coffee imports dropped. And one must bear in mind that Latin American countries use depreciated foreign currency from coffee sales to buy ever costlier U.S. products.

It is much more profitable to consume coffee than to produce it. In the United States and Europe coffee creates income and jobs and mobilizes substantial capital; in Latin America it pays hunger wages and sharpens economic deformation. It provides work for more than 600,000 people in the United States: those who distribute and sell Latin American coffee there earn infinitely more than the Brazilians, Colombians, Guatemalans, Salvadorans, and Haitians who plant and harvest it on the plantations. And incredible as it seems, coffee—so ECLA tells us—puts more wealth into European state coffers than it leaves in the hands of the producing countries. In effect, in 1960 and 1961 the total taxes levied on Latin American coffee by European Economic Community countries amounted to about $700 million, while supplier countries (in terms of the f.o.b. value of exports) only got $600 million.[30] The rich countries that preach free trade apply stern protectionist policies against the poor countries: they turn everything they touch—including the underdeveloped countries' own production—into gold for themselves and rubbish for others. The international coffee market operates so exactly like a funnel that Brazil recently agreed to impose high taxes on its soluble coffee exports, a reverse protectionism designed to protect the interests of competing U.S. manufacturers. Instant coffee made in Brazil is cheaper and better than that made by the flourishing U.S. industry; but then, of course, in a system of free competition some are freer than others.

In this kingdom of organized absurdity, natural disasters become blessings from heaven for the producing countries. They raise prices and permit the mobilization of accumulated reserves. Fierce frosts wrecked the 1969 harvest in Brazil and sealed the fate of many producers, especially the weakest, but at the same time pushed up coffee prices on the world market and appreciably lightened the "stock" of 60 million sacks—the equivalent of two-thirds of Brazil's external debt—which the state had accumulated to defend prices. The warehoused coffee, progressively deteriorating and losing value, could have ended up in a bonfire. It would not have been the first time. The collapse of prices and the shrinkage in consumption after the 1929 crisis caused Brazil to burn 78 million sacks; thus the efforts of 200,000 people during five harvests went up in flames. This was a typical crisis in a colonial economy: *it came from outside.* Apart from burning the coffee, the fall of the planters' and exporters' profits in the 1930s produced a bonfire in currency values. Such is the normal Latin American mechanism to "socialize the losses" of the export sector: losses of foreign currency are compensated in national currency through devaluation.

The consequences of rising prices are no better. While they lead to more sowing for more production, and multiply the area devoted to the fortunate crop, this acts as a boomerang since an abundance of the product demolishes prices and leads to disaster. Such was the fate of Colombia in 1958 when it harvested the coffee sown so enthusiastically four years earlier, and similar cycles have recurred throughout that country's history. Colombia is so dependent on coffee and its external price that "in Antioquia the marriage curve responds sensitively to the coffee-price curve. Par for the course in a dependent structure: even the propitious moment for a declaration of love on an Antioquian hillside is decided on the New York Stock Exchange."[31]

The Ten Years that Emptied Colombia's Veins

Back in the 1940s the noted Colombian economist Luis Eduardo Nieto Arteta wrote an apologia for coffee. Coffee had achieved what neither mines nor tobacco, nor indigo nor quinine, had managed to produce in the country's previous economic cycles: it had given birth to a mature and progressive order. Textile factories and other light industries had arisen in coffee-producing areas—Antioquia, Caldas, Valle del Cauca, Cundinamarca—and not by accident. A democracy made up of small farmers raising coffee had turned Colombians into "moderate and sober people. . . . The strongest premise for normality in the functioning of Colombian political life has been the attainment of our own kind of economic stability. Coffee has produced it, and with it tranquillity and moderation."[32]

Violence soon erupted again. For all the panegyrics, coffee had no magic with which to end Colombia's long history of revolt and bloody repression. This time—for ten years, from 1948 to 1957—small and large plantations, desert and farmland, valley and forest and Andean plateau were engulfed in peasant war; it put whole communities to flight, generated revolutionary guerrillas and criminal bands, and turned the country into a cemetery: it is estimated to have left a toll of 180,000 dead. The bloodbath coincided with a period of economic euphoria for the ruling class. But is the prosperity of a class really identifiable with the well-being of a country?

The violence began with a confrontation between Liberal and Conservative parties, but the dynamic of class hostilities steadily sharpened its class-struggle character. The Liberal leader Jorge Eliécer Gaitán—known half contemptuously and half fearfully to his own party's oligarchy as "The Wolf" or "The Idiot"—had won great popular prestige and threatened the established order. When he was shot dead, the hurricane was unleashed. First the spontaneous *bogotazo*—an uncontrollable human tide in the streets of the capital; then the violence spread to the countryside, where bands organized by the Conservatives had for some time been sowing terror. The bitter taste of hatred, long in the peasants' mouths, provoked an explosion; the government sent police and soldiers to cut off testicles, slash pregnant women's bellies, and throw babies in the air to catch on bayonet points—the order of the day being "don't leave even the seed." Liberal Party sages shut themselves in their homes, never abandoning their good manners and the gentlemanly tone of their manifestos, or went into exile abroad. It was a war of incredible cruelty and it became worse as it went on, feeding the lust for vengeance. New ways of killing came into vogue: the *corte corbata,* for example, left the tongue hanging from the neck. Rape, arson, and plunder went on and on; people were quartered or burned alive, skinned or slowly cut in pieces; troops razed villages and plantations and rivers ran red with blood. Bandits spared lives in exchange for tribute, in money or loads of coffee, and the repressive forces expelled and pursued innumerable families, who fled to seek refuge in the mountains. Women gave birth in the woods. The first guerrilla leaders, determined to take revenge but without clear political vision, took to destroying for destruction's sake, letting off blood and steam without purpose.

The names adopted by the protagonists of violence—Gorilla, Evil Shadow, The Condor, Redskin, The Vampire, Black Bird, Terror of the Plains—hardly suggest a revolutionary epic, yet the scent of social rebellion was in the couplets sung by their followers:

> I'm just a *campesino,*
> I didn't start the fight,
> But if they come asking for trouble,
> They'll get what's coming to them.

There is no doubt that indiscriminate terror, mixed with the cry for justice, had emerged in the Mexican Revolution. In Colombia many just ran amok, yet that violent decade gave birth to the political guerrillas who later raised the banner of social revolution over broad areas they came to occupy and control. Hounded by the repressors, the peasants took to the mountains to organize agriculture and self-defense. The so-called independent republics continued to offer refuge to the persecuted after Conservatives and Liberals signed a peace pact in Madrid. In an ambiance of toasts and mutual goodwill, the leaders of both parties agreed to take turns in power under a banner of national unity, and then began the "clean-up" operations against foci of subversion. In one of these operations alone—the crushing of the rebels in Marquetalia—1.5 million projectiles were fired, 20,000 bombs were dropped, and 16,000 soldiers were mobilized on the ground and in the air.

At the height of the violence one official said, "Don't bring me stories, bring me ears." Could the sadism of the repression and the ferocity of the war be explained clinically? Were they the result of inherent evil in the protagonists? A man who cut off the hands of a priest, set fire to his body and his house, and later cut him in pieces and threw him in a sewer, cried after the war was over: "I'm not guilty. Leave me alone." He had lost—yet in a certain sense retained—his reason: the horror of all the violence merely exposed the horror of the system. For coffee did not bring happiness and harmony as Nieto Arteta had prophesied. It is true that coffee opened up railroads, highways, and the Río Magdalena to navigation, and that thanks to coffee enough capital was accumulated to found some industries. But the ascendancy of coffee did not affect either the oligarchical social order or the dependence of the economy on foreign power centers; on the contrary, both became far more oppressive for Colombians. Toward the end of the violent decade, the United Nations published the results of a study of nutrition in Colombia (and there has been absolutely no improvement since then): 88 percent of Bogotá schoolchildren suffered from avitaminosis, 78 percent from riboflavinosis, and more than half were below normal weight; avitaminosis affected 71 percent of workers and 78 percent of Tensa Valley peasants.[33] The study showed "a marked insufficiency of protective foods—milk and its derivatives, eggs, meat, fish, and some fruits and vegetables—which together provide protein, vitamins, and salt." It is not only the flash of gunfire that reveals social tragedy. Statistics show that Colombia has seven times more homicides than the United States, and that one in every four Colombians of active age has no regular job. Every year 250,000 people come onto the labor market while industry fails to generate new jobs; the latifundio-minifundio system not only cannot absorb more labor, but it constantly banishes more people to swell the ranks of the unemployed in city slums. In Colombia over a million children do not attend school. This does not discourage the system from running forty-one public and private universities, each with its own faculties and departments, to educate the children of the elite and middle class.*

The World Market Casts Its Spell over Central America

Central American lands were comparatively unmolested up until the middle of the past century. In addition to food, the area produced cochineal and indigo with modest capital, a meager labor force, and few worries. Both the indigo plant and the cochineal bug, busily multiplying on the prickly surface of the nopal cactus, were in steady demand in European textile industries, but both of these natural pigments met a synthetic death around 1850, when German chemists invented aniline and other cheaper dyes. Thirty years after this victory of the laboratory over nature it was coffee's turn. Central America was transformed: by 1880 its newborn plantations were raising almost one-sixth of the world's coffee production. Coffee locked the region firmly into the world market. First English, then German, and finally U.S. buyers gave life to a native coffee bourgeoisie, which became the political power after

* Professor Germán Rama found that some of these venerable groves of academe contain in their libraries, like some precious patrimony, complete bound volumes of the Spanish edition of the *Reader's Digest.*[34]

the revolution led by Justo Rufino Barrios early in the 1870s. Agricultural specialization, dictated from abroad, set off a frenzy of land and labor grabbing: the Central American latifundio of today was born under the banner of free labor.

Great tracts of idle land—belonging to no one, or to the Church, or to the state—passed into private hands, and Indian communities were frenetically plundered. Peasants who declined to sell their land were hauled off into the army; plantations became human compost pits for Indians. The colonial order was revived with the forcible recruitment of labor and with laws against vagrancy, while fugitive workers were pursued with guns. Liberal governments modernized labor relations by introducing wages, but recipients of the wages became the property of upstart coffee planters. At no time in the ensuing century, of course, were periods of high prices reflected in wages, which have remained at the hunger level no matter how much was paid for the coffee. This helped prevent the development of any internal consumer market in Central America. As elsewhere, the ever expanding cultivation of coffee discouraged food-raising for the home market. These countries too were condemned to a chronic scarcity of rice, beans, corn, wheat, tobacco, and meat. A bleak subsistence agriculture barely survived on the high semi-barren lands to which the latifundio drove the Indians when it appropriated the lower and more fertile areas. The Indians who work on the plantations at harvest time spend part of the year on tiny mountain plots raising the corn and beans without which they could not survive. They are the world market's "labor reserve." Nothing has changed in a century: the latifundio and minifundio together make up a system based on ruthless exploitation of Indian labor. In general—but especially in Guatemala—this structure of labor force appropriation is visibly identified with racism: Indians suffer the internal colonialism of whites and mestizos blessed ideologically by the dominant culture, just as Central American countries suffer foreign colonialism.

Early in our century banana enclaves made their appearance in Honduras, Guatemala, and Costa Rica. A few railway lines financed by native capital had been built to take coffee to the ports. U.S. concerns took over these railroads and built others, to carry the products of their own plantations exclusively, while monopolizing electric light, the mails, telegraph and telephone, and—a no less important public service—politics: in Honduras a mule costs more than a deputy, and throughout Central America U.S. ambassadors do more presiding than presidents. The United Fruit Company swallowed up its competitors in the production and sale of bananas and became Central America's top latifundista, while its affiliates cornered rail and sea transport. It took over the ports and set up its own customs and police. The dollar in effect became the national currency of Central America.

The Filibusterers Come Aboard

In the geopolitical concept of imperialism, Central America is no more than a natural appendage of the United States. Not even Abraham Lincoln, who also contemplated annexation, could resist the "manifest destiny" of the great power to dictate to its contiguous areas.

In the middle of the nineteenth century the filibusterer William Walker, operating on behalf of bankers Morgan and Garrison, invaded Central America at the head of a band of assassins. With the obliging support of the U.S. government, Walker robbed, killed, burned, and in successive expeditions proclaimed himself president of Nicaragua, El Salvador, and Honduras. He restored slavery in the areas that suffered his devastating occupation, thus continuing his country's philanthropic work in the states that had just been seized from Mexico. He was welcomed back to the United States as a national hero. From then on invasions, interventions, bombardments, forced loans, and gun-point treaties followed one after the other. In 1912 President William H. Taft declared: "The day is not far distant when three Stars and Stripes at three equidistant points will mark our territory: one at the North Pole, another at the Panama Canal, and the third at the South Pole. The whole hemisphere will be ours in fact as, by virtue of our superiority of race, it already is ours morally."[35] Taft said that the correct path of justice in U.S. foreign policy "may well be made to include active intervention to secure for our merchandise and our capitalists opportunity for profitable investment."[36] In the same period ex-President Theodore Roosevelt loudly recalled his successful amputation of land from Colombia: "I took the Canal Zone and let Congress debate," said the proud Nobel Peace Prize winner as he related how he had invented Panama. Colombia soon afterward received $25 million in indemnity: it was the price of a country that was born so that the United States could have a route between two oceans.

U.S. concerns took over lands, customs houses, treasuries, and governments; Marines landed here, there, and everywhere to "protect the lives and interests of U.S. citizens"—the same holy-water formula that would be used to deodorize the Dominican Republic crime in 1965. General Smedley D. Butler, who headed many of the expeditions, indicated the sort of merchandise that was wrapped inside the flag when he wrote in 1935 of his own experience:

> I spent thirty-three years and four months in active service as a member of our country's most agile military force—the Marine Corps. I served in all commissioned ranks from a second lieutenant to major-general. And during that period I spent most of my time being a high-class muscle man for Big Business, for Wall Street, and for the bankers. In short, I was a racketeer for capitalism. . . . Thus I helped make Mexico and especially Tampico safe for American oil interests in 1914. I helped make Haiti and Cuba a decent place for the National City Bank to collect revenues in. . . . I helped purify Nicaragua for the international banking house of Brown Brothers in 1909–1912. I brought light to the Dominican Republic for American sugar interests in 1916. I helped make Honduras "right" for American fruit companies in 1903.[37]

In the first years of our century the philosopher William James passed the little-known judgment that the country had finally vomited the Declaration of Independence. To cite but one example: the United States occupied Haiti for twenty years and, in that black country that had been the scene of the first victorious slave revolt, introduced racial segregation and forced labor, killed 1,500 workers in one of its repressive operations (according to a U.S. Senate investigation in 1922), and when the local government refused to turn the Banco Nacional into a branch of New York's National City Bank, suspended the salaries of the president and his ministers so that they might think again. Alternating the "big stick" with "dollar diplomacy," similar actions were carried out in the other Caribbean islands and in all of Central America, the geopolitical space of the imperial *mare nostrum.*

The Koran mentions the banana among the trees of paradise, but the "bananization" of Guatemala, Honduras, Costa Rica, Panama, Colombia, and Ecuador suggests that it is a tree of hell. United Fruit became owner of the biggest latifundio in Colombia when a big strike broke out on the Atlantic coast in 1928. Banana workers were mowed down with bullets in front of a railroad station. "The forces of public order are authorized to punish with the aid of appropriate weapons," it was officially decreed, and no further decree was necessary to wipe the massacre from official memory.* Miguel Angel Asturias described the process of Central American conquest and plunder in his novel *The Green Pope*, about Minor Keith, the uncrowned king of the region, great white father of United Fruit, devourer of nations:

> "We have docks, railroads, land, buildings, and water. . . . The dollar circulates, English is spoken, and they fly our flag. . . . Chicago could not help but feel proud of that son who went off with a brace of pistols and returned to demand his position among the meat emperors, the railroad kings, the copper kings, the chewing-gum kings.[38] †

In *The 42nd Parallel* John Dos Passos traced the dazzling career of Keith and United Fruit:

> In Europe and the United States people had started to eat bananas, so they cut down the jungles through Central America to plant bananas, and built railroads to haul the bananas, and every year more steamboats of the Great White Fleet steamed north loaded with bananas, and that is the history of the American empire in the Caribbean, and the Panama canal and the future Nicaragua canal and the marines and the battleships and the bayonets.[40]

The land was as exhausted as the workers—the land was robbed of humus and the workers of their lungs—but there were always new lands to exploit and new workers to exterminate. Comic opera dictators watched over United Fruit's interests with knives between their teeth. Banana production eventually fell and the omnipotent corporation

---

* This is the theme of Alvaro Cepeda Samudio's novel *La casa grande* (1967), and also makes a chapter of Gabriel García Márquez's *One Hundred Years of Solitude:* "You must have been dreaming the officers insisted."

† The novel is one of Asturias's trilogy; the other two are *Strong Wind* and *Los ojos de los enterrados* (The Eyes of the Buried), published in Buenos Aires in the 1950s. Mister Pyle, a character in *Strong Wind,* says prophetically: "If instead of making new plantations, we buy fruit from the individual growers, it'll be much better for the future."[39] This is exactly the present situation in Guatemala: United Fruit imposes its banana monopoly through the selling end, a more effective and less risky method than direct production. It is worth noting that banana production fell sharply in the 1960s from the moment when United Fruit decided to sell and/or lease its Guatemalan plantations, then threatened by social agitation.

went through various crises; although cotton and sugar have pushed the banana off its privileged perch, Central America remains to this day a bonanza-sanctuary for adventurers. Bananas are still the main source of foreign currency for Honduras and Panama and, in South America, for Ecuador. Around 1929 Central America exported 38 million bunches and United Fruit paid Honduras a penny tax on each. There was no way to see that this mini-tax—which later rose slightly—was actually paid; nor is there today, for even now United Fruit exports and imports what it likes, operating outside the state customs system. The country's trade and payment balances are the works of fiction of exceptionally imaginative technicians.

The Crisis of the 1930s: "Killing an Ant Is a Greater Crime Than Killing a Man"

Coffee depended on the U.S. market, on U.S. consumption capacity, and on U.S. prices; bananas were a business of, by, and for the United States. Suddenly, in 1929, came the crisis. In the Caribbean, the New York stock market disaster which cracked the foundations of world capitalism fell like a huge block of stone into a puddle. Coffee and banana prices plummeted, along with sales. Peasants were evicted on all sides, unemployment soared, and a wave of strikes swept city and countryside; credit, investment, and public spending collapsed; and in Honduras, Guatemala, and Nicaragua, state employees' salaries were cut almost in half. Jackbooted dictators were the order of the day: in Washington it was the dawn of the Good Neighbor policy, but social agitation was boiling up everywhere and had to be sternly suppressed. For about twenty years—for some more, for some less—power would remain in the hands of Guatemala's Jorge Ubico Castañeda, El Salvador's Maximiliano Hernández Martínez, Honduras's Tiburcio Carías Andino, and Nicaragua's Anastasio Somoza.

The epic of Augusto César Sandino stirred the world. The long struggle of Nicaragua's guerrilla leader was rooted in the angry peasants' demand for land. His small ragged army fought for some years against 12,000 U.S. invaders and the National Guard. Sardine tins filled with stones served as grenades, Springfield rifles were stolen from the enemy, and there were plenty of machetes; the flag flew from any handy stick, and the peasants moved through mountain thickets wearing strips of hide called *huaraches* instead of boots. The guerrillas sang, to the tune of *Adelita:*

> In Nicaragua, gentlemen,
> the mouse kills the cat.

Neither the Marines' firepower nor the bombs dropped from planes sufficed to crush the rebels of Las Segovias; nor did the calumnies spread worldwide by Associated Press and United Press International, whose Nicaraguan correspondents were two North Americans who controlled the country's customs houses. In 1932 Sandino had a presentiment: "I won't live very long." A year later, under the influence of the Good Neighbor policy, hostilities ceased. The guerrilla leader was invited by the president to a decisive meeting in Managua, and on the way was killed in an ambush. The murderer, Anastasio Somoza, later said that U.S. Ambassador Arthur Bliss Lane had ordered the execution. Somoza, then head of the army, soon installed himself in power. He ruled Nicaragua for a quarter of a century and then bequeathed the job to his sons. Before wrapping the presidential sash across his breast, Somoza had conferred upon himself the Cross of Valor, the Medal of Distinction, and the Presidential Medal of Merit. Once in power he organized various massacres and grand celebrations for which he dressed up his soldiers in sandals and helmets like Romans. He became the country's biggest coffee producer, with forty-six plantations, and raised cattle on fifty-one additional haciendas. But he was never too busy to spread terror. During his long reign he lacked for nothing and even recalled with some wistfulness his youthful years when he had to forge gold coins to pay for his amusements.

The crisis brought tensions to a head, too, in El Salvador. Nearly half of Honduras's banana workers were Salvadorans, and many had to return to their country, where there was no work for anyone. A peasant rising in the Izalco region in 1932 quickly spread throughout western El Salvador. Hernández sent troops with modern equipment to deal with the "Bolsheviks." The Indians fought with machetes against machine-guns and the incident ended with 10,000 dead. Hernández, a vegetarian crank and theosophist, maintained that "killing an ant is a greater crime than killing a man, because a man is reincarnated after death while an ant dies once and for all."[41] He said he was protected by "invisible legions" who reported all plots and were in direct telepathic communication with the president of the United States. A pendulum clock showed him if food on a dish placed beneath it was poisoned, or showed places on a map where pirate treasure or political enemies were hidden. He used to send condolence notes to the parents of his victims, and deer pastured in the patio of his palace. He ruled until 1944.

Massacres were continual throughout the area. In Guatemala in 1933, Jorge Ubico shot one hundred trade union, student, and political leaders while restoring the laws against Indian "vagrancy." Each Indian had to carry a book listing his days of work; if these were deemed insufficient, he paid the debt in jail or by bending his back over the ground without pay for half a year. On the unhealthy Pacific coast men worked up to their knees in mud for $.30 a day and United Fruit explained that Ubico had forced it to cut wages. Just before the dictator fell in 1944, *Reader's Digest* ran a eulogistic article about him; this harbinger of the International Monetary Fund had avoided inflation by lowering wages from $1 to $.25 a day in the construction of the emergency military highway, and from $1 to $.50 for jobs on the air base in the capital. Ubico granted coffee and banana concerns permission to kill: "Plantation proprietors will be exempt from criminal responsibility. . . ." This decree—number 2,795—was revived in 1967 during the democratic and representative government of Julio César Méndez Montenegro (1966–1970).

Like all the Caribbean tyrants, Ubico thought he was Napoleon. He surrounded himself with busts and portraits of the Emperor who, he said, had the same profile. He believed in military discipline: he militarized post office employees, schoolchildren, and the symphony orchestra. Dressed in uniforms, the orchestra members played Ubico's selections, with techniques and instruments decided by him, for $9 a month. He felt that hospitals were for sissies, and patients who were poor as well as sick were put on the floors of corridors and passageways.

Who Started the Violence in Guatemala?

Ubico was swept off his pedestal in 1944 by a revolution of liberal hue, led by some young officers and middle-class university people. Juan José Arévalo, elected to the presidency, instituted a vigorous education plan and a new labor code to protect rural and city workers. Trade unions sprang tip; United Fruit, the virtually untaxed and uncontrolled owner of vast lands and of the railroad and port, was no longer omnipotent on its domains. In his farewell speech in 1951 Arévalo disclosed that he had had to deal with thirty-two conspiracies financed by the firm. The administration of Jacobo Arbenz Guzmán continued and extended the reforms. Highways and the new port of San José broke United Fruit's monopoly of transport and export. With national capital, and without begging from any foreign banker, various projects were launched to lead the country to independence. An agrarian reform law, aimed basically at developing a peasant capitalist economy and an agricultural capitalist economy in general, was approved in 1952. By 1954 over 100,000 families had benefited, although the law only affected idle lands and paid expropriated owners an indemnity in bonds. But since United Fruit was using a mere 8 percent of its land, which extended from ocean to ocean, its unused lands began to be distributed to the peasants. A frenetic international propaganda campaign was launched: "The Iron Curtain is falling over Guatemala," roared the radio, newspapers, and the bigwigs of the Organization of American States. Colonel Rodolfo Castillo Armas, a graduate of the Fort Leavenworth military post, invaded his own country with troops trained and equipped for the purpose by the United States, and with support from U.S.-piloted F-47 bombers. "We had to get rid of a Communist government which had taken over," Dwight D. Eisenhower said nine years later.[42] Testifying before a Senate subcommittee on July 27, 1961, the U.S. ambassador to Honduras said that the "liberating" operation in 1954 had been worked out by a team which included himself and the ambassadors to Guatemala, Costa Rica, and Nicaragua. Allen Dulles, then the number one man at the CIA, had cabled them his congratulations on a job well done. Dulles had previously been on United Fruit's board of directors, and a year after the invasion his seat was occupied by another CIA man, Walter Bedell Smith. Allen's brother, John Foster Dulles, had shown burning impatience at the OAS conference that approved the military expedition against Guatemala; it so happened that the United Fruit contracts in the Ubico era had been drafted in his law office.

Arbenz's fall started a conflagration in Guatemala which has never been extinguished. The same forces that bombed Guatemala City, Puerto Barrios, and the port of San José on the evening of June 18, 1954, are in power today. Foreign intervention was followed by a series of ferocious dictatorships—including the administration of Méndez, who lent democratic trappings to the tyranny. Arbenz's agrarian reform was blown to smithereens when Castillo Armas fulfilled his mission of returning the land to United Fruit and other expropriated landlords; Méndez promised agrarian reform but merely signed an authorization for landlords to carry guns and to use them.

The worst year in the orgy of violence begun in 1954 was 1967. Thomas Melville, a U.S. Catholic priest expelled from Guatemala, told the *National Catholic Reporter* in January 1968 that in little more than a year right-wing terrorist groups had murdered more than 2,800 intellectuals, students, trade union leaders, and peasants who were trying "to combat the sicknesses of Guatemalan society." Melville based his figure on information in the press, but most of the corpses never earned any report at all: they were poor Indians of no known name or habitat whom the army included—sometimes only as numbers—in its communiqués on its victories over subversion. Indiscriminate repression formed a part of the military "search and destroy" campaign against guerrilla movements. Under the newly adopted code, members of the security forces were not held responsible for homicides, and police and army communiqués were accepted as full proof by the courts. Plantation owners and managers had the legal status of local authorities, with the right to carry arms and form punitive squads. The systematic butchery set no teletypes humming; no news-hungry reporters flew to Guatemala, nor was any reproving voice heard. The world turned its back while Guatemala underwent a long Saint Bartholomew's night. All the men of the village of Cajón del Río were exterminated; those of Tituque had their intestines gouged out with knives; in Piedra Parada they were flayed alive; in Agua Blanca de Ipala they were burned alive after being shot in the legs. A rebellious peasant's head was stuck on a pole in the center of San Jorge's plaza. In Cerro Gordo the eyes of Jaime Velázquez were filled with pins. The body of Ricardo Miranda, thirty-eight holes in his head, and the head of Haroldo Silva were found beside the San Salvador highway. In Los Mixcos, Ernesto Chinchilla's tongue was cut out. In Ojo de Agua, the Oliva Aldana brothers, blindfolded and with hands tied behind backs, were pumped full of bullets. The head of José Guzmán was chopped into a mass of tiny pieces and scattered along the road. In San Lucas Sacatepéquez, the wells yielded corpses instead of water. On the Miraflores plantation, the men greeted the dawn without hands or feet. Threats were followed by executions or by shots without warning through the back of the neck. In the cities, the doors of the doomed were marked with black crosses. Occupants were machine-gunned as they emerged, their bodies thrown into ravines.

The violence did not stop after that: it has been a way of life in Guatemala ever since the period of humiliation and fury begun in 1954. Corpses—although not quite so many—continue to turn up in rivers and on roadsides, their featureless faces too disfigured by torture to be identified. The slaughter that is greater but more hidden—the daily genocide of poverty—also continues. In 1968 another expelled priest, Father Blase Bonpane, reported on this sick society in the *Washington Post:* "Of the 70,000 people who die each year in Guatemala, 30,000 are children. The infant mortality rate in Guatemala is forty times higher than in the United States."

The First Agrarian Reform: 150 Years of Defeat for José Artigas

It was the dispossessed of Latin America who, with spears and machetes, really fought against Spanish power at the dawn of the nineteenth century. Independence did not reward them; it betrayed the hopes of those who had shed their blood. Peace came, and with it a new era of daily misery. Landowners and businessmen increased their fortunes while poverty grew among the masses. The intrigues of Latin America's new masters grew, and the four viceroyalties of the Spanish empire blew up and gave birth to many new nations, splinters of a might-have-been national unity. The "nation," as the subcontinent's gentry conceived it, looked too much like a busy port, inhabited by the mercantile and financial clientele of the British Empire, with latifundios and mines in the background. A legion of parasites, who had received the War of Independence communiqués while dancing minuets in city salons, used British-made wineglasses to drink toasts to freedom of trade. The most pompous republican slogans of the European bourgeoisie came into fashion as our countries placed themselves at the service of English industrialists and French thinkers. But what sort of "national bourgeoisie" was ours, composed of landlords, big wheelers and dealers and speculators, frock-coated politicos, and intellectuals of borrowed cultures? Latin America quickly gave birth to bourgeois constitutions well varnished with liberalism, but there was no creative bourgeoisie in the European or U.S. style to accompany them, one which would undertake as its historical mission the development of a strong national capitalism. The bourgeoisies of our countries came into being as mere instruments of international capitalism, liberally oiled cogs in the global mechanism that bled the colonies and semicolonies. These shop-window bourgeois, moneylenders, and merchants who monopolized political power had no interest in developing local manufactures, which died in the egg when free trade opened the doors to the avalanche of British merchandise. Nor were their associates, the landlords, interested in resolving "the agrarian question," except to the extent that they could feather their own nests. The latifundio was consolidated on a foundation of plunder.

Economic, social, national frustration: a series of betrayals followed independence, and Latin America, split apart by its new frontiers, was doomed as before to monoculture and dependence. Agrarian reform was a demand from the beginning. In 1824 Simón Bolívar issued the Trujillo Decree, designed to protect the Indians and reorganize the land-ownership system in Peru. Its legal provisions in no way limited the Peruvian oligarchy's privileges, which remained intact despite the Liberator's good intentions, and the Indians were as exploited as they had been before. Earlier, Miguel Hidalgo and José María Morelos had been defeated in Mexico, and a century would pass before anything came of their demands for the emancipation of the dispossessed and the recovery of usurped lands.

Down south it was José Artigas who personified the agrarian revolution. This man, the victim of impassioned vilification by official historians, led the masses during the heroic years from 1811 to 1820, in the area now occupied by Uruguay and the Argentine provinces of Santa Fe, Corrientes, Entre Ríos, Misiones, and Córdoba. He wanted to lay economic, social, and political foundations for a Great Fatherland within the frontiers of the old Río de la Plata viceroyalty, and was the most important and clear-headed of the leaders who resisted the annihilating centralism of the port of Buenos Aires. He fought against Spanish and Portuguese, and his forces were finally crushed by a pincer movement from Rio de Janeiro and Buenos Aires—instruments of the British Empire—and by an oligarchy which, true to form, sold him out as soon as they saw the implications of his program of social demands.

Patriots took up arms to follow Artigas. They were mostly poor country people, rugged gauchos, Indians who rediscovered their dignity in the struggle, slaves who won freedom by joining the independence army. The cowboys' revolution set the pampas aflame. Buenos Aires's betrayal in leaving what is now Uruguay in the hands of Spanish power and Portuguese troops produced a mass exodus to the north. A people in arms became a people in flight: men and women, old people and children, abandoned everything to form an endless caravan of horses and carts behind their leader. Artigas called a halt on the Río Uruguay and soon set up his government. By 1815 he controlled a large area from his Purificación camp in Paysandú. "What do you think I saw?" an English traveler reported. "His Excellency the Señor Protector of half the New World sitting on the head of an ox beside a bonfire on the muddy soil of his ranch, eating barbecued meat and drinking gin from a cow's horn! A dozen ragged officers surrounded him. . . ."[43] Soldiers, aides-de-camp, and scouts rode in at the gallop from all directions. Pacing, hands behind his back, Artigas dictated the revolutionary decrees of his people's government. Two secretaries—carbon paper didn't exist—took notes. Thus was born Latin America's first agrarian reform; it was applied for a year in the "Eastern Province" (today's Uruguay) and then—after the oligarchy opened the doors of Montevideo to General Lecor, greeted him as a liberator, and conducted him beneath a canopy to a solemn honor-the-invader Te Deum in the Cathedral—smashed by a new Portuguese invasion. Artigas had earlier levied a tariff which heavily taxed foreign merchandise that competed with domestic products—manufactures and crafts which were substantially developed lay within the leader's dominions. At the same time, he stopped the taxation on the importation of means of production which were needed for economic development, and fixed a trifling duty on such Latin American products as Paraguayan *yerba mate* and tobacco. The gravediggers of the revolution were also to bury these tariff measures.

The agrarian code of 1815—free land, free men—was the most advanced and glorious of the many constitutions the Uruguayans would have. Artigas's code was no doubt influenced by the ideas of Pedro Rodríguez de Campomanes and Gaspar Melchor de Jovellanos in the reformist era of Charles III, but beyond question it was also a revolutionary response to the national need for economic recovery and social justice. It included expropriation and distribution of the lands of "bad Europeans and worse Americans," who emigrated because of the revolution and were never pardoned. Lands belonging to the revolution's enemies were expropriated without indemnity—and let it be recalled that these enemies owned the great majority of the latifundios. Children did not have to pay for the sins of their fathers: the code offered them the same as it offered poor patriots. Lands were distributed on the principle that "the most unfortunate will be the most privileged." Indians, in Artigas's view, had "the chief right." The essence of this agrarian reform was to settle the rural poor on the land, making a peasant out of the gaucho who was accustomed to a roving life in war and to clandestine activities and smuggling in peace. Subsequent La Plata basin governments would mercilessly suppress the gaucho, forcing him to work as a peon on big estates, but Artigas wanted to make him an owner of land: the rebel gauchos began to enjoy honest work, built ranches and corrals, and planted their first crops.

Foreign intervention wiped it all out. The oligarchy reared its head and took vengeance. The validity of Artigas' land distribution was legislatively repudiated. From 1820 until the end of the century, the poor patriots who had benefited from the agrarian reform were violently evicted. The only land they kept was enough to be buried in. The defeated Artigas had gone to Paraguay, to die alone after a long exile of austerity and silence. The land titles he had issued were without value: government attorney Bernardo Bustamante, for example, said that "the worthlessness of the said documents" was clear at first sight. Meanwhile, "order" restored, his government hastened to celebrate the first constitution of an independent Uruguay, that fragment of the Great Fatherland Artigas had vainly fought to consolidate.

The code of 1815 contained special clauses to avoid the accumulation of land in a few hands. In our day the Uruguayan countryside looks like a desert: 500 families monopolize half of all the land and, to crown their power, also control three-quarters of the capital invested in industry and banking. Agrarian reform projects pile up in the parliamentary cemetery while the countryside is depopulated: unemployment proliferates and the number of people occupied in agriculture steadily dwindles from one dramatic census to another. The country makes its living from wool and meat, but its pastures contain fewer sheep and fewer cows than at the beginning of our century. The backwardness of production methods is reflected in the low yields from livestock—dependent for food on periodic rains and natural soil fertility—and from crop farming. Meat production per animal is not even half that of France or Germany, and the same applies to milk in comparison with New Zealand, Denmark, and Holland. Every sheep produces a kilogram less wool than in Australia. Per hectare wheat yields are three times lower than in France, corn seven times lower than in the United States. The big landowners send their profits abroad, spend their summers at Punta del Este, and do not reside at their latifundios even in winter, paying occasional visits in their own airplanes. When the Asociación Rural was founded a century ago, two-thirds of its members already made their homes in the capital. The extensive production, left to nature and hungry peons, causes them no headaches.

And it certainly pays off. The rents and profits of cattle capitalists now amount to no less than $75 million a year.* Despite low yields,

---

* In the period of the rise of national industry, strongly subsidized and protected by the state, a large part of agricultural profits went into new factories. When industry entered its cycle of crisis, surplus capital from cattle-raising was diverted in other directions; Punta del Este's most useless and luxurious mansions were built on the nation's misfortune. Speculators then began feverishly fishing in the turbid waters of inflation. Above all, there was a flight of the capital and profits that the country produces year by year. According to official figures, between 1962 and 1966, $250 million fled Uruguay for safe Swiss and U.S. banks. There was also, two decades ago, the flight of young people from countryside to city, seeking jobs in developing industry. Today it continues by land or by sea to foreign countries, although their fate is of course not the

profits stay up because of extremely low costs. A landscape without people: the biggest latifundios provide work for barely two people per 1,000 hectares, and then not for the whole year. The always available labor supply accumulates miserably in hut settlements beside the ranches. The gaucho of folklore, the subject of paintings and poems, is a far cry from the peon who works the broad, hostile lands today. Instead of leather boots, he wears frayed sandals; instead of a wide belt adorned with gold or silver, an ordinary belt, or merely a knotted cord. The producers of meat have lost the right to eat it: rarely do these Creoles have access to the typical Creole roast, juicy tender meat turning golden over a fire. Misleadingly rosy international statistics notwithstanding, the truth is that pasta-and-chicken innards stew—no source of protein—is the basic diet of the Uruguayan *campesino.*

Artemio Cruz and the Second Death of Emiliano Zapata

Just a century after the Artigas land code, Emiliano Zapata introduced far-reaching agrarian reform in his zone of revolutionary jurisdiction in southern Mexico. It was five years after the dictator Porfirio Díaz had celebrated with huge fiestas the centenary of the Grito de Dolores, the beginning of the Mexican war of independence from Spain. The official Mexico of frock-coated gentlemen olympically ignored the real Mexico whose poverty fed their splendor. In this republic of outcasts, workers' wages had not risen by a centavo since the historic rising of the priest Miguel Hidalgo in 1810. In 1910, 800-odd latifundistas, many of them foreigners, owned almost all the national territory. They were urban princelings who lived in the capital or in Europe and very occasionally visited their estates—where they slept shielded by high, buttressed walls of dark stone. On the other side of the walls, the peons huddled in adobe hovels. Of a population of 15 million, 12 million depended on rural wages, almost all of which were paid at the hacienda

same. The capital is received with open arms, but the uprooted pilgrims have to face a cold and uncertain destiny. The Uruguay of 1971, shaken by profound crisis, is no longer the oasis of peace and progress that attracted European immigrants; it is a turbulent land condemning its own inhabitants to emigration. It produces violence and exports people as naturally as it produces and exports meat and wool.

company stores in astronomically priced beans, flour, and liquor. Prison, barracks, and vestry shared the task of combating the natural defects of the Indians who, as a member of one illustrious family put it, were born "weak, drunk, and thieving." With the worker tied by inherited debts or by legal contract, slavery was the actual labor system on Yucatán henequen plantations, on the tobacco plantations of the Valle Nacional, on Chiapas and Tabasco timberland and fruit orchards, and on the rubber, coffee, sugarcane, tobacco, and fruit plantations of Veracruz, Oaxaca, and Morelos. In a fine report on his visit, John Kenneth Turner wrote that "the United States has virtually reduced Díaz to a political dependency, and by so doing has virtually transformed Mexico into a slave colony of the United States."[44] U.S. capital made juicy profits directly or indirectly from its association with the dictatorship. "The Americanization of Mexico of which Wall Street boasts," wrote Turner, "is being accomplished and accomplished with a vengeance."[45]

In 1845 the United States had annexed the Mexican territories of Texas and California, where it restored slavery in the name of civilization. Mexico also lost the present states of Colorado, Arizona, New Mexico, Nevada, and Utah—more than half the country. The stolen territory was equal in size to present-day Argentina. "Poor Mexico!" it has been said ever since, "so far from God and so close to the United States!" After the invasion, the rest of Mexico's mutilated territory suffered from U.S. investments in copper, petroleum, rubber, sugar, banking, and transportation. Far from guiltless in the extermination of the Maya and Yaqui Indians on Yucatán henequen plantations—concentration camps where men, women, and children were bought and sold like mules—was the Standard Oil affiliate American Cordage Trust, which bought more than half the henequen and could sell it cheap at a handsome profit. But sometimes, as Turner discovered, the exploitation of slave labor was direct. A North American *administrador* bought press-ganged peons in lots at fifty pesos a head. He told Turner: "We always kept them as long as they lasted. . . . In less than three months we buried more than half of them."[46] *

* Mexico was the preferred country for U.S. investments: at the end of the century it had almost a third of the U.S. capital invested abroad. In Chihuahua state and in other northern areas, William Randolph Hearst, the "Citizen Kane" of Orson Welles's film, owned more than 3 million hectares.

Mexico's hour of revenge struck in 1910: the country rose in arms against Porfirio Díaz. An agricultural leader headed the insurrection in the south: he was Emiliano Zapata, purest of revolutionaries, most loyal to the cause of the poor, most determined to right the wrongs of society.

For agricultural communities throughout Mexico, the last decades of the nineteenth century had been a period of ruthless pillage. In Morelos, towns and villages were the victims of a bout of land-, water-, and labor-grabbing as sugarcane plantations expanded voraciously. Sugar haciendas dominated the life of the state, and their prosperity had brought with it modern mills, big distilleries, and railroad spurs. In Anenecuilco, where Zapata lived and to which he belonged body and soul, the plundered peasants claimed the soil they had worked for seven continuous centuries: they were there before Cortés arrived. But those who spoke up were marched off to forced labor in Yucatán. Throughout their state, whose good land belonged to seventeen families, they lived considerably worse than the polo ponies the latifundistas pampered in luxurious stables. A law in 1909, providing further seizure of land from its legitimate owners, was the last straw. Zapata, taciturn but famous as the state's best horsebreaker and respected by all for his honesty and courage, turned *guerrillero.* The men of the south quickly formed a liberating army.

Díaz fell and the revolution swept Francisco Indalecio Madero into power. Promises of agrarian reform soon disappeared in a fog of "institutionalism." On his wedding day, Zapata had to interrupt the party: the government had sent General Victoriano Huerta's troops to crush him. According to the learned pundits in the city, the hero had become a "bandit." In November 1911 Zapata proclaimed the Plan de Ayala and wrote: "I am resolved to struggle against everything and everybody."[47] The Plan noted that "the overwhelming majority of Mexican communities and citizens are owners of no more than the land they walk on," and proposed that the property of enemies of the revolution be nationalized, that lands usurped by the latifundista avalanche be returned to their legal owners, and that a third of the remaining hacendados' lands be expropriated. The Plan de Ayala became a magnet, drawing thousands upon thousands of peasants into Zapata's ranks. Zapata denounced "the infamous pretension" of reducing everything to a mere change of men in government: the revolution was not being made for that.

The struggle went on for nearly ten years—against Díaz, against Madero, against Huerta the assassin, and later against Venustiano Carranza. The long war years were also years of continual U.S. intervention: the Marines staged two landings and several bombardments, diplomatic agents framed a variety of political plots, and Ambassador Henry Lane Wilson successfully organized the murder of President Madero and his vice president. The successive shifts of power did not dilute the fury of the attacks against Zapata and his forces, for they were the real danger, the open expression of the class struggle deeply imbedded in the national revolution. Governments and newspapers clamored against "the vandal hordes" of the general from Morelos. Powerful armies were sent, one after the other, against him. Fire, massacre, and the devastation of villages proved equally futile. Men, women, and children were shot or hanged as "Zapatista spies," with proclamations of victory following the butcheries: the clean-up has succeeded! But in the nomadic revolutionaries' mountain camps in the south, bonfires soon blazed up again. More than once Zapata's forces counterattacked successfully up to the suburbs of the capital. After the fall of Huerta's regime, Zapata and Pancho Villa—the "Attila of the South" and the "Centaur of the North"—entered Mexico City as conquerors and arranged a temporary division of power. At the end of 1914, a brief period of peace enabled Zapata to put into force, in Morelos, an agrarian reform even more radical than that outlined in the Plan de Ayala. The founder of the Socialist Party and some anarchosyndicalist militants considerably influenced this process; they radicalized the leader's ideology without weakening his traditionalist roots, and afforded him indispensable organizational know-how.

The agrarian reform proposed to "destroy at the roots and forever the unjust monopoly of land, in order to realize a social state which guarantees fully the natural right which every man has to an extension of land necessary for his own subsistence and that of his family."[41] Lands taken from communities and individuals since the deamortization law of 1856 were restored; maximum limits were laid down for holding sizes, according to climate and fertility; and the lands of enemies of the revolution were declared national property. This last political decision had, as in the Artigas agrarian reform, a clear economic meaning: the latifundistas were the enemy. Technical schools, tool factories, and a rural credit bank were established; sugarmills and distilleries were nationalized and became public services. A system of local democracy put the reins of political power and of economic maintenance in the people's hands. Zapatista schools sprouted and spread, popular juntas were organized for defense and the promotion of revolutionary principles, and an authentic democracy took shape and gained in strength. The municipalities were nuclear units of government and the people elected their leaders, courts, and police. Military leaders had to submit to the wishes of organized civilian communities. Bureaucrats and generals no longer imposed methods of production and of living. The revolution tied itself to tradition and functioned "in conformity with the customs and usage of each pueblo . . . that is, if a certain pueblo wants the communal system, so it will be executed, and if another pueblo wants the division of land in order to admit small property, so it will be done."

In the spring of 1915 all the fields of Morelos were under cultivation, mostly with corn and food crops. Meanwhile food was short and hunger loomed in Mexico City. Carranza, who had won the presidency, also ordered a land reform, but his henchmen speedily cornered all its benefits. In 1916 Morelos's capital, Cuernavaca, and the Zapatista district were threatened by powerful forces. Crops now coming to fruition, minerals, hides, and machines were attractive booty for the advancing officers, who set fires as they came, and proclaimed "a work of reconstruction and progress."

A stratagem and a betrayal ended Zapata's life in 1919. A thousand men lying in ambush fired into his body. He died at the same age as Che Guevara. The legend of a sorrel horse, galloping alone southward through the mountains, survived him. But not only the legend: the resolve of all Morelos to "complete the reformer's work, avenge the martyr's blood, and follow the hero's example" found an echo throughout the country. Time passed and under the presidency of Lázaro Cárdenas (1934–1940), the Zapatista tradition regained life and vigor with the nationwide implementation of agrarian reform. Mainly during this administration, 67 million hectares owned by foreign or Mexican corporations were expropriated, and in addition to the land peasants received credits, education, and the means to organize their work. The economy and population had begun their accelerating rise; agricultural production multiplied while the whole country underwent modernization and industrialization. Cities expanded and the consumer market grew in breadth and depth.

But Mexican nationalism did not lead to socialism and consequently, like other countries that failed to take the decisive step, Mexico did not fully achieve its goals of economic independence and social justice. The million dead in the revolutionary war years had paid blood tribute "to a Huitzilopoxtli more cruel and insatiable than the one our ancestors worshiped: the capitalist development of Mexico under conditions imposed by subordination to imperialism."[49] The fading of the bright banners has been studied by a variety of scholars. Edmundo Flores writes in an official publication that "at the present time, 60 percent of Mexico's total population has incomes below $120 a year and goes hungry."[50] Eight million Mexicans consume almost nothing but beans, corn, tortillas, and chilis. The Tlatelolco massacre of some 500 students in 1968 is not the only evidence of the system's deep contradictions. Using official figures, Alonso Aguilar concludes that Mexico has some 2 million landless peasants, 3 million children not attending school, around 11 million illiterates, and 5 million who have no shoes. Collectively owned *ejido* land is continually being partitioned, and along with the multiplication of minifundios—which themselves become steadily more fragmented—a new type of latifundio system, and a new agrarian bourgeoisie engaged in large-scale commercial farming, have made their appearance. Local landlords and entrepreneurs, who have achieved a dominant position by trampling on the letter and spirit of the law, are in turn dominated: a recent book classifies them within the words "and Co." attached to Anderson, Clayton.[51] In the same book, Lázaro Cárdenas's son writes that "the camouflaged latifundios have been established, when possible, on the best and most productive lands."

Novelist Carlos Fuentes has reconstructed, in reverse chronological order, the life of a captain in Carranza's army who, in war and then in peace, uses gun and cunning to make his way to the top.[52] A man of humble origin, Artemio Cruz sheds the idealism and heroism of his youth as the years pass: he helps himself to land, founds and multiplies businesses, gets a seat in the Congress, and climbs the shining steps to the peaks of society, accumulating wealth, power, and prestige by wheeling and dealing, bribery, speculation, audacity, and the bloody repression of the Indians. His pilgrim's progress resembles that of the potently impotent party of the Mexican revolution which virtually monopolizes the country's political life in our time. Both have fallen upward.

The Latifundio Multiplies Mouths but Not Bread

Latin American agricultural and livestock production per capita is lower today than on the eve of World War II. During the thirty years since then, world production of food has grown in the same proportion as it has fallen in Latin America. The structure of backwardness in our countryside also functions as a structure of waste: waste of labor, of available land, of capital, of the product, and above all of the fleeting opportunities for development that history has offered. In almost all Latin American countries the latifundio—and its poor relation the minifundio—are the bottlenecks choking the growth of agriculture and the development of the whole economy. The private property system molds the production system: 1.5 percent of the agricultural landlords own half of all the cultivable land, and every year Latin America spends more than $500 million on importing food that its own broad and fertile lands could produce without difficulty. Hardly 5 percent of the total area is under cultivation: the lowest proportion—and consequently the greatest waste—on earth. Furthermore, yields from the small acreage that is cultivated are very low. In many areas there are more pointed-stick plows than tractors. The use of modern techniques—not only the mechanization of tasks, but the aid and stimulation of the soil with fertilizers, herbicides, seeds, pesticides, and artificial irrigation—is the exception rather than the rule. In a manner sometimes recalling the "Sun King" Louis XIV, the latifundio forms a constellation of power which, in Maza Zavala's apt phrase, multiplies mouths but not bread.[53] Instead of absorbing labor, the latifundio expels it: in forty years the proportion of rural workers in Latin America has fallen from 63 to 40 percent. There are plenty of technocrats, mechanically applying ready-made formulas, to tell us that this is a sign of progress: massive transfer of the peasant population accelerated urbanization. The unemployed continually vomited by the system do indeed pour into the cities and extend its suburbs. But the factories, which also create unemployment as they modernize, provide no refuge for this surplus and nonspecialized labor force. The scanty technical advances in the countryside sharpen the problem. Landlords increase their profits by adopting more modern ways to exploit their properties; as more hands become idle, the gap separating rich and poor only widens. For example, the introduction of motorized equipment eliminates more rural jobs than it creates. Malnutrition is the normal lot of Latin Americans who produce the food in dawn-to-dusk workdays; they receive paupers' wages while the income produced by the countryside is spent in the cities or sent abroad. A technical improvement that increases the soil's meager yields while leaving the property system intact is certainly no blessing to the peasants, despite its contribution to general progress. There is no rise in their wages, nor any participation in the crop. The countryside radiates poverty to the many and wealth to very few. Private airplanes soar over forlorn deserts, sterile luxury is spawned in fashionable resorts, and Europe teems with banknote-stuffed Latin American tourists who neglect to cultivate their lands but not their souls.

Paul Bairoch attributes the principal weakness of the third world's economy to the fact that its median agricultural productivity is only half what today's developed countries achieved on the eve of the Industrial Revolution.[54] In fact, for industry to expand harmoniously, a much greater increase in the production of food and agricultural raw materials is needed. Food because the cities keep growing and eating more; raw materials for the factories and for export, so that agricultural imports can be cut and foreign sales, which provide currency needed for development, increased. Furthermore, domestic consumption, which must expand if infant industries are to thrive, is enfeebled by the latifundio-minifundio system. Hunger wages in the countryside and the ever growing reserve army of unemployed encourage this weakness: the emigrants from the rural areas who come to beat on city doors keep pushing down the overall level of the workers' wages.

Ever since the Alliance for Progress trumpeted the need for agrarian reform to the four winds, the oligarchy and technocracy have tirelessly elaborated projects. Dozens of projects—fat ones, thin ones, broad and narrow ones—gather dust on the shelves of every Latin American parliament. No curse is attached anymore to the theme of agrarian reform: politicians have learned that the best way not to have it is to keep invoking it. The simultaneous processes of concentration and atomization of the land continue olympically in most of the countries.

Nevertheless, exceptions are beginning to break through. For the countryside is not merely a seed bed of poverty: it is also a seed bed of rebellion, and acute social tensions often lie concealed behind the apparent resignation of the masses. Brazil's Northeast, for example, impresses one at first as a kingdom of fatalism whose inhabitants consent to die of hunger as passively as they accept nightfall at the end of each day. Yet it is not so long, after all, since that mystical explosion when the Northeasterners fought beside their way-out Messiahs, raising cross and gun against armies to bring the Kingdom of Heaven to this world; nor since the *cangaceiros* created waves of violence. Fanatics and *bandoleiros,* seeking Utopia and vengeance, made a bed for the river of desperate peasant protest, even though it was still blind. The peasant leagues later recovered and deepened these fighting traditions.

The military dictatorship that seized power in Brazil in 1964 was prompt to announce its agrarian reform. Paulo Schilling has drawn our attention to the uniqueness of the Instituto Brasileiro de Reforma Agrária: instead of distributing land to the peasants, it proceeded to expel them and to restore to the latifundistas the acreage that had been spontaneously invaded or expropriated under previous governments. In 1966 and 1967, before press censorship was applied with greater rigor, the dailies used to report the spoliations, conflagrations, and persecutions with which the military police carried out the hardworking institute's orders. In 1964 Ecuador proclaimed another agrarian reform that deserves recognition: the government distributed unproductive land only, while facilitating the concentration of better land in the grip of the big landlords. Half of the land distributed by Venezuela's agrarian reform, beginning in 1960, was public property; big commercial plantations were untouched, and such generous indemnities were paid to expropriated latifundistas that they bought new land in other areas with the profits.

In 1968, a couple of years before his fall, Argentine dictator Juan Carlos Onganía tried to apply a new tax system to rural property. The idea was to tax unproductive "bare plains" more heavily than productive land.

The cattle oligarchy protested to high heaven and mobilized their own forces on the General Staff, and Onganía had to forget his heretical idea. Like Uruguay, Argentina's naturally fertile lands and benign climate have brought it relative prosperity in Latin America. But erosion does its remorseless work on the vast abandoned plains, which are neither farmed nor used for pasture, and the same occurs on a large part of the millions of hectares used for cattle-raising. This extensive method—again as in Uruguay, but to a smaller extent—was at the bottom of the crisis that shook the Argentine economy in the 1960s. Argentine latifundistas show no interest in technical innovations. Productivity is low because it suits them; the law of profit prevails over all others. Extending estates by buying new acreage is more remunerative and less risky than applying modern intensive techniques.* In 1931, the Sociedad Rural defended the horse against the tractor: "Cattle farmers! Working with horses on agricultural tasks is protecting your own and the country's interests!" Twenty years later it insisted: "It is easier, as a well-known military man has said, to put grass in a horse's stomach than gas in the tank of a heavy truck."[56] According to ECLA calculations, in proportion to arable acreage Argentina has sixteen times fewer tractors than France and nineteen times fewer than Britain. Also in proportion, the country consumes 140 times less fertilizer than West Germany.[57] Yields of wheat, corn, and cotton are much lower in Argentina than in developed countries.

Juan Domingo Perón had defied the interests of Argentina's landowning oligarchy by imposing the Statute of the Peon and compliance with a rural minimum wage. In 1944 the Sociedad Rural declared: "In fixing wages, it is essential to determine the standard of living of the ordinary peon. His material needs are sometimes so limited that the use to which any surplus will be put is of little social interest." The Sociedad Rural

---

* From the large-scale livestock owners' standpoint, artificial pasture means transferring capital into an investment that is larger, more risky, and at the same time less profitable than the traditional investment in extensive cattle-farming. Thus the private interest of the producer is in contradiction with the interest of society as a whole: the quality and yield of cattle can only improve, beyond a certain point, through the increase of nutrients in the soil. The country needs cows to produce more meat and sheep to produce more wool, but the landlords make greater profits from yields at the present level. In this matter, the conclusions of the University of Uruguay's Instituto de Economía are equally applicable to Argentina.[55]

continues to refer to peons as if they were animals, and its reflections on the workers' limited need to consume provide an unintentional key to the limitations of Argentine industrial development: the internal market neither expands nor deepens sufficiently. Perón's economic development policy never broke the structure of agricultural underdevelopment. In a speech at the Teatro Colón in June 1952, Perón denied any intention of agrarian reform, and the Sociedad Rural commented officially: "It was a masterly dissertation." In Bolivia, thanks to the agrarian reform of 1952, nutrition visibly improved over large areas of the *altiplano*—so much so that increases in height were noted among the peasants. Yet the Bolivian population as a whole still consumes barely 60 percent of the protein and 20 percent of the calcium necessary for a minimal diet; rural consumption is even more deficient than these average figures reveal. While agrarian reform can certainly not be called a failure, the division of altiplano land has not been enough to prevent Bolivia from spending one-fifth of its foreign currency on imported food.

The agrarian reform introduced in 1969 by the military government in Peru looked from the outset like a serious experiment. As for the Eduardo Frei administration's expropriation of some Chilean latifundios, it must at least be credited with opening a channel for the radical agrarian reform which the new president, Salvador Allende, is announcing as I write these pages.

The Thirteen Northern Colonies and the Importance of Not Being Born Important

In Latin America, private appropriation of land always came before its useful cultivation. The most backward aspects of the present property system are not the offspring of crises, but emerged in periods of great prosperity; inversely, periods of economic depression have tempered the voracity of the latifundistas in acquiring new acreage. In Brazil, for example, the decline of sugar and the virtual disappearance of gold and diamonds made possible, between 1820 and 1850, legislation providing that anyone who occupied land and made it produce acquired title to it. The rise of coffee as a new "king product" produced the 1850 Law of Lands, cooked to the taste of oligarchic politicians and military men and denying ownership of land to those who worked it when the great spaces of the interior, to the south and west, were being opened up. This law was subsequently "reinforced and ratified . . . by abundant legislation that decreed purchase as the only form of access to land, and created a civil registration system that would make it nearly impossible for a poor farmer to legalize his land, and stipulated as the sale value of the unoccupied government lands much higher price levels than the current ones for land already appropriated."[58]

U.S. legislation in the same period had the opposite aim: it was to promote the internal colonization of the country. Covered wagons rolled westward into virgin lands with pioneers who extended the frontier at the cost of slaughtered Indians. The Homestead Act of 1862 assured every family of ownership of a quarter section, a lot one-half mile square; each beneficiary committed himself to farm his parcel for a minimum of five years. The public domain was colonized with startling speed and the population grew and spread like a great oil smear. The fertile land that was to be had almost gratis drew European peasants like a magnet: they crossed the ocean and then the Appalachians onto the wide-open prairies. Thus it was free farmers who occupied the new central and western territories. As the country grew in extent and population, unemployment was avoided by the creation of farm jobs, and at the same time an internal market—the multitude of farmer-proprietors—was generated with substantial purchasing power to sustain industrial development.

In contrast, the rural workers who have pushed Brazil's frontier inland for more than a century have not been—and are not—free peasant families seeking a piece of land of their own, but (as Ribeiro notes) *braceros* contracted to serve latifundistas who have already taken possession of the great open spaces. The interior deserts have never been accessible, except in this way, to the rural population. Workers have hacked their way through the jungle with machetes to open up the country for the benefit of others. Between 1950 and 1960, sixty-five Brazilian latifundios absorbed a quarter of the new land brought under cultivation.

These two opposite systems of internal colonization reveal one of the most important differences between U.S. and Latin American development models. Why is the north rich and the south poor? The Río

Grande is much more than a geographical frontier. Is today's profound disequilibrium, which seems to confirm Hegel's prophecy of inevitable war between the two Americas, to be traced to U.S. imperialist expansion, or does it have more ancient roots? In fact, back in the colonial beginnings, north and south had already generated very different societies with different aims.* The *Mayflower* pilgrims did not cross the sea to obtain legendary treasures; they came mainly to establish themselves with their families and to reproduce in the New World the system of life and work they had practiced in Europe. They were not soldiers of fortune but pioneers; they came not to conquer but to colonize, and their colonies were settlements. It is true that a slave-plantation economy like Latin America's developed later south of the Delaware, but there was a difference: the center of gravity in the United States was from the outset the farms and workshops of New England, from which came the victorious armies of the Civil War. New England colonists, the original nucleus of U.S. civilization, never acted as colonial agents for European capitalist accumulation; their own development, and the development of their new land, were always their motivation. The thirteen colonies served as an outlet for the army of European peasants and artisans who were being thrown off the labor market by metropolitan development. *Free* workers formed the base of that new society across the ocean.

Spain and Portugal, on the other hand, had an abundance of *subjugated* labor in Latin America. Enslavement of the Indians was followed by the wholesale transplantation of Africans. Through the centuries, a legion of unemployed peasants was always available to be moved to production centers: as precious metal or sugar exports rose and fell, flourishing centers coexisted with centers of decay, and the latter provided labor for the former. This structure persists to our time; today, as yesterday, it means low wage scales because of the pressure of the unemployed on the labor market, and frustrates the growth of an internal consumer market. But also in contrast to the Northern Puritans, internal economic development was never the goal of the ruling classes of Latin American colonial society. Their profits came from outside; they were tied more to the foreign market than to their own domain.

* Lewis Hanke and the other authors of *Do the Americas Have a Common History?* stretch their imaginations in vain trying to find parallels between Northern and Southern historical processes.

Landlords, miners, and merchants had been born to fulfill the mission of supplying Europe with gold, silver, and food. Goods moved along the roads in only one direction: to the port and overseas markets. This also provides the key to the United States' expansion as a national unit and to the fragmentation of Latin America. Our production centers are not interconnected but take the form of a fan with a far-away vertex.

One might say that the thirteen colonies had the fortune of bad fortune. Their history shows the great importance of not being born important. For the north of America had no gold or silver, no Indian civilizations with dense concentrations of people already organized for work, no fabulously fertile tropical soil on the coastal fringe. It was an area where both nature and history had been miserly: both metals and the slave labor to wrest it from the ground were missing. Those colonists were lucky. Furthermore, the northern colonies, from Maryland to New England to Nova Scotia, had a climate and soil similar to British agriculture and produced exactly the same things. That is, as Sergio Bagú notes, they did not offer products *complementary* to the metropolis. The situation in the Antilles and the mainland Spanish-Portuguese colonies was quite different. Tropical lands produced sugar, tobacco, cotton, indigo, turpentine; a small Caribbean island had more economic importance for England than the thirteen colonies that would become the United States.

These circumstances explain the rise and consolidation of the United States as an economically autonomous system, one which did not drain abroad the wealth it produced. The ties between colony and metropolis were slender. In Barbados and Jamaica, on the other hand, only the capital necessary to replace worn-out slaves was reinvested. Thus it was not racial factors that decided the development of the one and the underdevelopment of the other: there was nothing Spanish or Portuguese about Britain's Antillean islands. The truth is that the economic insignificance of the thirteen colonies permitted the early diversification of their exports and set off the early and rapid development of manufacturing. Even before independence, North American industrialization had official encouragement and protection. And England took a tolerant attitude while it strictly forbade its Antillean islands to manufacture so much as a pin.

3. The Invisible Sources of Power

As Lungs Need Air, So the U.S. Economy Needs Latin American Minerals

In June 1969, when the astronauts had put the first human footprints on the moon, the father of that achievement, Werner von Braun, announced to the press a U.S. plan for a remote space station with functions that were less remote: he heralded an observation platform from which we will be able to examine all the wealth of the earth, including unknown petroleum, copper, and zinc deposits.

Petroleum continues to be our world's chief fuel, and the United States imports one-seventh of the petroleum it consumes. Bullets are needed to kill Vietnamese, and bullets need copper: the United States buys abroad one-fifth of the copper it uses. Shortages of zinc cause increasing anxiety: over half comes from abroad. Planes cannot be built without aluminum, and aluminum cannot be produced without bauxite: the United States has almost no bauxite. Its great steel centers—Pittsburgh, Cleveland, and Detroit—do not get enough iron from the Minnesota deposits, which are on the way to exhaustion, and there is no manganese within the United States: one-third of its iron and all of its manganese are imported. Nor has it any nickel or chrome of its own to produce jet engines. Tungsten is needed to make special steels and one-fourth of that is imported.

This growing dependence on foreign supplies produces the growing identification of the interests of U.S. capitalists operating in Latin America with U.S. national security. The internal stability of the world's greatest power is closely linked with its investments south of the Río Grande. About half of those investments are in the extraction of petroleum and minerals, indispensable for the U.S. economy in peace and war. In 1959, the chairman of the Chamber of Commerce International Department said: "Historically, one of the United States' chief reasons for investing abroad has been to develop natural resources, particularly minerals and more especially petroleum. It is quite obvious that incentives for this type of investment can only grow. Our needs for raw materials are continually increasing as the population expands and living standards rise. At the same time our domestic resources are depleted."[1] Government, universities, and big corporations invest astronomic amounts in scientific laboratories, which make new discoveries and inventions at a dizzy pace, but the new technology still has not found a substitute for the basic materials nature alone provides. At the same time, the materials necessary to meet the challenge of its industrial growth become increasingly scarce in the United States' own subsoil.

By-Products of the Subsoil: Coups d'État, Revolutions, Spy Dramas, etc.

The wealth of iron beneath Brazil's Paraopeba valley overthrew two presidents—Jânio Quadros and João Goulart—before Marshal Castelo Branco, who made himself dictator in 1964, graciously handed it over to the Hanna Mining Company. An earlier friend of the U.S. ambassador, President Eurico Dutra (1946-1951), had handed Bethlehem Steel the 40 million tons of manganese in the state of Amapá—one of the world's biggest deposits—for 4 percent of the income from exporting it. Since then Bethlehem has been moving the mountains to the United States so enthusiastically that in fifteen years' time Brazil may have no manganese for its own steel industry. Furthermore, thanks to the generosity of the Brazilian government, $88 of each $100 Bethlehem invests in mineral extraction are tax exempt, in the name of "regional development." As we can see, the experience of the lost gold of Minas

Gerais—"white gold, black gold, rotten gold," as the poet Manuel Bandeira wrote—has gone for nothing: Brazil continues the gratuitous self-plunder of its own natural sources of development.* In Bolivia, the Matilde mine contains lead, silver, and abundant zinc twelve times more pure than that in U.S. mines; between massacres of miners, dictator René Barrientos, who seized power in 1964, handed it over to Phillips Industries, a Dutch conglomerate. The firm was authorized to remove the crude zinc for processing in its refineries abroad, paying the state no less than 1.5 percent of the sale value. In Peru in 1968, page 11 of the agreement which President Fernando Belaúnde Terry had signed with a Standard Oil affiliate was mysteriously lost; General Juan Velasco Alvarado overthrew Belaúnde, took the reins, and nationalized the firm's wells and refinery. In Venezuela, the largest U.S. military mission in Latin America sits on Standard and Gulf's great petroleum lake. Argentina's frequent coups d'état erupt before or after each offer of oil concessions. Copper was a far from minor factor in the Pentagon's disproportionate military aid to Chile before the electoral victory of Salvador Allende's left coalition; U.S. copper reserves had fallen by more than 60 percent between 1965 and 1969. In 1964, Che Guevara showed me, in his office in Havana, that Batista's Cuba was not merely sugar: the Imperium's blind fury against the revolution was better explained, he thought, by Cuba's big deposits of nickel and manganese. The United States' nickel reserves subsequently fell by two-thirds when Nicaro Nickel was nationalized and President Johnson threatened an embargo on French metal exports if the French bought nickel from Cuba.

Minerals had much to do with the fall of Cheddi Jagan's socialist government, which at the end of 1964 had again won a majority of votes in what was then British Guiana. The country now called Guyana is the world's fourth producer of bauxite and Latin America's third producer of manganese. The CIA played a decisive role in Jagan's defeat. Arnold Zander, leader of the strike that served as a provocation and pretext to deny electoral victory to Jagan, afterward admitted publicly that his

* The Mexican government, on the other hand, saw in time that the country, one of the chief exporters of sulphur, was being emptied of it. Texas Gulf Sulphur and Pan-American Sulphur had insisted that the reserves still in their concessions were six times greater than they actually were. The government decided in 1965 to limit foreign sales.

union had dollars rained upon it from one of the CIA foundations. The new regime—very Western and very Christian—guaranteed the Aluminum Company of America (Alcoa) against any danger to its interests in Guyana: it could continue tranquilly removing the bauxite and selling it to itself at the same price as in 1938, although the price of aluminum had since soared.* The danger was indeed past. Arkansas bauxite costs twice as much as Guyana bauxite. The United States has very little bauxite on its own territory, but using cheap imported raw material it produces almost half of the world's aluminum.

The United States depends on foreign sources for most of the minerals it needs to maintain its ability to wage war. The jet engine, the gas turbine, and nuclear reactors have a great influence over the demand for materials only obtainable abroad, and there is a clear link between the imperative need for strategic minerals, indispensable for the maintenance of U.S. military-atomic power, and the massive purchase of land—usually by fraudulent methods—in Brazil's Amazonia. During the 1960s many U.S. firms, represented by professional adventurers and contrabandists, descended in a hectic "rush" upon these enormous forests, which under an agreement signed in 1964 had already been flown over and photographed by the U.S. air force. Scintillometers to detect deposits of radioactive minerals, electromagnetic devices for x-ray photography of subsoils rich in nonferrous minerals, and magnetometers to detect and measure the iron were all used. With the aid of a U.S. government geological survey, information and photos concerning the extension and depth of Amazonia's hidden wealth were put in the hands of interested private concerns. Gold, silver, diamonds, gypsum, hematite, magnetite, tantalite, titanium, thorium, bauxite, zinc, chrome, and mercury were detected. Photographing everything from the virgin forest of Mato Grosso to the southern Goiás plains, the intrepid lensmen (as ecstatically reported in the final Latin American edition of *Time* in 1967) captured God's-eye views showing lightning flashes of half a dozen distant storms on the same exposure as brilliant sunshine. The government had offered tax exemptions and other seductions to colonizers

* Arthur Davis, long-time chairman of Alcoa, died in 1962 leaving $300 million to charitable foundations, with the express condition that the money not be spent outside the United States. Not even through this channel could Guyana recover at least some of its stolen wealth.

of these wild, magical lands. Before 1967, according to *Time*, foreign capitalists had bought, at $.07 an acre, a tract larger than Connecticut, Rhode Island, Delaware, Massachusetts, and New Hampshire put together. "We must," said the director of the government's Amazonian development agency, "keep the doors wide open to foreign investment, for we need more than we can get." To justify the U.S. air force's aerophoto excursions, the government had previously declared it lacked the resources for the job. Again par for the course in Latin America: its resources are always surrendered to imperialism in the name of its lack of resources.

The Brazilian Congress managed to conduct an investigation which brought forth a voluminous report.[2] In this were listed cases of sale or usurpation of 20 million-odd hectares of land, forming so odd a shape that (said the investigating commission) "they constitute a cordon to isolate Amazonia from the rest of Brazil." The "clandestine exploitation of highly valuable minerals" appears in the report as one of the United States' chief motives for opening a "new frontier" in Brazil. Army testimony stresses "the interest of the U.S. government in maintaining under its control a vast tract of land for later use, whether for exploitation of minerals—especially radioactive ones—or as a base for organized colonization." Says the National Security Council: "A suspicious factor is that the areas occupied or being occupied by foreign elements are the same areas where sterilization campaigns for Brazilian women are carried on by foreigners." In fact, according to the newspaper *Correio da Manhã*, "more than twenty foreign religious missions, mainly of the U.S. Protestant church, are occupying Amazonia, functioning in places that are richest in radioactive minerals, gold, and diamonds. . . . They make extensive use of sterilization, using the intrauterine device, and teach English to the catechized Indians. . . . Their areas are surrounded by armed elements and no one can enter them."[3] Note that Amazonia is the largest of all the habitable deserts on our planet. *Birth control* has been introduced into this great empty space to avoid demographic competition by the very few Brazilians who live and reproduce in remote comers of the immense forests and plains.

General Riograndino Kruel told the congressional investigating commission that "contraband in materials containing thorium and uranium amounts to an astronomical one million tons." Shortly before, in 1966,

Kruel (then federal police chief) had denounced a U.S. consul's "insolent and systematic interference" in the open trial of four U.S. citizens accused of smuggling Brazilian atomic minerals. To the general's mind the fact that forty tons of radioactive minerals had been found in their possession was enough to convict them. Soon afterward three of the contrabandists mysteriously fled the country.

The smuggling was no new phenomenon, although it had greatly increased. Through clandestine leakage of rough diamonds alone, Brazil has for some years been losing more than $100 million a year. But the need to smuggle is only relative: legal concessions deprive Brazil, without any inconvenience, of most of its fabulous natural wealth. To give but one example—just a new bead on a long string—the world's largest niobium deposit, in Araxá, belongs to an affiliate of the Niobium Corporation of New York. Niobium is alloyed with various other metals which, because of their resistance to high temperatures, are used in constructing nuclear reactors, rockets, space ships, satellites, or simple jet planes. Along with the niobium, the concern incidentally extracts substantial quantities of tantalum, thorium, uranium, pyrochlore, and rare mineral-rich soils.

A German Chemist Defeats the Winners of the War of the Pacific

The story of the rise and fall of nitrates is a good illustration of Latin America's illusory fortunes in the world market: how transient the blissful breezes have always been, how crushing the catastrophes.

In the middle of the last century Malthus's dark prophecies hovered over the Old World. With Europe's population climbing steeply, it was urgently necessary to revive exhausted soil so that food production could grow in the same proportion. The value of guano as fertilizer was demonstrated in British laboratories, and after 1840 it began to be exported from Peru on a large scale. Since time immemorial pelicans and seagulls, feeding on the prodigious shoals of fish in the coastal currents, had been accumulating mountains of excrement rich in nitrogen, ammonia, phosphates, and alkaline salts: on these rainless shores the guano had remained in a pure state.* Soon after guano was launched in the international market, agricultural chemistry discovered even greater nutritive virtues in nitrate, and by 1850 it was being used intensively to fertilize European fields. Old World wheat-growing lands, impoverished by erosion, hungrily absorbed the cargoes of sodium nitrate shipped from Tarapacá (then in Peru) and later from Antofagasta (then in Bolivia).[5] Thanks to the sodium nitrate and the guano lying on Pacific coasts, almost within reach of the ships that came to fetch them, the specter of hunger departed from Europe.

The uncommonly arrogant Lima oligarchy continued enriching itself and amassing symbols of its power in the palaces and Carrara marble mausoleums which sprouted amid sandy deserts. Once it had been Potosí's silver that nourished the great families of the capital city; now they lived from bird-droppings and the shiny white clots in the nitrate fields—more vulgar means to the same elegant ends. Peru thought it was independent, but Britain had taken Spain's place. The country felt rich, according to José Carlos Mariátegui, and the state carelessly used up its credit, living prodigally and mortgaging its future to British high finance. In 1868, the state's expenditures and debts far exceeded the value of its sales abroad. The guano deposits served as guarantee for British loans, and Europe juggled prices. The plunder of the exporters created havoc; what nature had accumulated over millennia on the islands was squandered in a few years. Meanwhile, out on the nitrate fields the workers survived in hovels hardly higher than a man, made of stones, nitrate, rubble, and mud.

The exploitation of saltpeter rapidly spread into Antofagasta, although the business was not Bolivian but Peruvian and, more than Peruvian, Chilean. When the Bolivian government proposed to tax those nitrate fields on its territory, the Chilean army invaded the province, never to leave. Until then the desert had served as a damper on latent conflicts between Chile, Peru, and Bolivia, but now nitrates brought them to the boil. The War of the Pacific broke out in 1879 and lasted till 1883. Chile's armed forces, having occupied the Peruvian nitrate ports of Patillos, Iquique, Pisagua, and Junín in 1879, finally

---

* The guano producers, wrote Robert Cushman Murphy long after the boom, were the world's most valuable birds in their dollar yield for each digestive process: they surpassed Shakespeare's nightingale that sang on Juliet's balcony, the dove that flew from Noah's Ark, and, of course, the sad swallows of Gustavo Adolfo Bécquer.[4]

entered Lima as conquerors and the fortress of Callao surrendered the next day. The defeat brought mutilation and bloodletting to Peru. The national economy lost its two chief resources, productive forces were paralyzed, the currency collapsed, and foreign credit was cut off.* But, as Mariátegui notes, the collapse failed to wipe out the past: the colonial economic structure was untouched even though its sources of sustenance had been removed. As for Bolivia, it did not realize what the war had cost it: the most important copper mine today, Chuquicamata, lies in the province it lost to Chile. And the victors?

Nitrate and iodine accounted for 5 percent of Chile's income in 1880; ten years later, more than half came from the export of nitrates from the conquered territories. In the same period, British investments in Chile more than tripled: the nitrate region became a British factory. The English took over nitrates at bargain rates. The Peruvian government had expropriated the nitrate fields in 1875, paying for them in bonds; five years afterward, the war had reduced these documents to a tenth their former value. Such daring adventurers as John Thomas North and his partner Robert Harvey turned this to good account. While Chileans, Peruvians, and Bolivians exchanged bullets on the field of battle, the English bought up the bonds, thanks to credits graciously afforded them by the Bank of Valparaíso and other Chilean banks. The soldiers were fighting for them without knowing it. The Chilean government promptly rewarded the sacrifices of North, Harvey, Inglis, James, Bush, Robertson, and other industrious businessmen: in 1881—by which time half the bonds were in the hands of Britain's speculating wizards—it ordered the return of the nitrate fields to their "legitimate owners." Not one penny had left England to finance this masterpiece of looting.

In the early 1890s Chile was sending three-quarters of its exports to Britain and getting almost half of its imports from that country: its

* Peru lost the nitrate province of Tarapacá and some important guano islands, but retained guano deposits on the northern coast. Guano remained the chief fertilizer for Peruvian agriculture until the fishmeal boom wiped out the pelicans and seagulls after 1960. The fishing concerns, mostly from the United States, quickly destroyed the anchovy shoals near the coast to feed U.S. and European pigs and poultry with Peruvian fishmeal, and the guano-producing birds took off after the fishing boats, ever further out to sea. Without the strength to fly back, they fell in the ocean. Others stayed put, so that in 1962 and 1963 one could see flocks of pelicans hunting for food along Lima's main avenue; when they could no longer take wing, they died on the streets.

commercial dependence at the time was even greater than India's. The war had given Chile a world monopoly on natural nitrates, but the nitrate king was John Thomas North. One of his enterprises, the Liverpool Nitrate Company, was paying 40 percent in dividends. North had landed at Valparaíso in 1866 with only £10 in the pocket of his dusty old suit; thirty years later princes and dukes, top politicians and great industrialists, sat at table in his London mansion. He had appointed himself "Colonel" and, as befitted a gentleman of his standing, had joined the Conservative Party and the Kent Masonic Lodge. Lord Dorchester, Lord Randolph Churchill, and the Marquis of Stackpole graced his extravagant parties, where North danced in Henry VIII costume. Meanwhile, in his remote nitrate kingdom Chileans put in sixteen-hour workdays without even Sundays off, and were paid in script that lost about half its value at the company stores.

Between 1886 and 1890, the Chilean state under President José Manuel Balmaceda undertook the most ambitious development plan in its history. Balmaceda promoted some industries, carried out important public works, modernized education, took measures to break the British railroad monopoly in Tarapacá, and secured from Germany the only non-British loan Chile received in the whole of the past century. He announced in 1888 that the nitrate areas must be nationalized through the formation of Chilean enterprises, and refused to sell state-owned nitrate fields to the British. Three years later civil war broke out. North and his colleagues generously financed the rebels, and British warships blockaded the Chilean coast while the London press fulminated against Balmaceda, a "butcher" and "dictator of the worst stripe."* Balmaceda was defeated and killed himself. The British ambassador informed the Foreign Office: "The British community makes no secret of its satisfaction over the fall of Balmaceda, whose victory, it is thought, would have

* The Congress headed the opposition to the president—the weakness of many of its members for pounds sterling was notorious. The bribery of Chileans was "a custom of the country," according to the English, and North's associate Harvey described it thus at the trial of a lawsuit brought against him and other Nitrate Railways Company directors in 1897 by some small shareholders. Explaining a £100,000 expenditure on bribes, Harvey said: "The public administration in Chile, as you know, is very corrupt. . . . I don't say that one has to bribe judges, but I think many members of the Senate who were short of funds got some part of that money in exchange for their votes, and that it served to prevent the government from flatly refusing to listen to our protests and claims. . . ."[6]

implied serious harm to British commercial interests." State investments in roads, railways, colonization of new land, education, and public works promptly slumped as British enterprises extended their dominions.

On the eve of World War I, two-thirds of Chile's national income came from nitrate exports, but it was a prosperity which, far from developing and diversifying, only heightened the country's structural deformations. Chile functioned as an appendage of the British economy: the biggest supplier of fertilizer to the European market had no right to its own life. And then a German chemist, sitting in his laboratory, defeated the generals who had won the day on the battlefield. Perfection of the Haber process, which produces nitrates by fixing nitrogen from the air, decisively displaced Chilean nitrate and sent Chile's economy into a tailspin.

In the thirsty desert of Tamarugal, where the land dazzles one's eyes with its brilliance, I have stood beside the ruins of Tarapacá. During the boom there were 120 nitrate fields here; now only two remain in operation. Since the pampa is without moisture or moths, it was not only possible to sell the machinery as scrap, but also Oregon pine boards from the best houses, zinc sheets, and even intact nails, nuts, and bolts. Workers specializing in taking towns apart appeared on the scene: they were the only ones who could get a job in these razed and abandoned immensities. I saw the debris and the empty holes, the ghost towns, the dead tracks of the nitrate railway, the silent telegraph wires, the skeletons of nitrate fields mangled by the bombardment of years, the cemetery crosses buffeted at night by the cold wind, the whitish hills of slag piled up beside the excavations. "Here money flowed and everyone thought it would never stop," I was told by the surviving residents. They idealize the past as a paradise; even Sundays—which in 1889 did not exist for the workers, and were won later by determined strike action—are remembered with nostalgia. "Each Sunday on the nitrate pampa," a very old oldster said, "was a national fiesta for us, a new Independence Day every week." Iquique, the biggest nitrate port—"a first-class port," according to its official citation—was the scene of more than one massacre of workers, but its municipal theater in the Belle Époque style once drew Europe's best opera stars before they went to Santiago, the capital.

Copper Teeth in Chile's Flesh

Copper soon replaced nitrates as the pillar of Chile's economy, while U.S. predominance took the place of British. On the eve of the 1929 crisis, U.S. investments in Chile exceeded $400 million, almost all made in the exploitation and transport of copper. Anaconda and Kennecott, two concerns with close links as parts of a single world consortium, remained masters of the best copper deposits up until the Unidad Popular victory of 1970. In half a century they bled Chile of $4 billion, sent to their home offices under various headings; yet by their own inflated figures they invested no more than $800 million, almost all in profits taken from the country.* The hemorrhage kept growing as production grew, exceeding $100 million a year in recent times. The masters of copper were masters of Chile. On December 21, 1970, President Salvador Allende spoke to an excited multitude from the government palace balcony. He announced that he had just signed a constitutional reform project enabling the mines to be nationalized. In 1969, he said, Anaconda had garnered $79 million in profits from Chile—the equivalent of 80 percent of its global profits, although its investment in Chile was less than one-sixth its total investments abroad. The "bacteriological warfare" of the right—a planned propaganda campaign of terror to avoid nationalization of copper and other structural reforms proposed by the left—had been as intense as in previous elections. The newspapers had pictured heavy Soviet tanks rolling before La Moneda, the presidential palace; bearded *guerrilleros* dragging innocent youths off to death appeared on Santiago walls; every house waited for the bell to ring. . . . "Do you have four children? Two will go to the Soviet Union and two to Cuba," a *señora* explained. None of this worked; copper is "putting on poncho and spurs" and becoming Chilean.

The United States, its feet caught in the tangle of Southeast Asian wars, has not concealed its official displeasure at the trend in the southern Andes. But Chile is not within reach of a sudden Marine

* These firms process Chilean copper in their own distant plants. Anaconda, American Brass, Anaconda Wire & Cable, and Kennecott Wire & Cable are among the world's chief manufacturers of bronze and wire.

expedition, and Allende, after all, is president by every precept of representative democracy preached by Washington. Imperialism is in the first stages of a critical new cycle whose portents have shown themselves in economics; its function as world policeman becomes ever more costly and difficult. And the price war? Chilean products are now sold in several markets and new ones can be opened up in the socialist world; the United States lacks the means to set up a universal blockade of the copper Chile is exporting. Quite different, of course, was the situation in Cuba twelve years ago, when 100 percent of its sugar was destined for the U.S. market and was wholly dependent on U.S. prices. When Frei won the 1964 elections in Chile, the price of copper immediately rose; when Allende won the 1970 elections it was already falling and fell further. But copper, always subject to sharp price fluctuations, has in recent years enjoyed fairly high prices, and since demand exceeds supply, scarcity prevents any serious drop. While aluminum has substantially replaced copper as a conductor of electricity, aluminum also requires copper; furthermore, cheaper and more efficient substitutes have not been found to displace it from either the steel or the chemical industry, and copper remains the chief raw material used in gunpowder, brass, and wire manufacture.

Along the Andean slopes Chile has the world's greatest reserves of copper, a third of all those now known. Chilean copper generally appears with other metals, such as gold, silver, and molybdenum—an additional factor which stimulates its exploitation. And Chilean workers are cheap: their low costs in Chile more than compensated Anaconda and Kennecott for their high costs in the United States, and Chilean copper, through the device of "expenditures abroad," paid more than $10 million a year to maintain the offices in New York. The average wage in Chilean mines in 1964 was barely one-eighth of the basic Kennecott refinery wage in the United States, although the workers' productivity was the same. The foreign personnel in the big mines inhabit a world apart, a little state-within-a-state where only English is spoken and where newspapers are especially published for the inhabitants. The worker's productivity has grown as the companies have mechanized methods of exploitation. Since 1945 copper production has increased by 50 percent, but the number employed in the mines has fallen by one-third.

Nationalization will put an end to a state of affairs that had become intolerable for Chile, and prevent repetition in copper of the plunder and descent into the abyss of the nitrate cycle. The taxes the companies paid to the state did not begin to compensate for the remorseless draining of mineral resources which nature bestowed but will not renew. Furthermore, the taxes have decreased in relative terms since 1955, when a system of lower assessments for higher production was established, and since the Frei government's "Chileanization" of copper. In 1965 Frei made the state a partner of Kennecott and allowed the copper companies to almost triple their profits: tax assessments were based on an average price of $.29 per pound, although heavy global demand raised the actual price as high as $.70. Radomiro Tomic, the candidate chosen by the Christian Democrats to succeed Frei, admitted that the difference between the fictitious and the real price had lost Chile a vast sum in dollars. In 1969 the Frei government agreed to buy 51 percent of Anaconda's shares in half-yearly installments, on conditions that set off a new political scandal and further swelled opposition ranks. Anaconda's chairman had, according to the version given to the press, previously told the president of Chile: "Excellency, capitalists do not conserve their assets for sentimental motives but for economic reasons. It is commonplace for a family to keep a wardrobe because it belonged to a grandfather, but corporations don't have grandfathers. Anaconda can sell all of its assets. It only depends on the price that is paid."

But everywhere the nationalist tide runs faster, and the best of good humor cannot stop it; the lesser evil of "nationalization by agreement" had a short life. The structure of the international copper market is crumbling dangerously, and the four biggest producers—Chile, Zambia, the Congo, and Peru—have for some time been meeting to apply a common price-defense policy. At the end of 1969 the Peruvian affiliate of American Smelting & Refining signed a contract whereby the rich Cuajone mine, conceded to it years earlier, would remain in its possession. But despite some "traditional" clauses, the terms of the contract reflected the company's weakness and desperation in face of an international situation more unfavorable than ever to its interests. Under "normal" conditions, American Smelting would not have accepted the elimination of many of its privileges, which had made foreign mines all-powerful enclaves indifferent to Peru's economic development needs. Under the new conditions imposed by ascendant nationalism, the company hastened to proclaim its satisfaction with the terms of the agreement. Deep divergencies persist with regard to interpretation of the text, but the Peruvian government says that the recent state monopolization of mineral marketing also includes Cuajone copper. The state also reserves refining for its own projected plants, which will be obliged to hire and fulfill a work plan setting definite terms for investment and production. For not abiding by the terms of the new mining laws, Anaconda and American Smelting have lost their concessions at Cerro Verde and Michiquillay, two big reserves which had remained untouched for half a century.

TIN MINERS, UNDER AND ABOVE GROUND

Almost a century ago a man half dead from hunger battled against the rocks of Bolivia's desolate *altiplano.* A dynamite charge exploded. When he approached to pick up the pulverized bits of stone, he was dazzled by what he saw in his hands: sparkling fragments of the world's richest vein of tin. At dawn he mounted his horse and headed for Huanuni. Tests confirmed the value of his find. The tin could go straight from the vein to the port without the need for any concentration process. The man became the king of tin, and when he died *Fortune* described him as one of the ten multi-est multimillionaires on earth. His name was Simón Ituri Patiño. For years he sat in Europe making and unmaking Bolivian presidents and ministers, planning the hunger of his workers, organizing massacres, ramifying and extending his personal fortune: Bolivia was a country that existed for him, that was at his service.

Bolivia nationalized its tin after the heroic revolutionary days of 1952, but by then the super-rich mines had become poor. On the Juan del Valle mountain where Patiño found his dazzling vein, the degree of purity of the ore had fallen 120-fold. Of 156,000 tons of rock brought out every month, only 400 tons are now recovered. The total length of the perforations is twice the distance from the mine to La Paz: the mountain is an anthill pierced by countless galleries, passages, tunnels, and chimneys. It is on the way to becoming an empty shell. Every year it loses a little height, and the gradual process of collapse is eating away the crest; from a distance it looks like a cavitied molar.

Antenor Patiño not only collected a fat indemnity for the mines his father had almost exhausted, but he also kept control of the price and destination of the expropriated tin. He sat with fixed smile in his European mansion. "Mister Patiño is the affable Bolivian tin king," the society pages continued saying for years after nationalization.* For nationalization—a fundamental achievement of the 1952 revolution—has not changed Bolivia's role in the international division of labor. Bolivia has continued to export the crude mineral, and nearly all the tin is still refined in the Liverpool smelter of Williams, Harvey and Company, which belongs to Patiño. Nationalization of the production source of any raw material is not enough, as painful experience has taught. Even if a country has become nominal master of its own subsoil, it can remain as condemned to impotency as ever. Throughout its history Bolivia has produced crude minerals and refined speeches. Rhetoric and poverty abound: cheap writers and expensive sages have always dedicated themselves to absolving the guilty of all guilt. Of every ten Bolivians, six still cannot read, while half of the children do not attend school. In 1971 Bolivia was at last to get a tin smelter of its own in Oruro, after a chain of betrayals, sabotage, intrigues, and bloodshed stretching back into the mists of time.† This country that till now has

---

* The *New York Times* (August 13, 1969) described him thus in ecstatically reporting the vacation of the Duke and Duchess of Windsor at Patiño's sumptuous sixteenth-century castle near Lisbon. "We like to give the servants some peace and quiet," the hostess confessed, describing her daily program to Charlotte Curtis.

Then it is time to vacation in the Swiss mountains; photographers pursue counts and fashionable stars to St. Moritz. A fifty-year-old millionairess has just lost her second husband, a Ford vice-president: she smiles before the flashbulbs and announces her new romance with a youth who takes her by the arm and gazes at her with frightened eyes. Beside them in the magazine picture is another "in" couple. He is a stubby man with Indian features—thick eyebrows, hard eyes, squashed nose, prominent cheekbones: Antenor Patiño still looks like a Bolivian. In another magazine he appears dressed as an Oriental prince, complete with turban, among various real princes who have gathered in the palace of Baron Alexis de Rédé: Princess Margaret of Denmark, Prince Henry, María Pía de Savoia and her cousin Prince Miguel de Bourbon-Parma, Prince Lobckowitz, and other toilers in the vineyard.

† In July 1966, when General Alfredo Ovando announced an agreement with the German firm Klochner to install a state smelter, he saw a new destiny for "those poor mines which have only served, till now, to open pits in the lungs of our brothers the miners." As Sergio Almaraz

not been able to produce its own ingots can, however, boast of eight different law schools which turn out suckers of Indian blood in industrial quantities.

A story is told of Mariano Melgarejo, a dictator of a century ago, who forced the British ambassador to drink a barrelful of chocolate as punishment for sneering at a glass of local *chicha.* The ambassador was paraded down La Paz's main street sitting backward on a donkey and then shipped back to London. An infuriated Queen Victoria supposedly called for a map of South America, chalked an X over Bolivia, and pronounced sentence: "Bolivia does not exist." For the world, in effect, Bolivia did not exist then or later: the looting of its silver, and later of its tin, was no more than an exercise of the rich countries' natural rights. The tin can is, after all, as much the emblem of the United States as the eagle or apple pie. But the tin can is not merely a "pop" symbol; it is also, if unwittingly, a symbol of silicosis in the Siglo XX and Huanuni mines: Bolivians die with rotted lungs so that the world may consume cheap tin. Tinplate is made from tin, and the tin is worth nothing: a half-dozen people fix its global price. What does the Bolivian miner's bitter life matter to the consumer of preserves or the money-exchange manipulators? Most of the tin refined in the world is consumed in the United States: according to Food and Agricultural Organization figures, the average U.S. citizen consumes five times more meat and milk and twenty times more eggs than the inhabitant of Bolivia. And the miners are well below the national average. In the cemetery at Catavi, where blind people solicit pennies to pray for the dead, a forest of white crosses stand over small graves scattered among the dark headstones of adults. Of every two children born in the mining camps, one dies soon after

---

wrote, the men who give their lives for the mineral "do not own it. They never did, neither before nor after 1952. For tin has no immediate value except in ingots. The mineral, a heavy, earthy powder, serves no purpose except to be thrown into a smelter."[7]

Almaraz tells the story of an industrialist, Mariano Peró, who for more than thirty years fought a lone war to have Bolivian tin refined in Oruro and not in Liverpool. In 1946, a few days after the fall of nationalist President Gualberto Villarroel, Peró walked into the Quemado Palace. He had come to pick up two ingots of tin, the first produced in his Oruro smelter. There was no point in leaving the symbolic ingots to continue adorning the president's desk: Villarroel had been hanged from a lamppost in the Plaza Murillo, and with his fall the power of the oligarchy had been restored. Peró picked up the ingots and walked away with them. They were stained with newly dried blood.

opening its eyes. The other, the survivor, will surely grow up to be a miner. And before he is thirty-five he will have no lungs.

The cemetery creaks. Beneath the graves countless tunnels have been dug, with openings barely wide enough for the men who disappear into them, like rabbits, in search of tin. New deposits of tin have accumulated through the years in the tons upon tons of slag piled up in huge gray mounds across the landscape. When the violent rains pour from low clouds over Llallagua—where men drink themselves into a desperate stupor in the *chicha* taverns—one sees the unemployed crouching beside the dirt roads to collect the tin as it is washed down. Here, tin is an omnipresent canned god reigning over men and things. There is not only tin in the bowels of Patiño's old mountain; the black sparkle of cassiterite betrays its presence even in the adobe walls of the camps. There is tin, too, in the yellowish mud that slides off the slag, and in the poisoned water that flows from the mountains; it is in earth and rock, surface and subsoil, in the sands and pebbles of the Seco riverbed. In these dry and stony regions almost 13,000 feet above sea level, where no grass grows and everything—even the people—is the dark color of tin, men stoically endure their enforced separation from the joys of the world. The camps are a huddle of one-room dirt-floor shacks; the wind howls through cracks in the walls, cutting to the bone. A university study of the Colquiri mine found that of every ten boys questioned, six sleep in the same bed with their sisters. "Many of the parents," the report added, "feel embarrassed when their children observe them in the sexual act." There are no baths; the latrines are public sheds covered with filth and flies. People prefer to use open ash-dumps where, despite the accumulated garbage and excrement and the contentedly rooting pigs, at least air circulates. Likewise, the water supply is collective: people must await the moment of its arrival and hurry with gasoline tins and pots for a place in the queue at the public trough. The food is meager and bad. It consists of potatoes, beans, rice, dried potato starch, ground corn, and sometimes a little tough meat.

We were deep down inside the Juan del Valle mountain. Hours earlier the siren shrilly summoning workers of the first shift had resounded through the camp. Going from gallery to gallery inside the mine, we had passed from tropical heat to polar cold and back again to the heat, always—for hours—in the same poisoned air: humid, gas-filled, dusty, smoky. Breathing it we could understand why miners lose their senses of smell and taste in a few years. They all chew coca-leaf and ash as they work, and this too is part of the annihilation process, for coca, by deadening hunger and masking fatigue, turns off the alarm system which helps the organism stay alive. But the worst of it was the dust: circles of light from the miners' helmets danced dimly in the gloom, showing thick white curtains of deadly silica. It does not take long to do its work. The first symptoms are felt within a year, and in ten years one enters the cemetery. Late-model Swedish drills are used in the mine, but the ventilation system and work conditions have not improved with time.

Up on the surface, independent workers use twelve-pound wooden sledgehammers to conquer the rock, just as they did a century ago, as well as antique pumping devices and sifters to collect the mineral. They work like dogs and are paid in pennies, but they have the advantage of fresh air over the underground workers, prisoners sentenced without appeal to death by asphyxiation.

The din of the drills stopped and the workers took a break as we waited for more than twenty charges of dynamite to explode. Death in the mine can also be quick and thunderous: it is enough to miscount the number of detonations or to leave a wick burning longer than it should. Or a loose rock, a *tojo,* may crash on your head. Another form of death is by bullet: St. John's Night 1967 was the latest bead in a long rosary of massacres. At dawn soldiers took up kneeling positions on the hillsides and fired volley after volley into mining camps lit by bonfires for the fiesta.* But slow, silent death is the mine's speciality. Vomiting

* "When I sit up, I'm drunk. My eyes—see three or four of you. Can't feed myself. I'm just a baby, a child." Saturnino Condori, a veteran construction worker in the Siglo XX mining camp, lies in a Catavi hospital bed. He has been there four years, one of the victims of the St. John's Night massacre. He had been offered triple pay for working on Saturday, and he decided not to join in the *chicha* party like everyone else. He went to bed early. That night he dreamed that a gentleman was hurling spikes into his body: "Big spikes, they stuck in me." He awoke several times because of the rain of bullets that began whamming into the camp at 5 a.m. "My body felt all torn to bits, I had the shivers, and I was scared, scared—that's how it was. My old woman said to escape. But what did I do? I didn't go anywhere. Get going, she kept saying. Guns firing in the night, what's it about, what goes on, pap-pap-pap-pap-pap! And me waking and drowsing off and not escaping, and the old lady repeating, Get a move on, escape! What'll they do to me, I says to her, I'm a bricklayer, what could they want to do?" He woke again around eight and sat up in bed. A bullet tore through the roof and through his wife's hat, burying itself in his body and cracking his spinal column.

blood, coughing, the sensation of a leaden weight on the back and acute chest pains are the signs that herald it. After the medical diagnosis, pilgrimages to an endless chain of bureaucrats. You are allowed three months before eviction from your house.

After the explosions we could talk. The workers' cheeks bulged with coca and greenish juice oozed through their tight lips. A miner passed in a hurry, splashing up mud from between the rails of the gallery. "That's a new man," they told me. "See how fresh he looks in his army pants and yellow jacket? Just came on the job, and how he works! He still thinks he's smart. *Still doesn't feel anything.*"

The technocrats and bureaucrats do not die of silicosis, but they live off it. The general manager of the Corporación Minera Boliviana (COMIBOL) earns 100 times as much as a worker. From a slope that falls sharply to a riverbed, in the Llallagua region, one can see the María Barzola pampa. It was so named in honor of the militant woman worker who, the Bolivian flag sewn to her body, was machine-gunned at the head of a demonstration thirty years ago. Beyond the María Barzola pampa one can see Bolivia's best golf course—the one Catavi's engineers and chief officials use. Dictator René Barrientos had cut the miners' hunger wages in half in 1964 and at the same time had raised salaries for technicians and chief bureaucrats. The top-echelon salaries are secret—secret and paid in dollars. There is an all-powerful "advisory group" of technicians from the Inter-American Development Bank, the Alliance for Progress, and the foreign credit bank, who lay down the guidelines for the nationalized mines in Bolivia—to such an extent that COMIBOL, by now a state within a state, has become living propaganda against the nationalization of anything. The power of *la rosca,* the old oligarchy, has been replaced by that of a numerous "new class" which has devoted its best efforts to sabotaging the state-owned mines from within. The engineers not only torpedoed every project and plan for a national smelter, but helped to confine state mining within the limits of the old Patiño, Aramayo, and Hochschild deposits, accelerating the process of draining the reserves. Between the end of 1964 and April 1969, Barrientos, with the open complicity of technicians and managers, broke the sound barrier in the surrender of Bolivian subsoil resources to imperialist capital. Sergio Almaraz has told the story of tin concessions to the International Mining Corporation. With a mere $5,000 in declared capital, this pompously named enterprise secured a contract that enabled it to amass more than $900 million.[8]

Iron Teeth in Brazil's Flesh

The United States pays less for Brazilian and Venezuelan iron than for iron from its own subsoil. But this is not the key to the feverish desire for iron ore deposits abroad: more than just a business, capture of foreign mines is an imperative of national security. Steel cannot be made without iron, and 85 percent of U.S. industrial production contains steel in some form. As we have seen, the subsoil is becoming exhausted. When supplies from Canada were reduced in 1969, this was at once reflected in the increase of iron imports from Latin America.

Venezuela's Cerro Bolívar is so rich that its dirt is taken by U.S. Steel and loaded directly into the holds of U.S.-bound ships; its flanks betray the deep wounds that bulldozers are making in it. The company estimates that it contains some $8 billion worth of iron. In a single year, 1960, U.S. Steel and Bethlehem Steel realized a greater than 30 percent profit on their Venezuelan iron investment, and this profit equaled all the taxes paid the Venezuelan state in the decade since 1950. Since both firms sell the iron ore to their own steel mills in the United States, they have no interest in defending prices; on the contrary, it suits them that the raw material should be as cheap as possible. The world price of iron, which fell sharply between 1958 and 1964, has been relatively stable since and remains so; meanwhile, the price of steel has continued to rise. Steel is produced in the world's wealthy centers, iron in the poor suburbs; steel pays "labor aristocracy" wages, iron mere subsistence wages.

Thanks to information gathered and published by the International Geological Congress in Stockholm in 1910, U.S. businessmen could for the first time evaluate the amount of wealth in the subsoil of various countries. One of these—perhaps the most tempting—was Brazil. Many years later, in 1948, the U.S. embassy in Brazil created a new job: "minerals attaché." From the start he had at least as much work as the military or cultural attachés—so much, indeed, that two minerals attachés were soon appointed instead of one. Soon Bethlehem Steel received the splendid Amapá manganese deposits from Eurico Dutra's government. By 1952 Brazil had agreed, in a military pact with the United States, not to sell raw materials of strategic value—such as iron—to any socialist country. This was one of the causes of the tragic fall of President Getulio Vargas, who sold iron to Poland and to Czechoslovakia in 1953 and 1954 at much higher prices than the United States was paying. In 1957 Hanna Mining paid $6 million for most of the shares of the British firm St. John Mining, which had been exploiting Minas Gerais gold since the empire's early days. St. John operated in the Paraopeba valley, where the greatest iron reserves on earth, valued at $200 billion, are located. The British firm was not legally authorized to exploit this fabled wealth, and, under clear constitutional and legal clauses (which Duarte Pereira lists in his work on the subject), neither was Hanna. But as it was later realized, this was the business deal of the century.

At the time Hanna's chairman, George Humphrey, was a big wheel in the U.S. government—he was secretary of the treasury and director of the Export-Import Bank (Eximbank), the official bank for financing foreign trade operations. St. John had asked Eximbank for a loan, but nothing came of it until Hanna took over the firm. After that, successive Brazilian governments were subjected to fierce pressure: Hanna's directors, lawyers, and advisers—Lucas Lopes, José Luiz Bulhões Pedreira, Roberto Campos, Mario da Silva Pintos, Otavio Gouveia de Bulhões—were also top-level members of the Brazilian government and continued occupying posts as ministers, ambassadors, and directors of services in subsequent years. Hanna had picked its general staff sagaciously. The bombardment to recognize Hanna's right to exploit the iron which properly belonged to the state grew in intensity. On August 21, 1961, President Jânio Quadros signed a bill annulling the illegal rights extended to Hanna and restoring Minas Gerais iron to the national reserve. Four days later the armed forces made Quadros resign: "Terrible forces have risen against me," said the text of his resignation.

A popular rising in Pôrto Alegre, headed by Leonel Brizola, frustrated the military coup and put Quadros's vice-president, João Goulart, in power. But when a minister sought to implement the fatal decree against Hanna, U.S. Ambassador Lincoln Gordon wired Goulart, indignantly protesting the government's threatened strike against the interests of a

U.S. concern. The judiciary decreed Quadros's bill valid, but Goulart vacillated. Meanwhile, Brazil set the wheels in motion for a minerals transshipment depot in the Adriatic which would supply iron to various European countries, socialist and capitalist. Such a direct sale of iron ore implied an intolerable defiance of the big firms that manipulate global prices. The depot never materialized, but other nationalist measures—such as plugging the drain of the foreign concerns' profits—were implemented and proved to be detonators in an explosive political situation. The Damoclean sword of the Quadros bill remained hanging over Hanna's head. Finally, on the last day of March 1964, the coup d'état exploded in Minas Gerais, where the disputed iron deposits happened to be located. "For Hanna," commented *Fortune,* "the revolt that overthrew Goulart last spring arrived like a last-minute rescue by the 1st Cavalry."[9]

Hanna men moved in to occupy the vice-presidency and three ministries. On the day of the military revolt, the *Washington Star* had run an editorial that was at least prophetic: "Here is a situation in which a good, effective, old-style coup by conservative military leaders may well serve the best interests of all the Americas."[10] Goulart had still neither resigned nor left Brazil when President Lyndon Johnson, unable to restrain himself, sent his famous congratulatory telegram to Ranieri Mazzili, who had provisionally assumed the presidency: "The [North] American people have watched with anxiety the political and economic difficulties through which your great nation has been passing and have admired the resolute will of the Brazilian community to resolve these difficulties within a framework of constitutional democracy and without civil strife."[11] A little over a month later Ambassador Lincoln Gordon, on a euphoric tour of army barracks, said in a speech at the war college, the Escuela Superior de Guerra, that the success of the plot "might be included with the Marshall Plan proposal, the Berlin blockade, the defeat of Communist aggression in Korea, and the solution of the Cuban missile crisis as one of the most important moments of change in mid-twentieth century world history."[12] One of the U.S. embassy's military officials had offered material aid to the plotters shortly before the coup, and Gordon himself had suggested that the United States would recognize an autonomous government in São Paulo if it could maintain itself for two days. It is not worth detailing all the evidence of the importance of U.S. economic aid (we will take this up later), and of U.S. help on the military and trade union level, in the dénouement of these events.*

After it tired of throwing the books of Dostoevski, Tolstoy, Gorky, and other Russians into bonfires or into Guanabara Bay, and after it had sentenced countless Brazilians to exile, prison, or the grave, the Castelo Branco dictatorship got down to business: it gave away the iron and everything else. Hanna got its decree on December 24, 1964. This Christmas parcel contained not only total freedom to exploit the Paraopeba deposits in peace, but support for the firm's plans to open a port of its own sixty miles from Rio and to build a railroad to transport the iron. In October 1965, Hanna formed a consortium with Bethlehem Steel for joint exploitation of the iron deposits. The tireless Lincoln Gordon had finished the job, everyone could live happily ever after, and he left to preside over a university in Baltimore. In April 1966, after some months of vacillation, Johnson named John Tuthill as his replacement, explaining that he had delayed because Brazil needed a good economist.

U.S. Steel did not lag behind. Why should it be left off the party invitation list? Before long it teamed up with a state mining enterprise, the Companhia Vale do Rio Doce, which in effect became its official pseudonym. Resigning itself to *no more* than 49 percent of the shares, U.S. Steel thus got the Sierra de los Carajás iron deposit concession in Amazonia. Technicians say that it compares in size with Hanna–Bethlehem's bonanza in Minas Gerais. The Brazilian government, as usual, said that Brazil lacked the capital to exploit its own wealth.

The Black Curse of Petroleum

Along with natural gas, petroleum is today the chief fuel that keeps our world in motion; it is a raw material of rising importance for the

---

* According to a revealing article in *Selecciones del Reader's Digest,* thanks to the good offices of the American Institute for Free Labor Development, which has its headquarters in Washington, the Brazilian putschists could coordinate their troop movements by cable. The new military regime rewarded AIFLD by designating four of its graduates "to clean up the Red-dominated unions. . . ."[13]

chemical industry and is the basic strategic material for military activities. Nothing compares with this "black gold" as a magnet for foreign capital, nothing earns such lush profits, no jewel in the diadem of capitalism is so monopolized, and no businessmen wield the global political power of the great petroleum corporations. Standard Oil and Shell seat and unseat kings and presidents, finance palace plots and coups d'état, have innumerable generals, ministers, and James Bonds at their command, and make decisions about peace or war in every field and every language. Standard Oil of New Jersey (now Exxon) is the capitalist world's biggest industrial enterprise; outside the United States no industrial enterprise has greater power than Royal Dutch/Shell. Affiliates sell crude petroleum to subsidiaries which refine it and sell it to branch organizations for distribution: there is no loss of blood in the whole internal circulatory system of the cartel, which also owns the pipelines and most of the oil fleets on the seven seas. Prices are manipulated on a world scale to keep taxes low and profits high: the crude petroleum gets constantly cheaper, the refined constantly more expensive.

With petroleum, as with coffee or meat, rich countries profit more from the work of consuming it than do poor countries from the work of producing it. The ratio is ten to one: of the $11 that the derivatives of a barrel of petroleum sell for, countries exporting the world's most important raw material get a sum total of $1 from taxes and extraction costs. Countries in the developed zone, where the oil companies have their head offices, get the other $10, the sum total of their own taxes—eight times larger than those of the producing countries—and the costs and profits of transport, refining, processing, and distribution, monopolized by the big corporations.[14]

While petroleum from U.S. wells enjoys high prices and U.S. oil workers' wages are comparatively generous, the price of Venezuelan and Middle Eastern petroleum has been falling through the late 1950s and all through the 1960s. A barrel of Venezuelan petroleum, for example, cost $2.65 in 1957 and $1.86 as this chapter is written. The Rafael Caldera administration has promised to unilaterally fix the price much higher, but even by manipulating statistics it will not reach the 1957 level. The United States is at the same time the biggest producer and the biggest importer of petroleum. When most of the crude petroleum sold by the oil companies came from U.S. wells, the price was kept up;

but when, during World War II, the United States became a net importer and the cartel began applying a new policy, the price systematically sagged. An odd inversion of the "laws of the market": the price of petroleum falls as world demand rises and factories, automobiles, and generating plants multiply. And another paradox: while the price of petroleum falls, the price consumers everywhere pay for fuel rises. There is an enormous disproportion between the price of crude oil and that of its derivatives. This whole chain of absurdity is perfectly rational: no need to seek an explanation in supernatural forces. For, as we have seen, the oil business in the capitalist world is in the hands of an all-powerful cartel. The cartel was born in 1928, in a castle wreathed in Scottish mists, when Standard Oil of New Jersey, Shell, and Anglo-Iranian (now known as British Petroleum) agreed to divide up the planet. Standard Oil of New York (now Mobil), Standard Oil of California, Gulf, and Texaco joined later. Founded by Rockefeller in 1870, Standard Oil had split in 1911 into thirty-five different firms under the requirements of the Sherman Anti-Trust Act; the first of the teeming Standard family as we now know it is Standard Oil of New Jersey. Today its petroleum sales, added to those of Standard Oil of New York and Standard Oil of California, amount to half of the cartel's entire sales. The Rockefeller group of oil concerns is so vast that it accounts for one-third of all profits earned throughout the world by all U.S. corporations. Standard Oil of New Jersey, a typical multinational corporation, earns its biggest profits abroad, with Latin America bringing in more than the United States and Canada put together: south of the Río Grande its profit rate is four times higher. In 1957, more than half of its global profits came from its Venezuelan affiliates; in the same year Shell's Venezuelan affiliates accounted for half of Shell's world profits. These multinational corporations do not belong to the nations in which they operate: their multinationality consists in funneling a torrent of petroleum and dollars from the four points of the compass into the capitalist system's centers of power. They have no need to export capital to finance the expansion of their business; the profits taken out of poor countries not only flow directly to the few cities where their major coupon-clippers live, but they are partially reinvested to strengthen and extend the international operations network. The structure of the cartel implies the domination of many countries and the penetration of many governments; petroleum saturates presidents and dictators and further deforms the societies it conscripts into its service. It is the corporations, pencils on a terrestrial globe, that decide which zones will be exploited and which held in reserve, what price producers must get and consumers must pay. The natural wealth of Venezuela, and of other oil-bearing Latin American lands subjected to this organized looting, has become the chief instrument of political servitude and social degradation. This is a long story of infamies, of deeds of business prowess which have spread a black curse across the earth.

Cuba brought handsome peripheral profits to Standard Oil of New Jersey. Standard Oil bought crude oil from its Venezuelan affiliate, Creole Petroleum, and refined and distributed it on the island at prices that best suited it at each stage. When the Cuban Revolution was in full effervescence in October 1959, an official State Department note to Havana expressed concern about the future of U.S. investments in Cuba: bombardments by "pirate" planes from the north had already begun and relations were tense. In January 1960, President Eisenhower cut the Cuban sugar quota, and in February Fidel Castro signed a trade agreement with the USSR to exchange sugar for petroleum and other products at prices beneficial to Cuba. Standard Oil of New Jersey, Shell, and Texaco refused to refine Soviet petroleum, and in July the Cuban government nationalized them without compensation. The corporations, headed by Standard Oil, began a blockade, first boycotting qualified personnel, then machinery replacement parts, then transportation. The conflict was a test of sovereignty and Cuba emerged with flying colors. It simultaneously stopped being a star in the U.S. flag and a cog in the worldwide Standard Oil machine.

Twenty years earlier, Mexico had had its own experience of an international embargo decreed by Standard Oil of New Jersey and Royal Dutch/Shell: from 1939 to 1942 the cartel organized a blockade of Mexican petroleum exports and of supplies for its wells and refineries. President Lázaro Cárdenas had nationalized the oil concerns. Nelson Rockefeller, who had graduated as an economist in 1930 with a thesis on his own Standard Oil's virtues, journeyed to Mexico to negotiate an agreement, but Cárdenas would not budge. Standard Oil and Shell, having divided up Mexico by taking the north and the south respectively, defied Mexican Supreme Court rulings on the application of

Mexican labor laws; at the same time, they drained the famous Fajo de Oro deposits with startling speed and were making Mexicans pay more for their own petroleum than they received for what was sold in the United States and in Europe.* In a few months of feverish exporting, wells that could have continued producing for thirty or forty years were drained dry. "Nearly three decades of foreign operations had robbed Mexico of her richest oil deposits," writes Harvey O'Connor, "and left only a collection of antique refineries, depleted fields, ramshackle camps, the slum city of Tampico, and bitter memories."[15]

In less than twenty years production had dropped by 80 percent. Mexico was left with a decrepit industry, geared to foreign demand, and 14,000 workers; the technicians took off and even the transportation network disappeared. Cárdenas made recovery of the petroleum a national crusade and conquered the crisis with imagination and courage. Today Pemex (Petróleos Mexicanos), the enterprise created in 1938 to take charge of all production and marketing, is the largest nonforeign concern in Latin America. Although between 1947 and 1962 the Mexican government paid heavy indemnities to the expropriated corporations out of Pemex's profits, Mexico, as Jesús Silva Herzog has said, "is not the debtor of these pirate companies but their legitimate creditor."[16] In 1949 Standard Oil vetoed a loan the United States was going to make to Pemex, and years later, after generous indemnities had healed the wounds, Pemex had a similar experience with the Inter-American Development Bank.

Uruguay was the first Latin American country to install a state refinery. ANCAP was created in 1931, and the refining and sale of crude petroleum were to be among its chief functions. It was a national response to a long history of abuse by the international cartel on the Río de la Plata. At the same time, the state contracted to buy cheap petroleum from the USSR. The cartel immediately financed a campaign of calumny against the Uruguayan state concern and began threatening that no one would sell Uruguay machinery, it would find itself without any crude petroleum, the state was incompetent to run such a complicated

*This is still a normal phenomenon in various countries. In Colombia, for example, where petroleum is freely exported without any taxes, the state refinery buys Colombian petroleum from foreign concerns at a price 37 percent higher than the world price, and has to pay in dollars.

business. The palace coup of March 1933 exuded the smell of oil; the Gabriel Terra dictatorship annulled ANCAP's right to monopolize fuel imports, and in January 1938 it signed ominous "secret agreements"—still in effect—with the cartel, agreements which the public did not learn of for a quarter of a century. Uruguay has to buy 40 percent of its crude petroleum from whomever Standard Oil, Shell, Atlantic, or Texaco might indicate, at prices fixed by the cartel; and the state, while retaining the refining monopoly, has to pay all the corporations' costs, including publicity, executive salaries, and luxurious office furnishings. "Esso es progreso"—Esso is progress—warbles the TV, and the advertising barrage does not cost Standard Oil a cent. The Banco de la República's lawyer is also in charge of Standard Oil's public relations: the state pays him for both jobs.

In 1939 ANCAP's refinery—emasculated shortly after birth, as we have seen, but still an example of defiance to cartel pressure—was operating successfully. The chief of Brazil's Conselho Nacional del Petróleo, General Horta Barbosa, went to Montevideo and was exhilarated by what he saw: the Uruguayan refinery had paid off almost all of its installation costs in a single year. Thanks to the efforts of Barbosa and the enthusiasm of other nationalist military men, the Brazilian state enterprise was able to get under way in 1953, to the cry of "The petroleum is ours!" Today Petrobras is the biggest concern in Brazil.[17] It explores, extracts, and refines Brazilian petroleum. But Petrobras was also emasculated when the cartel appropriated two of its big sources of income. First, the distribution of gasoline, oils, kerosene, and various fuels, an enormous business which Esso, Shell, and Atlantic manage effortlessly by telephone and so profitably that it attracts more U.S. investment than anything in Brazil except the automobile industry. Second, the lush petrochemical industry, which the Castelo Branco dictatorship denationalalized a few years ago. Recently the cartel started a loud campaign to take the refining monopoly away from Petrobras. Petrobras's defenders recall that before 1953, when the field was wide open, private industry paid no attention to Brazilian petroleum,[18] and remind the short-memoried public of an episode that illustrates the goodwill of the monopolies. In 1960 Petrobras assigned two Brazilian technicians to head up a survey of the country's deposits. As a result of its reports, the little Northeastern state of Sergipe took the lead in petroleum production. Shortly before, in August, U.S. technician Walter Link, who had been chief geologist for Standard Oil of New Jersey, had received $500,000 from the Brazilian state for a pile of maps and an extensive report belittling the Sergipe deposits as "unviable": until then they had been rated "Grade B," and Link demoted them to "Grade C"; it was subsequently established that they were Grade A.[19] According to Harvey O'Connor, Link was said to have worked the whole time as a Standard Oil agent, intending in advance not to find any petroleum so that Brazil would remain dependent on imports from the Rockefeller affiliate in Venezuela.[20]

Likewise in Argentina, the foreign concerns and their native echoes have always insisted that the subsoil contains little petroleum, although investigations by technicians of Yacimientos Petrolíferos Fiscales (YPF), the state organization, have established beyond doubt that deposits exist beneath almost half of the national territory and the Atlantic coastal shelf. Each time talk of the Argentine subsoil's poverty becomes fashionable, the government makes a new concession to some member of the cartel. YPF has been the target of continuous and systematic sabotage since its inception. Until a few years ago, Argentina was one of the last historical settings for the interimperialist conflict between declining Britain and the ascendant United States. Cartel agreements did not prevent a dispute, sometimes involving violence, between Shell and Standard Oil over Argentina's petroleum: the coups d'état that have followed one after the other in the past forty years provide some eloquent coincidences. The Argentine Congress was ready to pass the oil nationalization law on September 6, 1930, when José Félix Uriburu's barracks putsch ousted nationalist leader Hipólito Irigoyen from the presidency. The Ramón Castillo government fell in June 1943 when it was signing an agreement to promote oil extraction by U.S. capitalists. In September 1955, Juan Domingo Perón went into exile when the Argentinian Congress was about to approve a concession to Standard Oil of California. Arturo Frondizi set off more than one acute crisis in the three branches of the armed services by announcing that the country's entire subsoil would be put up for bids by concerns interested in extracting petroleum. In August 1959 the offer was called off for lack of bidders. The plan was promptly revived and again called off in October 1960. Frondizi made various concessions to U.S. members of the cartel, and

British interests—decisive in the navy and in one political group in the army—played a part in his fall in March 1962. Arturo Illia annulled the concessions and was overthrown in 1966; Juan Carlos Onganía's hydrocarbons law the following year showed the United States to be the final victor in the internal struggle.

Petroleum has not only sparked coups d'état in Latin America: it also set off a war—the Chaco War of 1932–1935—between South America's two poorest peoples. René Zavaleta called the mutual massacre of Bolivians and Paraguayans "the war of the naked soldiers."[21] Louisiana Senator Huey Long shook the United States on May 30, 1934, with a violent speech accusing Standard Oil of New Jersey of provoking the conflict and of financing the Bolivian army so that it would appropriate the Paraguayan Chaco on its behalf. It needed the Chaco—which was also thought to be rich in petroleum—for a pipeline from Bolivia to the river. "These criminals," Long charged, "have gone down there and hired their assassins."* At Shell's urging, the Paraguayans marched to the slaughterhouse: advancing northward, the soldiers discovered Standard Oil's perforations at the scene of the dispute. It was a quarrel between two corporations, enemies and at the same time partners within the cartel, but it was not they who shed their blood. In the end Paraguay won the war but not the peace. Spruille Braden, the notorious Standard Oil agent, chaired the negotiating commission which retained for Bolivia and for Rockefeller thousands of square miles claimed by the Paraguayans.

Close to the battlefields of that war lie the oil wells and great natural gas deposits which Gulf Oil, the Mellon family concern, lost in Bolivia in October 1969. "The days of indignity for Bolivia are ended," cried Alfredo Ovando in proclaiming nationalization from the Quemado Palace balcony. Two weeks earlier, before he had taken power, Ovando had sworn to a group of nationalist intellectuals that he would nationalize Gulf; he had drafted the decree, signed it, and kept it undated in an envelope.†

---

* Long took off the adjectival brakes regarding Standard Oil, calling it "criminal . . . evil . . . wicked . . . domestic assassin . . . foreign assassin . . . international conspirator . . . a gang of rapacious highwaymen and thieves . . . a bunch of vandals and thieves."[22]

† Five months earlier, René Barrientos's helicopter had tangled fatally with telegraph wires in the Arque ravine. Human imagination could not have conceived of a more perfect death. The helicopter was a personal gift from Gulf Oil; the telegraph wires belong to the state. Burned up

In addition to decreeing nationalization, Ovando annulled the Petroleum Code, called the "Davenport Code" in homage to the lawyer who drafted it in English. In return for accepting it Bolivia had obtained a U.S. loan in 1956; on the other hand, Eximbank, private New York bankers, and the World Bank had always turned down requests for credit to develop YPFB, the state petroleum organization. The U.S. government always makes common cause with private oil corporations.* Under the Code, Gulf received a forty-year concession to the country's richest fields. The Code provided for ridiculously low state participation in the companies' profits: for many years, a mere 11 percent. The state became a partner in the concessionaire's expenses but had no control over the spending, making this the last word in giveaways: the state took the risks, Gulf took none. In the "letter of intention" signed by Gulf at the end of 1966, during the Barrientos dictatorship, it was even provided that in joint operations with YPFB, Gulf would recover 100 percent of the capital it invested in exploration of an area if petroleum was not found. If it was found, expenses would be recovered through later exploitation, but meanwhile would be charged to the state organization as liabilities. And Gulf would appraise the expenses to its own taste.[24] In this same "letter of intention," Gulf appropriated ownership of gas deposits which had never been conceded to it—the Bolivian subsoil contains much more gas than petroleum.

The party was not yet over. A year before Ovando expropriated Gulf in Bolivia, Velasco Alvarado had nationalized the deposits and refinery of Standard Oil of New Jersey's Peruvian affiliate, International Petroleum (IPC). Velasco had taken power at the head of a military junta and on the crest of a political scandal: the Belaúnde administration had "lost"

---

along with Barrientos were two suitcases full of money he was taking to distribute among the peasants, as well as some machine-guns which began spraying bullets around the flaming helicopter, preventing anyone from coming to the rescue as the dictator was roasted alive.

*Examples abound in recent and remote history. Irving Florman, U.S. ambassador to Bolivia, reported to the White House's Donald Dawson on December 28, 1950: "Since my arrival here I have worked diligently on the project of throwing Bolivia's petroleum industry wide open to American private enterprise, and to help our national defense program on a vast scale." He went on: "I knew that you would be interested to hear that Bolivia's petroleum industry and the whole land is now wide open for free American enterprise. Bolivia is, therefore, the world's first country to denationalize or to have nationalization in reverse, and I am proud to have been able to accomplish this for my country and the administration."[23]

the last page of the Talara agreement between the state and IPC. The vanished page contained the guarantee of the minimum price to be paid by IPC for crude petroleum produced at its refinery. The scandal did not end there. It was also disclosed that the Standard Oil subsidiary had swindled the state out of more than a billion dollars in unpaid taxes and other kinds of fraud and corruption over half a century. The head of IPC had had sixty interviews with President Belaúnde before reaching the agreement that sparked the military rising; for two years the U.S. State Department had suspended all aid to Peru while the negotiations proceeded, were broken off, and reopened.* There was hardly time to restore the aid since the submissive president's surrender sealed his fate. When the Rockefeller concern protested before a Peruvian court, people threw coins in its lawyers' faces.

Latin America is a Pandora's box; the tortured subcontinent's capacity to spring surprises is never exhausted. In the Andean region, military nationalism has come impetuously to the surface like a long-hidden subterranean river. The same generals who today are pursuing a contradictory but well-aimed policy of reform and patriotic affirmation were only yesterday mowing down *guerrilleros*. Thus many of the banners of the dead have been picked up by those who killed them. In 1965 the Peruvian officers were spraying guerrilla zones with napalm, their know-how supplied by IPC at the Las Palmas air base near Lima. The corporation could not foresee what lay in store for it.

Vultures over Lake Maracaibo

Though its participation in the world market has dwindled by half in the past decade, Venezuela is still the top petroleum exporter. Almost half the profits U.S. capitalists take from Latin America come from Venezuela. One of the world's richest countries, it is also one of the poorest and most violent. It boasts of Latin America's highest per-capita income and most complete and up-to-date highway network, and no country consumes as much Scotch whiskey per inhabitant. Immediately

*When the scandal broke, the U.S. embassy failed to observe a prudent silence. One of its officials even said that no original copy of the Talara agreement existed.[25]

exploitable iron, petroleum, and gas reserves in its subsoil could multiply by ten the wealth of every Venezuelan; the population of Germany or England could fit into its enormous virgin lands. In half a century, oil rigs have extracted an income double the resources of the Marshall Plan. Since the first well blew, the population has multiplied by three and the national budget by 100, but most of the people scramble for the plush minority's leavings, still as poor as when the country depended on cacao or coffee. The capital, Caracas, has grown 700 percent in thirty years: the old city of airy patios, central plaza, and silent cathedral is covered with skyscrapers as Lake Maracaibo is covered with oil wells. Today it is a supersonic, deafening, air-conditioned nightmare, a center of oil culture that might pass as the capital of Texas. Caracas chews gum and loves synthetic products and canned foods; it never walks, and poisons the clear air of the valley with the fumes of its motorization; its fever to buy, consume, obtain, spend, use, get hold of everything leaves it no time to sleep. From surrounding hillside hovels made of garbage, half a million forgotten people observe the sybaritic scene. The gilded city's avenues glitter with hundreds of thousands of late-model cars, but in the consuming society not everyone consumes. According to the census, half of Venezuela's children and youths do not go to school.

Every day Venezuela produces 3.5 million barrels of petroleum to move the capitalist world's industrial machinery, but four-fifths of the concessions owned by Standard Oil, Shell, Gulf, and Texaco are untouched reserves and over half the value of the exports never returns to the country. Creole (Standard Oil) publicity brochures point with pride to the corporation's Venezuelan philanthropies much as the Royal Guipuzcoan Company proclaimed its own virtues in the eighteenth century; the profits milked from this wonderful cow, in proportion to capital invested, are only comparable with those obtained by old-time slave merchants and pirates. No country has yielded as much for world capitalism in so short a time: the wealth drained from Venezuela, according to Domingo Alberto Rangel, exceeds what the Spaniards took from Potosí or the English from India. Some estimates put the real profits of Venezuelan oil concerns at 38 percent in 1961 and 48 percent in 1962, although the profit rates announced in their balance sheets were 15 percent and 17 percent respectively. The difference is attributable to the juggling of accounts and to hidden transfers. In the complex mechanism of the oil business, with its multiple simultaneous price systems, it is hard to estimate the profits hidden behind the artificial reduction of the price of crude oil—which from well to gasoline pump always circulates through the same veins—and the artificial raising of production costs which include fancy salaries and inflated publicity expenditures. But by official figures, Venezuela, far from receiving new investments from abroad, has experienced systematic de-investment in the past decade. It suffers an annual bloodletting of more than $700 million, "convicted and confessed" as "interest on foreign capital." The only new investments are provided by the country itself. Meanwhile, oil extraction costs are falling sharply as the companies use less labor. From 1959 to 1962 alone, the work force was cut by 10,000; somewhat more than 30,000 workers remained active, but by the end of 1970 petroleum only employed 23,000. Yet production has greatly increased in the decade.

Growing unemployment sharpened the crisis in the Lake Maracaibo oil camps, The lake is a forest of towers. Within these iron structures the endlessly bobbing pumps have for half a century pumped up all the opulence and all the poverty of Venezuela. Alongside, flames lick skyward, burning the natural gas in a carefree gift to the atmosphere. There are pumps even in houses and on street corners of towns that spouted up, like the oil, along the lakeside-towns where clothing, food, and walls are stained black with oil, and where even whores are known by oil nicknames, such as "The Pipeline," "The Four Valves," "The Derrick," "The Hoist." Here clothing and food cost more than in Caracas. These modern villages, of cheerless birth but quickened by the euphoria of easy money, have discovered that they have no future. When the wells die, survival becomes something of a miracle: skeletons of houses remain, oily waters lick abandoned shores and poison the fish. Mass firings and growing mechanization bring misfortune, too, to cities that live from exploiting still-active wells. "Oil has come and gone for us here," people were saying in Lagunillas in 1966. "It would have been better for us if these machines had never come. . . ." Cabimas, which for fifty years was Venezuela's biggest oil source and brought so much prosperity to Caracas and the oil companies, does not even have privies. It has two asphalt streets.

The euphoria began in the 1920s. Around 1917 oil co-existed in Venezuela with traditional latifundios, those enormous extensions of thinly populated or idle land where hacendados kept up production by whipping their peons or burying them alive up to the waist. At the end of 1922 the La Rosa well started gushing, 100,000 barrels a day, and the petroleum orgy was on. Lake Maracaibo sprouted rigs and derricks and was invaded by helmeted men; peasants swarmed in to build plank-and-oilcan huts on the bubbling ground and offer their muscles to petroleum. Plains and forests resounded for the first time with Oklahoma and Texas accents, and in the bat of an eye seventy-three companies were born. The carnival king of the concessions was Juan Vicente Gómez, an Andean cattleman who spent his twenty-seven years as dictator (1908-1935) making children and business deals. While the black geysers spouted on all sides, Gómez took petroleum shares from his bursting pockets to reward his friends, relations, and courtiers, the doctor who looked after his prostate, the generals who served as his bodyguard, the poets who sang his praises, and the archbishop who gave him a special dispensation to eat meat on Good Friday. The great powers covered Gómez's breast with gleaming decorations: the automobiles invading the world's highways needed food. The dictator's favorites sold concessions to Shell or Standard Oil or Gulf; the traffic in influence and bribes provoked speculation and set mouths watering for subsoil. Native communities were robbed of their lands and many farm families lost their holdings in one way or another. The petroleum law of 1922 was drafted by representatives of three U.S. firms. The oilfields were fenced in and had their own police. No one could enter without a company pass, and even the roads on which the oil was transported to the ports were barred to other traffic. When Gómez died in 1935, oil workers cut the barbed wire surrounding the camps and proclaimed a strike. The following years were dangerously explosive.

The fall of the Rómulo Gallegos government in 1948 ended three years of reform. The victorious military brass rapidly cut state participation in the petroleum extracted by cartel affiliates. Tax cuts in 1954 afforded Standard Oil $300 million in additional profits. A U.S. businessman had said in Caracas in 1953: "Here you have freedom to do what you like with your money; for me, this freedom is worth more than all political and civil freedoms put together."[26] When dictator

Marcos Pérez Jiménez was overthrown in 1958, Venezuela was one huge oilwell, surrounded by jails and torture chambers and importing everything from the United States: cars, refrigerators, condensed milk, eggs, lettuce, laws, and decrees. In 1957, the biggest of Rockefeller's enterprises, Creole, had declared profits equaling almost half its total investment. The ruling revolutionary junta raised the tax on its profits from 26 percent to 45 percent; in reprisal the cartel promptly lowered the price of Venezuelan petroleum and began to fire workers en masse. The price fell so low that despite the tax raise and increased oil exports, the state collected $60 million less in 1958 than in the previous year.

The governments that followed did not nationalize the oil industry, but neither did they grant new oil-extracting concessions to foreign companies until 1970. Meanwhile, the cartel speeded production from its Near Eastern and Canadian deposits; in Venezuela, prospecting for new wells virtually ceased and export was paralyzed. The policy of denying new concessions only made sense if the state petroleum corporation would fill the breach; but the corporation has only drilled a few wells here and there, confirming that it has no other function than that stated by President Rómulo Betancourt: "Not to achieve the dimension of a major enterprise, but to serve as intermediary for negotiations on the new concession formula." The new formula was proclaimed several times but never put into practice. In 1970, under the Christian Democratic regime of Rafael Caldera, progress was said to be well advanced toward signing "service contracts" under which the companies would explore and exploit 250,000 hectares in partnership with the state. Another form of fig-leaved imperialism, the mixed-enterprise system, had previously been used to deliver most of the petrochemical industry—synthetic rubber, polyethylene, ammonia, urea—to Union Carbide and a Standard Oil subsidiary.

The industrializing thrust that has taken shape and strength during the past two decades shows visible symptoms of exhaustion, of an impotence that is all too familiar in Latin America: the internal market, limited by the poverty of the masses, cannot sustain the development of manufactures beyond certain limits. At the same time, agrarian reform, initiated by the Acción Democrática administration, has traveled less than half of the road its creators promised to traverse.

Salvador Garmendia, the novelist who reinvented the prefabricated hell of this whole conquest culture, the culture of petroleum, wrote to me in the middle of 1969:

> Have you seen the apparatus that extracts crude petroleum? It looks like a big black bird whose sharp-pointed head rises and falls heavily day and night without stopping for a second: it is the only vulture that doesn't eat shit. What do we do when the characteristic sound of the sipper tells us there isn't any more oil? The grotesque overture is already beginning to be heard over Lake Maracaibo, where fabulous communities grew up overnight, with movies, supermarkets, dance halls, a profusion of whorehouses and gambling dens—where money had no value. I recently made a trip through there and felt claws in my stomach. The smell of death and decay overpowers the smell of oil. The towns are semi-deserted, wormeaten, ulcerated, the streets deep in mud, the stores dilapidated. One of the companies' old divers goes down every day with a saw to cut lengths of abandoned pipeline which he sells as old iron. People are beginning to talk about the "companies" as if conjuring up a golden fable. They live like acrobats on a tightrope of myths about the old days, when fortunes were squandered on a turn of the dice or a week-long drinking orgy. Meanwhile, the pumps continue bobbing up and down and the rain of dollars falls on Miraflores, the government palace, to be turned into superhighways and other cement monsters. Seventy percent of the country lives a totally marginal existence. In the cities an unconcerned, well-paid middle class stuffs itself with useless objects and makes a strident cult of imbecility and bad taste. The government recently announced with great fanfare that it had exterminated illiteracy. Sequel: in the recent electoral fiesta the registration lists showed a million illiterates between eighteen and fifty years of age.

Part II

Development Is a Voyage with More Shipwrecks than Navigators

4. Tales of Premature Death

A Declaration of Independence Hailed by British Warships

When George Canning, the brains of the British Empire, was celebrating its worldwide triumphs in 1823, the French chargé d'affaires had to swallow the humiliation of this remark: "Be yours the glory of victory followed by disaster and ruin, be ours the inglorious traffic of industry and an ever growing prosperity. . . . The age of chivalry is gone; and an age of economists and calculators has succeeded." London was entering a long period of festivity; Napoleon had finally been beaten some years earlier, and the curtain was rising on the era of Pax Britannica. In Latin America, the power of landlords and rich port merchants had been secured in perpetuity by independence, at the cost of the new-born countries' imminent ruin. The former Spanish colonies and Brazil were markets hungry for English textiles and pounds sterling at so much percent. Canning did not err when he wrote in 1824: "The deed is done, the nail is driven, Spanish America is free; and if we do not mismanage our affairs sadly, she is *English.*"[1]

The steam engine, the mechanical loom, and the perfection of textile machinery had precipitously matured Britain's Industrial Revolution. Factories and banks multiplied; the internal combustion engine modernized navigation and big ships sailed to the uttermost parts, expanding

British industry. The British economy paid with cotton textiles for the hides of Río de la Plata, the guano and nitrates of Peru, the copper of Chile, the sugar of Cuba, the coffee of Brazil. Throughout the nineteenth century industrial exports, freightage, insurance, interest on loans, and profits on investments fed British prosperity. Actually, much of the legal commerce between Spain and its colonies, before the wars of independence, was British-controlled—apart from the steady flow of contraband to Latin American coasts, effectively screened by the slave trade. The overwhelming majority of goods passing through Latin American customs houses was not Spanish. Spain's monopoly had never in fact existed: "The colony was already lost to the metropolis well before 1810, and the revolution was no more than political recognition of this state of affairs."[2]

British troops had taken Trinidad with but one casualty, but the commander of the expedition, Sir Ralph Abercromby, was convinced that other military conquests in Spanish America would not be so easy. Soon afterward, British invasions of Río de la Plata failed. The defeat confirmed Abercromby's view on the ineffectiveness of armed expeditions and the ripeness of the hour for diplomats, merchants, and bankers: a new liberal order in the Spanish colonies would offer Britain the opportunity to secure nine-tenths of Spanish American commerce.[3] Latin American lands burned with independence fever; after 1810, London applied a devious and two-faced policy which fluctuated with the need to favor British trade, keep Latin America from falling into United States or French hands, and avert Jacobin infection in the newly independent countries.

When the revolutionary junta was formed in Buenos Aires on May 25, 1810, British warships saluted it with a salvo of guns from the river. The captain of the *Mutine* made a glowing speech on His Majesty's behalf, and the jubilation warmed British hearts. Buenos Aires waited barely three days to repeal certain bans on trade with foreigners; twelve days later it cut the taxes on external sales of hides and fats or tallow from 50 to 7.5 percent. Six weeks later, the ban on exporting gold and silver coins was removed, so that they could flow tranquilly to London. A triumvirate replaced the junta in September 1811, and the export and import taxes were again reduced and in some cases abolished. After 1813, when the Assembly declared itself the sovereign authority, foreign traders were exempted from the obligation to sell their merchandise through native businessmen. In 1812, British traders were reporting to the Foreign Office that they had succeeded in replacing German and French textiles; they had also replaced Argentine textile production, which was strangled by the free-trade port. The same occurred with variations elsewhere in Latin America.

From Yorkshire, Lancashire, the Cheviot Hills, and Wales poured an endless stream of cotton and woolens, iron and leather, wood and porcelain goods. Manchester's looms, Sheffield's foundries, Worcester and Staffordshire potteries flooded Latin American markets. Free trade enriched the ports which lived from exports, lifted sky-high the extravagance of oligarchies determined to enjoy every known luxury, but ruined budding local manufacture and frustrated expansion of the internal market. Some weak and technically backward colonial industries had grown up despite metropolitan prohibitions, and were on the rise on the eve of independence as Spain's oppressive bonds loosened and war in Europe created a shortage of supplies. In the nineteenth century's first years, factories were recovering from the blow of the royal decree of 1778 authorizing free trade between Spanish and American ports. The resulting deluge of foreign goods had crushed colonial production of textiles, pottery, and metal objects, and the artisans had little time to get back on their feet; then independence flung open the door to free competition from Europe's already developed industries. Under the vacillating customs policies of independence governments, Latin American manufactures continued fitfully, with one foot in the grave and with no possibility of sustained long-term development.

The Dimensions of Industrial Infanticide

At the beginning of the nineteenth century Alexander von Humboldt estimated the value of Mexican manufactures—mostly textiles—at some 7 or 8 million pesos. Woolen and cotton cloth were turned out in specialized workshops: Querétaro had more than 200 looms and 1,500 workers; 1,200 cotton weavers worked in Puebla.[4] In Peru, the colony's crude products were never as perfect as the native textiles of Pizarro's time but economic performance was very great. The industry was based on forced labor by Indians who were locked into the shops from before dawn till late at night. This development—annihilated by independence—had been precarious but of some magnitude in Ayacucho, Cacamorsa, Tarma; the community of Pacaicasa, which formed one great weaving establishment with more than 1,000 workers, is now extinct, and Paucarcolla, which supplied a large area with wool blankets, is disappearing. In Chile, one of Spain's most far-flung possessions, isolation favored the development of industrial activity from the beginnings of colonial life. It had spinning mills, textile mills, and tanneries; all the ships of the South Seas were equipped with Chilean rigging and cordage; it manufactured metal objects, from retorts and guns to ornaments, fine tableware, and clocks, and built boats and vehicles. In Brazil, too, textile and metal works, which took their modest first steps in the eighteenth century, were wiped out by foreign imports. Both manufactures had managed to prosper despite obstacles imposed by Lisbon, but after 1807 the Portuguese monarchy, installed in Rio de Janeiro, was a toy in British hands and London had strength of a different order. "Until the ports were opened up," writes Caio Prado, "the shortcomings of Portuguese commerce had provided a protective barrier for a small local industry—a poor artisan industry, true, but enough to satisfy part of the local demand. This small industry could not survive free competition from abroad, even in the most insignificant products."[5]

Bolivia was the Río de la Plata viceroyalty's most important textile center. At the end of the century, according to Intendente Francisco de Viedma, 80,000 people in Cochabamba were engaged in making wool and cotton cloth and tablecloths. Oruro and La Paz also had factories which, together with those in Cochabamba, supplied blankets, ponchos, and warm flannel to the population, troops of the line, and frontier garrisons. From Mojos, Chiquitos, and Guarayos came the finest linen and cotton cloth, hats of straw, vicuna and lamb's fur, and cigars. "All these industries have disappeared in the face of competition with similar foreign-made articles," testified a book published on the first centenary of Bolivia's independence.[6]

In Argentina, the coast was the most backward and least populated region until independence moved the economic and political center of gravity from inland to Buenos Aires. Only one-tenth of the population lived in Buenos Aires, Santa Fe, and Entre Ríos at the beginning of the nineteenth century. A rudimentary native industry had slowly developed in the center and north while, as Procurador Larramendi observed in 1795, "not one craft or manufacture" existed on the coast. Textile workshops wove three types of ponchos, and factories produced sturdy carts, cigars and cigarettes, leather and shoe soles in Tucumán and Santiago del Estero—both pockets of underdevelopment today. All kinds of cloth, fine woolens, and clergymen's black flannel came from Catamarca; Córdoba turned out more than 70,000 ponchos, 20,000 blankets, and 40,000 Spanish yards of flannel a year, along with shoes and leather goods, sailing cinches and yards, carpeting and cordovan. The important tanneries and saddleries were in Corrientes. Salta was famous for its fine saddles; Mendoza produced between 2 and 3 million liters of wine a year, rivaling that of Andalusia; and San Juan distilled 350,000 liters of aguardiente a year. Mendoza and San Juan, situated between the Atlantic and the Pacific, were the "throat" of South American commerce.

Commercial agents from Manchester, Glasgow, and Liverpool toured Argentina and copied Santiagan and Córdoban ponchos and Corrientes leather goods, as well as the local wooden stirrups. Argentine ponchos cost seven pesos, Yorkshire ones three. The world's most advanced textile industry won at a gallop over the products of native looms, and it was the same with boots, spurs, iron grill work, bridles, and even nails. Interior Argentine provinces were ruined and promptly rose against the dictatorship of the port of Buenos Aires. The top merchants (Escalada, Belgrano, Pueyrredón, Vieytes, Las Heras, Cerviño) had assumed the power wrested from Spain, and trade enabled them to buy English silks and knives, fine Louviers cloth, Flanders lace, Swiss sabres, Dutch gin, Westphalian ham, and Hamburg cigars. In exchange, Argentina exported hides, tallow, bones, and salted meat, and the cattlemen of Buenos Aires province extended their markets thanks to free trade. The typical tough gaucho of the pampas was described thus in 1837 by the British consul in La Plata, Woodbine Parish: "Take his whole equipment—examine everything about him—and what is there not of raw hide that is not British? If his wife has a gown, ten to one it is made in Manchester; the camp-kettle in which he cooks his food, the earthenware he eats from, the knife, his poncho, spurs, bit, are all imported from England."[7] Argentina even received the stones for its sidewalks from Britain.

In about the same period James Watson Webb, U.S. ambassador in Rio de Janeiro, reported:

> In all of Brazil's haciendas the master and his slaves dress in the products of free labor, and nine-tenths of them are British. Britain supplies all the capital needed for internal improvements in Brazil and manufactures all the utensils in common use, from the spade on up, and nearly all the luxury and practical items from the pin to the costliest clothing. British pottery, British articles of glass, iron, or wood are as common as woolens and cotton cloth. Great Britain supplies Brazil with its steam and sailing ships, and paves and repairs its streets, lights its cities with gas, builds its railways, exploits its mines, is its banker, puts up its telegraph wires, carries its mail, builds its furniture, motors, wagons. . . .[8]

Free trade euphoria drove the port merchants wild: in those years Brazil also imported coffins (already lined) for the dead, riding saddles, crystal chandeliers, saucepans, and—most improbable of all for tropical coasts—ice skates; also wallets (although Brazil had no paper money) and an inexplicable quantity of mathematical instruments. The trade and navigation treaties signed in 1810 put a lower tax on English than on Portuguese imports, and their text was so barbarously translated from English that the word "policy," for example, was transmogrified into the Portuguese word for "police." The British in Brazil enjoyed a special code of justice which removed them from the jurisdiction of the national courts: Brazil was an unofficial member of the British economic empire.

A mid-century Swedish traveler arriving at Valparaiso witnessed the extravagance and ostentation free trade had produced in Chile: "The only way to rise in the world," he wrote, "is to submit to the dictates of Paris fashion magazines, to the black frock coat and all accessories thereof. . . . The *señora* buys a new hat that makes her feel eminently Parisian, while the husband dons a high, stiff cravat and imagines himself at the pinnacle of European culture."[9] Three or four British concerns had taken over the Chilean copper market and juggled prices in the best interests of foundries in Swansea, Liverpool, and Cardiff. The British consul general reported to his government in 1838 on the "prodigious growth" in sales of copper, which was exported "chiefly, if not entirely, in British ships or on behalf of Britons."[10] British businessmen monopolized commerce in Santiago and Valparaiso, and Chile was the second most important Latin American market for British products.

Latin America's big ports, through which the wealth of its soil and subsoil passed en route to distant centers of power, were being built up as instruments of the conquest and domination of the countries to which they belonged, and as conduits through which to drain the nations' income. While ports and capitals strove to be like Paris or London, behind them stretched the desert.

Protectionism and Free Trade: The Brief Flight of Lucas Alamán

The expansion of Latin American markets speeded accumulation of capital in the nursery gardens of British industry. The Atlantic had for some time been the main highway of world trade and the British had shrewdly capitalized on the location of their island—surrounded by ports, halfway between the Baltic and the Mediterranean, and facing out to the coasts of America. Britain was organizing a worldwide system and becoming the great factory supplying the planet: the entire world supplied it with raw materials and received its manufactured goods. The Empire had the greatest port and most potent financial apparatus of its time, the highest level of commercial specialization, a world monopoly on insurance and freight, and control of the international gold market. Friedrich List, father of the German customs union, once observed that free trade was Britain's chief export.* Nothing roused such British anger as protectionism, and they sometimes gave vent to it in violent language, as during the Opium War against China. But free trade only became revealed truth for them after they became sure of being the strongest power, and after they had developed their own textile industry under the umbrella of Europe's toughest protectionist legislation. In the difficult early days, when British industry was still at a disadvantage, an Englishman caught exporting raw wool was sentenced to lose his right

* This German economist, born in 1789, preached in the United States and his own country the doctrine of protectionism and industrial development. He killed himself in 1846, but his ideas took hold in both countries.

hand, and if he repeated the sin he was hanged. It was prohibited to bury a corpse without prior certification from the parish priest that the shroud came from a British factory.

"All the destructive phenomena which unlimited competition gives rise to within one country," wrote Marx, "are reproduced in more gigantic proportions on the world market."* Latin America's entry into the British orbit—which it would leave only to enter the U.S. orbit—took place within this general framework, and within it the dependence of the new independent countries was consolidated. Free circulation of merchandise, and of money for payment and transfer of capital, had dramatic consequences.

Vicente Guerrero came to power in Mexico in 1829, writes Chávez Orozco, "on the shoulders of the artisans' despair, fanned by the great demagogue Lorenzo de Zavala who loosed a hungry, desperate crowd on shops stuffed with British marketplace items." Guerrero soon fell amid the workers' indifference, since he did not want or was not able to dam up European merchandise, "the abundance of which spread unemployment among urban artisan masses who before independence—above all in periods of war in Europe—enjoyed modest comfort."[12] Mexican industry had been short of capital, labor, and modern techniques, had not been efficiently organized, and had lacked communications and transport to and from markets and supply sources. "The only things it probably had too much of," writes Alonso Aguilar, "were interference, restrictions, and every kind of obstacle."[13] Nevertheless, as von Humboldt noted, industry had grown when foreign trade was stagnant, sea communications were being interrupted or obstructed, and the manufacture of steel and the use of iron and mercury had begun. The liberalism that accompanied independence added new pearls to the British crown and paralyzed the textile and metallurgical workshops in Mexico City, Puebla, and Guadalajara.

Lucas Alamán, an able conservative politician, gave timely warning that the ideas of Adam Smith contained poison for the national economy, and set the stage, as minister, for a credit and loan bank to promote

* "If the free-traders cannot understand how one nation can grow rich at the expense of another, we need not wonder, since these same gentlemen also refuse to understand how within one country one class can enrich itself at the expense of another."[11]

industrialization. By taxing foreign cotton textiles, Mexico could buy machinery and equipment abroad in order to supply its own needs in cotton cloth. The country had the raw material and hydraulic power—cheaper than coal—and could train good workers quickly. The bank opened in 1830 and soon afterward modern cotton-spinning and weaving machinery from the best European factories arrived; the state also hired foreign experts in textile techniques. In 1844 the big Puebla plants produced 1.4 million lengths of heavy cotton. The country's new industrial capacity exceeded internal demand; the consumer market in the "kingdom of inequality," mostly consisting of hungry Indians, could not sustain the dizzying industrial growth. The effort to break the inherited colonial structure collided against this wall. Yet the industry had been so modernized that in 1840 U.S. textile mills averaged fewer spindles than did those in Mexico. Ten years later the ratio had been more than reversed. Political instability, pressure from British and French merchants and their powerful domestic partners, and the paltriness of an internal market strangled in advance by the mining and latifundista economy, wrecked the experiment. By 1850 Mexico's textile industry had stopped progressing. The creators of the credit and loan bank had broadened their field of action and, when the bank died, its credits also included woolen mills, carpet factories, and iron and paper producers. Esteban de Antuñano insisted on Mexico's need to create, as soon as possible, a national machine industry "to resist European egoism." The great merit of the Alamán-Antuñano industrializing cycle was that both men reestablished the identity between political independence and economic independence, and extolled industrialization as the only defense against powerful and aggressive nations. Alamán himself became an industrialist, building Mexico's biggest textile plant of the day (it still exists), and organizing fellow industrialists as a pressure group against successive free-trade governments.* But Alamán, conservative and Catholic, never took up the

* Various protectionist statements were published in 1850 in *El Siglo XIX:* "With the end of the conquest by Spanish civilization and its three centuries of military dominion, Mexico entered a new era, which can also be called conquest, but a scientific and mercatile one. . . . Its power is merchant shipping; its faith is absolute economic freedom; its mighty principle with less advanced people is the law of reciprocity. . . . 'Bring to Europe,' we were told, 'what manufactures you can (except, however, those we prohibit); and in return let us bring you what manufactures we can,

agrarian question since he felt ideologically linked to the old order. And he did not realize that industrial development was condemned in advance to remain up in the air, without bases of support, in that land of countless latifundios and general poverty.

THE MONTONEROS AND JUAN MANUEL DE ROSAS'S LEGACY OF HATE

Protectionism versus free trade, the country versus the port: this was the essence of the struggle in Argentina's nineteenth-century civil wars. Buenos Aires, which in the seventeenth century was no more than a big village with 400 houses, took power over the whole nation after the May revolution and independence. It was the only port: all that entered or left the country was forced to pass through it. Today the deformations that its hegemony imposed on the nation are plain to see: the capital and its suburbs embrace more than a third of the country's population and in various ways play the role of procurer to the provinces. In that period, with its monopoly on customs revenue, banks, and the issuance of currency, Buenos Aires prospered dizzily at the expense of the inland provinces. It appropriated the national customs receipts—almost all of the port city's income—for its own benefit, spending more than half on wars against the provinces—which thus paid for their own destruction.

From Buenos Aires's Sala de Comercio, founded in 1810, the British kept watch on shipping through telescopes; they supplied the city folk with fine cloth, artificial flowers, shoelaces, umbrellas, buttons, and chocolate, while the flood of ponchos and factory-made stirrups played havoc up-country. To appreciate the value the world market then placed on Río de la Plata hides, the imagination must travel back to an age when plastics and synthetic fabrics did not exist, even as a gleam in a chemist's eye. Nothing could equal the fertile coastal plains for grand-scale cattle production. In 1816, a new system was discovered for the indefinite preservation of hides by treatment with arsenic; at the same time,

---

though they may ruin your industries.' . . . If we adopted doctrines that they (our lords across the ocean and the Río Grande) give but do not take, our exchequer would perhaps benefit a little . . . but we would not be promoting the labor of the Mexican people but that of the English, Franch, Swiss and North American people."[14]

slaughterhouses were prospering and multiplying. Brazil, the Antilles, and Africa were opening their markets to imported dried meat, and as that product gained foreign consumers, Argentinians felt the change. Taxes were imposed on internal meat consumption and removed from exports; in a few years the price of calves tripled and ranches upped the value of their land. The gauchos were accustomed to hunting calves freely under the open sky of the unfenced pampa, to eating the best meat and discarding the rest with the sole obligation of delivering the hide to the owner. Things changed. Reorganization of production involved submitting the nomad gaucho to a new servile dependence: a decree in 1815 proclaimed every propertyless countryman a servant, with the obligation to carry a card and have it checked every three months by his master. Either he was a servant or a vagrant, and vagrants were forcibly recruited into frontier battalions. The untamed *criollo* of yore, who had served as cannon-fodder in patriot armies, was turned into a pariah, a wretched peon, or a buck private. Or else he got himself a weapon and joined the rebel *montonera* bands.* This fierce gaucho, dispossesed of

* The *montonera* band "is born in the plains like a whirlwind. It strikes, roars, and smashes like a whirlwind, and suddenly stops and dies like one."[15] In *Martín Fierro*, Argentina's most popular book, José Hernández (who was a federal soldier) puts the plight of the gaucho exiled from his haunts and persecuted by the authorities into song:

> The eagle lives in his nest,
> The tiger lives in the jungle,
> The fox in any cave,
> And in his fickle fortune,
> Only the gaucho lives a-wandering
> Wherever fate takes him.

Because:

> For him there are calabooses,
> For him grim prisons,
> Nothing he says is right,
> Although he has right a-plenty—
> The right of a wooden churchbell,
> The right of the poor.[16]

Jorge Abelardo Ramos notes that the two real surnames appearing in *Martín Fierro* are Anchorena and Gaínza—names representing the oligarchy that exterminated the armed *criollos;* today both have been fused into the family that owns the daily *La Prensa.*

The other face of *Martín Fierro* appears in Ricardo Güiraldes's *Don Segundo Sombra* (1939): here it is the domesticated gaucho, tied to his daily wage, fawning upon his master, a useful type for the folklore of nostalgia and pity.

everything except glory and anger, swelled the cavalry charges that repeatedly defied well-equipped armies sent from Buenos Aires. The rise of the capitalist cattle ranch in the damp coastal pampa subjected the whole country to the exporting of hides and meat, and went hand in hand with the dictatorship of the free-trade port. Until his defeat and exile, the Uruguayan José Artigas had been the outstanding leader of the *criollo* masses' struggle against merchants and landlords tied to the world market; years later Felipe Varela was able to set off a big rebellion in northern Argentina because, as he proclaimed, "to be a provincial is to be a beggar without country, liberty, or rights." His rising drew a response from the entire hinterland. He was the last of the *montoneros;* he died in 1870, tuberculous and in poverty.* In history as taught in Argentine schools, this defender of the "American Union"—the dream of reviving the fragmented Great Fatherland—remains as much a bandit as Artigas did until recently.

Born in a village lost among the Catamarca sierras, Varela had been an unhappy witness of the poverty inflicted on his province by the remote arrogant port. In 1824, when Varela was three, Catamarca could not pay the expenses of the delegates it sent to the Constituent Congress in Buenos Aires, and Misiones, Santiago del Estero, and other provinces were in similar plight. Catamarcan deputy Manuel Antonio Acevedo pointed to "the ominous change" brought about by foreign competition: "Catamarca has had to stand by helplessly, while its agriculture is primitive and costly, its industry without consumers . . . and its commerce by now almost nonexistent."[17] In 1830, the representative from Corrientes province, Brigadier General Pedro Ferré, summed up the possible consequences of the protectionism he advocated:

> Yes, certainly a few wealthy men will be deprived of fine wines and liquors with their dinners. . . . For the less well-off classes the difference will hardly be noticeable in the wines and liquors they now drink, only in the price, and consumption will go down, which is not such a bad thing. Our country folk won't wear English ponchos or carry British-made bolas and lassos; we won't get clothing, and other things we can make ourselves, from abroad; but on the other hand, the condition of all the Argentine communities will begin to be less miserable and the frightful poverty to which we are now condemned will no longer pursue us.[18]

---

* In 1870 Paraguay, the only Latin American country that still had not entered the imperialist prison, also fell in a bloodbath by foreign invaders.

In an important step toward reconstruction of the national unity that war had torn apart, the Juan Manuel de Rosas administration introduced a decidedly protectionist tariff. It banned the importation of iron and tinplate manufactures, riding equipment, ponchos, belts, wool or cotton waistbands, coarse woolen cloth, farm products, carriage wheels, tallow candles, and combs, and levied heavy duties on coaches, shoes, cordage, clothing, saddles, dried fruits, and alcoholic beverages. There was no tax on meat transported in Argentine flagships, and saddlery and tobacco-growing were encouraged. The effects were soon observable. Until the battle of Caseros that brought Rosas down in 1852, ships built in the Corrientes and Santa Fe yards sailed the rivers, more than one hundred factories prospered in Buenos Aires, and all travelers agreed on the excellence of Córdoba- and Tucumán-made textiles and shoes, Salta cigars and crafts, and Mendoza and San Juan wines and brandies. Tucumán cabinet-makers were exporting to Chile, Bolivia, and Peru. Ten years after passage of the law, the guns of British and French warships smashed the chains across the Río Paraná to open up the interior waterways that Rosas had kept firmly closed. Blockade followed the invasion.

Ten appeals from Yorkshire, Liverpool, Manchester, Leeds, Halifax, and Bradford, signed by 1,500 bankers, traders, and industrialists, had urged the British government to take measures against the restrictions on trade in La Plata. The blockade showed up the limitations of the national industries which, despite the progress made under the tariff law, were incapable of satisfying internal demand. Since 1841 manufacturing had in fact been languishing rather than gaining in vigor. Rosas represented above all the interests of the beef ranchers in Buenos Aires province, and no industrial bourgeoisie existed or was created to promote the development of a genuine national capitalism: the big ranch occupied the center of the economic stage, and no industrial policy could be independently and vigorously undertaken without destroying the omnipotence of the exporting latifundio. Basically, Rosas always remained true to his class. The best rider in the province, guitar-strummer, dancer, and noted horsebreaker, who on stormy starless nights chewed some blades of grass to locate his whereabouts, was himself a big ranch owner producing cured meat and hides, and the big landowners had made him their chief. The black legend that was later spun around his name cannot conceal the national and popular character of many of his administrative measures,* but class contradictions explain the lack—except for the customs-house surgery—of any dynamic, sustained industrial policy. This lack cannot be attributed to instabilities and shortages resulting from domestic wars and foreign blockade, for was it not in the whirlwind of a besieged revolution that Artigas, twenty years earlier, had combined in-depth agrarian reform with policies aimed at industrializing and uniting the country? In a substantial book, Vivian Trías has compared Rosas's protectionism with the series of measures spread by Artigas from the Banda Oriental (now Uruguay), between 1813 and 1815, to bring true independence to the area of the La Plata viceroyalty.[20] Rosas neither barred foreigners from trading in the internal market, nor returned to the nation the tariff revenues which Buenos Aires still appropriated, nor ended the dictatorship of the one and only port. But the nationalization of internal trade and the abolition of Buenos Aires's port and customs monopoly had been foundation stones—along with the agrarian question—of Artigas's policy. Artigas had wanted free navigation on internal waterways, but Rosas never gave the provinces this key to the door of foreign trade. Rosas also remained basically loyal to his privileged province. Despite all these limitations, the nationalism and populism of the "blue-eyed gaucho" still inspire hatred in Argentina's ruling classes. Rosas remains "guilty of treason to the fatherland"—as a never-annulled law of 1857 put it—and the country still refuses to provide a tomb for his bones, which are buried in Europe. His official image is that of an assassin.

With the suppression of Rosas's heresy, the oligarchy rediscovered its destiny. The chairman of the rural exhibition committee of 1858 opened the show with these words: "We, still in our infancy, are humbly content to send our products and raw materials to European markets so that they may be returned to us transformed by the powerful means at Europe's disposal. Raw materials are what Europe wants, so as to change them into rich artifacts."[21]

---

* In his well-known *Tablas de sangre*, José Rivera listed Rosas's crimes in order to horrify European sensibilities. According to *Atlas* (London), the British banking house of Samuel Lafone paid the writer a penny per corpse. Rosas had hit the Imperium hard by banning gold and silver exports, and had dissolved the National Bank, which was an instrument of British trade.[19]

The illustrious Domingo Faustino Sarmiento and other liberal writers saw in the rural *montonera* only a symbol of barbarism, backwardness, and ignorance, the anachronism of the countryside confronting urban civilization, the poncho and chaps against the frock coat, the spear and knife against the troops of the line, illiteracy against the school. Sarmiento wrote to President Bartolomé Mitre in 1861: "Don't try to economize on gaucho blood, it's all they have that is human. This is a fertilizer that must be made useful to the country." Such scorn and hatred were an expression of antipatriotism clearly tinged with political economy: "We are neither industrialists nor navigators," said Sarmiento, "and Europe will provide us for many centuries with its artifacts in exchange for our raw materials."[22] Beginning in 1862, Mitre launched a war of extermination against the provinces and their last leaders. Sarmiento was put in charge, and troops marched northward to kill gauchos, "biped animals of the most perverse stripe." In La Rioja, rebels under General "El Chacho" Peñaloza, whose influence extended over Mendoza and San Juan, put up one of the last stands against Buenos Aires, which felt that it was time to finish Peñaloza off. They cut off his head and nailed it up in the Plaza de Olta. The railroad and highways completed the collapse of La Rioja that had begun with the 1810 revolution: free trade had brought on a crisis for its craftsmen and had deepened the region's chronic poverty.

In the twentieth century, La Rioja peasants flee from their villages in the mountains and on the plains and flood into Buenos Aires to offer their labor: like the peasants of other poor provinces, they get no further than the city's outskirts, where they settle down beside 700,000 other inhabitants of the *"villas miserias"* and make out as best they can with crumbs from the great capital's banquet table. A few years ago sociologists asked the 150 survivors of a La Rioja village if they saw any change in their former neighbors who had left and returned on visits. Those who had remained said enviously that yes, Buenos Aires had improved the emigrants' clothing, manners, and way of speaking. Some also found the emigrants to be "whiter."[23]

How the War Against Paraguay Wrecked the Only Successful Attempt at Independent Development

The man sat beside me in silence. The strong noonday light outlined his sharp-nosed, high-cheekboned profile. We had left the southern frontier bound for Asunción in a bus for twenty persons which by some alchemy contained fifty. There was a halt after a few hours. We sat in an open patio under the shade of thick leaves. Before us stretched the blinding brilliance of the red earth, immense, unpopulated, untouched: from horizon to horizon nothing disturbed the transparency of the Paraguayan air. We smoked. My companion, a Guaraní-speaking peasant, strung together a few sad words in Spanish: "We Paraguayans are poor and few." He explained that he'd gone down to Encarnación to look for work but had found none. He'd managed to scrape up some pesos for the fare home. Years earlier, as a child, he'd tried his fortune in Buenos Aires and southern Brazil. Now it was cotton-picking time and many Paraguayan braceros were taking off, as they did every year, for Argentina. "But I'm sixty-three. All that crowd going after the jobs—my heart can't take it."

In the last twenty years, half a million Paraguayans have left their country once and for all. Poverty drives out the inhabitants of what was, until a century ago, South America's most advanced country. Today Paraguay's population is barely double what it was then and, with Bolivia, it is one of the poorest and most backward countries in the hemisphere. The woes of the Paraguayans stem from a war of extermination which was the most infamous chapter in South American history: the War of the Triple Alliance, they called it. Brazil, Argentina, and Uruguay joined in committing genocide. They left no stone unturned, nor male inhabitants amid the ruins. Although Britain took no direct part in the ghastly deed, it was in the pockets of British merchants, bankers, and industrialists that the loot ended up. The invasion was financed from start to finish by the Bank of London, Baring Brothers, and the Rothschild bank, in loans at exorbitant interest rates which mortgaged the fate of the victorious countries.

Until its destruction, Paraguay stood out as a Latin American exception—the only country that foreign capital had not deformed. The long, iron-fisted dictatorship of Gaspar Rodríguez de Francia (1814-1840) had incubated an autonomous, sustained development process in the womb of isolation. The all-powerful paternalist state filled the place of a nonexistent national bourgeoisie in organizing the nation and orienting its resources and its destiny. Francia had used the peasant masses to crush the Paraguayan oligarchy, and had established internal peace by erecting a *cordon sanitaire* between Paraguay and the other countries of the old La Plata viceroyalty. Expropriations, exilings, jails, persecutions, and fines had been used—not to consolidate the internal power of landlords and merchants, but for their destruction. Political liberties and the right of opposition neither existed nor would come into being later, but in that historical stage the lack of democracy only disturbed people who were nostalgic for lost privileges. There were no great private fortunes when Francia died, and Paraguay was the only Latin American country where begging, hunger, and stealing were unknown;* travelers of the period found an oasis of tranquillity amid areas convulsed by continuous wars. The U.S. agent Hopkins informed his government in 1845 that in Paraguay there was no child who could not read and write. It was also the only country that did not have its eyes riveted on the other side of the ocean. Foreign trade was not the axis of national life; liberal doctrine, the ideological expression of the global market, had no answer to the defiant attitude that Paraguay—forced by its inland isolation to grow inward—adopted from the beginning of the century. Extermination of the oligarchy enabled the state to gather its economic mainsprings into its own hands, to put this autarchic internal development policy into effect.

The succeeding governments of Carlos Antonio López and his son Francisco Solano continued and vitalized the task. The economy was in full growth. When the invaders appeared on the horizon in 1865, Paraguay had telegraphs, a railroad, and numerous factories manufacturing construction materials, textiles, linens, ponchos, paper and ink,

---

* In official histories, Francia appears as a star in a chamber of horrors. The optical distortions imposed by liberalism are not a monopoly of Latin America's ruling classes; many Left intellectuals who look at our countries' history through alien spectacles accept certain myths, canonizations, and excommunications of the Right. Pablo Neruda's *Canto General* pays moving homage to the Latin American peoples, but clearly reveals this distortion. Neruda pays no attention to Artigas, or to Carlos Antonio or Francisco López, and instead identifies with Sarmiento. He calls Francia a "leprous king" and is no more amiable with Rosas.[24]

crockery, and gunpowder. Two hundred foreign technicians, handsomely paid by the state, made a decisive contribution. From 1850 on, the Ibycui foundry made guns, mortars, and ammunition of all calibers; the arsenal in Asunción produced bronze cannon, howitzers, and ammunition. The steel industry, like all other essential economic activities, belonged to the state. The country had a merchant fleet, and the Asunción shipyard turned out many of the ships flying the Paraguayan flag on the Paraná and across the Atlantic and Mediterranean. The state virtually monopolized foreign trade; it supplied yerba maté and tobacco to the southern part of the continent and exported valuable woods to Europe. The trade balance produced a big surplus. With a strong and stable currency, Paraguay was wealthy enough to carry out great public works without recourse to foreign capital. It did not owe one penny abroad, yet was able to maintain the best army in South America, hire British technicians to serve the state instead of putting the state at their service, and send some university students to finish their studies in Europe. The economic surplus from agricultural production was not squandered by an oligarchy (which did not exist); nor did it pass into the pockets of middlemen and loan sharks, or swell the profits of the British Empire's freight and insurance men. The imperialist sponge, in short, did not absorb the wealth the country produced. Ninety-eight percent of Paraguayan territory was public property: the state granted holdings to peasants in return for permanently occupying and farming them, without the right to sell them. There were also sixty-four *"estancias de la patria,"* haciendas directly administered by the state. Irrigation works, dams and canals, and new bridges and roads substantially helped to raise agricultural production. The native tradition of two crops a year, abandoned by the conquistadors, was revived. The lively encouragement of Jesuit traditions undoubtedly contributed to this creative process.*

---

* Fanatical monks of the Society of Jesus, "the Pope's black guard," had become defenders of the medieval order against the new forces bursting upon the European stage. But in Hispanic America Jesuit missions developed along progressive lines. They came to cleanse by abnegation and ascetic example a Catholic Church which had surrendered to sloth and the untrammeled exploitation of the goods the Conquest had made available to the clergy. It was the Paraguayan missions that reached the highest level; in little more than a century and a half (1603-1768), they fully justified the aims of their founders. The Jesuits used music to draw in Guaraní Indians who had sought shelter in the forest, and who had stayed there rather than join in the "civilizing process" of the encomenderos and landlords. Thus 150,000 Guaranís were able to move back into their

The state pursued a tough protectionist policy—much reinforced in 1864—over national industry and the internal market; internal waterways were closed to the British ships which bombarded the rest of Latin America with Manchester and Liverpool products. British commerce did not hide its concern, not only because this last bastion of national resistance in the heart of the continent seemed invulnerable, but also and especially because of the dangerous example set to its neighbors by Paraguayan obstinacy. Latin America's most progressive country was building its future without foreign investment, without British bank loans, and without the blessings of free trade.

But as Paraguay progressed, so did its need to break out of its seclusion. Industrial development called for closer and more direct contacts with the international market and with sources of advanced techniques. Paraguay was effectively blockaded by Argentina on one side and Brazil on the other, and both could starve its lungs of oxygen by closing the river mouths (as did Rivadavia and Rosas) or imposing arbitrary taxes on its merchandise in transit. In any event, it was indispensable for the consolidation of the oligarchical state to cut short the scandal of this odious country, which was sufficient unto itself and objected to bowing down before British merchants.

Britain's minister in Buenos Aires, Edward Thornton, played a substantial role in preparing for the war. When it was about to break out, he participated as a government advisor in Argentine cabinet meetings, sitting beside President Mitre. The web of provocations and deceptions, which ended with a Brazilian-Argentine agreement that sealed Paraguay's fate, was woven under Thornton's fatherly gaze. Venancio Flores invaded Uruguay, aided in his intervention by its two

---

primitive community organization and revive their traditional arts and crafts. The latifundio system was unknown in the missions; the soil was cultivated partly to satisfy individual needs and partly to develop projects of common concern and to acquire the necessary work tools, which were common property. The Indians' life was intelligently organized; musicians and artisans, farmers, weavers, actors, painters, and builders gathered in workshops and schools. Money was unknown; traders were barred from entering and had to transact any business from hotels at an appropriate distance.

The Crown finally succumbed to the *criollo encomenderos'* pressure and the Jesuits were expelled from Latin America. Landlords and slave traders went in pursuit of the Indians. Corpses hung from trees in the missions; whole communities were sold in Brazilian slave markets. Many Indians took to the forest again. The Jesuits' libraries were used to fuel ovens or to make gunpowder cartridges.[25]

big neighbors, and after the Paysandú massacre he set up an administration in Montevideo subservient to Rio de Janeiro and Buenos Aires. The Triple Alliance was on the road. Paraguayan President Solano López had threatened war in the event of an attack on Uruguay: he knew that this would close an iron pincers around the throat of his country, corraled as it was by geography and the enemy. Nevertheless, liberal historian Efraím Cardozo stoutly maintains that López stood up to Brazil merely because he was offended: the emperor had refused him the hand of one of his daughters. The conflict was inevitable, but it was Mercury's work, not Cupid's.

The Buenos Aires press called López "the Attila of America": "He must be killed like a reptile," thundered the editorials. In September 1864, Thornton sent a long confidential report to London, datelined Asunción. He described Paraguay as Dante described the inferno, but put stress where it belonged: "Import duties on nearly all articles are 20 or 25 percent *ad valorem;* but since this value is calculated on the current price of the articles, the duty that is paid often amounts to 40 to 45 percent of the invoice price. Export duties are from 10 to 20 percent of value. . . ." In April 1865 the Buenos Aires English language daily, *The Standard,* was already hailing Argentina's declaration of war on Paraguay, whose president had "violated all the usages of civilized nations," and was announcing that Argentine President Mitre's sword "will hold high in its victorious course, in addition to the weight of past glories, the irresistible thrust of public opinion in a just cause." The treaty with Brazil and Uruguay was signed on May 1, 1865; its draconian terms were published a year later in the London *Times,* which got the text from banker-creditors in Argentina and Brazil. The future victors divided up the spoils of the vanquished in advance. Argentina was to get the whole territory of Misiones and the vast Chaco; Brazil got a fat slice west of its frontiers. Uruguay, ruled by a puppet of both powers, got nothing.

Mitre announced that he would take Asunción in three months, but the war lasted five years. It was a carnage from the beginning to end of the chain of forts defending the Río Paraguay. The "opprobrious tyrant" Solano López was a heroic embodiment of the national will to survive; at his side the Paraguayan people, who had known no war for half a century, immolated themselves. Men and women, young and old, fought like lions. Wounded prisoners tore off their bandages so that they would not be forced to fight against their brothers. In 1870 López, at the head of an army of ghosts, old folk, and children who had put on false beards to make an impression from a distance, headed into the forest. The invading troops set upon the debris of Asunción with knives between their teeth. When bullets and spears finally finished off the Paraguayan president in the thickets of Cerro Corá, he managed to say: "I die with my country!"—and it was true. Paraguay died with him. López had previously ordered the shooting of his brother and a bishop who accompanied him on this caravan of death. The invaders came to redeem the Paraguayan people, and exterminated them. When the war began, Paraguay had almost as large a population as Argentina. Only 250,000, less than one-sixth, survived in 1870. It was the triumph of civilization. The victors, ruined by the enormous cost of the crime, fell back into the arms of the British bankers who had financed the adventure. The slave empire of Pedro II, whose armies were filled with slaves and prisoners, nevertheless won more than 20,000 square miles of territory—plus labor, for the Paraguayan prisoners who were marched off to work on the São Paulo coffee plantations were branded like slaves. The Argentina of President Mitre, who had crushed his own federal leaders, came out with 36,000 square miles of Paraguayan territory, as well as other booty: "The prisoners and other war matériel we will divide in a convenient form," he wrote. Uruguay, where the heirs of Artigas had been killed or defeated and an oligarchy ruled, participated in the war as a junior partner and without reward. Some Uruguayan soldiers sent into the Paraguayan campaign had boarded the ships with bound hands. The financial bankruptcy of the three countries deepened their dependency on Britain. The Paraguay massacre left its mark on them forever.*

Brazil had performed the role the British had assigned it when they moved the Portuguese throne to Rio de Janeiro. Lord Canning's instructions to the ambassador, Viscount Strangford, early in the

* Solano López lives on in memory. When, in September 1969, Rio de Janeiro's National Historical Museum announced it would dedicate a window to the Paraguayan president, the military was furious. General Mourão Filho, who had set off the coup d'état in 1964, told the press: "A wind of madness is sweeping the country. . . . Solano López is a figure who should be erased forever from our history, as a paradigm of the uniformed South American dictator. He was a butcher who destroyed Paraguay, leading it into an impossible war."

nineteenth century, had been clear: make Brazil an emporium for British manufactures designed for consumption in all South America. Shortly before going to war, the Argentine president, inaugurating a new *British* railway line, made an impassioned speech: "What is the force driving this progress? Gentlemen, it is British capital!" In defeated Paraguay it was not only the population and great chunks of territory that disappeared, but customs tariffs, foundries, rivers closed to free trade, and economic independence. Within its shrunken frontiers, the conquerors implanted free trade and the latifundio. Everything was looted and everything was sold: lands and forests, mines, yerba maté farms, school buildings. Successive puppet governments were installed in Asunción by the occupation forces. The war was hardly over when the first foreign loan in Paraguay's history fell upon the smoking ruins. It was, of course, British. Its nominal value was £1 million, but a good deal less than half of this reached Paraguay; in ensuing years refinancing raised the debt to more than £3 million. The Opium War had ended in 1842 with a free-trade treaty signed in Nanking, consecrating the right of British traders to introduce the drug unrestrictedly into China; now the flag of free trade flew over Paraguay too. Cotton farming was abandoned and Manchester ruined textile production; the national industry never came back to life.

The Colorado Party, which now rules Paraguay, makes breezy mileage with the heroes' memory, but exhibits at the foot of its founding charter the signatures of twenty-two traitors to Solano López, "legionnaires" who served with the Brazilian occupation troops. Dictator Alfredo Stroessner, who has spent the last fifteen years turning Paraguay into a large concentration camp, did his military training under Brazilian generals, who sent him back with high marks and warm eulogies: "He is worthy of a great future. . . ." During his reign Stroessner has bestowed on Brazil and its U.S. masters the dominant place occupied in previous decades by Anglo-Argentine interests. Brazil and Argentina, which "liberated" Paraguay in order to gobble it up, have taken turns since 1870 enjoying the fruits of the plunder. But they have their own crosses to bear from the imperialist power of the moment. Paraguay has the double burden of imperialism and subimperialism. The British Empire used to be the main link in the chain of dependencies, but today the United States, understanding only too well the geopolitical importance of this country at the center of South America, maintains countless advisors who train and advise the armed forces, cook up economic plans, refashion the university to their taste, invent a new "democratic" policy for the country, and reward the generous services of the regime with burdensome loans.* Paraguay is also a colony of other colonies. Using agrarian reform as a pretext, the Stroessner government annulled the legal ban on selling frontier lands to foreigners, and today even state lands have fallen into the hands of Brazilian coffee latifundistas. The invading wave has crossed the Río Paraná with the complicity of the president, in partnership with Portuguese-speaking landowners. When I arrived at Paraguay's shifting northeastern frontier, I had banknotes engraved with the face of the defeated Solano López, but found that only those bearing the likeness of the victorious Emperor Pedro II are valid. After the passage of a century, the outcome of the War of the Triple Alliance takes on burning actuality. Brazilian guards demand passports from Paraguayan citizens who want only to move around in their own country. The flags and the churches are Brazilian. The land piracy also takes in the Guairá falls, the greatest potential source of energy in all Latin America; it is now called—in Portuguese—Sete Quedas. There, it has been announced, Brazil will build the world's largest hydroelectric station.

Subimperialism has a thousand faces. When President Johnson decided in 1965 to drown the Dominicans in blood, Stroessner sent along some Paraguayan soldiers to help him out. In a sinister jest, the battalion was called "Marshal Solano López." The Paraguayans were under a Brazilian general's orders, for it was Brazil that received the Judas honors: its General Panasco Alvim headed Latin America's uniformed accomplices in the massacre. There are other similar examples. Paraguay gave Brazil an oil concession on its territory, but the fuel distribution and petrochemical business in Brazil is in U.S. hands. The Brazilian Cultural Mission reigns over the philosophy and education departments of Paraguay's university, but North Americans now run Brazil's universities. The Paraguayan army's general staff receives advice not

---

* Before the 1968 elections General Stroessner visited the United States. "When I interviewed President Johnson," he told Agence France Presse, "I showed him that I had been fulfilling the prime ministerial function for twelve years by mandate of the polls. Johnson replied that was another reason for continuing to exercise it in the next period."

only from Pentagon technicians but also from Brazilian generals who, in turn, are to the Pentagon as an echo to a voice. Through open contraband channels, Brazilian industrial products invade the Paraguayan market, but the São Paulo factories that produce them have belonged to U.S. corporations since the denationalizing avalanche of recentyears.

Stroessner considers himself the heir to López. How can the Paraguay of a century ago be mentioned in the same breath with the Paraguay of today, the emporium of La Plata basin smuggling and the kingdom of institutionalized corruption? Yet at a political demonstration where the government party claimed both Paraguays at once to stormy applause and cheers, a boy openly hawked contraband cigarettes from a vendor's tray: the fervent gathering puffed nervously at Kents, Marlboros, Camels, and Benson & Hedges. The scanty middle class in Asunción drinks Ballantine's whiskey instead of Paraguayan aguardiente. In the streets one sees late-model luxury cars made in the United States or Europe, brought in as contraband or after payment of a trifling customs duty, moving beside ox-drawn carts slowly bringing fruit to the market: the soil is worked with wooden plows and the taxis are 1970 Impalas. Stroessner defines contraband as "the price of peace": the generals fill their pockets and hatch no plots. Industry, of course, enters its death throes before it can grow. The state does not even implement the decree requiring preference for domestic products in public spending. In this area the only triumphs proudly displayed by the government are the Coca-Cola and Pepsi-Cola plants, installed at the end of 1966 as a U.S. contribution to the progress of the Paraguayan people.

The state declares that it will only intervene directly in the creation of enterprises "when the private sector shows no interest,"[26] and the Banco Central informs the International Monetary Fund that it "has decided to establish a regime of free exchange and abolish restrictions on trade and on currency transactions." A booklet published by the Ministry of Industry and Trade advises investors that the country grants "special concessions to foreign capital." Foreign concerns are exempt from taxes and customs duties so as "to create a propitious climate for investment." The National City Bank of New York recovers all its invested capital in one year of business in Asunción. The foreign bank appropriates the national savings and extends external credits to

Paraguay, credits which further deform its economy and further mortgage its sovereignty. In the countryside, 1.5 percent of proprietors own 90 percent of the cultivated land, and less than 2 percent of the total land area is under cultivation. The official colonization plan in the Caaguazú triangle offers hungry peasants more graves than gain.* The fatherland denies its children the right to work and daily bread, and Paraguayans emigrate en masse.

The furnaces of the Ibycui foundry, where the cannon used in the defense of the invaded fatherland was forged, were constructed in a place now called Mina-cué, which means "It was mine" in Guaraní. There, among the swamps and mosquitos, near a crumbling wall, you can still see the base of a chimney blown up by the invaders a century ago, and pieces of rusted steel that were part of the structure. The few ragged peasants who live in the area don't even know which war it was that caused the destruction, but they say that sometimes at night you can hear the sounds of machinery and hammers, the roar of cannon, and the shouts of soldiers. The Triple Alliance has been a great success.

How Loans and Railroads Deformed the Latin American Economy

René Chateaubriand, France's foreign minister under Louis XVIII, wrote in presumably well-informed disgust: "In the hour of emancipation the Spanish colonies turned into some sort of British colonies."[27] He cited some figures. Between 1822 and 1826, he said, Britain had extended to the liberated Spanish colonies ten loans for a nominal value of around £21 million, but after deduction of interest and middlemen's commissions scarcely £7 million had actually reached Latin America. At the same time, more than forty limited stock companies had been created in London to exploit Latin America's natural resources—mines,

* Many peasants have finally opted to return to the minifundio region in the center of the country, or have joined the new exodus to Brazil, where they offer their cheap labor to Curitiba and Mato Grosso yerba maté plantations or Paraná coffee plantations. Most desperate is the plight of the pioneer, who finds himself face to face with the jungle, totally without technical know-how or credit assistance, with government-"granted" lands from which he must wrest enough to eat *and* to meet his payments—for if he fails to pay the stipulated price he does not get the land title.

agriculture—and to establish public service enterprises. Banks mushroomed in Britain: in one year, 1836, forty-eight were founded. British railroads appeared in Panama around mid-century, and the first streetcar line in Latin America was inaugurated by a British firm in 1868 in the Brazilian city of Recife. The Bank of England also directly financed government treasuries: Latin American public bonds actively circulated, with their crises and booms, in the British financial market. Their public services in British hands, the new states from their inception faced a flood of military expenditures and also had to cope with external payment deficits. Free trade involved a frenzied increase in imports, especially of luxury articles; governments contracted debts, which in turn called for new loans, so that a minority could live fashionably. The countries were mortgaging their future in advance, moving away from economic freedom and political sovereignty. Except in Paraguay (whose contrary effort was crushed), the process was similar throughout Latin America—and still is, although the creditors and the mechanisms are different. The need for external financing became, like the addict's need for morphine, indispensable. Holes were dug for the sake of filling them. Nor is the deterioration of commercial terms of exchange a phenomenon peculiar to our own day. According to Celso Furtado, the prices of Brazilian exports fell 40 percent between 1821 and 1830 and between 1841 and 1850, while foreign import prices remained stable: Latin America's vulnerable economies compensated for the decline with loans.[28]

"The finances of these young states," writes Robert Schnerb, "are not sound. . . . They must resort to inflation, which produces depreciation of the currency, and to onerous loans. These republics' history may be said to be that of the economic obligations they incur to the all-absorbing world of European finance."[29] In fact, bankruptcies, payment suspensions, and desperate refinancing were frequent. Pounds sterling ran out like water between the fingers. Of the £1 million loan that the Buenos Aires government negotiated with Baring Brothers in 1824, Argentina received only £570,000, and that not in gold (as stipulated) but in paper. The loan consisted of drafts on orders sent to British businessmen in Buenos Aires, who had no gold with which to pay since their real mission was to send all precious metals that came their way to London. So Argentina received paper but was required to pay in gold;

it was not until early in this century that Argentina canceled the debt, which successive refinancings had inflated to £4 million. Buenos Aires province had been completely mortgaged—all its revenues, all its public lands—as guarantee of payment. As the finance minister in the period when the loan was contracted said: "We are not in a position to take measures against foreign trade, particularly British, because we are bound to that nation by large debts and would expose ourselves to a rupture which would cause much harm. . . ." The use of debt as an instrument of blackmail is not, as we can see, a recent U.S. invention.

Such usurious operations put bars around free nations. By the middle of the nineteenth century, servicing of the foreign debt absorbed almost 40 percent of Brazil's budget, and every country was caught in the same trap. Railroads formed another decisive part of the cage of dependency: when monopoly capitalism was in flower, imperialist influence extended into the colonial economies' remote backyards. Many of the loans were for financing railroads to bring minerals and foodstuffs to export terminals. The tracks were laid not to connect internal areas one with another, but to connect production centers with ports. The design still resembles the fingers of an open hand: thus railroads, so often hailed as forerunners of progress, were an impediment to the formation and development of an internal market. The imperialist nations also achieved this in other ways, especially through a tariff policy cut to the British pattern. For example, freightage on articles processed in the Argentine interior was much higher than on unfinished goods. Railroad charges became a curse that made it impossible to manufacture cigarettes in tobacco-growing areas, to spin and weave in wool centers, or to finish wood in forest zones. True, the Argentine railroad developed the Santiago del Estero timber industry, but with such results that a local author groaned: "Oh, that Santiago had never had a tree!"[30] The cross-ties were made of wood, and charcoal served as fuel; the lumber camps created by the railroad broke up rural communities, destroyed agriculture and cattle-farming by razing pastureland and shade trees, enslaved several generations of Santiagans in the forests, and furthered depopulation. The mass exodus has not stopped and today Santiago del Estero is one of Argentina's poorest provinces. When the railroads switched to fuel oil, the region was plunged into a deep crisis.

It was not British capital that laid the first tracks across Argentina, Brazil, Chile, Guatemala, Mexico, and Uruguay. Nor in Paraguay, as we have seen; but the railroads built by the Paraguayan state, with the help of European technicians, passed into British hands after the defeat. The other countries' railroads went the same way without producing a single centavo of new investment; furthermore, the state contracts took care to assure the companies a minimum profit level, to avoid possible unpleasant surprises. Decades later, at the end of World War II, when the railroads yielded no more dividends and had fallen into relative disuse, the public authorities got them back. Almost all of the states bought the scrap iron from the British and thus nationalized the companies' losses.

When the railroads were booming, the British concerns had often obtained considerable land concessions on either side of the tracks, in addition to the railbeds themselves and the right to build new branch lines. The land was an additional business bonanza. A fabulous gift to the Brazilian railway in 1911 led to the burning of countless huts and the eviction or death of peasant families in the concession area. It was this that triggered off the "Contestado" revolt, one of the greatest outbursts of popular fury in Brazilian history.

Protectionism and Free Trade in the United States: A Success Due Not to an Invisible Hand

When the Triple Alliance was announcing Paraguay's imminent destruction in 1865, General Ulysses S. Grant was celebrating Lee's surrender at Appomattox. The Civil War brought victory to Northern industrialists—unblushing protectionists—over the free-trade cotton and tobacco planters of the South. Thus the outbreak of the war that sealed Latin America's colonial fate coincided with the end of the war that enabled the United States to consolidate its position as a world power. As the newly elected president said:

> For centuries England has relied on protection, has carried it to extremes, and has obtained satisfactory results from it. There is no doubt that it is to this system that it owes its present strength. After two centuries, England has found it convenient to adopt free trade because it thinks that protection can no longer offer it anything. Very

> well then, gentlemen, my knowledge of our country leads me to believe that within two hundred years, when America has gotten out of protection all that it can offer, it too will adopt free trade.[31]

Two and a half centuries earlier, adolescent English capitalism had sent to its North American colonies its men, its capital, its way of life, its incentives, and its projects. The thirteen colonies, safety valves for Europe's surplus population, soon turned to account the "handicap" of their poor soil and subsoil, and from early days developed an industrializing philosophy which the metropolis did little to discourage. In 1631 the recently arrived colonists in Boston launched a thirty-ton sloop, *Blessing of the Bay,* which they had built themselves, and from then on the shipping industry grew rapidly. White oak, abundant in the woods, was ideal for the framing and hulls; decks, bowsprits, and masts were made of pine. Massachusetts subsidized production of hemp for rigging and ropes, and also encouraged local manufacture of canvas and sails. To the north and south of Boston the coasts were dotted with prosperous shipyards. The colonial governments extended subsidies and premiums to all kinds of manufacture. There were incentives to promote the production of flax and wool, raw materials for crude fabrics which, if not over-elegant, were weatherproof and *national.* To exploit Lynn iron deposits, the first foundry went into operation in 1643; soon Massachusetts was supplying iron to the whole region. When the stimuli to textile production seemed insufficient, this colony opted for compulsion: in 1855 it imposed heavy penalties on any family failing to keep at least one spinning wheel continuously active. In the same period each county of Virginia had to select children for instruction in textile manufacture. It was also prohibited to export hides, so that these could be used domestically for making boots, belts, and saddles.

Economic historian Edward Kirkland wrote that the handicaps with which colonial industry must contend come from every direction except British colonial policy. Indeed, 3,000 miles' distance and the difficulties of communication made proscriptive legislation lose nearly all its force and favored the trend toward self-sufficiency. The Northern colonies sent no gold, silver, or sugar to England, while their consumption needs produced an excess of imports which had somehow to be checked. Trade across the ocean was light; hence development of local manufactures was indispensable for survival. England paid such scant attention to these colonies in the eighteenth century that they were able to introduce the latest metropolitan techniques into their factories, turning restrictive colonial pacts into scraps of paper. This was far from true of the Latin American colonies, which delivered their air, water, and salt to ascendant European capitalism and, in return, received a largesse of the finest and costliest luxury goods to pamper their ruling classes. The only expanding activities in Latin America were those oriented toward export, and so it continued in succeeding centuries: the economic and political interests of the mining and landlord bourgeoisie never coincided with the need for internal economic development, and businessmen were linked less with the New World than with foreign markets for the metals and foodstuffs they wanted to sell and with foreign sources of the manufactured articles they wanted to buy.

When the United States declared its independence, it had the same population as Brazil. The Portuguese metropolis—as underdeveloped as the Spanish—exported its underdevelopment to the colony. Throughout the eighteenth century, Brazil's economy had been orchestrated into the British symphony as imperial supplier of gold. This function was reflected in the colony's class structure. Unlike the United States, Brazil's ruling class was not made up of farmers, manufacturing entrepreneurs, and domestic businessmen. The chief interpreters of ruling-class ideals in the two countries, Alexander Hamilton and the Viscount de Cairú (one of the main figures influencing the opening of the ports in 1808), expressed the difference clearly. Both had been disciples, in England, of Adam Smith. But while Hamilton had become a champion of industrialization and a promoter of state protection for national industry, Cairú believed in the invisible hand that worked the magic of liberalism: *laissez faire, laissez passer, laissez vendre.*[33]

By the end of the eighteenth century, the United States had the world's second merchant fleet, consisting entirely of ships built in its own yards, and its textile and steel mills were in surging growth. Soon afterward its machine industry got under way, eliminating the need for its factories to buy capital goods abroad. The zealous Mayflower pilgrims had laid the foundations of a nation in the New England countryside; along its coast of deep bays and great estuaries an industrial bourgeoisie had continuously grown and prospered. In this, as we have seen, the Antilles trade—including the sale of African slaves—had played a major role, but the U.S. achievement would not have happened if it had not been kindled from the outset by a fierce nationalist flame. George Washington had advised in his farewell address that the United States should pursue a lone course. Emerson proclaimed in 1837: "We have listened too long to the courtly muses of Europe. . . . We will walk on our own feet; we will work with our own hands; we will speak our own minds."[34]

Public funds broadened the internal market. The states built roads and railroads, bridges and canals. In mid-century, the state of Pennsylvania participated in launching more than 150 mixed-economy enterprises, in addition to administering the $100 million invested in public works. The military operations which grabbed more than half of Mexico's territory also contributed substantially to the country's progress. But the state participated in the development process with more than capital investment and the military costs of expansion; in the North a tough protectionist policy had been inaugurated. The landlords of the South, on the contrary, were free traders. Cotton production doubled every ten years, and while it brought a large commercial income to the whole country and fed Massachusetts's modern textile mills, it depended above all on European markets. The Southern aristocracy, like that of Latin America, was primarily linked to the world market; 80 percent of the cotton spun in European mills came from the toil of Southern slaves. When abolition of slavery was added to Northern industrial protectionism, the contradiction set off the war. North and South confronted each other as two opposed worlds, two historical eras, two antagonistic philosophies of the national destiny. The twentieth century won this nineteenth-century war.

> Let every free man sing . . .
> Old King Cotton is dead and buried,

sang a poet of the victorious army. After General Lee's defeat customs duties—which had been raised during the conflict to provide revenue and had remained in force to protect the industry of the victors—became sacred. Congress voted the ultra-protectionist "McKinley" tariff in 1890, and the Dingley Act further hiked customs duties in 1897. Soon afterward the developed countries of Europe felt obliged to erect customs barriers against the invasion of dangerously competitive U.S.

manufactures. The word "trust" had been coined in 1882: petroleum, steel, foodstuffs, railroads, and tobacco were dominated by monopolies that advanced with giant strides.*

Before the Civil War Grant had participated in the plunder of Mexico; after it he was a protectionist president: all part of the same process of national affirmation. Northern industry was conducting the orchestra of history and, as political master of the state, seeing to its interests from the seat of power. The agricultural frontier moved westward and southward at the expense of Indians and Mexicans, but it was with small holdings, not latifundios, that it filled the new open spaces. The promised land not only attracted European peasants; masters of the most varied crafts and workers skilled in mechanics, metallurgy, and steel production also came from Europe to enrich the country's industrialization. By the end of the century the United States was the leading industrial power; in thirty years after the Civil War its factories had multiplied its production capacity by seven. It produced as much coal as Britain and twice as much steel, and had nine times as many miles of railroad. The center of the capitalist world was beginning to move.

After World War II the United States began to emulate Britain in exporting the doctrine of free trade and free competition, so that other people could consume. The International Monetary Fund and World Bank emerged together to deny to underdeveloped countries the right of protecting their national industries, and to discourage state action in those countries. Infallible curative properties were attributed to private enterprise. But the United States did not abandon an economic policy which still remains rigidly protectionist, and which listens carefully to the voice of history: in the North the disease was never confused with the remedy.

---

* The South became an internal colony of Northern capitalists. After the war, propaganda for spinning-mill construction in the two Carolinas, Georgia, and Alabama assumed the dimension of a crusade. But this was no victory for a moral cause, and no pure humanitarianism fathered the new industries; the South offered cheaper labor and power and soaring profits, sometimes amounting to 75 percent. Capital flowed from the North to tie the South to the system's center of gravity. The tobacco industry, concentrated in North Carolina, was directly under the Duke trust, headquartered in New Jersey to take advantage of more favorable laws; in 1907 Tennessee Coal & Iron, which exploited Alabama's iron and coal, came under the control of U.S. Steel, which from then on arranged prices and thus eliminated irksome competition. At the beginning of our century the South's per capita income had fallen to half of what it was before the Civil War.[35]

5. The Contemporary Structure of Plunder

An Impotent Talisman

Of all the direct private investment in Latin America coming from abroad, less than one-fifth was from the United States when Lenin wrote *Imperialism* in the spring of 1916. Today, nearly three-quarters is from the United States. What was the imperialism Lenin knew? The rapacity of industrial centers seeking world markets for their merchandise; the fever to capture all possible sources of raw materials; the plunder of iron, coal, and petroleum; the railroads which linked the control of dominated areas; the voracious loans of the financial monopolies; the military expeditions; the wars of conquest. It was an imperialism that poisoned any place where a colony or semi-colony might dare to build a factory of its own. Industrialization was the privilege of the metropolis; in the poor countries it was incompatible with the rich countries' system of domination. The end of World War II found European interests in full retreat from Latin America, and U.S. investments triumphantly advancing. Since then there has been an important change in the focus of investment. Step by step, year by year, capital put into public services and mining has lost importance, while investments in petroleum and, above all, in manufacturing have grown in proportion. At the present time $1 of every $3 invested in Latin America is invested in industry.*

In return for insignificant investments, the affiliates of giant corporations jump over customs barriers erected—paradoxically—against foreign competition, and take over the internal industrializing process. They export factories or, not infrequently, corner and devour those already existing. For this they can rely on the enthusiastic aid of most local governments and on the power of extortion with which international credit organizations endow them. Imperialist capital captures markets *from within*, appropriating the key sectors of local industry: it conquers or constructs the decisive strongholds from which to control the rest. The OAS describes the process thus: "Latin American enterprises continue in control of already established and less sophisticated industries and techniques, while private investment from the United States—and probably from other industrialized countries also—rapidly increases its participation in certain dynamic industries, which require a relatively high technical level and are more important in determining the course of economic development."[1] Thus the dynamism of U.S. factories south of the Río Grande is much more intense than that of Latin American industry in general. The figures for the three biggest countries are eloquent: with an index of 100 in 1961, Argentina's industrial product amounted to 112.5 in 1965, while in the same period sales by U.S.-affiliated concerns rose to 166.3. For Brazil the equivalent figures are 109.2 and 120; for Mexico, 142.2 and 186.8.

The interest of the imperialist corporations in appropriating Latin American industrial growth and capitalizing it for their own benefit does not, of course, imply a disinterest in traditional forms of exploitation. It is true that United Fruit's railroad in Guatemala stopped being profitable, and that nationalization by Brazil was splendid business for Electric Bond and Share and International Telephone and Telegraph, which received indemnities in pure gold for rusty installations and museum-piece machinery. But if public services are abandoned for more profitable activities, raw materials are a different matter. How would the Imperium make out without Latin America's oil and minerals? Despite the relative decline in mining investment, the U.S. economy

---

* Forty years ago U.S. investment in transformation industries was only 6 percent of the total U.S. capital invested in Latin America. In 1960 it grazed the 20 percent mark, and has continued rising to become nearly one-third of the total.

cannot, as we have seen, do without the vital supplies from the south and the juicy profits they bring. Furthermore, the investments that turn Latin American factories into mere cogs in the giant corporations' machinery do not in any way alter the international division of labor. There is no change in the system of intercommunicating arteries through which capital and merchandise circulate between poor countries and rich countries. Latin America continues exporting its unemployment and poverty: the raw materials that the world market needs, and on whose sale the regional economy depends. Unequal exchange functions as before: hunger wages in Latin America help finance high salaries in the United States and Europe. Brazil, despite its industrialization, continues substantially dependent on coffee exports, Argentina on sales of meat; Mexico exports very few manufactures.

There are always politicians and technocrats ready to show that the invasion of "industrializing" foreign capital benefits the area invaded. In this version, the new-model imperialism comes on a genuinely civilizing mission, is a blessing to the dominated countries, and the true-love declarations by the dominant power of the moment are its real intentions. Guilty consciences are thus relieved of the need for alibis, for no one is guilty: today's imperialism radiates technology and progress, and even the use of this old, unpleasant word to define it is in bad taste. But when imperialism begins exalting its own virtues we should take a look in our pockets. We find that the new model does not make its colonies more prosperous, although it enriches their poles of development; it does not ease social and regional tensions, but aggravates them; it spreads poverty even more widely and concentrates wealth even more narrowly; it pays wages twenty times lower than in Detroit and charges prices three times higher than in New York; it takes over the internal market and the mainsprings of the productive apparatus; it assumes proprietary rights to chart the course and fix the frontiers of progress; it controls national credit and orients external trade at its whim; it denationalizes not only industry but the profits earned by industry; it fosters the waste of resources by diverting a large part of the economic surplus abroad; it does not bring in capital for development but takes it out. As various ECLA reports have shown, the hemorrhage of profits from direct U.S. investments in Latin America has been five times greater in recent years than the infusion of new investments. To enable the corporations to take out their profits, Latin American countries mortgage themselves to foreign banks and international credit organizations, thus multiplying the flow of the next bloodlettings. The result is the same for industrial investment as it is for the "traditional" kind.

In the rigid framework of a global capitalism integrated around the big U.S. corporations, the industrialization of Latin America has increasingly less to do with progress and national liberation. The talisman was robbed of its power in the decisive defeats of the past century, when ports triumphed over interiors and free trade crushed new-born national industries. And the twentieth century produced no bourgeoisie strong and creative enough to reshoulder the task and follow it through to its end. Every effort petered out halfway to the goal. What happened to Latin America's industrial bourgeoisie was what happens to dwarfs: it became decrepit without having grown. Our bourgeois of today are agents and functionaries of prepotent foreign corporations. Truth compels us to admit that they never did anything to deserve a better fate.

The Guards Themselves Open the Gates: The Guilty Sterility of the National Bourgeoisie

The present structure of industry in Argentina, Brazil, and Mexico—the three touted poles of Latin American development—shows deformations characteristic of a *reflected* development. With rare exceptions, the satellization of industry in other, weaker countries has been easily achieved. There is certainly nothing competitive about a capitalism that today exports factories as well as merchandise and capital, that penetrates and hogs everything: this is a global industrial conglomeration by capitalism in the age of the multinational corporation, of the giant monopoly embracing every kind of activity in every corner of the earth. U.S. capital is more tightly concentrated in Latin America than in the United States itself; a handful of concerns control the overwhelming majority of investments. For them the nation is not a task to undertake, a flag to defend, or a destiny to fulfill: it is no more than a hurdle to leap—for sovereignty can be inconvenient—or a succulent fruit to devour. But is the nation a destiny to fulfill to the ruling classes in each country? The grand march of imperialist capital has found local industry defenseless and unaware of its historic role. The bourgeoisie has enlisted in the foreign invasion force without shedding tears or blood; and with the Latin American economy getting steadily weaker over the past two decades, the state's influence upon it has been reduced to an all-time low by the good offices of the International Monetary Fund. U.S. corporations went into Europe like conquistadors and grasped the reins of the old continent's development so firmly that before long, we are told, U.S. industry in Europe will be the world's third industrial power after the United States and the USSR.[2] If the European bourgeoisie, with its tradition and power, has not been able to dam the flood, what hope is there that, at this stage of history, Latin America's bourgeoisie will lead the impossible venture of independent capitalist development? In fact, the denationalization process in Latin America has been much speedier and cheaper and has had far worse consequences.

The growth of Latin American manufacturing was sparked, in our century, from outside, rather than by planned national development policies. It has not been a maturing of productive forces; nor was it the result of an explosion of internal conflicts—conflicts allegedly "overcome"—between landlords and an ascendant artisan class, for that class was short-lived. Latin American industry was delivered from the very womb of the agro-export system, in response to an acute disequilibrium provoked by the fall of external trade. Two world wars, and especially the capitalist depression that followed "Black Friday" in October 1929, abruptly and violently curtailed the region's exports and consequently its capacity to import. Prices of suddenly scarce foreign industrial products soared. No industrial class free from traditional dependency emerged: the manufacturing impetus came from capital accumulated by landlords and importers. It was the big cattlemen who imposed exchange controls in Argentina. The chairman of the Sociedad Rural, who had become minister of agriculture, said in 1933: "The isolation in which we have been placed by a dislocated world obliges us to manufacture here what we can no longer buy in countries that buy from us."[3] Coffee hacendados hurried to put much of their capital accumulated from external trade into the industrialization of São Paulo: "In contrast with the industrialization of already developed countries," a government document said, "Brazil's industrialization was not a slow process, a part of a general process of economic transformation. It was rather a rapid and intense phenomenon, superimposed on the previously existing socioeconomic structure without entirely modifying it, giving rise to the profound sectoral and regional differences which characterize Brazilian society."[4]

From the start, the new industry dug itself in behind protective customs barriers erected by the governments, and it grew thanks to measures taken by the state to restrict and control imports, fix special exchange rates, avoid taxation, buy or finance production surpluses, build roads for the transport of raw materials and merchandise, and create or extend sources of energy. The nationalist and broadly popular governments of Getulio Vargas (1930–1945 and 1951–1954), Lázaro Cárdenas (1934–1940), and Juan Domingo Perón (1946–1955) expressed the need of Brazilian, Mexican, and Argentine industry to "take off," to develop or consolidate according to place and period. In Latin America, the "spirit of enterprise" that defines certain basic characteristics of the industrial bourgeoisie in developed capitalist countries was a characteristic of the state, especially in these decisive periods. Instead of the social class for which history clamored with small success, it was the government of the populist *caudillos* that embodied the nation and gave the masses political and economic access to the benefits of industrialization. The industrial bourgeoisie hatched in this incubator did not differ essentially from previous ruling classes. Perón, for example, inspired panic in the Unión Industrial—whose leaders, not without reason, saw the ghost of the provincial *montoneras* reappearing in the rebellion of the Buenos Aires suburban proletariat. Before Perón defeated it in the February 1946 elections, the conservative coalition received a famous check from the industrialists' leader; ten years later, when Perón fell, it was again clear to them that their contradictions with the oligarchy—of which they for better or worse formed a part—were not fundamental. In 1956 the Unión Industrial made a united front with the Sociedad Rural and the Bolsa de Comercio in defense of free association, free enterprise, freedom to trade, and freedom to hire. In Brazil, an important sector of the manufacturing bourgeoisie closed ranks with the forces that drove Vargas to suicide. The Mexican experience had distinctive characteristics and promised much more to the Latin American process of change than it finally contributed. The

Cárdenas nationalist cycle was the only one that broke lances with the landlords by carrying out the agrarian reform for which the country had agitated since 1910. In other countries—not merely in Argentina and Brazil—industrializing governments left the latifundio structure intact, so that it continued to strangle the internal market and agricultural production.*

Generally speaking, industry landed as an airplane does, without affecting the airport: conditioned by and serving the needs of a previously existing internal market, it never broadened that market enough to make great structural changes possible. Industrial development required more and more imports of machinery, spare parts, fuel, and intermediate products,† but exports, the source of foreign currency, could not pay for these since they came from an activity condemned to backwardness by its masters. Under the Perón regime, the Argentine state achieved a monopoly of grain exports but did not touch the land-ownership system; nor did it nationalize the big U.S. and British meatpacking plants or the wool exporters. Thus the official push toward heavy industry was extremely weak and the state did not realize in time that if it did not give birth to a technology of its own, its nationalist policy would take flight with clipped wings. By 1953 Perón, who had come to power in direct confrontation with the U.S. ambassador, was giving Milton Eisenhower a rousing welcome and soliciting the cooperation of foreign capital in promoting dynamic industries.** The need

---

* Chile, Colombia, and Uruguay also did some industrializing as a substitute for importing in the periods referred to here. Uruguayan President José Batlle y Ordóñez (1903–1907 and 1911–1915) had previously been a prophet of the bourgeois revolution in Latin America. Uruguay put the eight-hour day into law before the United States. Batlle's welfare-state experiment was not limited to implementation of the most advanced social laws of the time; it also gave a strong impetus to cultural development and mass education, and nationalized public services and various economically important productive activities. But it neither touched the power of the landlords, nor nationalized banking or foreign trade. Today Uruguay suffers the consequences of the prophet's perhaps inevitable omissions and of his successors' betrayals.

† "The transfer of a particular product to internal production only 'substitutes' for part of the aggregate value previously generated outside the economy. . . . To the extent that consumption of this 'substituted' product expands rapidly, the resultant demand for imports can rapidly overtake the foreign-currency economy. . . ."[5]

** The minister of economic affairs replied thus to a representative of the magazine *Visión* on November 27, 1953:

"Apart from the oil industry, what other industries does Argentina want to develop with the

for a "partnership" between national industry and the imperialist corporations became pressing as substitution for imported manufactures was speeded up and as the new factories required rising levels of technology and organization. The same trend emerged in Getulio Vargas's industrialization plan, and was dramatized in Vargas's final tragic decision. Foreign oligopolies, with their ultramodern technology, steadily and not very secretly took over the national industry of all Latin American countries, including Mexico, by the sale of manufacturing techniques, patents, and new equipment. Wall Street had definitely taken the place of Lombard Street, and it was the U.S. concerns which settled down to enjoy superpower in the region. To this penetration of the manufacturing field was added ever increasing interference in banking and commerce: the Latin American market was being integrated into the internal market of the multinational corporations.

In 1965 Roberto Campos, economic czar of the Castelo Branco dictatorship, announced that "the era of charismatic leaders surrounded by a romantic aura is giving place to a technocracy."[7] The U.S. embassy had directly participated in the coup against the João Goulart government; the fall of Goulart, Vargas's heir in style and aim, rang down the curtain on populism and mass politics. "We are a beaten, dominated, conquered, destroyed nation," a friend wrote to me from Rio de Janeiro some months after the success of the military plot: the denationalization of Brazil meant iron-fisted rule by an unpopular dictatorship. Capitalist development could no longer be fitted in with the great mass mobilization around a *caudillo* like Vargas. To contain runaway inflation at the expense of the greater poverty of the poor, the regime had to ban strikes and destroy unions and parties, to jail, torture, and kill, to cut workers' wages by any means necessary. A survey in 1966–1967 showed that 84 percent of Brazil's big industrialists thought the Goulart government's economic policy had been harmful. Undoubtedly, among them were those captains of the national bourgeoisie Goulart tried to lean on in order to stem the imperialist bloodletting of the national economy. The

---

cooperation of foreign capital?"

"To be precise, let us cite in order of priority oil. . . . Secondly, the steel industry. . . . Heavy chemistry. . . . Manufacture of transport units. . . . Manufacture of tires and axles. . . . And construction of diesel engines."[6]

same process of repressing and strangling the people occurred under Onganía in Argentina—actually, it had begun with Perón's defeat in 1955, just as in Brazil it began with the shot that killed Vargas in 1954. In Mexico, too, denationalization of industry coincided with increasingly repressive policies by the party that monopolizes the government.

As Fernando Henrique Cardoso has noted, light or "traditional" industry, which grew under the benevolent protection of populist governments, requires increased consumption by the masses, the people who buy shirts or cigarettes.[8] But "dynamic" industry—the production of intermediate and capital goods—is directed toward a restricted market, one which has the big concerns and the state at its top: a few consumers with big financial resources. Dynamic industry, now in foreign hands, rests upon and subordinates previously existing traditional industry. In the traditional sectors, technologically at a low level, national capital retains some strength; the less the capitalist is tied to international modes of production by technological and financial dependence, the more he tends to favor agrarian reform and the raising of mass consumer-power through the trade union struggle. On the other hand, those with closest foreign connections, representing dynamic industry, simply want strengthened bonds between the dependent countries' islands of development and the world economic system, and they subordinate internal transformations to this priority. Here are the throats from which the song of the industrial bourgeoisie emerges, as is shown in all the recent Argentine and Brazilian surveys Cardoso uses as raw material. The big businessmen are firmly opposed to agrarian reform; most of them deny that the manufacturing sector has different interests from the rural sector and believe that nothing is more important for industrial development than the cohesion of all productive classes and the strengthening of the Western bloc. Only 2 percent of the great industrialists in Argentina and Brazil think the workers are of primary political importance. Most of those interviewed were "national entrepreneurs"; and most were bound hand and foot to foreign power centers by the myriad bonds of dependency.

Could anything else be expected at this point? The industrial bourgeoisie is a dominant class dominated in turn from abroad. The chief latifundistas on the Peruvian coast, now being expropriated by the Velasco Alvarado government, are also owners of thirty-one transformation industries and many other assorted enterprises. The situation is similar in all the other countries: a few hundred families own the factories and lands, the large businesses and banks.[9] Mexico is no exception: the national bourgeoisie, subordinated to big U.S. concerns, is much more afraid of mass pressure than of imperialist oppression, in whose bosom it is developing without independence—and without the creative imagination attributed to it—and has efficiently multiplied its interests.* In Argentina, the founder of the Jockey Club, center of latifundista social prestige, was also the leading industrialist, and thus an immortal tradition was born at the end of the past century.† Manufacturers with fattened bank accounts marry landlords' daughters to gain entry to the oligarchy's most exclusive salons, or buy land for the same purpose; and not a few cattle ranchers have—at least in boom periods—invested capital surpluses accumulated in their hands in industry. Faustino Fano, who made a good part of his fortune as a textile merchant and industrialist, held the presidency of the Sociedad Rural for four terms before his death in 1967: "Fano destroyed the false contradiction between agriculture and industry," his press obituaries proclaimed. Industrial surpluses are turned into cows. The powerful Di Tella brothers sold their auto and refrigerator factories to foreign capitalists and now raise prize bulls for Sociedad Rural shows. Half a century ago the Anchorena family, which owned Buenos Aires province up to its borders, built one of the city's biggest metallurgical plants.

In Europe and the United States, the industrial bourgeoisie made a very different kind of entrance onto the stage of history, and grew and consolidated its power in quite a different way.

---

* As Alonso Aguilar says: "Mexican capitalists are more and more versatile and ambitious. With business freedom as their point of departure for acquiring wealth, they—or at least the most prominent—enjoy a network of channels through which to multiply and interweave their interests by friendships, business partnerships, marriage compaternity *[compadrazgo]* of children, extension of mutual favors, membership in certain clubs or groups, frequent social gatherings and, of course, affinity in their political positions."[10]

† He was Carlos Pellegrini. The Jockey Club honored him by publishing his speeches; those in which the industrialists' point of view were supported were omitted.[11]

Which Flag Flies Over the Machinery?*

The old woman stooped and fanned the fire with her hand. Back bent, wrinkled neck extended, she looked like an ancient black tortoise. But her ragged dress certainly gave less protection than a shell, and, after all, it was only the years that made her so slow. Behind her the wall of her hovel, made of bits of wood and tin, sagged like its occupant; beyond were similar hovels of the São Paulo slum. Before her the water for coffee was boiling in a blackened kettle. She lifted a small tin can to her lips and, before drinking, shook her head and shut her eyes. "*O Brasil é nosso,*" she said—Brazil is ours. In the center of the same city, and at that same moment, the executive director of Union Carbide was thinking the same thing—but in another language—as he raised a crystal glass to drink to the firm's capture of still another Brazilian plastics factory. One of the two was mistaken.

Since 1964 Brazil's successive military dictators have marked the anniversaries of the various state enterprises by announcing their imminent denationalization, now known as "recuperation." Ministers flock to celebrate every opening of a foreign factory. Law 56,570, passed on July 6, 1965, reserved the petrochemical industry for the state; Law 56,571, passed the same day, annulled Law 56,570, opening up petrochemicals to private investment. Thus directly, or through "partnership" with the state, Dow Chemical, Union Carbide, the Rockefeller group, and Phillips Petroleum won the most coveted "filet mignon," the oil derivatives industry in which a boom in the 1970s was anticipated. What happened in the few hours between the two laws? Rustling curtains, footsteps in the hallway, desperate bangings on the door, green bills in swift motion, a flurry in the palace: from Shakespeare to Brecht, many would have enjoyed describing it. A government minister admits: "In Brazil, apart from the state itself, and with honorable exceptions, only foreign capital is strong."[12] And the government does its best to avoid any irksome competition with U.S. and European corporations.

Foreign capital for manufacturing began copiously flowing into Brazil in the 1950s, and got a strong impetus from the development plan President Juscelino Kubitschek put into effect between 1957 and

* "Which flag flies" is part of a famous saying by José Artigas. (Trans.)

1960. Those were the days of growth euphoria. Brasilia emerged as if from a magician's cauldron, in a wilderness where the Indians had not yet heard of the wheel; highways and great dams were built; automobile factories produced a new car every two minutes. The industrial curve climbed steeply. Doors were flung open to foreign investment, the dollar invasion was hailed, the dynamism of progress was felt in the air. Banknotes circulated before the ink dried; the leap forward was financed by inflation and a heavy external debt that would be unloaded on the backs of successor governments. A special type of exchange for remitting profits to the foreign concerns' head offices and amortizing their investment was introduced and guaranteed by Kubitschek. The state assumed co-responsibility for payment of debts contracted abroad by these concerns, and arranged a cheap dollar for amortization and interest on these debts: according to an ECLA report, over 80 percent of all investment between 1955 and 1962 came from state-guaranteed loans.[13] In other words, more than four-fifths of these concerns' investments came from foreign banks and became a further addition to the Brazilian state's millstone of external debt. Special benefits were also granted for the importation of machinery.* National enterprises did not enjoy the benefits extended to General Motors and Volkswagen.

The denationalizing effects of this seduction of imperialist capital emerged in the findings of the university's Instituto de Ciencias Sociales when it investigated Brazil's great economic groupings.[15] Of conglomerates with capital exceeding 4 billion cruzeiros, more than half were foreign and most were U.S.-owned; of those with more than 10 billion cruzeiros, twelve were foreign and five Brazilian. "The bigger the economic group, the more likely it is to be foreign," concluded Mauricio Vinhas de Queiroz in analyzing the results of the investigation. Equally or more eloquent was the fact that of the twenty-four Brazilian groups with over four billion in capital, only nine were not linked by shareholdings

---

* Eugênio Gudin, an economist much in favor of foreign investment, estimates that under this heading alone Brazil made a present to U.S. and European concerns of no less than $1 billion. According to Moacir Paixão, privileges extended to the auto industry in the period of its inception were equivalent to the national budget. Paulo Schilling notes that while the Brazilian state showered benefits on the big international corporations, permitting them maximum profits with maximum investments, it refused help to the Fábrica Nacional de Motores, created in the Vargas period.[14] Later, during the Castelo Branco regime, this state enterprise was sold to Alfa Romeo.

to U.S. or European capital, and two of the nine had interlocking foreign directorships. The survey showed that ten economic groups had a virtual monopoly in their respective lines, and that of these, eight were affiliates of big U.S. corporations.

But all this was child's play compared to what came later. Between 1964 and mid-1968, fifteen auto and auto parts factories were swallowed up by Ford, Chrysler, Willys Overland, Simca, Volkswagen, and Alfa Romeo. In the electric-electronic sector, three important Brazilian concerns passed into Japanese hands. Wyeth Laboratories, Bristol Meyers, Mead Johnson, and Lever Brothers gobbled various laboratories, reducing national production of drugs to one-fifth the market. Anaconda pounced on nonferrous metals and Union Carbide on plastics, chemicals, and petrochemicals; American Can, American Machine and Foundry, and other colleagues took over six Brazilian machine and metallurgical concerns; the Companhia de Mineração Geral, owner of one of Brazil's biggest metallurgical plants, was bought for a song by a Bethlehem Steel–Chase Manhattan–Standard Oil consortium. A parliamentary commission set up to investigate the matter reached some sensational conclusions, but the military regime closed the doors of Congress and the findings never got to the Brazilian public.*

Under Castelo Branco, an investment-guarantee agreement was signed which gave foreign concerns virtual extraterritoriality: taxes on their profits were cut and they were given extraordinary credit facilities, while tourniquets applied by the Goulart government to the profits drain were removed. The dictatorship hawked the country to foreign capitalists as a pimp offers a woman, and put the stress where it belonged: "The treatment of foreigners in Brazil is among the most liberal in the

---

* The commission found that in 1968 foreign capital controlled 40 percent of the capital market in Brazil, 62 percent of external trade, 82 percent of ocean transport, 67 percent of external air transport, 100 percent of motor vehicle production, 100 percent of tire manufacturing, more than 80 percent of the pharmaceutical industry, about 50 percent of the chemical industry, 59 percent of machinery and 62 percent of auto parts production, 48 percent of aluminum and 90 percent of cement production. Half of the foreign capital was that of U.S. concerns, followed by German. It is interesting to note in passing the increasing weight of the Federal Republic of Germany's investments in Latin America. Of every two autos made in Brazil, one comes from the Volkswagen plant, the biggest in the whole region. The first auto factory in South America was German—Mercedes-Benz Argentina, founded in 1951. The German firms Bayer, Hoechst, BASF, and Schering control a substantial part of Latin America's chemical industries.

world . . . no general restrictions are in effect with reference to the nationality of owners, partners, or shareholders. . . . There is no limit to the percentage of the registered capital that may be remitted as profit. . . . No limitation is placed on the repatriation of capital, and reinvestment of profits is considered as an increase of the original capital. . . ."[16]

Argentina competes with Brazil for the role of imperialist-investment favorite, and its military regime did not lag in singing the benefits during the same period. In his 1967 speech defining Argentine economic policy, Juan Carlos Onganía reaffirmed that the hens granted equal opportunity to the fox: "Foreign investments in Argentina will be considered on an equal footing with investments of internal origin, in accordance with the traditional policy of our country which has never discriminated against foreign capital."[17] As in Brazil, Argentina puts no limitations on the entrance of foreign capital, its movement within the national economy, the export of profits, or the repatriation of capital; payments for patents, royalties, and technical assistance are made freely. The government exempts the concerns from taxes and extends to them special exchange rates, in addition to many other stimuli and exemptions. Between 1963 and 1968, fifty important Argentine enterprises—twenty-nine of which passed into U.S. hands—were denationalized in such varied sectors as steel, autos and auto parts, petrochemicals, chemicals, the electrical industry, paper, and cigarettes. In 1962 two private-capital Argentine concerns, Siam Di Tella and Industrias Kaiser Argentinas, were among the five biggest industrial enterprises in Latin America; in 1967 both had been generously surrendered to imperialist capital. Of the country's largest enterprises, those with sales exceeding 7 billion pesos a year, half the total value of the sales belongs to foreign firms, one-third to the state, and barely one-sixth to private companies with Argentine capital.[18]

Almost one-third of U.S. investment in Latin American manufacturing is in Mexico, which also puts no restrictions on the transfer of capital and the repatriation of profits; its exchange restrictions are conspicuous in their absence. The obligatory "Mexicanization" of capital, under which nationals must hold the majority of shares in some industries, has, according to the Secretary of Industry and Commerce, "generally speaking been well received by foreign investors, who have publicly recognized various advantages in the creation of mixed enterprises." He continued: "It should be noted that even internationally renowned enterprises have adopted this form of partnership in companies they have established in Mexico, and it should also be stressed that the policy of Mexicanization of industry has not only not discouraged foreign investment in Mexico, but that after this investment flow broke a record in 1965, the volume reached in that year was again exceeded in 1966."[19] Of the hundred most important enterprises in Mexico in 1962, fifty-six were wholly or partly controlled by foreign capital, twenty-four belonged to the state, and twenty to private Mexican capital. These twenty accounted for slightly more than one-seventh of the hundred concerns' total sales volume.[20] Big foreign concerns now control more than half the capital invested in computers, office equipment, machinery, and industrial equipment; General Motors, Ford, Chrysler, and Volkswagen have consolidated their power over the auto industry and its network of auxiliary factories; the new chemical industry belongs to Du Pont, Monsanto, Imperial Chemical Industries (British), Allied Chemical, Union Carbide, and Cyanamid; the chief laboratories are in the hands of Parke-Davis, Merck, Ross Laboratories (a subsidiary of Abbott), and Squibb; the influence of Celanese plastics is decisive in the manufacture of manmade fibers; Lever Brothers and Anderson, Clayton have an increasing hold on edible oils; and foreign capital participates overwhelmingly in the production of cement, cigarettes, rubber and its derivatives, housewares, and assorted foods.

Bombardment by the International Monetary Fund Helps the Conquerers to Land

Testifying before the parliamentary commission on the denationalization of Brazilian industry, two government ministers admitted that indigenously owned factories had been put at a disadvantage by the Castelo Branco regime's measure permitting the direct inflow of external credit. They were referring to the famous Order 289 of early 1965, which allowed foreign concerns operating in Brazil to get loans from abroad at 7 or 8 percent interest, with a government-guaranteed exchange arrangement in case the cruzeiro was devalued. Brazilian concerns had to pay almost 50 percent interest on credits they obtained—with difficulty—at home. The inventor of the measure, Roberto Campos, offered this explanation: "Obviously the world is unequal. Some are born intelligent, some stupid. Some are born athletes, others crippled. The world is made up of small and large enterprises. Some die early, in the prime of life; others drag themselves criminally through a long useless existence. There is a basic fundamental inequality in human nature, in the condition of things. The mechanism of credit cannot escape this. To postulate that national enterprises must have the same access to foreign credit as foreign enterprises is simply to ignore the basic realities of economics. . . ."* According to this brief but meaty "Capitalist Manifesto," the law of the jungle is the natural code governing human life; injustice does not exist, for what we know as injustice is merely an expression of the cruel harmony of the universe: poor countries are poor because . . . they are poor; our fate is written in the stars and we are born only to fulfill it. Some are condemned to obey, others are appointed to command. Some put their necks out and others put on the rope. The author of this theory was the creator of International Monetary Fund policy in Brazil.

As in other Latin American countries, application of IMF formulas opened the gates to let foreign conquerers into an already scorched land. From the end of the 1950s economic recession, monetary instability, the credit drought, and a decline in internal purchasing power all helped to capsize national industry and put it at the mercy of imperialist corporations. With the magical incantation of "monetary stabilization," the IMF—which not disinterestedly confuses the fever with the disease, inflation with the crisis of existing structures—has imposed on Latin America a policy that accentuates imbalances instead of easing them. It liberalizes trade by banning direct exchanges and barter agreements; it forces the contraction of internal credits to the point of asphyxia, freezes wages, and discourages state activity. To this program it adds sharp

* This testimony appeared in the report of a parliamentary commission investigating transactions between national and foreign enterprises, dated September 6, 1968. Soon afterward Campos published a curious interpretation of the Peruvian government's nationalist stance. According to him, the Velasco Alvarado government's expropriation of Standard Oil was no more than an "exhibition of masculinity." The only objective of nationalism, he wrote, is to satisfy the human being's primitive need for hate. However, he added that "pride does not generate investments or increase the flow of capital. . . ."[21]

monetary devaluations which are theoretically supposed to restore the currency to its real value and stimulate exports. In fact, the devaluations merely stimulate the internal concentration of capital in the ruling classes' pockets and facilitate absorption of national enterprises by foreigners who turn up with a fistful of dollars.

In all Latin America, the system produces much less than the necessary monetary demand, and inflation results from this structural impotence. Yet the IMF, instead of attacking the causes of the production apparatus's insufficient supply, launches its cavalry against the consequences, crushing even further the feeble consumer power of the internal market: in these lands of hungry multitudes, the IMF lays the blame for inflation at the door of excessive demand. Its stabilization and development formulas have not only failed to stabilize or develop; they have tightened the external stranglehold on these countries, deepened the poverty of the dispossessed masses—bringing social tensions to the boiling point—and hastened economic and financial denationalization in the name of the sacred principles of free trade, free competition, and freedom of movement for capital. The United States, which itself operates an enormous protectionist system—tariffs, quotas, internal subsidies—has never earned a glance from the IMF. Toward Latin America, on the other hand, the IMF is inflexible: for this it was brought into the world. As soon as Chile accepted the first IMF mission in 1954, the country swarmed with its "advisors"; and today most of the governments blindly follow its directives. The therapy makes the sick man sicker, the better to dose him with the drug of loans and investments. The IMF extends loans or flashes the indispensable green light for others to extend them. Born in the United States, headquartered in the United States, and at the service of the United States, the Fund effectively operates as an international inspector without whose approval U.S. banks will not loosen their pursestrings. The World Bank, the Agency for International Development, and other philanthropic organizations of global scope likewise make their credits conditional on the signature and implementation of the receiving governments' "letters of intention" to the all-powerful Fund. All the Latin American countries put together do not have half as many votes as the United States in the direction of the policy of this supreme genie of world monetary equilibrium. The IMF was created to institutionalize Wall Street's financial dominion over the whole planet, when the dollar first achieved hegemony as international currency after World War II. It has never been untrue to its master.

It is true that the Latin American national bourgeoisie, with its vocation for living above its income, has done little to stop the avalanche of foreigners; but it is also true that imperialist corporations have used a bewildering range of demolition methods. With the IMF's preliminary bombardment facilitating the penetration, some enterprises were taken by a mere telephone call, after a sharp drop in the stock market, in exchange for a little oxygen in the form of shares, or by calling in some debt for supplies or for the use of patents, brand names, or technical innovations. Such debts, multiplied by currency devaluations—which oblige local enterprises to pay more in national currency for their commitments in dollars—thus become a death trap. Technological dependency costs dearly; the corporations' know-how includes expertise in the art of devouring one's neighbor. One of the last of the Mohicans of Brazilian national industry remarked shortly before the military government sent him into exile: "Experience shows that the profit from sales by a national enterprise often never reaches Brazil, but remains, bearing interest, in the financial market of the purchasing country."[22] The creditors collect by taking over the installations and machinery of the debtors. Banco Central do Brasil figures show that no less than one-fifth of new industrial investments in 1965, 1966, and 1967 was in reality a conversion of unpaid debts into investment.

On top of the financial and technological blackmail is the unfair "free" competition between strong and weak. As part of a global structure, the big-corporation affiliate can permit itself the luxury of losing money for a year, or two, or whatever is necessary. Prices fall, and it sits down to wait for the victim to surrender. The banks collaborate in the siege: the national enterprise is less solvent than it looked, supplies are denied it, and it soon raises the white flag. The local capitalist becomes a junior partner or functionary of his conquerors. Or else he brings off the most coveted feat—he retrieves his property in the form of shares in the foreign concern and ends his days as a well-heeled coupon-clipper. An eloquent story with regard to price "dumping" is that of Union Carbide's capture of the Brazilian tape factory, Adesite. Scotch Tape, part of the multitentacled Minnesota Mining and

Manufacturing, began steadily lowering the price of its products in Brazil. Adesite's sales kept going down. The banks cut off credit. Scotch Tape continued lowering its prices—by 30 percent, then by 40 percent. Then Union Carbide appeared on the scene and bought the desperate Brazilian concern for a song. Later Union Carbide and Scotch Tape got together to share the national market: they divided up Brazil, taking half each, and agreed to digest what they had eaten by raising the price of tape by 50 percent. The antitrust law of the old Vargas days had been annulled years earlier.

The Organization of American States admits that the abundant financial resources of U.S. affiliates "in times of very low liquidity for national enterprises, has on occasion enabled some national enterprises to be acquired by foreign interests." In fact, the scarcity of financial resources, sharpened by the IMF-imposed contraction of internal credit, smothers local factories. But the same OAS document tells us that no less than 95.7 percent—80 percent in the case of manufacturing industries—of the funds U.S. enterprises require for their normal functioning and development in Latin America come from *Latin American* sources in the form of credits, loans, and reinvested profits.

The United States Is Generous with Other People's Savings: The Invasion of the Banks

The siphoning off of national resources into imperialist affiliates is largely explained by the recent proliferation of U.S. branch banks pushing up their heads throughout Latin America like mushrooms after rain. The offensive against local savings in satellite countries is linked with the United States' chronic balance-of-payments deficit, which compels the restriction of its own investments abroad, and with the dollar's dramatic deterioration as a world currency. Latin America provides the saliva as well as the food, and the United States limits its contribution to the mouth. The denationalization of industry has turned out to be a gift.

According to the International Banking Survey, there were seventy-eight branches of U.S. banks south of the Río Grande in 1964. By 1967 there were 133; they had $810 million in deposits in 1964 and $1.27 million in 1967.[23] In 1968 and 1969 the foreign bankers' advance picked up speed: today First National City alone has 110 branches scattered through seventeen Latin American countries—the figure includes various recently acquired local banks. Chase Manhattan Bank acquired the Banco Lar Brasileiro (34 branches) in 1962, the Banco Continental (42 branches, in Peru) in 1964, the Banco del Comercio (120 brances, in Colombia and Panama) and the Banco Atlántida (24 branches, in Honduras) in 1967, and the Banco Argentino de Comercio in 1968. The Cuban Revolution had nationalized twenty U.S. banking agencies, but the bankers more than recovered from this blow: in 1968 alone more than seventy U.S. bank affiliates were opened in Central America, the Caribbean, and the smaller South American countries.

No one knows the precise extent of the simultaneous growth of parallel activities—subsidiaries, holding companies, finance companies, agencies. What is known is that an equal or greater amount of Latin American funds have been absorbed by banks which, while not operating openly as branches, are controlled from abroad through decisive blocks of shares or by the opening of conditional external lines of credit.

This banking invasion has served to divert Latin American savings to the U.S. enterprises established in the region, while national enterprises are strangled by lack of credit. The public relations departments of the various U.S. banks operating abroad unblushingly announce that their chief aim in the countries in which they operate is to channel internal savings into the multinational corporations which are their head offices' clients. Let us indulge in a flight of the imagination: could a Latin American bank establish itself in New York and capture the national savings of the United States? The bubble explodes: such an outrage is expressly prohibited. U.S. banks, through numerous branches, dispose of Latin America's national savings at their pleasure. Latin America watches as the United States takes over its finances as tenderly as does the United States itself. In June 1966, however, the Banco Brasileiro de Descontos consulted its shareholders about a great and vigorous nationalist step which it proposed to take. It printed the phrase *"Nós confiamos em Deus"* on all its documents. The bank pointed with pride to the fact that the dollar bears the motto "In God We Trust."

The credit policies of such Latin American banks as have not been captured, infiltrated, or surrounded by foreign capital follow the same lines as National City, Chase Manhattan, and Bank of America affiliates: they, too, prefer to meet the requirements of foreign industrial and commercial enterprises, which enjoy solid guarantees and operate on a large-volume basis.

An Empire That Imports Capital

The Government Economic Action Program worked out by Roberto Campos anticipated that, in response to such a benevolent policy, foreign capital would flow in to promote development and would contribute to economic and financial stability in Brazil.[24] * New direct investments from abroad of $100 million were announced for 1965; $70 million arrived. There were assurances that the projections for 1965 would be surpassed in succeeding years, but the conjuring was in vain. In 1967, $76 million came in; the flight of profits and dividends, together with payments for technical aid, patents, royalties, and the use of brand names, amounted to more than four times the new investment. And on top of all this there were the clandestine remittances. The Banco Central admits that $120 million left Brazil in 1967 outside of legal channels. As we can see, far more went out than came in. Actually, new investments in the key years of industrial denationalization—1965, 1966, 1967—were well below the 1961 level.† Most U.S. capital in Brazil is invested in industry, but it amounts to less than 4 percent of global U.S. investment in manufacturing. In Argentina it is a bare 3 percent; in Mexico 3.5 percent. Swallowing up Latin America's biggest

* Speaking on December 22, 1966, at Mackenzie University in São Paulo, Campos insisted: "Since economies in the process of organization lack resources to dynamize themselves—for the simple reason that if they had them they would not be backward—it is right to accept the aid of all who want to run with us the risks of the marvelous adventure that is progress, in order to receive from it a part of the fruits."

† According to the Ministry of Planning and Economic Coordination, "The flow of interest, profits and dividends, royalties, and technical assistance payments from Brazil has shown a marked increase since 1965, when legislation altering the foreign investment law of 1962 became effective."[25]

industrial establishments has not meant great sacrifices for Wall Street. It has brought in few dollars and taken out many.

"Under modern capitalism, when monopolies prevail, the export of *capital* has become the typical feature," wrote Lenin.[26] In our day, as Baran and Sweezy have pointed out, imperialism *imports* capital from the countries it operates in. In the period 1950–1967, new U.S. investments in Latin America (not including reinvested profits) totaled \$3.921 billion. Profits and dividends sent abroad in the same period totaled \$12.819 billion. The siphoned-off profits were more than three times the new capital invested in the region.* According to ECLA, the profit bloodletting has since increased to five times the new investments; Argentina, Brazil, and Mexico have suffered the greatest widening of this escape hatch. But this is a conservative calculation. A substantial part of the funds repatriated as debt amortization is in fact identical with profits on investments, and the figures include neither remittances abroad for patents, royalties, and technical-aid payments, nor other invisible transfers customarily concealed under the rubric "errors and omissions."† Nor do these figures take into account the profits that accrue to the corporations when they inflate the prices of the supplies they ship to their affiliates and—with equal enthusiasm—inflate their costs of operation.

The enterprises are equally imaginative with respect to the investments themselves. In effect, as the technical progress fever keeps shortening the periods of fixed capital renewal in advanced economies, most of the installations and factory equipment exported to Latin America have already completed a cycle of their useful life in their place of origin. Thus they have been partly or wholly amortized. This factor in investment abroad is overlooked: the value arbitrarily placed upon machinery is often a small fraction of what it is if the wear it has previously undergone is taken into account. Furthermore, the head office has no reason to involve itself in the expense of producing in Latin America the

---

* President Kennedy has already admitted that in 1960, "from the under-developed world, which needs capital—we took in \$1,300,000,000 and we sent out in capital for investment \$200,000,000. . . ."[27]

† Between 1955 and 1966, for example, the mysterious "errors and omissions" amounted to over \$1 billion in Venezuela, \$743 million in Argentina, \$714 million in Brazil, and \$310 million in Uruguay.[28]

goods formerly sold to it from afar. And Latin American governments undertake to prevent this by advancing resources to the local affiliate, which has access to local credit from the moment it puts up a sign on the lot chosen for its factory. It gets exchange privileges for its imports—purchases the enterprise customarily makes from itself—and in some countries can even be assured of a special exchange arrangement to pay its external debts, which are often debts to the financial arm of the same corporation. A Brazilian magazine estimated that foreign currency input by the auto industry in Argentina between 1961 and 1964 was 3.5 times more than would have been needed to build seventeen thermoelectric and six hydroelectric stations, with a total power of more than 2,200 megawatts; and that it equaled in value the machinery and equipment that the dynamic industries would have to import over an eleven-year period to produce a 2.8 percent annual increment in product per inhabitant.[29]

Technocrats Are Better Hold-Up Artists Than Marines

In taking out many more dollars than they bring in, the enterprises whet the region's chronic dollar hunger; the "benefited" countries are decapitalized instead of capitalized. And here the loan mechanism goes to work. International credit organizations are important in helping to dismantle the weak citadels of nationally capitalized industry and in solidifying neocolonial structures. "Aid" works like the philanthropist who put a wooden leg on his piglet because he was eating it bit by bit. The U.S. balance-of-payments deficit is the result of military spending and foreign aid, and is a critical sword of Damocles over U.S. prosperity. *At the same time,* it makes that prosperity possible: the Imperium sends forth its Marines to save its monopolists' dollars; more effectively, it sends its technocrats and loans to extend business and assume raw materials and markets.

At its global center of power the capitalism of our day exhibits a clear identity of interest between private monopolies and the state apparatus. Multinational corporations make direct use of the state to accumulate, multiply, and concentrate capital, to deepen the technological revolution, to militarize the economy, and by various means to assure success in the crusade to control the capitalist world. The Export-Import Bank (Eximbank), AID, and other smaller organizations function in this role, as do some purportedly international organizations in which the United States has unchallenged hegemony: the International Monetary Fund, its twin the International Bank for Reconstruction and Development (IBRD), and the Inter-American Development Bank (IDB). These assume the right to decide the economic policy of countries asking for credits, pouncing successfully on the countries' central banks and decisive ministers. They get hold of all the secret economic and financial data, draft and impose national laws, and ban or authorize steps proposed by governments whose course they chart down to the last detail.

International charity does not exist; it begins at home, for the United States as for everyone else. The role of foreign aid is primarily domestic—the U.S. economy aids itself—and it was defined by none other than Roberto Campos, when he was the ambassador for Goulart's nationalist government, as a program of broadening foreign markets to absorb U.S. surpluses and alleviate superproduction in U.S. exporting industries. In the early days of the Alliance for Progress, the U.S. Department of Commerce pointed to its successful creation of new businesses and job sources for private enterprise in forty-four states.[30] In January 1968, President Johnson assured Congress that more than 90 percent of U.S. foreign aid in 1969 would be applied to financing purchases in the United States, and that he had personally and directly intensified efforts to increase this percentage. In October 1969 cables sizzled with statements by Carlos Sanz de Santamaría, chairman of the Alliance's Inter-American Committee, who said in New York that the aid had turned out to be excellent business for the U.S. economy and for its treasury. After the disequilibrium of the U.S. balance of payments became critical at the end of the 1950s, loans were conditioned upon buying U.S. industrial goods, usually costing more than similar products from other countries. More recently, certain mechanisms were put into effect, among them "negative lists" to see that the credits are not used for exporting articles which the United States can sell on the world market under good competitive conditions without recourse to auto-philanthropy. Subsequent "positive lists" have made possible the sale through "aid" of certain U.S. manufactures at prices from 30 to 50 percent higher than the same goods from other sources.

"Tied aid" (so called by the OAS document cited earlier) bestows "a general subsidy on U.S. exports." In Brazil, "sales of U.S. capital exporters are faced with increasing competition from other exporters . . . [and] are at a serious disadvantage unless they can take advantage of the more liberal financing available under the various aid programs."[31] When, in a speech late in 1969, Richard Nixon promised to "untie" the aid, he referred only to the possibility of alternative purchases in Latin American countries. Such had been the case with the loans that the Inter-American Development Bank granted and charged to its Special Operations Funds. But experience shows that the United States—or the Latin American affiliates of its corporations—always ends up as the chosen supplier in the contracts. Loans from AID and Eximbank, and most of those from the IDB, also require that at least half of the shipments be made in U.S. bottoms. Freight rates on U.S. ships run as much as double those of other available shipping lines. The firms insuring the transported merchandise, and the banks through which the operations are effected, are also usually U.S.-owned.

The OAS has made a revealing estimate of the extent of *real* aid received by Latin America. When chaff is separated from grain, one must conclude that a mere 38 percent of the *nominal* aid can be considered as *real* aid. Only one-fifth of the authorized total of loans for industry, mining, and communications, and compensatory credits, constitutes aid. In the case of Eximbank, the aid travels from south to north: the financing it extends, says OAS, means not aid but extra costs for the region in view of the inflated prices of U.S. articles exported via the bank.

Latin America provides most of the ordinary capital resources of the IDB. But IDB documents carry the Alliance for Progress emblem in addition to its own insignia, and the United States is the only member country with veto power; the votes of the Latin American countries, in proportion to their contributions of capital, fall short of the two-thirds majority necessary for important resolutions. In his famous report to President Nixon in August 1969, Nelson Rockefeller admitted that "while the United States' veto power over IDB loans has not been used, the threat of its use for political purposes has influenced decisions." On most of the loans it extends, the IDB imposes the same conditions as do openly U.S. organs: the money must be spent on U.S. merchandise, at least half of which must be transported in ships flying the Stars and

Stripes—and the Alliance for Progress is expressly mentioned in the publicity. The IDB determines the tariff and tax policy of the services it touches with its fairy wand: it decides how much must be charged for water and fixes the taxes for water mains and housing on the basis of proposals by U.S. consultants named with its gracious approval. It approves work plans, drafts the bidding terms, administers the funds, and keeps watch on how the job is done.* In the task of restructuring higher education in the region according to the standards of cultural neocolonialism, the IDB has played a fruitful role. Its loans to universities block the possibility of modifying laws and statutes without its knowledge and permission; at the same time, it imposes specific pedagogical, administrative, and financial reforms.† In the case of a difference of opinion, the OAS's general secretary names the arbitrator.

Agency for International Development contracts not only mandate U.S. merchandise and freightage, but also ban trade with Cuba and North Vietnam and make the administrative tutelage of AID technicians obligatory. To compensate for the divergence of price between U.S. tractors or fertilizers and those more cheaply obtainable on the world market, the elimination of taxes and customs duties for products imported with credits is stipulated. AID aid includes jeeps and modern weapons for use by the police in safeguarding law and order in the countries concerned. Not for nothing is one-third of the credits payable immediately, while the other two-thirds are conditional on approval by the IMF—whose recipes normally kindle a fire of social agitation. And as if the IMF had not succeeded in dismantling all the mechanisms of sovereignty as one dismantles a watch, AID generally throws in the requirement of approval of specific laws and decrees. AID is the chief vehicle for Alliance for Progress funds. To cite but one example of the labyrinths of generosity, the Alliance's Inter-American Committee got the Uruguayan government to sign a commitment whereby the income and expenditures of state bodies, and the official policy on tariffs, wages, and investments, would pass under the control of this foreign organization.[32]

---

* For example, in Uruguay, the text of the contract signed on May 21, 1963, between the IDB and the Montevideo departmental government for the extension of water mains.

† For example, in Bolivia, the text of the contract signed on April 1, 1966, between the IBD and San Simón University, Cochabamba, to improve the teaching of agricultural sciences.

But the most pernicious conditions rarely appear in the published texts of contracts and commitments, and are hidden in secret codicils. The Uruguayan parliament never knew that in March 1968 the government had agreed to limit rice exports in that year so that the country could receive flour, corn, and sorghum under the U.S. agricultural surplus law.

Numerous daggers glint beneath the cloak of aid to poor countries. Teodoro Moscoso, who was chairman of the Alliance for Progress, confessed: "It may happen that the United States needs the vote of a particular country in the UN or the OAS, and it is possible that the government of that country [following the sacred tradition of cold war diplomacy] may ask a price in exchange."[33] In 1962 the Haitian delegate to the OAS Punta del Este conference changed his vote in return for a new airport, and thus the United States got its majority in its attempt to expel Cuba.* Ex-director Miguel Ydígoras Fuentes of Guatemala said he had to threaten the United States with withholding his country's vote at Alliance for Progress conferences to make the United States keep its promise to buy more Guatemalan sugar.[35]

It might at first sight seem paradoxical that during the Goulart regime Brazil was the country most favored by the Alliance for Progress. But the paradox vanishes as soon as one realizes the internal distribution of the aid received: Alliance credits were sown in Goulart's path like explosive mines. Carlos Lacerda, governor of Guanabara and at that time leader of the extreme right, got seven times more than all of the Northeast: Guanabara, with scarcely 4 million inhabitants, was thus able to create beautiful gardens for tourists on the shores of the world's most spectacular bay, while the Northeast remained the open sore of Latin America. In June 1964, after the coup d'état that successfully put Castelo Branco in power, Thomas Mann, undersecretary of state for international affairs and right arm of President Johnson, explained: "The United States distributed among the efficient governors of certain Brazilian states the aid that had been destined for the government of Goulart, thinking to finance democracy in this way; Washington

---

* The Duvalier dictatorship was also promised, as a token of gratitude, a road out to the airport. Several authors agree that this was a case of bribery.[34] But the United States did not keep its promise to Haiti, and "Papa Doc" Duvalier, guardian of death in voodoo mythology, felt he had been swindled. The old sorcerer is said to have invoked the Devil's aid to bring vengeance on President Kennedy, and to have smiled contentedly when the bullets in Dallas felled the president.

gave no money for the balance of payments or the federal budget, because that could directly benefit the central government."[36] The U.S. administration had decided to deny any kind of cooperation to Belaúnde's government in Peru "unless it would give the desired assurances of following an indulgent policy towards the IPC. This Belaúnde refused to do and, as a result, by late 1965 he was still not receiving the share of Alliance for Progress funds that his government has earned the right to expect."[37] Later, as we know, Belaúnde compromised—and lost both oil and power: he had obeyed in order to survive. In Bolivia, U.S. loans did not provide a centavo for the country to build its own tin smelter, so that crude tin continued journeying to Liverpool and from there, smelted, to New York. "Aid" gave birth to a parasitic commercial bourgeoisie, inflated the bureaucracy, built large edifices and modern auto highways and other white elephants in a country that competes with Haiti for the highest rate of infant mortality in Latin America. The credits from the United States and its "international" organs denied Bolivia the right to accept Soviet, Czech, and Polish offers to create a petrochemical industry, extract and smelt zinc, lead, and iron, and install smelters for tin and antimony. At the same time, Bolivia was obliged to import products exclusively from the United States. When the Movimiento Nacionalista Revolucionario (MNR) government finally fell, its foundations eaten away by U.S. aid, U.S. Ambassador Douglas Henderson began to attend René Barrientos's cabinet meetings regularly.

The loans indicate as precisely as thermometers the general business climate of each country, and help clear political rainclouds or revolutionary storms from the blue sky of the millionaires. "The United States," announced a group of businessmen led by David Rockefeller in 1963, "will arrange its economic aid program in countries showing the greatest inclination to favor the investment climate, and will withdraw aid from other countries not showing a satisfactory performance."* The text of the foreign aid law provides categorically for the suspension of aid to any government that has

* David Rockefeller's daughter Peggy decided shortly afterward to go and live in a Rio de Janeiro *favela* called Jacarezinho. Her father, one of the world's richest men, went to Brazil to look after his multimillion-dollar affairs and personally visited the humble family house Peggy had chosen; he sampled the modest dinner and discovered with alarm that the house leaked and

"nationalized, expropriated, or acquired property or control of property belonging to any U.S. citizen, or any corporation, society, or association" that belongs not less than 50 percent to U.S. citizens.[38] * Not for nothing does the Alliance for Progress Trade Committee include among its most distinguished members top executives of Chase Manhattan, National City Bank, Standard Oil, Anaconda, and Grace. AID clears the road for U.S. capitalists in many ways—for instance, by requiring approval of agreements guaranteeing investments against possible loss through wars, revolutions, insurrections, or monetary crises. In 1966, according to the U.S. Department of Commerce, U.S. private investors received these guarantees in fifteen Latin American countries, for one hundred projects involving more than $300 million, under the AID Investment Guaranty Program.[39]

ADELA is not a Mexican revolutionary song, but the name of an international investment consortium. It was started by First National City Bank, Standard Oil of New Jersey, and the Ford Motor Company. The Mellon group joined enthusiastically, and so did major European corporations because, as Senator Jacob Javits remarked, "Latin America provides an excellent opportunity for the United States to show, by inviting Europe to 'enter,' that it does not seek a dominant or exclusive position."[40] In its 1968 annual report ADELA offered special thanks to the IDB for the parallel loans it had extended to promote the consortium's

---

rats entered under the door. On his departure he left a check with a string of zeros on the table. Peggy lived there for some months, collaborating with the Peace Corps. The checks kept coming in, each one worth as much as the master of the house could earn by ten years' work. When Peggy finally left, the Jacarezinho house and family had been transformed. Never had the *favela* known such opulence. Peggy had come straight from heaven. It was like having won all the lotteries at once. The master of the house then became the mascot of the regime. TV and radio reportage, newspaper and magazine articles, publicity ran wild: the man was a model whom all Brazilians should imitate. He had emerged from poverty thanks to his indomitable will to work and his capacity to save: look, look, he doesn't spend what he earns on booze, and now he has a TV, a refrigerator, new furniture, shoes for the kids! The propaganda left out one detail: the visit of Peggy, the fairy godmother. Brazil has 90 million inhabitants and the miracle had been performed for only one of them.

* It is no accident that this legal text explicitly refers to measures adopted against U.S. interests "on January 1, 1962, or a later date." On February 16, 1962, Governor Leonel Brizola had expropriated the phone company, a subsidiary of ITT, in the Brazilian state of Rio Grande do Sul, and this had hardened relations between Washington and Brasilia. The firm did not accept the indemnity proposed by the government.

business in Latin America, and also saluted the performance along the same lines of the International Finance Corporation, an arm of the World Bank. ADELA is in continuous contact with both institutions to avoid duplication of effort and to evaluate investment opportunities.[41]

Many more examples of such holy alliances could be given. In Argentina, Latin American contributions to the resources of the IDB have served as very convenient loans benefiting such concerns as the Electric Bond and Share affiliate Petrosur (over $10 million for construction of a petrochemical complex), and The Budd Company (Philadelphia) affiliate Armetal (to finance an auto parts plant). AID credits made possible the expansion of Richfield's chemical plant in Brazil, and Eximbank extended loans to ICOMI, a Bethlehem Steel affiliate in the same country. Also in Brazil, contributions from the Alliance for Progress and the World Bank enabled the Dutch Phillips Industries to install Latin America's biggest complex of fertilizer factories in 1966. It all comes under the heading of "aid"—and all adds further to the weight of external debt on the countries so favored.

In the first days of the Cuban Revolution, Fidel Castro took the problem of rebuilding foreign currency reserves drained by the Batista dictatorship to the World Bank and the IMF; they replied that he must first accept a stabilization program, which implied—as it did everywhere else—the dismantling of the state and a freeze on structural reform.[42] The World Bank and the IMF function in close harmony and for common ends; they were born together at Bretton Woods. The United States has one-fourth of the votes in the World Bank: the twenty-two countries of Latin America have less than one-tenth. The World Bank responds to the United States like thunder to lightning.

As the Bank explains it, most of the loans are for building roads and other communications links, and for developing sources of electrical energy, an essential condition for the growth of private enterprise. In effect, these infrastructure projects facilitate the movement of raw materials to ports and world markets and the progress of already denationalized industry in the poor countries. The World Bank believes that

> to the greatest extent practicable, competitive industry should be left to private enterprise. This is not to say that the Bank has an absolute bar against loans to government-owned industries, but it will undertake such financing only in cases where private capital is not available, and if it is satisfied, after thorough examination,

that the government's participation will be compatible with efficient operation and will not have an unduly deterrent effect upon the expansion of private initiative and enterprise.

Loans are conditional upon application of the IMF stabilizing formula and prompt payment of the external debt, and are incompatible with policies of control of the enterprises' profits, "so restrictive that the utilities cannot operate on a sound basis, still less provide for future expansion."[43] Since 1968 the World Bank has to a considerable extent channeled its loans toward birth-control promotion, educational plans, agro-business, and tourism.

Like all the other one-armed bandits of international high finance, the Bank is also an efficient instrument of extortion for the benefit of very specific circles. Its chairmen since 1946 have been prominent U.S. businessmen. Eugene R. Black, chairman from 1949 to 1962, later became a director of several private corporations, one of which—Electric Bond and Share—is the world's top monopolist of electrical energy.* By chance or otherwise, in 1966 the World Bank made Guatemala accept a "gentlemen's agreement" with Electric Bond and Share as a condition for implementing the Jurún-Marinalá hydroelectric project: the agreement was to pay the firm a fat indemnity for possible damages in a river basin site which had been given it as a present some years earlier, and included a state commitment not to interfere with Electric Bond and Share in its fixing of electricity rates. By chance or otherwise, the World Bank, in 1967, made Colombia pay a $36 million indemnity to the Electric Bond and Share affiliate Compañía Colombiana de Electricidad for its old, recently nationalized machinery. The Colombian state thus bought what belonged to it—but the concession to the enterprise had run out in 1944. Three World Bank chairmen are stars in the Rockefeller power constellation. John J. McCloy, who presided from 1947 to 1949, moved on into a director's chair at Chase Manhattan Bank. His successor, Black, crossed the road in the opposite direction, coming from the Chase Manhattan board. Black was succeeded in 1963 by another Rockefeller man, George D. Woods. By chance or otherwise, the World

* According to Black, "Foreign aid stimulates the development of new overseas markets for U.S. companies and orients national economies toward a free enterprise system in which U.S. firms can prosper."[44]

Bank directly participates—with one-tenth of the capital and substantial loans—in the biggest Rockefeller venture in Brazil: South America's most important petrochemical complex, Petroquímica União.

More than half the loans Latin America receives come—after the IMF's green light—from private and official U.S. sources; international banks also provide an important percentage. The IMF and the World Bank put more and more pressure on Latin American countries to reshape their economies and finances in terms of payment of the foreign debt. But the fulfillment of commitments—the essence of international good conduct—gets more and more difficult and at the same time more necessary. The region is experiencing the phenomenon that economists call the "debt explosion." It is a strangulating vicious circle. Loans increase, investments follow investments, so that payments grow for amortization, interest, dividends, and other services. To pay off these debts, new injections of foreign capital are resorted to, generating bigger commitments, and so on and on. Servicing the debt consumes a growing proportion of income from exports, which in any case, due to the unremitting fall of prices, cannot finance the necessary imports; new loans to enable the countries to supply themselves thus become as indispensable as air to the lungs. In 1955 one-fifth of exports went for amortization, interest, and profit on investments; the proportion has kept growing and is approaching the explosion point. In 1968 these payments amounted to 37 percent of exports.[45] If Latin America continues resorting to foreign capital to fill the "trade gap" and finance the flight of profits on imperialist investment, by 1980 no less than 80 percent of the foreign currency will remain in foreign creditors' hands, and the total debt will be more than six times the value of exports. The World Bank had foreseen that in 1980 debt-servicing payments would completely cancel out the flow of new foreign capital to the underdeveloped world. But in fact the flow of new loans to Latin America in 1965 was already less than the capital drained out merely as amortization and interest to fulfill previous commitments.

The Organized Inequality of the World Market Is Unchanged by Industrialization

The exchange of merchandise, along with loans and direct investments abroad, are the straitjacket of the international division of labor. Third world countries exchange rather more than one-fifth of their exports among each other, and three-quarters of their foreign sales are made to the imperialist centers whose tributaries they are. Most Latin American countries are identified in the world market with a single raw material or foodstuff.* Latin America has abundant wool, cotton, and natural fibers, and a traditional textile industry, but only a 0.6 percent share in European and U.S. purchases of yarns and fabrics. The region has been condemned to sell primary products to keep foreign factories humming; and it happens that those products "are mostly exported by strong consortiums with international connections, which have the necessary world-market relations to place their products under the most convenient conditions"[48]—the most convenient *for them,* suiting the interests of the buyer countries: that is to say, *at the lowest prices.* In international markets there is a virtual monopoly of demand for raw materials and of supply of industrial products, while suppliers of basic products, who are also buyers of finished goods, operate separately. The former, grouped around, and dominated by, the United States—which consumes almost as much as all the rest of the world—are strong; the latter are isolated and weak: the oppressed competing against the oppressed. The so-called free play of supply and demand in the so-called international market does not exist; the reality is a dictatorship of one group over the other, always for the benefit of the developed capitalist

---

* In the three years 1966–1968, coffee earned Colombia 64 percent of its total export income, Brazil 43 percent, El Salvador 48 percent, Guatemala 42 percent, and Costa Rica 36 percent. Bananas earned 61 percent of its foreign currency for Ecuador, 54 percent for Panama, and 47 percent for Honduras. Nicaragua depended 42 percent on cotton, the Dominican Republic 56 percent on sugar. Meat, hides, and wool brought Uruguay and Argentina 83 percent and 38 percent respectively of their foreign currency. Copper was responsible for 74 percent of Chile's commercial income and for 26 percent of Peru's; for Bolivia tin represented 54 percent of the value of its exports, and 93 percent of Venezuela's foreign currency came from petroleum.[46]

As for Mexico, it "depends more than 30 percent on three products, more than 40 percent on five products, and more than 50 percent on ten products, mostly unmanufactured and having their main outlet in the U.S. market."[47]

countries. The decision-making centers, where prices are fixed, are in Washington, New York, London, Paris, Amsterdam, Hamburg, in cabinet meetings and on the stock exchanges. It means little or nothing that international agreements have been signed to protect the prices of wheat (1949), sugar (1953), tin (1956), olive oil (1956), and coffee (1962). A glance at the descending curve of these products' relative value shows that the agreements have only been symbolic excuses offered by strong countries when the prices of the weak countries' products sank scandalously low. What Latin America sells gets constantly cheaper and—also in relative terms—what it buys gets constantly dearer.

For the price of twenty-two bullocks, Uruguay could have bought a Ford Major tractor in 1954; today more than twice as many are needed. A group of Chilean economists who made a survey for the trade unions calculated that, if the price of Latin American exports had risen since 1928 at the same rate as the price of imports, Latin America would have received $57 billion more for its sales abroad between 1958 and 1967 than it actually received.[49] Without going back that far, and taking 1950 prices as a base, the United Nations estimates that due to exchange deterioration Latin America lost more than $18 billion in the decade 1955-1964. The fall continued after that. The "trade gap"—the difference between import needs and income from exports—will continue to widen if present external trade structures do not change, and each year the abyss gets deeper. If in the immediate future the region attempted to slightly step up its development pace over that of the past fifteen years—which has been snail-slow—the import needs it would confront would considerably exceed the foreseeable growth of its foreign currency income from exports. According to the Instituto Latinoamericano de Planificación Económica y Social, the trade gap will rise to $4.6 billion in 1975 and to $8.3 billion in 1980. This last figure is no less than half the value of exports foreseen for that year. Thus the Latin American countries, hats in hand, will be knocking ever more desperately on the doors of the international loan sharks.

Arghiri Emmanuel holds that the curse of low prices does not weigh upon particular products but upon particular countries.[50] After all, coal—until recently one of Britain's chief exports—is no less a raw material than wool or copper, and there is more labor in sugar than in Scotch whiskey or French wine. Sweden and Canada export timber, a raw material, at excellent prices. According to Emmanuel, the world market bases the trading inequality on the exchange of more work-hours in poor countries for less work-hours in rich countries: the key to the exploitation is that while there is an enormous difference between the wage levels of the poor and rich countries, it is not accompanied by differences of the same magnitude in the productivity of the work. It is the low wages that determine the low prices, says Emmanuel, not the reverse: the poor countries export their poverty—further impoverishing themselves in the process—while the rich countries get the opposite result. According to Samir Amin, if the products exported by underdeveloped countries in 1966 had been produced by developed countries with the same techniques but with their much higher wage levels, the prices would have differed to such an extent that the developed countries would have received $14 billion more.[51]

Certainly the rich countries have used and are using tariff barriers to protect their high wage scales in areas in which they cannot compete with poor countries. The United States uses the IMF, the World Bank, and GATT (General Agreement on Tariffs and Trade) agreements to impose the free trade and free competition doctrine on Latin America, forcing the reduction of multiple exchanges, quotas, and import and export permits, and of tariffs and customs duties. But it in no way practices what it preaches. In the same way that it discourages state activity in other countries while protecting monopolies at home through a vast subsidy and privileged-price system, in its foreign trade the United States practices an aggressive protectionism with high tariffs and severe restrictions. Customs duties are combined with other taxes, and with quotas and embargoes. What would happen to the prosperity of Midwest cattlemen if the United States permitted access to its internal market—without tariffs and fanciful sanitary prohibitions—of better and cheaper meat from Argentina and Uruguay? Iron enters the U.S. market freely, but if it has been converted into ingots it pays $16 a ton, and the tariff rises in direct proportion to the stage of refinement. The same is true for copper and countless other products: let bananas be dried, tobacco cut, cacao sweetened, timber sawed, or dates stoned, and tariffs are implacably piled on them. In January 1969, the U.S. government ordered the suspension of purchases of Mexican tomatoes—which give jobs to 170,000 peasants in Sinaloa state—until Florida tomato growers got the Mexicans to raise the price to avoid competition.

But the most startling contradiction between theory and reality in the world market emerged in the open "soluble coffee war" in 1967. It then became clear that *only the rich countries* have the right to exploit for their own benefit the "natural comparative advantages" which theoretically determine the international division of labor. The sensationally expanding soluble coffee market is in the hands of Nestlé and General Foods: before long, it is believed, these two will be supplying more than half the coffee consumed in the world. The United States and Europe buy coffee beans in Brazil and Africa, concentrate it in their industrial plants, and sell it worldwide in soluble form. Brazil, the biggest coffee producer, does not have the right to compete by exporting its own soluble coffee, thereby taking advantage of its obviously lower costs and providing an outlet for the surpluses which it once destroyed and now stores in state warehouses. Brazil only has the right to supply the raw material to enrich foreign factories. When Brazilian factories—a mere 5 in a world total of 110—began offering soluble coffee on the international market, they were accused of unfair competition. The rich countries yelled to high heaven and Brazil accepted a humiliating imposition: it placed a huge internal tax on its soluble coffee to put it out of the running in the U.S. market.

In erecting customs, tax, and sanitation barriers against Latin American products, Europe does not lag behind. The Common Market piles on import duties to defend the high internal prices of its agricultural products, and at the same time subsidizes those products in order to export them at competitive prices: it finances the subsidies with what it gets from the duties. Thus the poor countries pay their rich customers to compete against them. The price of a pound of sirloin in Buenos Aires or Montevideo is multiplied by five when it hangs from a butcher's hook in Hamburg or Munich. As a Chilean government delegate at an international conference justifiably complained: "The developed countries are willing to let us sell them jet planes and computers, but nothing that we have any likelihood of being able to produce."[52]

Imperialist investments in Latin American industry have in no way modified the terms of its international trade. The region continues to die as it exchanges its primary products for the specialized products of metropolitan economies. The expansion of sales by U.S. concerns south of the Río Grande is concentrated in local markets, not in exports. Indeed, the proportion that is exported has tended to shrink: according to the OAS, U.S. affiliates exported 10 percent of their total sales in 1962 and only 7.5 percent three years later.[53] * Trade in Latin American industrial products only grows *inside* Latin America: in 1955, manufactures were 10 percent of the exchange among countries of the area; in 1966 the proportion had risen to 30 percent.

John Abbink, head of a U.S. technical mission in Brazil, had a prophetic moment in 1950: "The United States must be prepared to 'guide' the inevitable industrialization of the undeveloped countries if we want to avoid the shock of intensive economic development outside U.S. aegis. . . . Industrialization, if not controlled in some way, would bring a substantial reduction of U.S. export markets."[56] Indeed, would not industrialization—even though teleguided from abroad—substitute national products for merchandise that each country previously had to import? Celso Furtado has noted that to the extent that Latin America advances in substitution for more complex imported products, "dependence on input from the head offices tends to increase." Between 1957 and 1964, the sales of U.S. affiliates doubled while their imports—apart from equipment—more than tripled. According to Celso Furtado, "This tendency would seem to indicate that 'substitutive' efficiency is a declining function of industrial expansion controlled by foreign countries."[57]

Dependence is not broken but undergoes a qualitative change: the United States today sells to Latin America a greater proportion of more sophisticated and technologically higher-level products. "In the long run," the Department of Commerce says, "as Mexican industrial production goes up, opportunities are greater for additional U.S. exports of industrial raw materials or components. . . ."[58] Argentina, Mexico,

* A thorough survey of U.S. subsidiaries in Mexico, made for the National Chamber Foundation in 1969, showed that half the concerns answering the questionnaire were barred by their U.S. head offices from selling their products abroad. The affiliates had not been set up for that.[54]

The relation between exports of manufactures and gross industrial product did not exceed 2 percent in 1963 in Argentina, Brazil, Peru, Colombia, and Ecuador; it was 3.7 percent in Mexico and 3.2 percent in Chile.[55]

and Brazil are very good customers for industrial machinery, electrical machinery, motors, equipment, and spare parts made in the United States. The affiliates of big corporations supply themselves from their head offices at deliberately inflated prices. As Ismael Viñas and Eugenio Gastiazoro have written about foreign auto concerns in Argentina: "Paying for these imports at very high prices, they sent funds abroad. The payments were often so large that the enterprises not only showed a loss (despite the prices for which cars were sold here), but began to go bankrupt, with rapid depreciation of shares held in the country. . . . The result was that of the twenty-two enterprises 'established,' ten now remain, some on the brink of bankruptcy."[59]

Thus for the corporations' greater glory their subsidiaries dispose of the scanty foreign currency of the Latin American countries. The operating plan of satellized industry does not differ much from the traditional system of imperialist exploitation of raw materials. Antonio García maintains that "Colombian" export of crude petroleum has in fact always been the physical transfer of crude oil from a U.S. oil field to refining, marketing, and consumption centers in the United States, and "Honduran" or "Guatemalan" banana export has been a transfer by U.S. companies from certain colonial plantations to certain U.S. marketing and consumption areas.[60] But the "Argentine," "Brazilian," and "Mexican" factories—to mention only the most important—also occupy an economic space that has nothing to do with their geographical location. Along with many other threads, they make up an international web of corporations whose head offices transfer profits from one country to another, invoicing sales above or below the real prices according to the direction in which they want the profits to flow.* The mainsprings of external trade thus remain in the hands of U.S. or European concerns, which orient the countries' trade policies according to the criteria of governments and directorates outside Latin America. Just as U.S. affiliates do not export copper to the USSR, nor sell oil to Cuba, neither do they get raw materials and machinery from the cheapest and most convenient sources.

---

* The mechanism is certainly not new. The Anglo meatpacking plant has always run at a loss in Uruguay in order to get subsidies from the state and pyramid the profits of its 6,000 London butcher shops, where each pound of Uruguayan meat sells for four times the price at which Uruguay exports it.[61]

This efficient coordination of global activities, completely outside of any "free play of market forces," is not of course translated into lower prices for local consumers, but into profits for foreign shareholders. The auto industry is a graphic example. Latin American countries offer an abundant and extremely cheap labor force and an official policy in every way favoring expansion of investments—free gifts of land, privileged electricity rates, state rediscounts to finance sales on credit, easily accessible money; and as if this were not enough, some countries have even exempted the companies from income or sales taxes. Control of the market is further facilitated in advance by the magical prestige attached, in the eyes of the middle classes, to makes and models promoted by global publicity campaigns. Yet far from making Latin American-produced cars cheaper than those produced in the companies' home countries, all these factors make them far more expensive. True, Latin American markets are much smaller; but it is also true that in these countries the corporations' appetite for profits is more leonine than anywhere else. A Ford Falcon made in Latin America costs three times as much as in the United States,[62] an Argentine-made Valiant or Fiat more than double its price in the United States or in Italy,[63] and the same goes for the relation between the Brazilian Volkswagen and its price tag in Germany.[64]

The Goddess Technology Doesn't Speak Spanish

Congressman Wright Patman considers that 5 percent of the shares in a big corporation can often suffice for an individual, family, or economic group to control it.[65] If 5 percent is enough to control one of the United States' mighty enterprises, what percentage is needed to dominate a Latin American enterprise? In fact, it can be done with less: the "mixed" company, one of the few remaining objects of pride for the Latin American bourgeoisie, merely adorns foreign power with a national capital participation that may constitute the majority but is never decisive over the foreign elements. Often the state itself goes into partnership with an imperialist enterprise which, thus transformed into a "national" concern, gets all the desirable guarantees and a cooperative—even an affectionate—climate. The "minority" participation of foreign capital is usually justified by the need for technical and patent transfers. The Latin American bourgeoisie, a bourgeoisie of merchants lacking any creative character, umbilically tied to the power of the land, prostrates itself before the goddess technology. If foreign shareholdings (however small) and technological dependence (rarely small) are evidence of denationalization, how many factories can really be considered national in Latin America? In Mexico, for example, foreign owners of the technology often demand shares in an enterprise, in addition to decisive technical and administrative controls, the sale of the product to specific foreign middlemen, and the importation of machinery and other goods from their head offices, in return for contracts to transmit patents or "know-how."[66] And not only in Mexico. Countries of the so-called Andean Group (Bolivia, Colombia, Chile, Ecuador, and Peru) have worked out a plan for common treatment of foreign capital in the area, stressing rejection of technology-transfer contracts that contain such clauses. But to countries that will not accept the plan, it proposes that foreign concerns holding patents should fix the prices of products resulting from the patents, or ban their export to specific areas.

The first system of patents to protect ownership of inventions was created almost four centuries ago by Sir Francis Bacon. Bacon liked to remark that "Knowledge is power," and it has since become clear how right he was. There is little universality in scientific universals; objectively they are confined within the frontiers of the advanced nations. Latin America does not apply the results of scientific research to its own advantage for the simple reason that it has none; consequently it is condemned to suffer the technology of the powerful, which attacks and removes natural raw materials, and is incapable of creating its own technology to sustain and defend its own development. The transplantation of the advanced countries' technology not only involves cultural—and, most definitely, economic—subordination. It has also been shown, after four and a half centuries' experience of proliferating modernized oases amid deserts of backwardness and ignorance, to resolve none of the problems of underdevelopment. This vast region of illiterates invests 200 times less than the United States invests in technological research. There are less than 1,000 computers in Latin America and 50,000 in the United States; the electronic models and programming languages that Latin America imports are, of course, designed and created in the United States. Latin American underdevelopment is not a stage on the road to development, but the counterpart of development elsewhere; the region "progresses" without freeing itself from the structure of its backwardness and, as Manuel Sadosky points out, the "advantage" of not participating in progress with its own programs and goals is illusory.[67] * The symbols of prosperity are symbols of dependence. Modern technology is received as railroads were received in the past century, at the service of foreign interests which model and remodel the colonial status of these countries. "What happens to us is what happens to a watch that loses time and is not regulated," Sadosky writes. "Although its hands continue moving forward, the difference grows between the time it shows and the real time."

On a small scale, Latin American universities turn out mathematicians, engineers, and programmers who can only find work in exile: we give ourselves the luxury of providing the United States with our best technicians and ablest scientists, who are lured to emigrate by the high salaries and broad research possibilities available in the north. At the same time, whenever a Latin American university or center of higher learning tries to stimulate the basic sciences, to lay the foundations for a technology that is not copied from foreign patterns and interests, a timely coup d'état destroys the experiment on the pretext that it is an incubator of subversion. The University of Brasilia, crushed in 1964, was an example of this. And the truth is that the armor-plated archangels who guard the established order are not mistaken: an autonomous cultural policy, when it is genuine, requires and promotes deep changes in all existing structures.

The alternative is to depend on foreign sources: to imitate, apelike, the advances spread by the great corporations, which monopolize the most modern techniques of creating new products and improving the quality or reducing the cost of existing ones. The electronic brain has infallible methods of calculating costs and profits, and thus Latin

* To illustrate the nature of the developmental illusion, Sadosky cites the testimony of an OAS specialist: "'The underdeveloped countries,' says George Landau, 'have some advantages over developed countries because when they introduce some new process or technique they usually select the most advanced of its type, and thus reap the benefit of years of investigation and the fruit of considerable investments that more industrialized countries had to make to achieve those results.'"

America imports production techniques designed to economize on labor, although it has labor to spare and in several countries the unemployed may soon be the overwhelming majority. And thus our own impotence puts the progress of the region at the will or whim of foreign investors. For obvious reasons, control of the technological levers gives the multinational corporations a hold on other decisive levers of our economy. The head offices never, of course, give their affiliates the latest innovations or promote an independence which would not suit them. A survey made by *Business International* for the IDB concluded that "clearly the subsidiaries of international corporations operating in the region make no significant efforts in the direction of 'research and development.' In fact, most of them lack any department for this purpose and only in very rare cases take on the job of technical adaptation, while another small minority of enterprises—almost invariably located in Argentina, Brazil, and Mexico—undertake modest research activities."[68] Raúl Prebisch notes that "U.S. enterprises in Europe install laboratories and undertake research which helps strengthen the scientific and technical capacity of those countries, something that has not happened in Latin America," and makes a very serious point: "For lack of specialized knowledge ('know-how') on the part of national entrepreneurs, most of the transferred technology consists of techniques that are in the public domain but are licensed as specialized knowledge."[69]

Technological dependence costs dearly in more ways than one: in hard-cash dollars, for instance, although the companies' versatile sleight-of-hand in declaring their remittances abroad makes the amount hard to estimate. Official figures nevertheless indicate that the dollar drain for technical aid to Mexico rose fifteen-fold between 1950 and 1964, while in the same period new investments were not even doubled. Three-quarters of the foreign capital in Mexico today is in manufacturing industry, a rise from one-quarter in 1950. This concentration of resources in industry implies only a reflected modernization, using second-hand technology, for which the country pays as if it were the very latest. The auto industry has drained $1 billion from Mexico in one way or another, but a United Auto Workers leader wrote after touring the new General Motors in Toluca: "It was worse than archaic. Worse, because it was deliberately archaic, with the obsolescence carefully built in. . . . Mexico's plants are deliberately equipped with low-production machinery."[70] * What should we say of the gratitude Latin America owes to Coca-Cola and Pepsi, which collect astronomical industrial licensing fees from their concessionaries for providing them with a paste that dissolves in water and is mixed with sugar and carbonation?

Surplus People, Surplus Regions

"Grow with Brazil." Display ads in New York newspapers exhort U.S. businessmen to join the precipitous growth of the giant of the tropics. The city of São Paulo sleeps with its eyes open. The din of development shatters its eardrums; factories and skyscrapers, bridges and highways, sprout with the suddenness of tropical plants. But if accuracy had a place in publicity, the slogan would be: "Grow *at the expense of* Brazil." Despite its deceptive splendors, this development is a banquet to which few are invited and whose main dishes are reserved for foreign stomachs. Brazil already had 90 million inhabitants and will double that number by the end of the century, but its modern factories economize on labor and, in the hinterland, the intact latifundio is no more promising a source of jobs. A small boy in rags gazes with shining eyes at the world's longest tunnel, recently opened in Rio de Janeiro. The ragged boy is rightly proud of his country, but he is illiterate and steals in order to eat.

Throughout Latin America the invasion of foreign capital for manufacturing, received with so much enthusiasm, has sharpened the contrast between "classical models" of industrialization as described by the developed countries' historians, and the process characteristic of our part of the world. The system vomits men, but in Latin America industry sacrifices labor more than it does in Europe. There is no coherent relation between the labor available and the technology applied, unless the convenience of using one of the world's cheapest labor forces can be

* The foreign affiliates are, however, far more modern than the national enterprises. For example, in the textile industry—one of the last bastions of national capital—the degree of automation is abysmally low. According to ECLA reports, in 1962 and 1963 four European countries invested six times more in new equipment for their textile industries than all of Latin America invested for that purpose in 1964.

so described. Rich land, richer subsoil, poverty-stricken people, in this kingdom of abundance and dereliction: the legion of workers the system sweeps onto the roadside frustrates the development of an internal market and holds down the wage level. The perpetuation of the established landholding system not only aggravates the chronic problem of low rural productivity through waste of land and capital in large unproductive haciendas, and of labor in proliferating minifundios; it also involves a copious and increasing stream of unemployed workers toward the cities. Rural underemployment turns into urban underemployment. Bureaucracy grows, slums spread out as bottomless sewers for people robbed of the right to work. Factories cannot absorb the surplus labor, but the existence of this huge, always available reserve army keeps wages fifteen or twenty times lower than those of workers in the United States or Germany. Wages can remain low while productivity rises, and productivity rises at the expense of cuts in the labor force. The nature of "satellized" industrialization is to exclude: in this region with the highest demographic growth rate on earth, the masses multiply at dizzying speed but the development of dependent capitalism—a voyage with more shipwrecks than navigators—marks many more people "surplus" than it is able to use. The proportion of workers in manufacturing industry to Latin America's active population falls rather than rises: in the 1950s, 14.5 percent were factory workers; today it is only 11.5 percent. In Brazil, according to a recent study, the total number of new jobs that need to be created will average 1.5 million *a year* during the next decade.[71] Yet the total number of workers employed by factories in Brazil, Latin America's most industrialized country, is barely 2.5 million.

A myriad of laborers flees the poorest areas of each country: the cities attract and cheat whole families with hopes of work, of a chance to better their condition, of a place in the magic circle of urban civilization. But hallucinations do not fill stomachs. The city makes the poor even poorer, cruelly confronting them with mirages of wealth to which they will never have access—cars, mansions, machines as powerful as God or the Devil—while denying them secure jobs, decent roofs over their heads, full plates on the midday dinner table. At least 25 percent of Latin American city populations, according to a United Nations estimate, live in "quarters that fall short of modern standards of urban construction"[72]—a technician's lengthy euphemism for slums: the *favelas* of Rio de Janeiro, the *callampas* of Santiago de Chile, the *jacales* of Mexico, the *barrios* of Caracas, the *barriadas* of Lima, the *villas miserias* of Buenos Aires, and the *cantegriles* of Montevideo. In tin, mud, and board, hovel-colonies on the cities' outskirts sprout new additions every night; the marginal populations drawn by poverty and hope keep piling up. *Huaico* means landslide in the Quechua language, and that is what Peruvians call the human avalanche let loose from the mountains upon the coastal capital: nearly 70 percent of Lima's inhabitants come from the provinces. In Caracas they are called *toderos* because they do a bit of everything (*todo*). The surplus people get an occasional nibble at a job, or perform sordid or illegal tasks; they become servants, sell lemonade or what-have-you, get pick-and-shovel or bricklaying or electrical or sanitary or wall-painting odd-jobs, beg, steal, mind parked cars—available hands for whatever turns up. Since the human surplus grows faster than the "integrated" element, the United Nations survey foresees that within a few years "the makeshift camps will house the majority of the urban population." *The defeated will be the majority.* Meanwhile, the system prefers to hide the dirt under the rug. It is clearing the *favelas* from the bay area and the *villas miserias* from the national capital at gunpoint, sweeping the human surplus out of sight by the thousands upon thousands. Rio de Janeiro and Buenos Aires conjure away the spectacle of the poverty the system produces: soon only the mastications of prosperity, but not its excrement, will be seen in these cities where the wealth created by all of Brazil and Argentina is squandered.

The international system of domination suffered by each country is reproduced within each. The concentration of industry in particular areas reflects the previous concentration of demand in the big ports or export zones. Eighty percent of Brazilian industry is located in the southeastern triangle—São Paulo, Rio de Janeiro, and Belo Horizonte—while the famished Northeast participates less and less in the national industrial product. Two-thirds of Argentine industry is in Buenos Aires and Rosario. Montevideo embraces three-quarters of Uruguayan industry, as do Santiago and Valparaíso in Chile. In Lima and its port is concentrated 60 percent of Peruvian industry.[73] The growing relative backwardness of the great hinterlands, submerged in poverty, is not, as some maintain, due to their isolation, but on the contrary to direct or indirect exploitation by the old colonial centers now converted into industrial centers. According to an Argentine trade union leader: "A century and a half of our history has witnessed the violation of all the solidarity agreements, the breaking of the faith sworn in hymns and constitutions, the domination of the provinces by Buenos Aires. Armies and customs houses, laws made by few and endured by many, governments that with some exceptions have been agents of foreign powers, built this proud metropolis that accumulates wealth and power. But if we seek the explanation of that grandeur and the penalty of that pride, we will find it in the missionaries' *yerba mate* plantations, in the dead communities of the Forestal Land, Timber, and Railways Company, in the despair of Tucumán sugarmills and Jujuy mines, in the abandoned ports of the Paraná, in the exodus from Berisso:* a whole map of misery surrounding a center of opulence secured by the exercise of an internal domination which can no longer be dissimulated or accepted."[74] In his study of the development of Brazilian underdevelopment, Andre Gunder Frank observed that while Brazil is a U.S. satellite, the Northeast plays internally the role of satellite to the "internal metropolis" located in the southeast. The polarization shows itself in numerous phenomena: not only in the concentration of the immense majority of private and public investments in São Paulo, but also in the city's fraudulent appropriation—through unfavorable trade exchange, an arbitrary price policy, privileged internal tax scales, and a massive cornering of skilled brain and labor power—of capital generated in the whole country.

Dependent industrialization further concentrates income at the regional and social level. The wealth it generates does not spread through the whole country or the whole society, but consolidates and deepens existing inequalities. Not even its own—ever less numerous—"integrated" workers benefit to an equal extent from industrial growth; the fruits of higher productivity, bitter for so many, go to the highest strata of the social pyramid. In Brazil between 1955 and 1966, the mechanical, electrical, communications, and auto industries raised productivity by about 130 percent, but in the same period their workers' wages only grew 6 percent in real value. Latin America offers cheap labor: in 1961 the

* Berisso is a meatpacking center with high unemployment. (Trans.)

average hourly wage in the United States was $2; in Argentina it was $.32, in Brazil $.28, in Colombia $.17, in Mexico $.16, and in Guatemala barely $.10. Since then the gap has widened. To earn what a French worker gets in one hour, the Brazilian now has to work 2.5 days. A little more than ten hours' work gets the U.S. worker the equivalent of a month's work by a Brazilian. And to earn more than a Rio de Janeiro worker gets for an eight-hour day, the British or German workers puts in less than half an hour. Latin America's low wage scale is reflected in the low prices the region gets for its raw materials in the international market, to the benefit of consumers in the rich countries. In the internal markets, where denationalized industry sells manufactured goods, prices are kept high to maintain the inflated profits of the imperialist corporations.

All economists agree on the importance of growing demand as a catapult of industrial development. But Latin America's foreign-dominated industry shows no interest in widening and deepening the mass market, for this could only be achieved on the basis of practical steps to transform the socioeconomic structure, which would involve troublesome political storms. With trade unions dominated or annihilated or tamed in the more industrialized cities, the growth of a wage earner's purchasing power is too small, and prices of industrial articles do not go down. This, then, is a vast region with an enormous *potential* market and a *real* market shrunken by the poverty of its masses. The consumers to whom big auto and refrigerator plants direct their products are only 5 percent of the Latin American population. Hardly one in four Brazilians can really be considered a consumer. Forty-five million Brazilians have the same combined income as 900,000 privileged citizens at the other end of the social scale.[75]*

---

* According to this same ECLA study, "A significant process of progressive income redistribution took place in Argentina in the years prior to 1953. Of the three years for which more detailed information is available, this was precisely the one in which there was least inequality, while it was much greater in 1959 . . . in Mexico, in the more extended period from 1940 to 1964 . . . there are indications to suggest that the loss was not only relative but also absolute for 20 percent of the lowest-income families."

THE INTEGRATION OF LATIN AMERICA UNDER THE STARS AND STRIPES

Some innocents still believe that all countries end at their frontiers. They say that the United States has little or nothing to do with Latin American integration, for the simple reason that the United States is not a member of the Latin American Free Trade Area (LAFTA), or of the Central American Common Market. Integration, they say, is as the liberator Simón Bolívar wanted it: it goes no further than the border separating Mexico from its powerful northern neighbor. Those who sustain this seraphic notion suffer from a form of amnesia which may not be wholly disinterested. They forget that a legion of pirates, merchants, bankers, Marines, technocrats, Green Berets, ambassadors, and captains of industry have, in a long black page of history, taken over the life and destiny of most of the peoples of the south, and that at this moment Latin America's industry lies at the bottom of the Imperium's digestive apparatus. "Our" union makes "their" strength to the extent that our countries, not having broken from the molds of underdevelopment and dependence, integrate their own respective serfdoms.

Official LAFTA documents exalt the role of private capital in the development of integration—and we have seen in previous chapters in whose hands that private capital lies. In mid-April 1969, the Consultative Council on Business Affairs met in Asunción. Among other things, it reaffirmed "the orientation of the Latin American economy, in the sense that economic integration of the zone must be achieved fundamentally on the basis of the development of private enterprise." It recommended that the governments introduce common legislation for the formation of "multinational enterprises, made up predominantly [sic] of capital and entrepreneurs from the member states." All the keys were handed over to the thief. Back in April 1967, in the final declaration of the Punta del Este conference—on which Lyndon Johnson himself placed his golden seal—the creation of a common market of shares was even proposed, a kind of integration of stock exchanges, so that enterprises located anywhere in Latin America could be purchased anywhere in Latin America. Official documents went so far as to recommend openly the denationalization of public enterprises. The first gathering of the meat industry within LAFTA, in Montevideo in April

1969, resolved "to request the governments . . . to study suitable methods to achieve progressive transference of state meatpacking plants to the private sector." At the same time, the Uruguyan government, one of whose members chaired the meeting, pursued an all-out policy of sabotage of the state-owned Frigorífico Nacional packing plant in favor of those privately owned by foreigners.

Tariff disarmament, which is gradually freeing the circulation of merchandise within the LAFTA area, is intended to reorganize the distribution of Latin American production centers and markets for the benefit of the great multinational corporations. The "escalation economy" now prevails: the first phase, carried out during these recent years, has seen the consolidation of foreign power over the launching platforms—the industrialized cities—from which the regional market as a whole is to be dominated. The enterprises in Brazil with the greatest interest in Latin American integration are precisely the foreign ones and, above all, the most powerful ones.[76] Of the multinational corporations—mostly U.S.-owned—replying to an all-Latin American questionnaire sent out by the IDB, more than half were planning or proposing that their activities in the second half of the 1960s be in the extended LAFTA market, creating or strengthening regional departments.[77] * In September 1969, Henry Ford II announced at a Rio de Janeiro press conference that he wanted to join in the Brazilian economic process "because the situation is very good. Our initial participation consisted of purchasing Willys Overland do Brasil." He said he would be exporting Brazilian vehicles to several Latin American countries. Caterpillar Tractors— "a firm that has always treated the world as one single market," according to *Business International*—took advantage of the tariff reductions as soon as they were negotiated, and in 1965 was already supplying various South American countries with bulldozers and tractor spare parts from its plant in São Paulo. With equal speed, Union Carbide began showering electrotechnical products on Latin American countries from its Mexican factory, availing itself of customs, tax, and advance-deposit exemptions in the LAFTA area.[78]

---

*Sixty-four percent of the enterprises, taking advantage of LAFTA concessions, were exporting within the region chemical products and petrochemicals, artificial fibers, electronic materials, industrial and agricultural machinery, office equipment, motors, measuring instruments, steel pipes, and other products.

The Latin American countries—impoverished, incommunicado, decapitalized, and facing serious structural problems within their own frontiers—progressively dismantle their economic, financial, and fiscal barriers in the monopolies' favor. The result is that the monopolies, which are still strangling each country separately, can move outward and consolidate a new division of labor on a regional scale by specializing their activities by countries and spheres of activity, fixing optimum sizes for their affiliated enterprises, reducing costs, eliminating competitors outside the area, and stabilizing markets. The affiliates of the multinational corporations can point to the conquest of the Latin American market in certain spheres and under certain conditions not affecting the global policies of their head offices. As we saw in an earlier chapter, the international division of labor continues functioning as it always did for Latin America: the changes are only within the region. The presidents declared at Punta del Este that "foreign private initiative will be able to perform an important function to assure achievement of the objectives of integration," and they agreed that the IDB should increase "the sums available for export credits in intra-Latin American trade."

Fortune in 1967 assessed the "enticing new opportunities" which the Latin American Common Market opens to northern business: "In many a boardroom, the common market is becoming a serious element in planning for the future. Ford Motor do Brasil, which makes Galaxies, thinks it could mesh nicely with Ford of Argentina, which makes Falcons, thus deriving economies of scale by producing both cars for larger markets. Kodak, which now makes photographic paper in Brazil, would like to make exportable film in Mexico and cameras and projectors in Argentina."[79] The magazine cited other examples of "rationalizing" or "expanding" operations by corporations such as ITT, General Electric, Remington Rand, Otis Elevator, Worthington, Firestone, Deere, Westinghouse, Air Brake, and American Machine and Foundry. Nine years ago Raúl Prebisch, a vigorous advocate of LAFTA, wrote: "Another argument I often hear, from Mexico to Buenos Aires, passing through São Paulo and Santiago, is that the Common Market will offer foreign industry opportunities for expansion that it does not now have in our limited markets. . . . It is feared that the benefits offered by the Common Market will be taken advantage of principally by foreign industry, and not by national industries. . . . I shared and share this fear, not only in imagination but because I have verified the reality of that fact in practice."[80] This verification did not prevent Prebisch from later signing a document concerning integration in progress in which it is stated that "foreign capital undoubtedly has an important role in the development of our economies,"[81] and proposing that mixed companies be founded in which "the Latin American entrepreneur may participate efficiently and equitably." Equitably? Yes, "equality of opportunity" must of course be preserved. Anatole France aptly said that the law in its majestic equality forbids the rich as well as the poor from sleeping under bridges, begging in the streets, and stealing bread. But it happens that on this planet and in this epoch one enterprise alone, General Motors, employs as many workers throughout the world as the entire active population of Uruguay, and earns in a single year four times as much money as the whole gross national product of Bolivia.

The corporations know, from their experience of previous integrations, the advantages of acting as "insiders" in the capitalist development of other areas. The fact that the total sales of worldwide U.S. affiliates are six times the value of U.S. exports tells its own story.[82] In Latin America as elsewhere, the United States' inconvenient antitrust laws do not apply. Here, with full impunity, countries become pseudonyms for the foreign concerns that dominate them. The first LAFTA implementation agreement was signed in August 1962 by Argentina, Brazil, Chile, and Uruguay, but in fact it was an agreement between IBM, IBM, IBM, and IBM. It eliminated import duties in the four countries on computers and their components, while raising duties on these machines imported from outside the area: IBM "suggested to the governments that if they eliminated duties on trade between themselves, it would build plants in Brazil and Argentina. . . ."[83] Mexico added its signature on the second agreement: this time it was RCA and Phillips (Dutch) which promoted the exemption for radio and TV equipment. And so on. The ninth agreement, in the spring of 1969, divided the Latin American market in electrical generating, transmission, and distribution equipment between Union Carbide, General Electric, and Siemens (German).

The Central American Common Market, an effort to join the rachitic and deformed economies of five countries, has served to blow down with one puff the feeble national producers of cloth, paint, medicines, cosmetics, and biscuits, and to expand the profits and trading orbit of General Tire and Rubber, Procter and Gamble, Grace, Colgate-Palmolive, Sterling Products, and National Biscuit. In Central America, liberation from customs duties has also gone hand in hand with raising the barriers against "external foreign" competition (as it might be called) so that "internal foreign" firms may sell at higher prices and greater profits: "The subsidy received through tariff protection exceeds the total value added by the domestic production process."[84]

No one has a better sense of proportion than these foreign enterprises: their own and other enterprises' proportions. What, for example, would be the point of installing a big auto plant, steel blast furnaces, or an important chemical factory in Uruguay, Bolivia, Paraguay, or Ecuador, with their minuscule markets? The springboard sites are chosen elsewhere on the basis of the size and growth potential of the internal markets. FUNSA, the Uruguayan tire plant, depends substantially on Firestone but it is Firestone's affiliates in Brazil and Argentina that expand with a view to integration. The growth of the Uruguayan plant is braked, applying the same criterion that determines that Olivetti, the Italian firm invaded by General Electric, will make its typewriters in Brazil and its calculating machines in Argentina. "The efficient assignment of resources requires an unequal development of the different parts of a country or region," says Paul Rosenstein-Rodan, and an integrated Latin America will also have its Northeasts and its poles of development.[85] Weighing the eight years of life of the Montevideo Treaty which sparked LAFTA, the Uruguayan delegate said that "differences in degrees of development" between the various countries "tend to sharpen," for the mere increase of trade in an interchange of reciprocal concessions can only augment the previously existing inequality between privileged poles and submerged areas. The Paraguayan ambassador made a similar complaint: absurdly, he said, the weak countries were subsidizing the industrial development of the free trade zone's most advanced countries, absorbing their high internal costs through customs exemptions. He added that the deterioration of the terms of trade punished his country as severely within LAFTA as outside it: "For every ton of products imported from the zone, Paraguay pays with two." The reality, said the spokesman for Ecuador, was that of "eleven countries in different degrees of development, which means greater or lesser capacities to take advantage of the free trade area and leads to polarization of the benefits and handicaps." The Colombian ambassador drew "just one conclusion: the program of liberation benefits the three big countries in conspicuous disproportion."[86] * As integration proceeds, the small countries will be renouncing their customs income—which in Paraguay finances nearly half the national budget—in exchange for the doubtful advantage of receiving, for example, cars from São Paulo, Buenos Aires, or Mexico made by the same firms that sell them from Detroit, Wolfsburg, or Milan at half the price.† This is the solid fact beneath the frictions increasingly provoked by the integration process. The successful emergence of the Andean Pact, bringing together the Pacific nations, is one result of the three big countries' visible hegemony in the broader framework of LAFTA: the small countries propose to unite separately.

But despite all the problems, thorny as they may appear, the markets expand as the satellites keep bringing new satellites into their orbit of dependent power. Under the Castelo Branco dictatorship, Brazil signed an agreement guaranteeing foreign investments which saddles the state with the risks and handicaps of each business deal. Significantly, the official who arranged the agreement defended its humiliating conditions before Congress with the statement that "in the near future Brazil will be investing capital in Bolivia, Paraguay, or Chile and will then need agreements of this type."[89] ** In the Brazilian governments following the coup d'état of 1964, a tendency has in fact developed to assign to Brazil a "sub-imperialist" function vis-à-vis its neighbors. A very influential military clique pictures the country as the great administrator of U.S. interests in the region, and calls on Brazil to become the same sort of boss over the south as the United States is over Brazil itself. In this connection, General Golbery do Couto e Silva has invoked a new

---

* Integration as a simple process of reducing trade barriers will maintain "highly developed enclaves within a generally depressed continent," according to the director of UNCTAD.[87]

† The auto industry is 100 percent foreign in Brazil and Argentina, and mainly foreign in Mexico.[88]

** For example, Uruguay agreed to increase its imports of machinery from Brazil in exchange for such favors as a supply of Brazilian electrical energy to northern Uruguay. Today the Uruguayan departments of Artigas and Rivera cannot raise their consumption of energy without Brazil's permission.

"manifest destiny": "All the more so," wrote this ideologue of "subimperialism" in 1952, "when our manifest destiny does not conflict in the Caribbean with that of our northern elder brothers. . . ." The General is now chairman of Dow Chemical in Brazil. Certainly the desired subdominion structure has plentiful historical antecedents, from the annihilation of Paraguay on behalf of British bankers after the war of 1865 to the sending of Brazilian troops, just a century later, to head the solidarity operation when U.S. Marines invaded Santo Domingo.

Recent years have seen a revival of the competition between the agents for imperialist interests installed in the Brazilian and Argentine governments on the troublesome question of continental leadership. Everything suggests that Argentina is in no condition to resist the powerful Brazilian challenge: Brazil has double the land area and four times the population, produces nearly three times as much steel, double the cement, more than double the electric energy, and renews its merchant fleet fifteen times as fast. Furthermore, in the past two decades, its rate of economic growth has been considerably greater than Argentina's. Until recently Argentina produced more cars and trucks than Brazil, but at the present rate Brazil's auto industry will be three times larger than Argentina's by 1975 and its fleet—equal to Argentina's in 1966—will be as big as that of all Latin America put together. Brazil offers foreign investors its far-flung potential market, its fabulous natural wealth, the strategic importance of its territory—sharing boundaries as it does with all the South American countries except Ecuador and Chile—and all the conditions for U.S. enterprises on its soil to advance with seven league boots. It has cheaper and more abundant labor than its rival: the average wage level is three times lower than in Argentina and the unemployed run into the millions. It is no accident that one-third of the processed and semiprocessed products sold within the LAFTA zone come from Brazil. This is the country called upon to become the axis of all Latin America's liberation or servitude. Perhaps Senator Fulbright was not aware of the full significance of his words when, in public statements in 1965, he attributed to Brazil the mission of directing the Common Market of Latin America.

As Simón Bolívar Prophesied: "We Shall Never Be Happy, Never!"

For U.S. imperialism to be able to "integrate and rule" Latin America today, it was necessary for the British Empire to help divide and rule us yesterday. An archipelago of disconnected countries came into being as a result of the frustration of our national unity. When the peoples in arms won independence, Latin America stood on the stage of history with a common bond of tradition between its diverse regions, territorially united, speaking two languages of the same origin, Spanish and Portuguese. But lacking one essential condition to form one great nation—economic community.

The poles of prosperity that flourished to supply Europe's need for metals and foodstuffs were not interconnected: the ribs of the fan had their vertex across the ocean. People and capital were displaced according to the rising and falling fate of gold or sugar, silver or indigo, and only the ports and the capitals, the leeches of the productive regions, had a permanent existence. Latin America was born as a single territory in the imaginations and hopes of Simón Bolívar, José Artigas, and José de San Martín, but was broken in advance by the basic deformations of the colonial system. The oligarchies of the free trade ports consolidated this structure of fragmentation, which was their source of profit: those sagacious traders could not incubate the national unity that was the essence of the European and U.S. bourgeoisie. Throughout the past century the British, Spain's and Portugal's heirs since before independence, perfected this structure by means of diplomats' white-gloved intrigues, bankers' extortions, and the merchants' capacity for seduction. "For us the fatherland is America," Bolívar proclaimed; but Gran Colombia was divided into five countries and the liberator died defeated: "We shall never be happy, never!" he said to General Urdaneta. Betrayed by Buenos Aires, San Martín stripped off the insignia of command and Artigas, who called his soldiers Americans, went to a solitary exile's death in Paraguay: the Río de la Plata viceroyalty had been divided into four. Francisco de Morazán, creator of the federal republic of Central America, died before a firing squad,* and the

*As Gregorio Bustamante Maceo described it: "He ordered them to ready their arms, bared

waist of America was split into five pieces—Panama, the canal with the rank of republic invented by Teddy Roosevelt, was added later.

Today the world sees the result: any of the multinational corporations operates with more coherence and sense of unity than the congeries of islands that is Latin America, broken up by so many frontiers and such a lack of communication. What integration can be achieved among themselves by countries that have not even been able to integrate internally? Each country suffers from deep fissures in its own body, bitter social divisions and unresolved tensions between its great marginal deserts and its urban oases. The drama is reproduced on the regional level. The railroads and highways, created to transport foreign products by the shortest routes, still bear irrefutable witness to Latin America's impotence or incapacity to make the national dream of its heroes come true. Brazil has no permanent land connections with three of its neighbors, Colombia, Peru, and Venezuela; Atlantic seaboard cities have no direct cable communications with Pacific cities, so that telegrams between Buenos Aires and Lima, or Rio de Janeiro and Bogotá, have to go through New York; the same with telephone communications between the Caribbean and the south. Each Latin American country still identifies itself with its own port—a negation of its roots and real identity—to such an extent that almost all intraregional trade goes by sea: inland transport is virtually nonexistent. Furthermore, the global freight cartel fixes rates and itineraries to suit itself, and Latin America merely endures the exorbitant charges and ridiculous routes. Of the 118 regular shipping lines operating in the region only seventeen fly regional flags; freightage bleeds the Latin American economy of $2.6 billion a year.[92] Thus merchandise shipped from Pôrto Alegre to Montevideo arrives faster if it goes via Hamburg, and the same for Uruguayan wool bound for the United States; freightage from Buenos Aires to a Mexican gulf port is more than 25 percent lower if the shipment goes

---

his head, ordered them to aim, corrected the aim, gave the command to fire, and fell; still he raised his bleeding head and said, I am alive; another volley ended his life."[91]

In the plaza of Tegucigalpa, the band plays light music every Sunday night at the foot of Morazán's bronze statue. But the inscription is wrong; this is not the equestrian likeness of the champion of Central American unity. The Hondurans who went to Paris soon after the shooting to commission a sculptor on the government's behalf spent the money on a spree and ended up buying a statue of Marshal Ney in the flea market. Central America's tragedy rapidly became farce.

via Southampton.[93] Shipment of timber from Mexico to Venezuela costs more than double the shipment of timber from Finland to Venezuela, although the maps still insist that Mexico is closer. A direct shipment of chemical products from Buenos Aires to Tampico in Mexico costs far more than if it is routed via New Orleans.[94]

What the United States set out to achieve for itself, and did achieve, is certainly different. Seven years after their independence, the thirteen colonies had doubled their territory, already extending beyond the Alleghenies to the banks of the Mississippi, and four years after that they forged their unity by creating a common market. Purchase of the Louisiana Territory from France in 1803 again doubled the land area; then came Florida and, at midcentury, the invasion and amputation of half of Mexico in the name of "manifest destiny." Then the purchase of Alaska and the usurpation of Hawaii, Puerto Rico, and the Philippines. The colonies made themselves a nation, and the nation made itself an empire, putting into practice aims clearly expressed and pursued from the remote days of the "founding fathers." While the north of America grew, developing internally within its expanding frontiers, the south developed outwardly and blew into fragments like a grenade.

In the present process of integration we neither re-encounter our origins nor come nearer to our goals. Bolívar prophesied shrewdly that the United States seemed fated by Providence to plague America with woes in the name of liberty. General Motors or IBM will not step graciously into our shoes and raise the old banners of unity and emancipation which fell in battle; nor can heroes betrayed yesterday be redeemed by the traitors of today. It is a big load of rottenness that has to be sent to the bottom of the sea on the march to Latin America's reconstruction. The task lies in the hands of the dispossessed, the humiliated, the accursed. The Latin American cause is above all a social cause: the rebirth of Latin America must start with the overthrow of its masters, country by country. We are entering times of rebellion and change. There are those who believe that destiny rests on the knees of the gods; but the truth is that it confronts the conscience of man with a burning challenge.

Part III

Seven Years After

Seven years have gone by since *Open Veins of Latin America* was first published.

This book was written to have a talk with people. A non-specialized writer wanted to tell a non-specialized public about certain facts that official history, history as told by conquerors, hides or lies about.

The most heartening response came not from the book pages in the press but from real incidents in the streets. The girl who was quietly reading *Open Veins* to her companion in a bus in Bogotá, and finally stood up and read it aloud to all the passengers. The woman who fled from Santiago in the days of the Chilean bloodbath with this book wrapped inside her baby's diapers. The student who went from one bookstore to another for a week in Buenos Aires's Calle Corrientes, reading bits of it in each store because he hadn't the money to buy it.

And the most favorable reviews came not from any prestigious critic but from the military dictatorships that praised the book by banning it. For example, *Open Veins* is unobtainable either in my country, Uruguay, or in Chile; in Argentina the authorities denounced it on TV and in the press as a corrupter of youth. As Blas de Otero remarked, "They don't let people see what I write because I write what I see."

I don't think there is a vanity in the pleasure I have had, as time went by, in seeing that *Open Veins* has not been a mute book.

I know I can be accused of sacrilege in writing about political economy in the style of a novel about love or pirates. But I confess I get a pain from reading valuable works by certain sociologists, political experts, economists, and historians who write in code. Hermetic language isn't the invariable and inevitable price of profundity. In some cases it can simply conceal incapacity for communication raised to the category of intellectual virtue. I suspect that boredom can thus often serve to sanctify the established order, confirming that knowledge is a privilege of the elite.

Something similar occurs, one might add, with a certain militant literature aimed at a public of the converted. For all its revolutionary rhetoric, a language that mechanically repeats the same clichés, adjectives, and declamatory formulas for the same ears seems conformist to me. It could be that this parochial literature is as remote from revolution as pornography is remote from eroticism.

One writes to try and answer the questions that buzz in one's head, obstinate flies that disturb one's sleep; and what one writes can take on collective sense when it coincides in some way with the social necessity for a reply. I wrote *Open Veins* to spread some ideas of other people, and some experiences of my own, which might dispel a little of the fog from questions always pursuing us: Is Latin America a region condemned to humiliation and poverty? Condemned by whom? Is God, is Nature, to blame? The oppressive climate, racial inferiority? Religion, customs? Or may not its plight be a product of history, made by human beings and so, unmakable by human beings?

Veneration for the past has always seemed to me reactionary. The right chooses to talk about the past because it prefers dead people: a quiet world, a quiet time. The powerful who legitimize their privileges by heredity cultivate nostalgia. History is studied as if we were visiting a museum; but this collection of mummies is a swindle. They lie to us about the past as they lie to us about the present: they mask the face of reality. They force the oppressed victims to absorb an alien, dessicated, sterile memory fabricated by the oppressor, so that they will resign themselves to a life that isn't theirs as if it were the only one possible.

Open Veins seeks to portray the past as something always convoked by the present, a live memory of our own day. A search for keys in past history to help explain our time—a time that also makes history—on the basis that the first condition for changing reality is to understand it. This is no catalog of heroes, dressed as if for a masked ball, who die in battle making long solemn pronouncements; rather it probes for the sound and footprints of the multitudes who traced the paths we walk today. *Open Veins* has its roots in reality but also in other books—better books than this one—which have helped us recognize what we are so as to know what we can be, and see where we come from so as to reckon more clearly where we're going. That reality and those books show that underdevelopment in Latin America is a consequence of development elsewhere, that we Latin Americans are poor because the ground we tread is rich, and that places privileged by nature have been cursed by history. In this world of ours, a world of powerful centers and subjugated outposts, there is no wealth that must not be held in some suspicion.

In the years since the first edition of *Open Veins,* history has not ceased to be a cruel mistress to us.

The system has multiplied hunger and fear; wealth has become more and more concentrated, poverty more and more widespread. That is recognized by the documents of specialized international organizations, in whose aseptic vocabulary our oppressed territories are "countries in process of development" and the pitiless impoverishment of the working class is "regressive income distribution."

The international Moloch-machine has kept on grinding: countries at the service of commodities, people at the service of things.

With the passage of time methods of exporting crises are perfected. Monopoly capital reaches its highest peak of concentration, and international domination of markets, credits, and investments makes possible the systematic and growing transfer of contradictions: the outposts pay the price for the prosperity of the centers.

The international market remains one of the master keys to this operation. There the multinational corporations impose their dictatorship—multinational (as Paul Sweezy explains) because they operate in many countries, yet highly and assuredly national in ownership and control. The global organization of inequality is not affected by the fact that (for example) Brazil now exports Volkswagens to other South American countries and to the distant markets of Africa and the Middle

East. In the last analysis it is the German Volkswagen concern that has considered it more convenient to export cars to certain markets from its Brazilian affiliate: the low production costs and cheap labor are Brazilian, the high profits are German.

Nor is the straitjacket magically broken when some raw material manages to escape from the curse of low prices. This has been the case with petroleum since 1973. Isn't petroleum an international business? Standard Oil of New Jersey (now known as Exxon), Royal Dutch/Shell, Gulf. Are they Arabian or Latin American enterprises? Who takes home the lion's share? The hubbub raised against oil-producing countries has in fact been most revealing. They dared defend their prices and immediately became the scapegoats for inflation and unemployment in Europe and the United States. Did the most developed countries ever consult with anyone before raising the price of any of their products? For twenty years the price of oil sagged and sagged. Its paltry market quotation represented a giant subsidy for the world's great industrial centers whose products at the same time got dearer and dearer. Relative to the ceaseless price rises of U.S. and European products, the new price of oil has no more than brought it back to its 1952 levels. Crude oil merely recovered in 1973 the purchasing power it had two decades earlier.

Among the important events of these seven years was the nationalization of oil in Venezuela. It didn't break Venezuela's dependency with respect to refining and marketing, but it opened a new space of autonomy. From soon after its birth the state concern Petróleos de Venezuela took first place among Latin America's 500 biggest enterprises. It began seeking markets apart from the traditional ones and rapidly found fifty new customers.

But as always when the state takes over a country's principal wealth, it is appropriate to ask who runs the state. Nationalization of basic resources doesn't in itself imply redistribution of income for the majority's benefit, nor does it necessarily endanger the power and privileges of the dominant minority. In Venezuela the economy of waste and extravagance continues intact. The neon-lit center is as resplendent as ever with the squandermania of a multimillionaire class. In 1976 imports rose by 25 percent, largely to finance the super-luxury articles which inundate the Venezuelan market. Commodity fetishism as a symbol of power, human existence reduced to competitive and consumer relationships. In the ocean of underdevelopment the privileged minority apes the lifestyle and fashions of the richest members of the world's most opulent societies. In the bedlam of Caracas, as in New York, commodities that are "natural" by definition—air, light, silence—become ever costlier and costlier. "Watch out," warns Juan Pablo Pérez Alfonso, patriarch of Venezuela's nationalism and prophet of the recovery of its oil, "one can die from indigestion as well as from hunger."[1]

I finished writing *Open Veins* in the last days of 1970.

In the last days of 1977 Juan Velasco Alvarado died on an operating table. His coffin was carried shoulder-high to the cemetery by the greatest multitude ever seen in the streets of Lima. Born in a humble house in north Peru's dry lands, General Velasco Alvarado had headed a process of social and economic reforms. It was the deepest and most far-reaching attempt at change in his country's recent history. After the 1968 revolt the military government pushed a genuine agrarian reform and opened a road to recovery of the natural resources usurped by foreign capital. But some time before Velasco Alvarado died, the funeral of the revolution had been held. The creative process had a fleeting life: it ended up strangled by the blackmail of loan sharks and merchants and by the implicit fragility of any paternalistic project with no organized popular base.

On the eve of Christmas, 1977, while General Velasco Alvarado's heart was beating its last in Peru, the fist of another general who in no way resembled him pounded on a desk in Bolivia. General Hugo Banzer, dictator of Bolivia, said NO to amnesty for the prisoners, the exiled, and the fired workers. Four women and fourteen children, who had come to La Paz from the tin mines, then started a hunger strike.

"This isn't the moment," pronounced the wiseacres. "We'll let you know when. . . ."

The women sat down on the floor.

"We're not asking you," they said, "we're telling you. The decision has been taken. Up there at the mine it's a permanent hunger strike. You get born and the hunger strike starts right then and there. And that's where we have to die too. It's slower, but we have to die too."

The government reacted with castigations and threats, but the hunger strike let loose forces that were long pent up. All Bolivia was shaken and showed its teeth. Ten days later there were no longer four women and fourteen children: 1,400 workers and students had gone on hunger strike. The dictatorship felt the ground wobbling beneath its feet. And the general amnesty was won.

Thus two Andean countries crossed the frontier between 1977 and 1978. Further north in the Caribbean, Panama awaited the promised liquidation of the colonial status of its canal after thorny negotiations with the new U.S. government; and in Cuba the people were having a party: the unconquered socialist revolution was celebrating its first nineteen years of life. A few days later in Nicaragua a furious multitude poured out into the streets. Dictator Somoza, son of dictator Somoza, peered out through the keyhole. Various businesses were put to the torch by the angry people. One of them, Plasmaféresis by name, specialized in vampirism. This concern which went up in smoke at the beginning of 1978 was the property of Cuban exiles, and its business was selling Nicaraguan blood to the United States. (In the blood business, as in all others, what the producers receive is barely a tip. The Hemo Caribbean outfit, for example, pays Haitians $3 per liter of blood, which it resells for $25 in the U.S. market.)

In August of 1976 Orlando Letelier published an article describing the terror of the Pinochet dictatorship and the "economic liberty" of small privileged groups as two sides of the same coin.[2] Letelier, who had been a minister in Salvador Allende's government, was exiled in the United States. There he was blown to pieces shortly afterwards.[3] He submitted in his article that it was absurd to talk of free competition in an economy such as Chile's, subjected to the monopolies which play with prices at their whim, and laughable to mention workers' rights in a country where genuine unions are outside the law and the military junta fixes wages by decree. Letelier described the massive destruction of gains made by the Chilean people during the Popular Unity government. The dictatorship had returned to their former owners half of the industrial monopolies and oligopolies which Allende nationalized, and put the other half up for sale. Firestone had bought the national tire factory, Parsons and Whittemore, a big paper plant. The Chilean economy, wrote Letelier, is more concentrated and monopolized now than on the eve of the Allende government.[4] *Business free as never before, people in jail as never before; in Latin America free enterprise is incompatible with civil liberties.* Free market? The price of milk has not been controlled in Chile since early in 1975. The result is as expected. Two firms dominate the market. The price of milk for consumers went up immediately by 40 percent, while for the producers it went down by 22 percent.

Infant mortality, substantially reduced during the Popular Unity regime, rose dramatically with Pinochet. When Letelier was assassinated in a Washington street, one quarter of Chile's population was getting no income and survived thanks to foreign charity or their own stubbornness and guile.

The abyss that exists in Latin America between the well-being of the few and the misery of the many is infinitely greater than in Europe or the United States. Hence the methods necessary to maintain it are much more ruthless. Brazil has an enormous and excellently equipped army but devotes only 5 percent of the national budget to education. In Uruguay half the budget now goes for the armed forces and police, and the function of one fifth of the active population is to watch, trail, and punish the others.

Undoubtedly among Latin America's most important and tragic events of these years of the seventies was the military insurrection that overthrew Salvador Allende's democratic government on September 11, 1973, and submerged Chile in a bath of blood.

A little earlier, in June, a coup d'état in Uruguay had dissolved the parliament, put unions outside the law, and banned all political activity.[5]

In March of 1976 the Argentine generals returned to power: the government of Juan Domingo Perón's widow had become a stench and it fell, unregretted and unsung.

The three southern countries are today a festering sore upon the globe, cronic bad news. Torture, kidnapping, murder, and exile have become the daily round. These dictatorships are tumors to be extirpated from healthy organs—or are they the pus that betrays the infection of the system?

There is always, I believe, a close relationship between the intensity of the threat and the brutality of the response. I doubt if present events in Brazil and Bolivia can be grasped without taking into account the experience of the João Goulart and Juan José Torres regimes. Before they fell, these governments had put into effect a series of social reforms and promoted a nationalist political economy, during a process that was cut off in 1964 in Brazil and in 1971 in Bolivia. *In the same way we could well say that Chile, Argentina, and Uruguay are expiating the sin of hope.* The cycle of deep changes under Allende, the banners of justice that mobilized Argentina's working masses and rose high during the short-lived Héctor Cámpora government in 1973, and the stepped-up politicization of Uruguayan youth, were all challenges not to be tolerated by a system that was impotent and in crisis. The potent oxygen of liberty was explosive for the specters, and the pretorian guard was summoned to save law and order. The clean-up plan is a plan of extermination.

The Congressional Record of the United States is replete with irrefutable evidence of interventions in Latin America. Guilt-ridden consciences purge themselves in the imperial confessionals. Recently official admissions of U.S. responsibility for various disasters have multiplied. Full public confessions have proved among other things that the U.S. government directly participated in Chilean politics by bribery, espionage, and blackmail. The strategy for the crime was planned in Washington. Kissinger and the intelligence services were carefully preparing the fall of Allende ever since 1970. Millions of dollars were distributed among enemies of the legal Popular Unity government. That, for example, was how the truck owners in 1973 could keep going their long strike which paralyzed much of the country's economy. The assurance of impunity loosens tongues. When the coup took place against Goulart, the United States had in Brazil its largest embassy anywhere on earth. Lincoln Gordon, the ambassador, admitted to a journalist thirteen years later that his government had long been financing the forces opposing the reforms. "What the hell," said Gordon, "that was more or less a habit in those days. . . . The CIA used to dole out political funds."[6] In the same interview Gordon explained that when the coup took place the Pentagon had a huge aircraft carrier and four supply ships stationed off the Brazilian coast "in case the anti-Goulart forces should ask for our help." That help, he said, "wouldn't be just moral. We would back them up logistically, with supplies, munitions, oil."

Since President Jimmy Carter announced a policy of human rights, it has become the custom for Latin American regimes imposed by U.S. intervention to formulate indignant pronouncements against U.S. intervention in their internal affairs.

The U.S. Congress resolved in 1976 and 1977 to suspend economic and military aid to various countries. But most U.S. external aid doesn't go through the congressional filter. So despite pronouncements, resolutions, and protests General Pinochet's regime got $290 million of direct U.S. aid in 1976 without congressional authorization. When General Videla's dictatorship in Argentina was a year old it had received $500 million from private U.S. banks and $415 million from two institutions (World Bank and Bank for International Development) in which the United States has decisive influence. Argentina's special rights for International Monetary Fund loans, $64 million in 1975, had risen to $700 million two years later.

President Carter's concern about the butchery in some Latin American countries seems healthy, but the present dictators are not self-taught: they have learned the techniques of repression and the arts of government at academies run by the Pentagon in the United States and the Panama Canal Zone. These courses are still being given today, and no change is known to have been made in their content. The Latin American military men who are now causing a scandal in the United States have been good pupils. A few years ago when he was defense secretary, Robert McNamara, now president of the World Bank, spelled it out: "They are the new leaders. I don't need to expatiate on the value of having in leadership positions men who have previously become closely acquainted with how we Americans think and do things. Making friends with those men is beyond price."[7]

One wonders if those who made us paralytic might offer us a wheelchair?

The bishops of France speak about another sort of responsibility, deeper and less visible: "We, who belong to nations purporting to be the world's most advanced, form a part of those who benefit from exploitation of the developing countries. We do not see the sufferings that this inflicts on the flesh and spirit of entire peoples. We help to reinforce the division of the present world in which the domination of poor by rich, of weak by strong, is conspicuous. Do we know that our squandering of resources and raw materials would not be possible without the control of international exchange by the Western countries? Do we not see who profits from the arms traffic, of which our country has provided sad examples? Do we perhaps understand that the militarization of poor countries' regimes is one of the consequences of economic and cultural domination by the industrialized countries, where life is ruled by the lust for profits and the power of money?"[8]

Dictators, torturers, inquisitors: the terror has its officials, just as it has post offices and banks, and they apply it because it is necessary. It isn't a case of a plot by the perverse. General Pinochet may look like a figure in Goya's "black art," a prize specimen for psychoanalysts, or the inheritor of a savage tradition from the banana republics. But the clinical or folkloric roots of this or that dictator, which provide seasoning for history, are not history. Who would dare maintain today that World War I broke out because of the complexes of Kaiser Wilhelm, who had one arm shorter than the other? As Bertolt Brecht wrote at the end of 1940 in his working diary: "In democratic countries the violent character inherent in the economy doesn't show itself; in authoritarian countries the same holds true for the economic character of violence."

In Latin America's southern lands the centurions have taken over power as a function of the needs of the system: the terrorism of the state is put into action when the dominant classes can pursue their business by no other means. *Torture wouldn't exist in our countries if it weren't effective; formal democracy would continue if it could be guaranteed not to get out of the hands that hold power.* In difficult times democracy becomes a crime against national security—that is, against the security of internal privilege and foreign investment. Our devices for mincing human flesh are part of an international machinery. The whole society is militarized, the state of exception is made permanent, and the repressive apparatus is endowed with hegemony by the turn of a screw in the centers of the imperial system. When crisis begins to throw its shadow, the pillage of poor countries must be intensified to guarantee full employment, public liberties, and high rates of development in the rich countries. *The sinister dialectic of victim-hangman relations: a structure of successive humiliations that starts in international markets and financial centers and ends in every citizen's home.*

Haiti is the poorest country in the Western hemisphere. It has more foot-washers than shoeshiners: little boys who, for a penny, will wash the feet of customers lacking shoes to shine. Haitians, on the average, live a bit more than thirty years. Nine out of every ten can't read or write. For internal consumption the barren mountain sides are cultivated. For export, the fertile valleys: the best lands are given to coffee, sugar, cacao, and other products needed by the U.S. market. No one plays baseball in Haiti, but Haiti is the world's chief producer of baseballs. There is no shortage of workshops where children assemble cassettes and electronic parts for a dollar a day. These are naturally for export; and naturally the profits are also exported, after the administrators of the terror have duly got theirs. The slightest breath of protest in Haiti means prison or death. Incredible as it sounds, Haitian workers' wages lost 25 percent of their wretched real value between 1971 and 1975.[9] Significantly, in that period a new flow of U.S. capital into the country began.

I recall an editorial in a Buenos Aires daily a couple of years ago. An old conservative newspaper was bellowing with fury because some international document depicted Argentina as an underdeveloped country. How could a cultured, European, prosperous, white society be measured by the same yardstick as a poor black country such as Haiti?

Of course the differences are enormous, although they have little to do with the analytical categories of Buenos Aires's arrogant oligarchy. But with all the diversities and contradictions one could mention, Argentina isn't outside the vicious circle that strangles the Latin American economy as a whole. No intellectual exorcism can remove it from the reality that, to a greater or smaller extent, the other countries of the region share with it.

General Videla's massacres are, after all, no more civilized than those of "Papa Doc" Duvalier or his successor to the throne, although in Argentina the technological level of the repression is higher. Essentially both dictatorships act at the service of the same objective: *to supply cheap labor to an international market that demands cheap products.*

Fresh from taking power, the Videla dictatorship hastened to ban strikes and decree freedom of prices while putting wages behind bars. Five months after the coup d'état, the new foreign investment law put foreign and national enterprises on an equal footing. Thus free competition put an end to the unfair handicap suffered by certain multinational corporations vis-à-vis local concerns—for example, poor unprotected General Motors, whose world sales volume equals the entire gross national product of Argentina. Also now liberated, with gossamer limitations, is the remission of profits abroad and the repatriation of invested capital.

When the regime was a year old the real value of wages had fallen by 40 percent. The feat was accomplished by terror. "Fifteen thousand disappeared, 10,000 jailed, 4,000 dead, tens of thousands exiled—that is the naked balance sheet of the terror," as the writer Rodolfo Walsh totted it up in an open letter. Walsh sent the letter on March 29, 1977, to the three chiefs of the governing junta. On the same day he was kidnapped and disappeared.

Unimpeachable sources confirm that a diminutive part of the new direct foreign investments in Latin America really comes from their country of origin. According to a U.S. Department of Commerce survey[10] a mere 12 percent of the funds comes from the enterprises' U.S. headquarters, 22 percent comes from profits made in Latin America, and the remaining 66 percent from internal-credit, and above all international-credit, sources. The proportion is similar for investments of European or Japanese origin. And it must be borne in mind that 12 percent of investment coming from the enterprises' headquarters is often nothing more than the result of transfer of already used machinery or simply reflect the arbitrary appraisal placed by the enterprises upon their industrial "know-how," their patents, and their brand names. Thus the multinational corporations not only usurp the internal credit of countries where they operate, in exchange for a distinctly dubious capital contribution, but also multiply those countries' external debts.

Latin America's external debt in 1975 was almost three times greater than in 1969.[11] In 1975 approximately half of Brazil's, Mexico's, Chile's, and Uruguay's incomes from exports went for amortization and interest on the debt, and for paying the profits of foreign concerns operating in those countries. Servicing of debt and profit remittances in that year swallowed 55 percent of Panama's exports and 60 percent of Peru's.[12] In 1969 every Bolivian owed $137 to foreigners; in 1977, $483. The inhabitants of Bolivia weren't consulted, nor did they see a centavo of those loans that put the rope around their necks.

Citibank doesn't appear as a candidate on any list, in the few Latin American countries that still have elections; and none of the generals who run the dictatorships is named International Monetary Fund. But whose is the hand that executes, whose the mind that gives the orders? He who lends, commands. In order to pay, more must be exported; and more must be exported in order to finance imports and to confront the hemorrhage of profits and "royalties" that the foreign concerns drain into their central coffers. The increase of exports, whose purchasing power shrinks, implies hunger wages. Massive poverty, the key to success for an economy skewed to the outside, prevents such growth of the internal consumer market as is necessary for smooth economic development. Our countries are becoming echoes and losing their own voice. They depend on others, they exist to the extent that they respond to others' needs. And in turn the remodeling of the economy as a function of external demand brings us back to the original hangman's rope: it opens the doors for pillage by foreign monopolies and forces us to seek new and larger loans from the international bankers. *The vicious circle is perfect: foreign debt and foreign investment oblige us to multiply exports that they themselves devour. The task can't be accomplished with gentlemanly matters. To fulfill their function as hostages of foreign prosperity, Latin American workers must be held prisoner, either inside or outside the bars of the jails.*

Savage exploitation of labor is not incompatible with intensive technology. It never was, in our countries: consider the legions of Bolivian workers who left their lungs in the Oruro mines in the time of Simón Patiño in a system of wage-slavery, yet with very modern machinery. The "tin baron" knew how to combine the highest levels of technology in his day with the lowest levels of wages.[13]

Furthermore in our day, importation of the most advanced economies' technology coincides with expropriation of locally capitalized industries by the all-powerful multinationals. The capital-centralizing movement is achieved by "ruthless wiping out of 'obsolete' entrepreneurial levels which, not by accident, are precisely those of national ownership."[14] The speeded-up denationalization of Latin American industry carries with it a growing technological dependency. Technology, the decisive key to power, is monopolized in the capitalist world by the metropolitan centers. It comes to us second-hand but those centers charge for the copies as if they were the originals. In 1970 Mexico paid twice as much as in 1968 for importation of foreign technology. Between 1965 and 1969 Brazil doubled its payments, and so did Argentina over the same period.

Technology transfer swells the astronomical foreign debts and has devastating effects on the labor market. In a system organized to drain off profits abroad, the labor force of "traditional" enterprise has ever less opportunities for employment. In exchange for a dubious shot in the arm for the rest of the economy, the islets of modern industry sacrifice workers as they reduce the labor time necessary for production. The existence of a large and growing army of unemployed in turn facilitates the destruction of the real value of wages.

Even the documents of the UN's Economic Commission for Latin America (ECLA) now talk about a new international division of labor. The technicians hazard the hope that, within a few years, Latin America will perhaps export as much manufactures as it now sells raw materials and food.

> The wage differentials between developed countries and those in development, including Latin America, may bring about a new division of activities between countries, displacing from the former to the latter for competitive reasons those industries in which labor costs are very important. Labor costs for manufacturing industry, for example, are generally much lower in Mexico or Brazil than in the United States.[15]

Sparkplug of progress or neocolonial adventure? Electrical and non-electrical machinery is already one of Mexico's chief exports. And in Brazil, the sale abroad of vehicles and armaments grows. Some Latin American countries are experiencing a new stage of industrialization, largely induced and oriented by foreign needs and the foreign masters of the means of production. Won't this be another chapter to add to our long history of "development toward the outside"? In world markets the constantly rising prices don't correspond generically with "manufactured products" but with commodities of a more sophisticated and technological nature which is exclusive to the more developed economies. *Whatever Latin America sells—raw materials or manufactures—its chief export product is really cheap labor.*

Hasn't our experience throughout history been one of mutilation and disintegration disguised as development? Centuries ago the conquest cleared our lands to plant crops for export and annihilated the indigenous populations in the mines to satisfy the demand abroad for silver and gold. The diet of the pre-Columbian population that could survive the exterminations *deteriorated* as the foreigners progressed. In our day the people of Peru produce fishmeal very rich in protein, for the cattle of the United States and Europe, but proteins are conspicuously absent from the diet of most Peruvians. The Volkswagen affiliate in Switzerland plants a tree for every car it sells—gracious ecological gesture—while the Volkswagen affiliate in Brazil uproots thousands of acres of forest to dedicate them to intensive production of meat for export. The Brazilian people, who very rarely eat meat, sell more and more meat abroad. Recently Darcy Ribeiro remarked to me that there isn't much difference between a "Volkswagen republic" and a "banana republic." For every dollar produced from exporting bananas, just eleven cents remain in the producing country,[16] and of those eleven cents only a meager part goes to the plantation workers. Do the proportions change when a Latin American country exports automobiles?

Slave ships no longer ply the ocean. Today the slavers operate from the ministries of labor. African wages, European prices. What are the Latin American coups d'état but successive episodes in a war of pillage? The dictators hardly grasp their scepters before they invite foreign concerns to exploit the local, cheap, and abundant work force, the unlimited credit, the tax exemptions, and the natural resources that await them on a silver tray.

Employees of the Chilean government's emergency plan get a wage equivalent to $30 a month. A kilo of bread costs half a dollar, so they get two kilos of bread a day. The minimum monthly wage in Uruguay and Argentina is the present equivalent of six kilos of coffee. In Brazil it is $60 a month but the *boias frias,* migrant rural workers, get from fifty cents to $1 a day on the coffee, soybean, and other export-crop plantations. The fodder consumed by Mexican cattle contains more protein than the diet of *campesinos* who tend them. The meat of these cattle is destined for a few privileged mouths within the country and above all for the international market. Agriculture for export flourishes in Mexico beneath the shield of a generous policy of credits and official facilities, while the amount of protein available per inhabitant fell between 1970 and 1976, and in rural areas only one of every five Mexican kids has normal weight and height.[17] In Guatemala rice, corn, and beans for internal consumption are left to the will of God, but coffee, cotton, and other export products absorb 87 percent of the credit. Of every ten Guatemalan families who work at raising and harvesting coffee, the country's chief source of foreign exchange, hardly one gets a minimally adequate diet.[18] In Brazil only 5 percent of agricultural credit goes for rice, beans, and manioc, which constitute the basic diet of Brazilians; the rest goes for export products.

The recent collapse of world sugar prices did not, as it once did, set off a famine among Cuba's *campesinos.* In Cuba malnutrition no longer exists. On the other hand the almost simultaneous rise of world coffee prices did nothing to ease the chronic poverty of Brazilian coffee workers. The rise in coffee prices in 1976—a euphoria brought about by frosts that devastated Brazilian crops— "was not directly reflected in wages," as a high official of the Brazilian Coffee Institute recognized.[19]

Actually export crops are not in themselves incompatible with the welfare of the population, nor do they in themselves contradict an "inward" economic development. Sugar sales abroad have in fact given Cuba leverage to create a new world in which all have access to the fruits of development, and solidarity is the axis of human relations.

So we know who is condemned to pay for the crisis of system-adjustment. The prices of most of the products Latin America sells decline implacably in relation to the prices of what it buys from countries that monopolize technology, trade, investment, and credit. To make up the difference and meet the obligations to foreign capital, *Latin America must cover in quantity what it loses in price.* In this framework the southern dictatorships have cut workers' wages in half and turned every production center into a forced labor camp. *The workers also have to compensate for the fall in value of their labor power, which is the product they sell in the market. They must make up in quantity—quantity of hours—what they lose in purchasing power of their wages. The laws of the international market are thus reproduced in the microworld of every Latin American worker's life.* For workers who have "the luck" to count on a regular job, the eight-hour day exists only in the dead letter of the laws. They often work ten, twelve, even fourteen hours; and not a few have lost their Sundays.

Simultaneously on-the-job accidents have multiplied—human blood offered on the altar of productivity. Three examples in Uruguay at the end of 1977:

• Railroad quarries producing stones and ballast double their output. In early spring, fifteen workers die in a gelignite explosion.

• Lines of unemployed outside a fireworks factory; children working on the production lines; records broken. On December 20, an explosion: five workers dead, dozens wounded.

• At 7 a.m. on December 28, workers refuse to enter a fish-canning factory because they smell a strong odor of gas. They are threatened: if they don't go in, they lose their jobs. They continue to refuse. Renewed threats: we'll call in the army. The firm has already summoned the army on other occasions. The workers enter. Four dead, many hospitalized. Ammonia gas was escaping.[20]

Maria Carolina de Jesus was born amid garbage and vultures.

She grew, suffered, worked hard; loved men, had kids. She kept a notebook where she jotted down, in crude handwriting, an account of her tasks and her days.

A journalist happened to read the notebooks and Maria Carolina de Jesus became a famous writer. Her book *Quarto de Despejo,** diary of five years in a sordid São Paulo slum, was read in forty countries and translated into thirteen languages.

A Cinderella in Brazil, transformed into a global consumer product, Maria Carolina de Jesus left the slum to tour the world, be interviewed and photographed and garlanded by critics, regaled by the gentry and received by presidents.

---

* Published in English as *Child of the Dark* (New York: Dutton, 1962).

The years passed. Early in 1977, on a Sunday morning, Maria Carolina de Jesus died, amid garbage and vultures. No one remembered the woman who had written: "Hunger is the dynamite of the human body."

She who had lived on leftovers could ephemerally become one of the elect. She was allowed to sit at the table. After the dessert, the magic was broken. And while her dream lasted, Brazil had continued to be a country where one hundred workers are injured every day in work accidents and where four of every ten children are obliged from birth to become beggars, thieves, or magicians.

The statistics may wear a smile, but the people get taken. In systems organized upside down, when the economy grows, social injustice grows with it. In the most successful phase of the Brazilian "miracle," infant mortality rose in the slums of the country's wealthiest city. The sudden oil boom in Ecuador brought color TV instead of schools and hospitals.

The cities swell up to the point of explosion. In 1950 Latin America had six cities with a population of more than a million. In 1980 it will have twenty-five.[21] On the edges of great urban centers the hordes of workers expelled from the countryside share the fate that the system reserves for "surplus" city youth. In the Latin American picaresque style the hustlers perfect ways to survive. "The productive system has demonstrated patent insufficiency to generate productive employment which absorbs the region's growing labor force, especially the large contingents of urban labor. . . ."[22]

An International Labor Organization study recently showed that Latin America has more than 110 million persons in a condition of "serious poverty." Seventy million of them can be considered "indigent."[23] What percentage of the population eat less than they need? In the technicians' language, those receiving "incomes below the cost of minimal balanced diet" are 42 percent of the population of Brazil, 43 percent of Colombians, 49 percent of Hondurans, 31 percent of Mexicans, 45 percent of Peruvians, 29 percent of Chileans, 35 percent of Ecuadoreans.[24]

How to stifle the rebellious explosion of the great condemned majorities? How to head off those explosions? How to avoid those majorities becoming ever larger, if the system doesn't function for them? Leaving aside charity, the police remains.

In our countries the terror industry pays dearly, like any other, for foreign "know-how." U.S. repression technology, tested at the four corners of the earth, is bought and applied. But it would be unjust not to credit Latin America's ruling classes with a certain creative capacity in this field.

Independent economic development was beyond the capacity of our bourgeoisies, and their attempts to create a national industry had a short low flight, like a hen's. Throughout our historical process the masters of power have likewise demonstrated their lack of political imagination and their cultural sterility. On the other hand they did know how to set up a giant fear machine and have made their own contributions to the technique of exterminating persons and ideas. In this sense the recent experience of the Río de la Plata countries is revealing.

"The task of disinfection will take us a long time," the Argentine brass warned when they took the stage. The armed forces were successively summoned by Uruguay's and Argentina's ruling classes to crush the forces of change, tear them up by the roots, perpetuate the internal orders of privilege, and generate economic and political conditions that would seduce foreign capital: scorched earth, tranquility and order, workers cheap and meek. There is nothing more orderly than a cemetery. The population immediately became the internal enemy. Any sign of life, of protest, or even mere doubt, is a dangerous challenge from the standpoint of military doctrine and national security. So complicated mechanisms of prevention and punishment have been developed.

A deep rationality lurks behind appearances. *To operate effectively, the repression must appear arbitrary.* Apart from breathing, any human activity can constitute a crime. In Uruguay torture is applied as a routine system of interrogation: *anyone may be its victim*, not only those suspected or guilty of acts of opposition. *In this way panic fear of torture is spread through the whole population, like a paralyzing gas that invades every home and implants itself in every citizen's soul.*

In Chile the hunt for human prey left a balance of 30,000 dead, but in Argentina they don't shoot: they kidnap. The victims "disappear." The invisible armies of the night carry out the task. There are no corpses and no one is responsible. In this way the bloodbath has the more impunity for not being "official," *and thus collective anxiety is more potently spread around. No one renders accounts, no one offers explanations.*

Each crime builds horrible uncertainty in persons close to the victim and is also a warning for everyone else. State terrorism aims to paralyze the population with fear.

To get a job and keep it in Uruguay, one needs to stay in the good graces of the military. In a country where it's so tough to find work outside of the barracks and police stations, this not only serves to drive into exile a good part of the 300,000 citizens listed as leftists. *It is also useful as a threat hanging over those who stay.* Montevideo newspapers often feature public penitences and declarations by citizens who beat their breasts just in case: "I have never been, I am not, I never will be. . . ."

In Argentina it is no longer necessary to ban any book by decree. The new Penal Code penalizes, as always, the writer and publisher of a book considered subversive. But it also penalizes the printer (so that no one will dare to print a text that is merely doubtful) and the distributor and the bookstore (so that no one will dare sell it); and as if this weren't enough, it also penalizes the reader, so that no one will dare read it, much less keep it. Thus the consumer of a book gets the same treatment the law applies to consumers of drugs.[25] *In this program for a society of deaf mutes, each citizen has to become his own Torquemada.*

In Uruguay it is a crime not to inform on your neighbor. Students entering the university swear in writing that they will denounce anyone who indulges on campus in "any activity outside the functions of study." The student assumes co-responsibility for whatever occurs in his presence. *In this program for a society of sleepwalkers, all citizens must be their own and others' policeman.* However, the system—with good reason—is mistrustful. There are 100,000 police and soldiers in Uruguay, but there are also 100,000 informers. Spies work the streets, cafes and buses, factories and high schools, offices and the university. Anyone voicing a complaint about life being so expensive and so hard ends up in jail: he or she has committed a "crime against the moral force of the Armed Forces," for which the price is three to six years behind bars.

In the January 1978 referendum, one voted "Yes" for the Pinochet dictatorship by marking a cross beneath the Chilean flag. To vote "No," one put the cross beneath a black rectangle.

The system would like to be confused with the country. The system *is* the country, says the official propaganda that bombards the citizenry day and night. The enemy of the system is a traitor to the fatherland. Capacity for indignation against injustice and a desire for change are proofs of desertion. In many Latin American countries, citizens who aren't exiled beyond the frontiers live as exiles on their own soil.

But even while Pinochet celebrated his victory, strikes which the dictatorship called "collective labor absenteeism" were breaking out all over Chile, despite the terror. The great majority of kidnapped and disappeared people in Argentina are workers who performed some union activity. The limitless popular imagination keeps hatching new forms of struggle—the "Sad Faces Workday," the "Angry Faces Workday"—and solidarity finds new channels for the escape from fear. Numerous unanimous strikes occurred in Argentina through 1977, when fear of losing one's life was as real as the risk of losing one's job. A stroke of the pen can't destroy the power of response of an organized working class with a long fighting tradition. In May of the same year, when the Uruguayan dictatorship was balancing up its program of emptying minds and performing collective castration, it was forced to recognize that "37 percent of the country's citizens are still interested in politics."[26]

In these lands we are not experiencing the primitive infancy of capitalism but its vicious senility. Underdevelopment isn't a stage of development, but its consequence. Latin America's underdevelopment arises from external development, and continues to feed it. A system made impotent by its function of international servitude, and moribund since birth, has feet of clay. It pretends to be destiny and would like to be thought eternal. All memory is subversive, because it is different, and likewise any program for the future. The zombie is made to eat without salt: salt is dangerous, it could awaken him. The system has its paradigm in the immutable society of ants. For that reason it accords ill with the history of humankind, because that is always changing. And because in the history of humankind every act of destruction meets its response, sooner or later, in an act of creation.

References

Notes to Introduction: 120 Million Children in the Eye of the Hurricane, pp. 1-8

1. Woodrow Wilson, as quoted in Scott Nearing and Joseph Freeman, *Dollar Diplomacy* (1925; reprint ed., New York: Monthly Review Press, 1966).
2. *Life,* 29 March 1968, p. 83.
3. Lyndon B. Johnson, in a speech on the twentieth anniversary of the United Nations, San Francisco, June 25, 1965.

Notes to Chapter 1: Lust for Gold, Lust for Silver, pp. 11-58

1. *The Adventures of Marco Polo,* Richard J. Walsh, ed. (New York: John Day, 1948), p. 143.
2. Daniel Vidart, *Ideología y realidad de América* (Montevideo, 1968).
3. *The Log of Christopher Columbus' First Voyage to America in the Year 1492* (London: W.H. Allen & Co., Ltd., n.d.).
4. Quoted in Luis Nicolau D'Olwer, *Cronistas de las culturas precolombinas* (México, 1963).
5. Gonzalo Fernández de Oviedo, *Historia general y natural de las Indias* (Madrid, 1959).
6. According to the Indian informants of Fray Bernardino de Sahagún in the Florentine Codex, cited in Miguel León-Portilla, *Visión de los vencidos* (México, 1967).
7. See Rafael Pineda Yáñez, *La isla y Colón* (Buenos Aires, 1955).
8. According to the anonymous authors of Tlatelolco and the informants of Sahagún, cited in Léon-Portilla, *Visión de los vencidos.*
9. Léon-Portilla, *El reverso de la conquista: relaciones aztecas, mayas e incas* (México, 1964).
10. Ibid.
11. Earl J. Hamilton, *American Treasure and the Price Revolution in Spain,*

1501-1650 (1934; reprint ed., New York: Octagon, 1965).

12. Quoted in Gustavo Adolfo Otero, *Vida social en el coloniaje* (La Paz, 1958).

13. These are the words of José de Gálvez, Charles III's Visitor-General in New Spain, as quoted in John Lynch, *Spanish Colonial Administration, 1782-1810* (London: Athlone Press, 1958).

14. Ernest Mandel, *Marxist Economic Theory*, 2 vols. (New York: Monthly Review Press, 1968), 2: 443-44.

15. Ernest Mandel, "La teoría marxiana de la acumulación primitiva y la industrialización del Tercer Mundo," *Amaru* (Lima), April-June 1968.

16. Celso Furtado, *The Economic Development of Latin America: A Survey from Colonial Times to the Cuban Revolution* (Cambridge: Cambridge University Press, 1970), p. 11

17. J. Beaujeau-Garnier, *L'économie de l'Amérique Latine* (Paris, 1949).

18. Sergio Bagú, *Economía de la sociedad colonial: ensayo de historia comparada de América Latina* (Buenos Aires, 1949).

19. Alexander von Humboldt, *Political Essay on the Kingdom of New Spain* (London, 1811), Book II, Chapter VII, p. 22.

20. Andre Gunder Frank, *Capitalism and Underdevelopment in Latin America* (New York and London: Monthly Review Press, 1967).

21. Alvaro Alonso Barba, *Arte de los metales* (Potosí, 1967).

22. Otero, *Vida social.*

23. Humboldt, *Political Essay*, Book IV, Chapter XI. See also Fernando Carmona, Introduction to Diego López Rosado, *Historia y pensamiento económico de México* (Mexico, 1968).

24. Don Joseph Ribera Bernárdez (Count Santiago de La Laguna), *Descripción breve de la muy noble y leal ciudad de Zacatecas,* in Gabriel Salinas de la Torre, *Testimonios de Zacatecas* (Mexico, 1946).

25. John Collier, *The Indians of the Americas* (New York: W.W. Norton, 1947), p. 138.

26. Emilio Romero, *Historia económica del Perú* (Buenos Aires, 1941).

27. Enrique Finot, *Nueva historia de Bolivia* (Buenos Aires, 1946).

28. According to a member of the United States Soil Conservation Service, cited in Collier, *The Indians of the Americas,* p. 53.

29. Daniel Valcárcel, *La rebelión de Túpac Amaru* (Mexico, 1947).

30. Alexander von Humboldt, *Ansichten der Natur (Aspects of Nature),* vol. II; quoted in Adolf Meyer-Abich et al., *Alejandro de Humboldt, 1769–1859* (Bad Godesberg, 1969).

31. Ernest Gruening, *Mexico and Its Heritage* (New York: Appleton-Century-Crofts, 1928), p. 38.

32. Arturo Bonilla Sánchez, "Un problema que se agrava: la subocupación rural," in *Neolatifundismo y explotación, de Emiliano Zapata a Anderson Clayton & Co.* (México, 1968).

33. René Dumont, *Lands Alive* (New York: Monthly Review Press, 1965), p. 10.

34. "Don Volcán necesita carne humana bien tostadita," in Carlos Guzmán Boeckler and Jean-Loup Herbert, *Guatemala: una interpretación histórico-social* (México, 1970).

35. As quoted in C.R. Boxer, *The Golden Age of Brazil 1695–1750* (Berkeley and Los Angeles: University of California Press, 1962), p. 163.

36. As quoted in ibid., pp. 184–85.

37. Ibid., p. 165.

38. Esteban Montejo, *The Autobiography of a Runaway Slave*, ed. Miguel Barnet (New York: World Publishing, 1969), p. 42.

39. Boxer, *The Golden Age of Brazil*, p. 219. For further information see Joaquím Felício dos Santos, *Memórias do Distrito Diamantino* (Rio de Janeiro, 1956).

40. Augusto de Lima Jr., *Vila Rica de Ouro Prêto: síntese histórica e descritiva* (Belo Horizonte, 1957).

41. Franklin de Oliveira, *A tragédia da renovação brasileira. Minas Gerais e São Paulo: a miséria dentro do progresso* (Rio de Janeiro, 1970).

Additional Bibliography for Chapter 1

Aguilar Monteverde, Alonso. *Dialéctica de la economía mexicana.* México, 1968.

Banco de Comercio. *La economía del estado de Guanajuato.* México, 1968.

——— *La economía del estado de Zacatecas.* México, 1968.

Baran, Paul A. The *Political Economy of Growth.* New York: Monthly Review Press, 1962.

Cañete y Domínguez, Pedro Vicente. *Potosí colonial: guía histórica, geográfica, política, civil y legal del gobierno e intendencia de la provincia de Potosí.* La Paz, 1939.

Capitan, L., and Lorin, H. *El trabajo en América, antes y depués de Colón.* Buenos Aires, 1948.

Capoche, Luis. *Relación general de la Villa Imperial de Potosí.* Madrid, 1959.

Chávez Orozco, Luis. *Revolución industrial—revolución política.* México: Biblioteca del Obrero y Campesino, n.d.

de Martínez Arzana y Vela, Nicolás. *Historia de la Villa Imperial de Potosí.* Buenos Aires, 1943.

Elliott, J. H. *Imperial Spain.* London, 1963.

Furtado, Celso. *The Economic Growth of Brazil.* Berkeley & Los Angeles: University of California Press, 1963.

Galeano, Eduardo. *Guatemala: Occupied Country.* New York and London: Monthly Review Press, 1969.

Gerbi, Antonio. *La disputa del Nuevo Mundo.* Mexico, 1960.

Halperin Donghi, Tullio. *Historia contemporánea de América Latina.* Madrid, 1969.

Hanke, Lewis. *Estudios sobre fray Bartolomé de Las Casas y sobre la lucha por la justicia en la conquista española de América.* Caracas, 1968.

Hawkes, Jacquetta. "Prehistoria." In *Historia de la Humanidad.* Buenos Aires: UNESCO, 1966.

Huamán Poma. "El primer nueva crónica y buen gobierno." In *El reverso de la conquista: relaciones aztecas, mayas, e incas,* edited by Miguel Léon Portilla. México, 1964.

Manchester, Allan K. British *Preeminence in Brazil: Its Rise and Fall.* Chapel Hill, N.C.: University of North Carolina Press, 1933.

Marmolejo, Lucio. *Efemérides guanajuatenses, o datos para fomar la historia de la cuidad de Guanajuato.* Guanajuato, 1883.

Molins, Jaime. *La ciudad única.* Potosí, 1951.

Mora, José María Luis. *México y sus revoluciones.* México, 1965.

Mousnier, Roland. *Los siglos xvi y xvii. Historia general de las civilizaciones,* edited by Maurice Crouzet, vol. 4. Barcelona, 1967.

Ots Capdequí, J.M. *El estado español en la Indias.* México, 1941.

Quesada, Vicente G. *Crónicas potosinas.* París, 1890.

Ramos, Jorge Abelardo. *Historia de la nación latinoamericana.* Buenos Aires, 1958.

Ribeiro, Darcy. *The Americas and Civilization.* New York: Dutton, 1971.

Ruas, Eponina. *Ouro Prêto: sua história, seus templos e monumentos.* Rio de Janeiro, 1950.

Simonsen, Roberto S. *História econômica do Brasil 1500–1820.* São Paulo, 1962.

Turner, John Kenneth. *Barbarous Mexico.* 1910; reprint ed. Austin: University of Texas Press, 1969.

Vázquez Franco, Guillermo. *La conquista justificada.* Montevideo, 1968.

Vicens Vives, J. *Historia social y económica de España y América.* Barcelona, 1957.

Notes to Chapter 2: King Sugar and Other Agricultural Monarchs, pp. 59-133

1. According to investigations by Pernambuco's Instituto Joaquim Nabuco de Pesquisas Sociais, cited by Kit Sims Taylor, "Brazil's Northeast: Sugar and Surplus Value," *Monthly Review,* March 1969.
2. René Dumont, *Lands Alive* (New York: Monthly Review Press, 1965), p. 34.
3. Karl Marx, "On the Question of Free Trade," in *The Poverty of Philosophy* (New York: International Publishers, 1963), p. 223.
4. As quoted in Tadeusz Lepkowski, *Haití* (Havana, 1968), vol. I.
5. Manuel Moreno Fraginals, *El ingenio* (Havana, 1964).
6. See José Pedro Barrán and Benjamín Nahum, *Historia rural del Uruguay moderno, 1851–1885* (Montevideo, 1967).
7. Enrique Ruiz García, *América Latina: anatomía de una revolución* (Madrid, 1966).
8. Fidel Castro, "History Will Absolve

Me" (Havana, n.d.).

9. Quoted in K.S. Karol, *Guerrillas in Power: The Course of the Cuban Revolution* (New York: Hill and Wang, 1970), p. 224.

10. L. Capitán and H. Lorin, *El trabajo en América, antes y después de Colón* (Buenos Aires, 1948).

11. Adam Smith, *The Wealth of Nations,* Cannon edition (New York: Modern Library, 1937), p. 591.

12. Daniel P. Mannix, in collaboration with Malcolm Cowley, *Black Cargoes: A History of the Atlantic Slave Trade, 1518–1865* (New York: Viking, 1962), p. 22.

13. Quoted in ibid., p. 48.

14. For documentation of this information, see Eric Williams, *Capitalism and Slavery* (Chapel Hill: University of North Carolina Press, 1944).

15. Philip Reno, *The Ordeal of British Guiana* (New York: Monthly Review Press, 1964), p. 4.

16. Décio de Freitas, "A guerra dos escravos," unpublished manuscript.

17. Esteban Montejo, *The Autobiography of a Runaway Slave,* ed. Miguel Barnet (New York: World Publishing, 1969), pp. 44 and 45.

18. Roberto C. Simonsen, *História económica do Brasil, 1500–1820* (São Paulo, 1962).

19. Moreno Fraginals, *El ingenio.*

20. Quoted in Rodolfo Teófilo, *Historia da sêca do Ceará, 1877–1880* (Rio de Janeiro, 1922).

21. Agence France Presse, 21 April 1970.

22. Aurélio Pinheiro, *A margem do Amazonas* (São Paulo, 1937).

23. Domingo Alberto Rangel, *El proceso del capitalismo contemporáneo en Venezuela* (Caracas, 1968).

24. ECLA, *Economic Survey of Latin America, 1969* (New York: United Nations, 1970).

25. José Carlos Mariátegui, *Seven Interpretive Essays on Peruvian Reality* (Austin and London: University of Texas Press, 1971).

26. OAS, Inter-American Committee for Agricultural Development, *Peru: Land Tenure Conditions and Socio-Economic Development of the Agricultural Sector* (Washington, 1966).

27. Quoted in Mario Arrubla, *Estudios sobre el subdesarrollo colombiano* (Medellín, 1969).

28. Data from Banco Central, Instituto Brasileiro do Café, and the United Nations Food and Agricultural Organization. See *Fator* (Rio de Janeiro), November–December 1968.

29. According to a Federal Trade Commission investigation, cited in Cid Silveira, *Café: un drama na economia nacional* (Rio de Janeiro, 1962).

30. ECLA, *El comercio internacional y el desarrollo de América Latina* (México/Buenos Aires, 1964).

31. Arrubla, *Estudios sobre el subdesarrollo colombiano.*

32. Luis Eduardo Nieto Arteta, *Ensayos sobre la economía colombiana*

(Medellín, 1969).

33. United Nations, *Analysis and Projections of Economic Development*, vol. III, in *Economic Development of Colombia* (New York, 1957).

34. Germán W. Rama, "Educación y movilidad social en Colombia," *Eco* (Bogotá), December 1969.

35. William Howard Taft, as quoted in Gregorio Selser, *Diplomacia, Garrote y Dólares en América Latina* (Buenos Aires: Editorial Palestra, 1962), pp. 46–47; retranslated from the Spanish.

36. Quoted in Leo Huberman, *Man's Worldly Goods* (New York: Monthly Review Press, 1952), p. 265.

37. Ibid.

38. Miguel Angel Asturias, *The Green Pope* (New York: Delacorte, 1971), pp. 134–35.

39. Miguel Angel Asturias, *Strong Wind* (New York: Delacorte, 1968), p. 47.

40. John Dos Passos, *The 42nd Parallel* (New York: Harper & Brothers, 1930), p. 252.

41. William Krehm, *Democracia y tiranías en el Caribe* (Buenos Aires, 1959).

42. Speech to the American Booksellers Association, Washington, D.C., 10 June 1963, cited in David Wise and Thomas B. Ross, *The Invisible Government* (New York: Random House, 1964), p. 166.

43. J.P. and W.P. Robertson, *Letters on Paraguay* (London: John Murray, 1838).

44. John Kenneth Turner, *Barbarous Mexico* (1910; reprint ed., Austin: University of Texas Press, 1969), p. 219.

45. Ibid., p. 223.

46. Ibid., p. 225.

47. John Womack, Jr., *Zapata and the Mexican Revolution* (New York: Vintage, 1968), p. 127.

48. Ibid., pp. 228–29.

49. Fernando Carmona, *El drama de América Latina: el caso de México* (México, 1964).

50. Edmundo Flores, "¿Adónde va la economía de México?" *Comercio exterior* (México), January 1970.

51. Rodolfo Stavenhagen, Fernando Paz Sánchez, Cuauhtémoc Cárdenas, and Arturo Bonilla, *Neolatifundismo y explotación: de Emiliano Zapata a Anderson Clayton & Co.* (México, 1968).

52. Carlos Fuentes, *The Death of Artemio Cruz* (New York: Farrar Straus, 1964).

53. D.F. Maza Zavala, *Explosión demográfica y crecimiento económico* (Caracas, 1970).

54. Paul Bairoch, *Diagnostic de l'évolution économique du Tiers Monde, 1900–1966* (Paris, 1967).

55. Instituto de Economía de la Universidad del Uruguay, *El proceso económico del Uruguay: contribución al estudio de su evolución y perspectivas* (Montevideo, 1969).

56. Quoted in Dardo Cúneo, *Comportamiento y crisis de la clase empresaria* (Buenos Aires, 1967).

57. ECLA, *Economic Survey of Latin America, 1964 and 1966,* and ECLA/FAO Agricultural Division

in collaboration with the Inter-American Development Bank, *El uso de fertilizantes en América Latina* (Santiago de Chile, 1966).

58. Darcy Ribeiro, *The Americas and Civilization* (New York: Dutton, 1971), p. 211.

Additional Bibliography for Chapter 2

Aguilar Monteverde, Alonso, and Carmona, Fernando. *México: riqueza y miseria.* México, 1968. Bagú, Sergio. *Economía de la sociedad colonial: ensayo de historia comparada de América Latina.* Buenos Aires, 1949.

Baltra Cortés, Alberto. *Problemas del subdesarrollo económico latinoamericano.* Buenos Aires, 1966. Banco Cafetero. *La industria cafetera en Colombia.* Bogotá, 1962.

Carneiro, Edison. *O quilombo dos Palmares.* Rio de Janeiro, 1966.

de Castro, Josué. *The Geography of Hunger.* Boston: Little Brown, 1952.

de la Torre, Nelson. *Evolución económica de la Banda Oriental.* Montevideo, 1967.

———. *Estructura económico-social de la Colonia.* Montevideo, 1968.

de la Torre, Nelson; Rodríguez, Julio C; and Sala de Touron, Lucía. *Artigas: tierra y revolución.* Montevideo, 1967.

de Oliveira, Franklin. *Revolución y contrarrevolución en el Brasil.* Buenos Aires, 1965.

Duarte Pereira, Osny. *¿Quem faz as leis no Brasil?* Rio de Janeiro, 1966.

Facó, Rui. *Cangaceiros e fanáticos.* Rio de Janeiro, 1965.

Flores, Ana María. *La magnitud del hambre en México.* México, 1961.

Furtado, Celso. *The Development of Underdevelopment.* Berkeley & Los Angeles: The University of California Press, 1964.

———. *The Economic Development of Latin America: A Survey from Colonial Times to the Cuban Revolution.* New York: Cambridge University Press, 1970.

———. *The Economic Growth of Brazil.* Berkeley & Los Angeles: The University of California Press, 1963.

———*Um projecto para o Brasil.* Rio de Janeiro, 1969.

Galeano, Eduardo. "Los dioses y los diablos en las favelas de Río." *Amaru,* June 1969.

———. *Guatemala: Occupied Country.* New York & London: Monthly Review Press, 1969.

———. "Uruguay: Promise and Betrayal." In *Latin America: Reform or Revolution?* edited by James Petras and Maurice Zeitlin. New York: Fawcett, 1969.

Guzmán Boeckler, Carlos, and Herbert, Jean-Loup. *Guatemala: una interpretación histórico-social.* México, 1970.

Guzmán Campos, Germán; Fals Borda, Orlando; Umaña Luna, Eduardo. *La violencia en Colombia: estudio de un proceso social.* Bogotá, 1963-64.

Harlow, Vincent T. *History of Barbados.* Oxford, 1926.

Inter-American Committee for

Agricultural Development. *Guatemala: Land Tenure Conditions and Socio-Economic Development of the Agricultural Sector.* Washington, 1965.

Jenks, Leland H. *Our Cuban Colony.* New York: Vanguard Press, 1928.

Julien, Claude. *America's Empire.* New York: Pantheon, 1971.

Kirkland, Edward C. *A History of American Economic Life.* 1932; reprint ed. New York: Appleton, 1969.

Monbeig, Pierre. *Pionniers et planteurs de São Paulo.* Paris, 1952.

Núñez Jiménez, A. *Geografía de Cuba.* Havana, 1959.

Ortiz, Fernando. *Cuban Counterpoint: Tobacco and Sugar.* New York: Vintage, 1970.

Panorama Económico Latinoamericano (Havana), September 1963.

Prado, Caio Jr. *Formação do Brasil contemporaneo.* São Paulo, 1942.

———. *Historia económica del Brasil.* Buenos Aires, 1960.

Prensa Latina, 13 October 1970. *Report by Cuba to the Eleventh Food and Agricultural Organization Regional Conference.*

Rangel, Domingo Alberto. *Capital y desarrollo.* Caracas, 1969.

Reyes Abadie, Washington; Bruschera, Oscar H.; and Melogno, Tabaré. *El ciclo artiguista.* Montevideo, 1968.

Rodrigues, Nina. *Os africanos no Brasil.* Rio de Janeiro, 1932.

Schilling, Paulo. "Un nuevo genocidio." *Marcha* (Montevideo), 10 July 1970.

Seers, Dudley; Bianchi, Andrés; Jolly, Richard; and Wolff, Max. *Cuba: The Economic and Social Revolution.* Chapel Hill: The University of North Carolina Press, 1964.

Selser, Gregorio. *Diplomacia, garrote y dólares en América Latina.* Buenos Aires, 1962.

———. *Sandino, general de hombres libres.* Buenos Aires, 1959.

Silva Herzog, Jesús. *Breve historia de la Revolución Mexicana.* México/Buenos Aires, 1969.

Torres-Rivas, Edelberto. *Interpretación del desarrollo social centroamericano.* Santiago de Chile, 1969.

Trías, Vivian. *Reforma agraria en el Uruguay.* Montevideo, 1962.

United Nations Food and Agricultural Organization. *Yearbook of Production, 1965.*

Wettstein, Germán, and Rudolf, Juan. "La sociedad rural." *Nuestra Tierra* (Montevideo), no. 16 (1969).

Notes to Chapter 3: The Invisible Sources of Power, pp. 134-70

1. Philip Courtney, paper presented to the Second International Congress on Savings and Investment, Brussels, 1959.
2. Parliamentary Investigation Commission report of the sale of Brazilian land to physically or juridically foreign persons, Brasilia, 3 June 1968.
3. *Correio da Manhã* (Rio de Janeiro), 30 January 1968.

4. Quoted in Emilio Romero, *Historia económica del Perú* (Buenos Aires, 1949).

5. Oscar Bermúdez, *Historia del salitre desde sus orígenes hasta la Guerra del Pacífico* (Santiago de Chile, 1963).

6. Hernán Ramírez Necochea, *Balmaceda y la contrarrevolución de 1891* (Santiago de Chile, 1969).

7. Sergio Almaraz Paz, *El poder y la caída: el estaño en la historia de Bolivia* (La Paz/Cochabamba, 1967).

8. Almaraz Paz, *Réquiem para una república* (La Paz, 1969).

9. "Immovable Mountains," *Fortune*, April 1965, p. 63.

10. Quoted in Mário Pedrosa, A *opção brasileira* (Rio de Janeiro, 1966).

11. *New York Times*, 3 April 1964.

12. According to the daily *0 estado de São Paulo*, 4 May 1964.

13. Eugene Methvin in *Selecciones del Reader's Digest*, December 1966.

14. According to data published by the Organization of Petroleum Exporting Countries and quoted in Francisco Mieres, *El petróleo y la problemática estructural venezolana* (Caracas, 1969).

15. Harvey O'Connor, *World Crisis in Oil* (New York: Monthly Review Press, 1962), p. 112.

16. Jesús Silva Herzog, *Historia de la expropiación de las empresas petroleras* (México, 1964).

17. See *Conjuntura econômica* (Rio de Janeiro), no. 9, 1970, for a list of the fifty biggest enterprises; Petrobras heads the list.

18. *Correio da Manhã*, February 19, 1967, published a long excerpt from the report.

19. Statement by Márcio Leite Cesarino, an engineer, in *Correio da Manhã*, 28 January 1967.

20. O'Connor, *World Crisis in Oil*, p. 172.

21. René Zavaleta Mercado, *Bolivia: el desarrollo de la conciencia nacional* (Montevideo, 1967).

22. Quoted in *Guaranía* (Buenos Aires), November 1934.

23. *NACLA Newsletter* (New York), February 1969. The *Newsletter* published a photostat of this letter, taken from the Truman Library.

24. Marcelo Quiroga Santa Cruz, quoted in *Revista jurídica* (Cochabamba), special edition, 1967.

25. See Richard N. Goodwin, "Letter from Peru," *New Yorker*, 17 May 1969.

26. *Time* (Latin American edition), 11 September 1953.

Additional Bibliography for Chapter 3

Alameda Ospina, Raúl. *Esquina* (Bogotá), 1968.

Alves, Hermano. "Aerofotogrametria." *Correio da Manhã* (Rio de Janeiro), 8 June 1967.

Araujo, Orlando. *Operación Puerto Rico sobre Venezuela*. Caracas, 1967.

Baran, Paul A. and Sweezy, Paul M. *Monopoly Capital*. New York: Monthly Review Press, 1966.

Brito, Federico. *Venezuela siglo XX.* Havana, 1967.

Cademartori, José. *La economía chilena.* Santiago de Chile, 1968.

Duarte Pereira, Osny. *Ferro e indepêndencia: um desafio à dignidade nacional.* Rio de Janeiro, 1967.

ECLA. *Economic Survey of Latin America 1969.* New York/Santiago de Chile, 1970.

Falcón Urbano, M. A. *Desarrollo e industrialización de Venezuela.* Caracas, 1969.

Geyer, Georgie Anne. "Seized U.S. Oil Firm Made Napalm." *New York Post,* 7 April 1969.

Julien, Claude. *America's Empire.* New York: Pantheon, 1971.

Krehm, William. *Democracia y tiranías en el Caribe.* Buenos Aires, 1959.

Lieuwen, Edwin. *The United States and the Challenge to the Security of Latin America.* Columbus: Ohio State University Press, 1966.

Magdoff, Harry. *The Age of Imperialism.* New York: Monthly Review Press, 1969.

Maza Zavala, D. F.; de la Plaza, Salvador; Mejía, Pedro Esteban; and Montiel Ortega, Leonardo. *Perfiles de la economía venezolana.* Caracas, 1964.

Mariátegui, José Carlos. *Seven Interpretive Essays on the Peruvian Reality.* Austin and London: University of Texas Press, 1971.

O'Connor, Harvey. *The Empire of Oil.* New York: Monthly Review Press, 1955.

Quintero, Rodolfo. *La cultura del petróleo.* Caracas, 1968.

Ramírez Necochea, Hernán. *Historia del imperialismo en Chile.* Santiago de Chile, 1960.

Rangel, Domingo Alberto. *El proceso del capitalismo contemporáneo en Venezuela.* Caracas, 1968.

Reno, Philip. "Aluminum Profits and Caribbean People." *Monthly Review,* October 1963.

———. *The Ordeal of British Guiana.* New York: Monthly Review Press, 1964.

Samhaber, Ernst. *Sudamérica, biografía de un continente.* Buenos Aires, 1946.

Schilling, Paulo R. *Brasil para extranjeros.* Montevideo, 1966.

Siekman, Philip. "When Executives Turn Revolutionaries." *Fortune,* July 1964.

Stacchini, José. *Mobilização de audácia.* São Paulo, 1965.

Suttie, R.I. "Copper Substitution." In *Finance and Development.* Washington, D.C.: International Bank for Reconstruction and Development, June 1969.

Tanzer, Michael. *The Political Economy of International Oil and the Underdeveloped Countries.* Boston: Beacon Press, 1969.

Trías, Vivian. *Imperialismo y petróleo en el Uruguay.* Montevideo, 1963.

Uslar Pietri, Arturo. "¿Tiene un porvenir la juventud venezolana?" *Cuadernos Americanos* (Mexico), March–April 1968.

Vera, Mario and Catalán, Elmo. *La*

encrucijada del cobre. Santiago de Chile 1965.

Notes to Chapter 4: Tales of Premature Death, pp. 173-204

1. Letter from Canning to Lord Grenville, as quoted in William W. Kaufmann, *British Policy and the Independence of Latin America, 1804–1828* (New Haven: Yale University Press, 1951), p. 178.
2. Manfred Kossok, *El Virreinato del Río de la Plata: su estructura económico-social* (Buenos Aires, 1959).
3. H.S. Ferns, *Britain and Argentina in the Nineteenth Century* (Oxford: Clarendon Press, 1960), p. 11.
4. Alexander von Humboldt, *Political Essay on the Kingdom of New Spain* (London, 1811), Book IV, Chapter XII.
5. Caio Prado Jr., *Historia económica del Brasil* (Buenos Aires, 1960).
6. The University Society, *Bolivia en el primer centenario de su independencia* (La Paz, 1925).
7. Sir Woodbine Parish, *Buenos Ayres and the Provinces of the Río de la Plata* (London: John Murray, 1839), p. 338.
8. Paulo Schilling, *Brasil para extranjeros* (Montevideo, 1966).
9. Gustavo Beyhaut, *Raíces contemporáneas de América Latina* (Buenos Aires, 1964).
10. Hernán Ramírez Necochea, *Historia del imperialismo en Chile* (Santiago de Chile, 1960).
11. Karl Marx, "On the Question of Free Trade," in *The Poverty of Philosophy* (New York: International Publishers, 1963), p. 223.
12. Luis Chávez Orozco, *La industria de transformación mexicana, 1821–1867.* Colección de documentos para la historia del comercio exterior de México, vol. 7 (México: Banco Nacional de Comercio Exterior, 1962).
13. Alonso Aguilar Monteverde, *Dialéctica de la economía mexicana* (México, 1968).
14. Banco Nacional de Comercio Exterior, Colección, vol. 3.
15. Dardo de la Vega Díaz, *La Rioja Heroica* (Mendoza, 1965).
16. Literal translation. (Trans.)
17. Quoted in Miron Burgin, *The Economic Aspects of Argentine Federalism, 1820–1852* (Cambridge, MA: Harvard University Press, 1946), p. 141.
18. Juan Alvarez, *Las guerras civiles argentinas* (Buenos Aires, 1912).
19. John F. Cady, *La intervención extranjera en el Río de la Plata* (Buenos Aires, 1943).
20. Vivian Trías, *Juan Manuel de Rosas* (Montevideo, 1970).
21. Speech by Gervasio A. de Posadas, cited in Dardo Cúneo, *Comportamiento y crisis de la clase empresaria* (Buenos Aires, 1967).
22. Domingo Faustino Sarmiento, *Facundo* (Buenos Aires, 1952).
23. Mario Marguls, *Migración y marginalidad en la sociedad argentina* (Buenos Aires, 1968).
24. Pablo Neruda, *Obras completas,* vol.

I (Buenos Aires, 1967), section entitled "La Arena traicionada."

25. Jorge Abelardo Ramos, *Historia de la nación latinoamericana* (Buenos Aires, 1968).

26. National Technical Planning Secretariat, *Plan nacional de desarrollo económico y social* (Asunción, 1966).

27. Quoted in R. Scalabrini Ortiz, *Política británica en el Río de la Plata* (Buenos Aires, 1940).

28. Celso Furtado, *The Economic Growth of Brazil* (Berkeley & Los Angeles: University of California Press, 1963), p. 117.

29. Robert Schnerb, *Le XIXe. siècle: l'apogée de l'expansion européenne, 1815–1914* (Paris, 1968).

30. J. Eduardo Retondo, *El bosque y la industria forestal en Santiago del Estero* (Santiago del Estero, 1962).

31. Quoted in Andre Gunder Frank, *Capitalism and Underdevelopment in Latin America* (New York and London: Monthly Review Press, 1967), p. 164, and retranslated from the Spanish.

32. Edward C. Kirkland, *A History of American Economic Life* (1932; reprint ed., New York: Appleton, 1969).

33. Furtado, *Economic Growth of Brazil*, p. 109.

34. Ralph Waldo Emerson, "The American Scholar," in *The Complete Essays and Other Writings of Ralph Waldo Emerson* (New York: Modem Library, 1950), pp. 62–63.

35. See C. Vann Woodward, *Origins of the New South, 1879-1913* (Baton Rouge: Louisiana State University Press, 1951).

Additional Bibliography for Chapter 4

Alberdi, Juan Bautista. *Historia de la guerra del Paraguay*. Buenos Aires, 1962.

Alen Lascano, Luis C. *Imperialismo y comercio libre*. Buenos Aires, 1963.

Bazán, Armando Raúl. "Las bases sociales de la montonera." *Revista de historia americana y argentina* (Mendoza), 1962/1963.

Bazant, Jan. "Estudio sobre la productividad de la industria algodonera mexicana en 1843-1845." In *Colección de documentos para la historia del comercio exterior de México*. México: Banco Nacional de Comercio Exterior, 1962.

Box, Pelham Horton. *Los orígenes de la Guerra de la Triple Alianza*. Buenos Aires/Asunción, 1958.

Busaniche, José Luis. *Rosas visto por sus contemporáneos*. Buenos Aires, 1955.

Cardozo, Efraím. *El imperio del Brasil y el Río de la Plata*. Buenos Aires, 1961.

Chaves, Julio César. *El Presidente López*. Buenos Aires, 1955.

Levene, Ricardo. "Introduction" to *Docuntentos para la historia argentina* (1919). Buenos Aires, 1962.

Manchester, Alan K. *British Preeminence in Brazil: Its Rise and Fall*. Chapel Hill: University of North Carolina Press, 1933.

Mitre, Bartolomé and Gómez, Juan Carlos. *Cartas polémicas sobre la guerra del Paraguay.* Buenos Aires, 1940.

Normano, J. F. *Evolução econômica do Brasil.* São Paulo, 1934.

Ortega Peña, Rodolfo and Duhalde, Eduardo Luis. *Felipe Varela contra el Imperio Británico.* Buenos Aires, 1966.

Pereyra, Carlos. *Francisco Solano López y la guerra del Paraguay.* Buenos Aires, 1945.

Pérez Acosta, Juan F. *Carlos Antonio López, obrero máximo: labor administrativa y constructiva.* Asunción, 1948.

Pierce, H. H. *The Railroads of New York: A Study of Government Aid, 1826–1875.* Cambridge: Harvard University Press, 1953.

Ramírez Necochea, Hernán. *Antecedentes económicos de la independencia de Chile.* Santiago de Chile, 1959.

Rippy, J. Fred. *British Investments in Latin America: A Case Study in the Operation of Private Enterprise in Retarded Regions, 1822–1949.* Minneapolis: University of Minnesota Press, 1959.

Romero, Emilio. *Historia económica del Perú.* Buenos Aires, 1949.

Rosa, José María. *La guerra del Paraguay y las montoneras argentinas.* Buenos Aires, 1965.

Santos Martínez, Pedro. *Las industrias durante el Virreinato, 1776–1810.* Buenos Aires, 1969.

Véliz, Claudio. "La mesa de tres patas." *Desarrollo económico* (Santiago de Chile), September 1963.

Notes to Chapter 5: The Contemporary Structure of Plunder, pp. 205-61

1. OAS Secretariat-General, *El financiamiento externo para el desarrollo de la América Latina* (Washington, 1969); restricted document of the Sixth Annual Meeting of the Inter-American Economic and Social Council at the Ministerial Level.

2. J.-J. Servan-Schreiber, *The American Challenge* (New York: Atheneum, 1968), p. 3.

3. Quoted in Alfredo Parera Dennis, "Naturaleza de las relaciones entre las clases dominantes argentinas y las metrópolis," *Fichas de investigación económica y social* (Buenos Aires), December 1964.

4. Ministry of Planning and Economic Coordination, *A industrialização brasileira: diagnóstico e perspectivas* (Rio de Janeiro, 1969).

5. Maria de Conceição Tavares, *O processo de substituição de importações, como modelo de desenvolvimento recente na América Latina* (Rio de Janeiro: ECLA/ILPES, n.d.).

6. Reply of the Minister of Economic Affairs to a representative of the magazine *Visión,* 27 November 1953; quoted in Parera Dennis, "Naturaleza de las relaciones."

7. Quoted in Octavio Ianni, *O colapso do populismo no Brasil* (Rio de Janeiro, 1968).

8. Fernando Henrique Cardoso, *Política e desenvolvimento em*

sociedades dependentes: ideologias do empresariado industrial argentino e brasileiro (São Paulo, 1968).

9. For irrefutable examples, see Ricardo Lagos Escobar, *La concentración del poder económico. Su teoría. Realidad chilena* (Santiago de Chile, 1961); and Vivian Trías, *Reforma agraria en el Uruguay* (Montevideo, 1962).

10. Alonso Aguilar Monteverde, in Alonso Aguilar Monteverde et al., *El milagro mexicano* (México, 1970).

11. See Dardo Cúneo, *Comportamiento y crisis de la clase empresaria* (Buenos Aires, 1967).

12. Speech by Minister Hélio Beltrão to the Asociación Comercial de Rio de Janeiro, as reported in *Correio do Povo,* May 24, 1969.

13. ECLA/BNDE, *Quince años de política económica en el Brasil* (Santiago de Chile, 1965).

14. Paulo Schilling, *Brasil para extranjeros* (Montevideo, 1966).

15. Maurício Vinhas de Queiroz, "Os grupos multibilionarios," *Revista do Instituto de Ciências Sociais* (Universidade Federal do Rio de Janeiro), January 1965.

16. *New York Times,* 19 January 1969, p. 12E.

17. Sergio Nicolau, *La inversión extranjera directa en los países de la ALALC* (México, 1968).

18. ECLA, *Economic Survey of Latin America 1968* (New York: United Nations, 1969).

19. *Visión,* 3 February 1967.

20. José Luis Ceceña, *Los monopolios en México* (México, 1962).

21. *O Globo,* 25 February 1969.

22. Fernando Gasparian in *Correio da Manhã,* 1 May 1968.

23. *Journal of Commerce,* International Banking Survey, 25 February 1968.

24. Ministry of Planning and Economic Coordination, *Programa de Ação Econômica do Govêrno,* Rio de Janeiro, November 1964.

25. *International Commerce,* 24 April 1967, p. 26.

26. V.I. Lenin, *Imperialism: The Highest Stage of Capitalism* in *Selected Works,* vol. V (New York, n.d.), p. 56.

27. Speech to the AFL-CIO Congress in Miami, as reported in the *New York Times,* 8 December 1961, p. 18.

28. ECLA, *Estudio económico de América Latina 1968* (New York/Santiago de Chile, 1969).

29. *Fichas de investigación económica y social,* June 1965.

30. *International Commerce,* 3 February 1963, p. 21.

31. Ibid., 17 July 1967, p. 10.

32. This document was published in the daily *Ya* (Montevideo), 28 May 1970.

33. *Panorama* (Centro de Estudios y Documentación Sociales, México), November-December 1965.

34. Irving Pflaum, *Arena of Decision: Latin American Crisis* (Englewood Cliffs, NJ: Prentice Hall, 1964); John Gerassi, *The Great Fear in Latin America* (New York: Macmillan, 1965).

35. Georgie Anne Geyer, in *Miami Herald*, 24 December 1966.

36. Statement to a House of Representatives subcommittee, cited in Nelson Werneck Sodré, *História militar do Brasil* (Rio de Janeiro, 1965).

37. Frederick B. Pike, *The Modern History of Peru* (New York: Praeger, 1967), p. 319.

38. Hickenlooper Amendment, Section 620 of the Foreign Assistance Act.

39. *International Commerce*, 10 April 1967, p. 44.

40. *NACLA Newsletter* (New York), May-June 1970.

41. ADELA Annual Report, quoted in ibid.

42. Harry Magdoff, *The Age of Imperialism* (New York and London: Monthly Review Press, 1968), pp. 145–46.

43. World Bank, IFC, IDA, *Policies and Operations* (Washington, D.C., 1962).

44. Eugene R. Black, "The Domestic Dividends of Foreign Aid," *Columbia Journal of World Business*, no. 1, 1965, p. 23.

45. ECLA, *Economic Survey of Latin America*, 1968, 1969.

46. Ibid.

47. Pablo González Casanova, *La democracia en México* (México, 1965).

48. Marco D. Pollner, in INTAL/BID, *Los empresarios y la integración de América Latina* (Buenos Aires, 1967).

49. Central Unica de Trabajadores de Chile, *América Latina, un mundo que ganar* (Santiago de Chile, 1968).

50. Arghiri Emmanuel, *Unequal Exchange* (New York: Monthly Review Press, 1972).

51. Samir Amin, *L'accumulation à l'échelle mondiale* (Paris, 1970).

52. *New York Times*, 3 April 1968.

53. OAS Secretariat-General, *El financiamiento externo.*

54. Miguel S. Wionczek, "La inversión extranjera privada en México: problemas y perspectivas," *Comercio exterior* (México), October 1970.

55. Aldo Ferrer in INTAL/BID, *Los empresarios.*

56. *Jornal do Comercio* (Rio de Janeiro), 23 March 1950.

57. Celso Furtado, *Um projeto para o Brasil* (Rio de Janeiro, 1968).

58. *International Commerce*, 24 April 1967.

59. Ismael Viñas and Eugenio Gastiazoro, *Economía y dependencia, 1900–1918* (Buenos Aires, 1968).

60. Antonio García, "Las constelaciones del poder y el desarrollo latinoamericano," *Comercio exterior*, November 1969.

61. Guillermo Bernhard, *Los monopolios y la industria frigorífica* (Montevideo, 1970).

62. Statement made by President Salvador Allende as reported in Agence France Presse dispatch, 12 December 1970.

63. *La Razón* (Buenos Aires), 2 March 1970.

64. "Resultados de indústria automobilística," special study in *Conjuntura econômica*, February 1969.

65. *NACLA Newsletter*, April-May 1969.

66. Miguel S. Wionczek, "La trasmisión de la tecnología a los países en desarrollo:proyecto de un estudio sobre México," *Comercio exterior*, May 1968.

67. Manuel Sadosky, "América Latina y la computación," *Gaceta de la Universidad* (Montevideo), May 1970.

68. Quoted in Gustavo Lagos et al., *Las inversiones multinacionales en el desarrollo y la integración de América Latina* (Bogota, 1968).

69. Raúl Prébisch, "La cooperación internacional en el desarrollo latinoamericano," *Desarrollo* (Bogotá), January 1970.

70. Leo Fenster in *The Nation*, 2 July 1969.

71. F.S. O'Brien, *The Brazilian Population and Labor Force in 1968*, Ministry of Planning and Economic Coordination document for internal discussion.

72. ECLA, *Estudio económico de América Latina, 1967* (New York/Santiago de Chile, 1968).

73. Ibid.

74. Raimundo Ongaro, "Letter from Prison," *De Frente* (Buenos Aires), 25 September 1969.

75. ECLA, *Estudio sobre la distribución del ingreso en América Latina* (Santiago de Chile, 1967).

76. Vinhas de Queiroz, "Os grupos multibilionarios."

77. Lagos et al., *Las inversiones multinacionales*.

78. "LAFTA: Key to Latin America's 200 Million Consumers." *Business International*, June 1966.

79. "A Latin-American Common Market Makes Common Sense—for U.S. Business Too," *Fortune*, June 1967, p. 56.

80. Raúl Prébisch, "Problemas de la integración económica," *Actualidades económicas financieras* (Montevideo), January 1962.

81. Raúl Prébisch et al., *Proposiciones para la creación del Mercado Común Latinoamericano*, document presented to President Frei in 1966.

82. United States Department of State, Office of External Research, *The Multinational Corporation* (Washington, D.C., 1969).

83. "LAFTA: Key to Latin America's 200 Million Consumers."

84. Roger Hansen, "Time of Trial for the 'Other' Common Market," *Columbia Journal of World Business* (September–October 1967), cited in *NACLA Newsletter*, January 1970.

85. Paul N. Rosenstein-Rodan, *Reflections on Regional Development*, cited in Lagos et al., *Las inversiones multinacionales*.

86. LAFTA Permanent Executive Committee, Extraordinary Sessions, July and September 1969, *Apreciaciones sobre el proceso de integración de la ALALC [LAFTA]* (Montevideo, 1969).

87. Sidney Dell, "Obstacles to Latin American Integration," in *The*

Movement Toward Latin American Unity, ed. Ronald Hilton (New York: Praeger, 1969).

88. LAFTA, *La industria automotriz en la ALALC [LAFTA]* (Montevideo, 1969).

89. Vivian Trías, *Imperialismo y geopolítica en América Latina* (Montevideo, 1967).

90. Golbery do Couto e Silva, *Aspectos geopolíticos do Brasil* (Rio de Janeiro, 1952).

91. Gregorio Bustamante Maceo, *Historia militar de El Salvador* (San Salvador, 1951).

92. ECLA, *Los fletes marítimos en el comercio exterior de América Latina* (Santiago de Chile, 1968).

93. Enrique Angulo H., in *Integración de América Latina: experiencias y perspectivas* (México, 1964).

94. Sidney Dell, *Latin American Common Market* (New York: Oxford University Press, 1966).

Additional Bibliography for Chapter 5

Aguilar Monteverde, Alonso, and Carmona, Fernando. *México, riqueza y miseria.* México, 1968.

Baptista Gumucio, Mariano, et al. *Guerrilleros y generales sobre Bolivia.* Buenos Aires, 1968.

Baran, Paul A., and Sweezy, Paul M. *Monopoly Capital.* New York: Monthly Review Press, 1966.

Bourricaud, François; Bravo Bresani, Jorge; Favre, Henri; and Piel, Jean. *La oligarquía en el Perú.* Lima, 1969.

Canelas, Amado. *Radiografía de la Alianza para el atraso.* La Paz, 1963.

Ceceña, José Luis. *México en la órbita imperial.* México, 1970.

Cheprakov, V.A. *El capitalismo mono-polista de estado.* Moscow, n.d.

ECLA. *El financiamiento externo de América Latina.* New York/Santiago de Chile:United Nations, 1964.

Frank, Andre Gunder. *Capitalism and Underdevelopment in Latin America.* New York and London: Monthly Review Press, 1967.

García Lupo, Rogelio. *Contra la ocupación extranjera.* Buenos Aires, 1968.

Gunther, John. *Inside South America.* New York: Harper & Row, 1967.

Instituto Latinamericano de Planificación Económica y Social. *La brecha comercial y la integración latinoamericana.* México/Santiago de Chile, 1967.

Inter-American Development Bank. *Annual Report, 1969.* Washington, 1970.

Jalée, Pierre. *The Pillage of the Third World.* New York and London: Monthly Review Press, 1968.

Lichtensztejn, Samuel and Couriel, Alberto. *El FMI y la crisis económica nacional.* Montevideo, 1967.

Lízano F., E. "El problema de las inversiones extranjeras en Centro América." *Revista del Banco Central* (Costa Rica), September 1966.

Maggiolo, Oscar J. In *Hacia una política cultural autónoma para América Latina.* Montevideo, 1969.

Martins, Luciano. *Industrialização, burguesia nacional e desenvolvimento.*

Rio de Janeiro, 1968.

Quijano, Carlos. "Las victimas del sistema." *Marcha* (Montevideo), 23 October 1970.

Romanova, Z. *La expansión económica de Estados Unidos en América Latina.* Moscow, n.d.

Trías, Vivian. *La crisis del imperio.* Montevideo, 1970.

Urquidi, Victor L. In *Obstacles to Change in Latin America,* edited by Claudio Véliz, et al. New York: Oxford University Press, 1965.

Notes to Part III: Seven Years After pp. 265-87

1. Interview with Jean-Pierre Clerc, *Le Monde* (Paris), 8-9 May 1977.

2. *The Nation* (New York), 28 August 1976.

3. The crime occurred in Washington on 21 September 1976. Various Uruguayan, Chilean, and Bolivian political exiles had previously been murdered in Argentina. Most noteworthy among them were General Carlos Prats, key figure in the Allende government's military setup, whose car blew up in a Buenos Aires garage on 27 September 1974; General Juan José Torres, who had headed a short-lived anti-imperialist government in Bolivia and was riddled with bullets on 15 June 1976; and the Uruguayan legislators Zelmar Michelini and Héctor Gutiérrez Ruiz, kidnapped, tortured, and murdered in Buenos Aires between 18 and 21 March 1976.

4. The agrarian reform, started under the Christian Democratic government and deepened by Popular Unity, was also destroyed. See María Beatriz de Albuquerque W., "La agricultura chilena: modernización capitalista o regresión a formas tradicionales? Comentarios sobre la contra-reforma en Chile," *Ibero-Americana,* vol. 6, no. 2, 1976, Institute of Latin American Studies, Stockholm.

5. Three months later there were elections in the university. They were the only elections remaining. The dictatorship's candidates got 2.5 percent of the university votes. So to defend democracy, the dictatorship added substantially to the jail population and handed over the university to the 2.5 percent.

6. *Veja* no. 444 (São Paulo), 9 March 1977.

7. U.S. House of Representatives, Committee on Appropriations, Foreign Appropriations for 1963, Hearings 87th Congress, 2nd Session, Part I.

8. *Déclaration de Lourdes* (October 1976).

9. *Le Nouvelliste* (Port-au-Prince, Haiti), 19-20 March 1977. Data cited by Agustín Cueva in *El desarrollo del capitalismo en América Latina* (México: Siglo XXI, 1977).

10. Ida May Mantel, *Sources and Uses of Funds for a Sample of Majority-Owned Foreign Affiliates of U.S. Companies, 1966-1972,* U.S. Dept. of Commerce, *Survey of Current Business,* July 1975.

11. United Nations, Economic Commission for Latin America, *El*

desarrollo económico y social y las relaciones externas de América Latina (Santo Domingo, Dominican Republic), February 1977.

12. Money, which has its little wings, travels without a passport. A sizable part of the profits generated by the exploitation of our resources escapes to the United States, Switzerland, Federal Republic of Germany, or other countries where it performs a circus somersault and returns to our shores converted into loans.

13. Agustín Cueva, *El desarrollo.*

14. Ibid.

15. United Nations, ECLA, *El desarrollo económico.*

16. UNCTAD, *The Marketing and Distribution System for Bananas,* December 1974.

17. "Reflexiones sobre la desnutrición en México," *Comercio Exterior,* Banco Nacional de Comercio Exterior, S.A., vol. 28, no. 2 (México), February 1978.

18. Roger Burbach and Patricia Flynn, "Agribusiness Targets Latin America," *NACLA Report,* vol. 13, no. I (New York), January-February 1978.

19. Ibid.

20. Data from trade union and journalism sources published in *Uruguay Informations,* nos. 21 and 25 (Paris).

21. United Nations, ECLA, *El desarrollo económico.*

22. Ibid.

23. *ILO, Empleo, crecimiento y necesidades esenciales* (Geneva, 1976).

24. United Nations, ECLA, *El desarrollo económico.*

25. In Uruguay the inquisitors have modernized themselves: an odd mixture of Middle Ages and capitalist business sense. The military don't burn books: now they sell them to paper factories, which shred and convert them into pulp for return to the consumer market. It isn't true that Marx is not available to the public. True, not in the form of books, but in the form of paper napkins.

26. Press conference of President Aparicio Méndez, 21 May 1977 in Paysandú. "We are saving the country from the tragedy of political passion," said the President. "Good folk don't talk about dictatorships, don't think about dictatorships, and don't claim human rights."

INDEX

Abbink, John, 241
Abercromby, Ralph, 174
Acevedo, Manuel Antonio, 184
ADELA (investment consortium), 233-34
Africa, 15, 28. *See also* Slave trade
Agency for International Development (AID), 221, 230
Agrarian reform: Artigas uprising, 115-20; Guatemala, 113-15; Paraguay, 195; Zapata, 120-25
Agricultural products, 59-133. *See also specific products*
Aguilar, Alonso, 125, 180, 216*n*
Alamán, Lucas, 37, 179-82
Allende, Salvador, 130, 144, 145, 272-73, 274
Alliance for Progress, 5, 7, 127, 152, 228, 230, 231, 233
Aluminum, 134, 137, 145. *See also* Bauxite
Aluminum Company of America (Alcoa), 137
Alvarado, Pedro de, 16, 18, 19
Alvim, Panasco, 195
Amado, Jorge, 93*n*
Amazonia. *See* Brazil
American Coffee Corporation, 96
American Cordage Trust, 121
American Smelting and Refining, 146, 147
Amin, Samir, 239
Anaconda (Wire and Cable), 144, 146, 147
ANCAP (Uruguayan state refinery), 160-61
Andean Group, 244
Anderson, Clayton and Company, 95, 96, 125
Angola, 54
Animal products, 69, 176, 177, 178, 184
Antilles, 15, 28, 38, 62, 86
Arabs, 12, 25
Arbenz Guzmán, Jacobo, 113, 114
Arévalo, Juan José, 113
Argentina, 4, 32, 43, 48, 48*n*, 61, 128-30, 188, 193-94,199, 210, 226, 246, 271, 275; American aid to, 273;

censorship, 284; civil wars, 182-86; disappearance in, 276; foreign capital, 218; importation of technology, 278; industrial output, 208; nineteenth century British relations, 177-78, 185; petroleum, 136, 162; repression in, 283; strikes, 285; textiles, 177; wages and prices, 279; wheat, 95
Artigas, José, 115-20, 124, 184, 186, 259
Atahualpa, 17, 19
Atlantic Oil Company, 161
Aztecs, 18-20, 43-44

Bagú, Sergio, 44, 79
Bahamas, 11
Bairoch, Paul, 127
Balaguer, Joaquín, 78*n*
Ball, George W., 5
Balmaceda, Jose Manuel, 142
Bananas, 94, 100, 107; "bananization," 108-11
Bandeira, Manuel, 136
Bank for International Development, 273
Banking: international, 223-36
Bank of England, 198
Banzer, Hugo, 271
Baran, Paul, 29-30, 226
Barba, Alvaro Alonso, 32-33
Barbados, 59, 60, 62, 65, 82
Barbosa, Horta, 161
Barrientos, René, 136
Batista, Fulgencio, 70, 75, 77, 136
Bauxite, 134, 136, 137. *See also* Aluminum
Beet sugar, 71
Belaunde Terry, Fernando, 136
Belgium, 6
Betancourt, Rómulo, 169
Bethlehem Steel Company, 57, 135, 153-54, 156
Birth control. *See* Family planning
Black, Eugene, 235
Blacks, 28-31, 38; Brazil, 52-55; cotton plantations, 94; religion in Brazil, 86; sugar plantations, 59-60, 65-67. *See also* Slaves; Slave trade
Blood: as commodity, 270
Bolívar, Simón, 116, 252, 261
Bolivia, 6, 22-23, 32, 42, 88*n*, 188, 251*n*, 269-70, 272; agrarian reform, 130; debt, 277; labor exploitation, 277; minerals, 136; mining industry, 147-53; nitrates, 140; petroleum, 163-65; textiles, 176
Bonaparte, Napoleon, 66, 173
Bonaparte, Pauline, 66
Bosch, Juan, 78*n*
Botí, Regino, 73
Bourgeoisie: national capital participation of, 242; role in Latin America of, 208-14, 222
Brazil, 3, 4, 6, 38, 43, 178, 192, 193-94, 206, 207, 208, 210, 211, 212-13, 222-23, 224, 225, 226, 229, 231-32, 272; African cults, 86; agrarian reform, 128; agricultural exports, 280; cacao, 92-94; coffee, 96-98, 240, 280; cotton, 94-96; debt, 276-77; first Portuguese communities, 16; food costs, 64; foreign capital, 215-19; fruit plantations, 61; gold, 49, 56, 137, 202; importation of technology, 278; Indians, 49; iron, 153-56; mining, 52-55; nineteenth century British relations, 178, 193-94, 199-200; petroleum, 161-62; rubber, 61, 87-91; slavery, 52-55, 86; soil ravagement, 61-65; sugar, 60-62; textiles, 178; U.S. control of

minerals, 135-39, 153-54; Volkswagen production in, 269-70; wages and prices, 279-80
Brecht, Bertolt, 274
Britain. *See* England
British Petroleum (Anglo-Iranian), 158
Brizola, Leonel, 154
Bueno do Prado, Bartolomeu, 84
Butler, Smedley D., 108

Cacao (chocolate), 31, 61, 79, 80, 91-94, 166
Cairú, Viscount de, 202
Caldera, Rafael, 169
Calderón, Francisco García, 90*n*
Calvinism, 24
Cámpora, Héctor, 272
Campos, Roberto, 212, 220*n*, 225, 228
Canada, 95
Canary Islands, 59
Canning, George, 173
Capital: import and export, 225-27. *See also* Banking; Direct foreign investments; Loans
Capoche, Luis, 39, 40
Caracas (Venezuela), 61, 91
Carca Indians, 47
Cárdenas, Lázaro, 124, 125, 159-60, 210, 211
Cardoso, Fernando Henrique, 213
Cardozo, Efraím, 192
Carpentier, Alejo, 66*n*
Carranza, Venustiano, 123, 124
Carter, Jimmy, 273
Castillo Armas, Rodolfo, 113, 114
Castro, Fidel, 72, 73, 74, 76, 236
Castro, Josué de, 4
Catholicism. *See* Roman Catholicism
Cattle, 65, 91
Censorship, 284
Central America: effects of world market on, 105-7; fruit plantations, 61, 100. *See also specific countries*
Central American Common Market, 258
Central Intelligence Agency (CIA), 136-37, 272
Cepeda Samudio, Alvaro, 109*n*
Cervantes Saavedra, Miguel de, 26-27
Ceylon, 89
Chaco War, 163
Charles II, 39, 80
Charles III, 47
Charles V, 24, 25, 26, 79, 83
Charruas Indians, 47-48
Chateaubriand, René, 197
Chile, 3, 6, 32, 42, 178, 211*n*; agrarian reform, 130; American aid to Pinochet, 273; copper, 136, 141, 144-47, 174; debt, 278-79; nitrates, 140-43; Pinochet dictatorship, 270-71, 285; poverty, 282; relations with England, 178-79; repression in, 283; textiles, 176; wages and prices, 279
China, 23
Chocolate. *See* Cacao
Chrome, 134, 137
CIA, 136-37, 272
Cigars, 176, 177
Citibank, 277
Cities: population growth, 284; poverty in, 248-49
Class: role of national bourgeoisie, 208-15, 224; terrorism and state and, 274-75. *See also* Labor
Coca (cocaine), 47, 151, 152
Cochineal, 105
Coffee, 61, 79, 80, 88, 209; Brazil, 96, 97-99, 174, 240, 282; prices, 99-102
Colbert, Jean-Baptiste, 24, 79

Colombia, 42, 48, 100, 211*n*, 260; civil war, 102-5; coffee, 98-99, 102; labor market and unemployment, 105; petroleum, 242; poverty, 282
Columbus, Christopher, 11, 12, 13-14, 15, 48, 59
Columbus, Diego, 83
Commodities: transport and delivery system, 260-61
Commodity fetishism: as symbol of power, 271
Common Market, 240
Copper, 1, 134; Chile, 136, 141, 144-47, 178
Cortés, Hernán, 8, 13, 14, 15, 16, 18-19, 42, 43, 122
Costa Rica, 97; bananas, 106
Cotton, 61, 79, 80, 94-96, 97
Creole Oil Company, 169
Crowder, Enoch, 70
Cruz, Artemio, 125-26
Cuba, 2, 15*n*, 54*n*, 270, 280; African cults, 86; changes in economy, 74-78; education, 73; minerals, 72; nickel, 136; petroleum, 159; revolution, 72, 76, 159, 224, 234; slave revolts, 84-85; sugar, 67-78
Currency: disposal by multinational corporations of, 242
Cuzco (Peru), 19, 20, 44, 47

Dantas, Maneca, 93
Davis, Arthur, 137*n*
Debt: Latin American external, 276-77
Diamonds, 94, 130, 137; Minas Gerais, 54-55, 56; smuggling, 138
Díaz, Porfirio, 120-21, 122
Díaz del Castillo, Bernal, 13
Direct foreign investments, 215-19, 276; International Monetary Fund, 220-23
Disease, 18, 37, 46-47, 49, 50, 54, 58, 63, 87, 90, 98, 152
Dominican Republic, 59, 61, 65, 77-78, 83; U.S. Marines, 108
Dos Passos, John, 109
Dow Chemical, 215
Dulles, Allen, 74, 113
Dulles, John Foster, 114
Dumont, René, 15*n*, 48, 64
Dutra, Eurico, 135
Duvalier, Francois, 275

Economic Mission for Latin America (ECLA). *See* United Nations
Ecuador, 6, 42, 100; agrarian reform, 128; bananas, 61, 110; cacao, 94; poverty, 282
Education: Cuba, 73; higher, 245
Eisenhower, Dwight D., 6, 113, 159
Eisenhower, Milton, 211
Electric Bond and Share, 206, 234, 235
Eliécer Gaitán, Jorge, 103
Elizabeth I, 26, 80
El Salvador, 6, 97, 98, 107, 111
Emerson, Ralph Waldo, 203
Emmanuel, Arghiri, 238
Engels, Frederick, 38
England, 6; Brazilian gold, 55-57; cacao, 93-94; coffee, 105; commerce with Latin America, 173-75; cotton, 94; exports, 26, 177-78; Industrial Revolution, 173-74; industry, 60, 173-79; loans to Latin America, 197-200; Methuen Treaty, 55; nineenth century Argentine relations, 174-78, 185; nineteenth century Brazilian relations, 178, 193-94, 199-200; protectionism, 200-4; slave trade, 79-82
Estrada Palma, Tomás, 72
Export-Import Bank (Eximbank), 228,

229
External debt, 276-77
Exxon. *See* Standard Oil of New Jersey

Family planning, 5, 138
Ferdinand (King of Aragon), 12, 25
Ferré, Pedro, 184
Ferreira Machado, Simão, 52
Firestone, 270
Flores, Edmundo, 125
Ford, Henry, II, 253
Ford Foundation, 6
Foreign aid: United States, 227-36
Foreign capital. *See* Direct foreign investments
Foreign investments. *See* Direct foreign investments
Fortune, 254
Fraginals, Manuel Moreno, 67
France, 4, 28, 60, 136
Francia, Gaspar Rodríguez de, 188-89
Francisco Sugar Company, 74
Franco, Francisco, 25
Frank, Andre Gunder, 31-32, 250
Free trade and protectionism, 179-82, 200-4; IMF and, 220-23; market inequality and, 237-43; nineteenth century, 175-82
Frei, Eduardo, 130
Fuentes, Carlos, 125-26
Fuentes, Miguel Ydígoras, 77, 231
Furtado, Celso, 30, 56, 198, 241

García, Antonio, 242
García, Gregorio, 41
Garmendia, Salvador, 170
General Agreement on Tariffs and Trade (GATT), 239
General Motors, 276
Ginés de Sepúlveda, Juan, 41
Gold, 1, 11, 13, 14, 15, 18-20, 24, 29, 37, 60, 144; Brazilian, 49, 56, 130, 137; Mexican exports, 36; Minas Gerais, 51-58; Nicaraguan, 47
Gómez, Juan Vicente, 168
Good Neighbor policy, 110-11
Goodyear, Charles, 88
Gordon, Lincoln, 272
Goulart, Jango, 272
Goulart, João, 135, 212, 217
Grant, Ulysses S., 200, 204
Great Britain. *See* England
Guadeloupe, 59, 65
Guanajuato (Mexico), 36-37, 60
Guano, 139-41, 174. *See also* Nitrates
Guaraní Indians, 190*n*
Guatemala, 7, 19, 77, 112, 206, 231; agricultural exports, 280; bananas, 106, 108; coffee, 97, 98; cotton, 95; Indians, 50; years of violence, 113-15
Guevara, Ernesto Che, 70, 78, 124, 136
Guinea, 83
Gulf Oil Company, 158, 163-64, 166, 168, 268
Guyana (British Guiana), 136-37
Gypsum, 137

Haiti, 2, 6, 12-13, 15, 59, 60, 65, 108; coffee, 97, 98; poverty, 275; revolution, 66; slave settlement, 83; voodoo, 86
Hamilton, Alexander, 202
Hancock, Thomas, 88
Hanna Mining Company, 57, 135, 154-56
Harvey, Robert, 141
Hawkins, John, 80
Hearst, William Randolph, 121*n*
Hematite, 137

Hemo Caribbean, 270
Henequen, 61, 121
Henry VIII, 26
Hernández Martínez, Maximiliano, 110, 111-12
Hidalgo, Miguel, 46, 116, 120
Hides, 174, 186
Holland, 56; cacao, 94; Dutch Guiana, 83-84; industry, 60; slave revolts, 83-84; slave trade, 56, 62, 80
Holy Inquisition, 12, 24
Homestead Act (1862), 131
Honduras, 106, 107, 108, 110; poverty, 282
Huayna Cápaj, 21
Huerta, Victoriano, 122-23
Humboldt, Alexander von, 8, 31, 36-37, 45, 175, 180
Humphrey, George, 154

IMF. *See* International Monetary Fund
Imperialism: early twentieth century nature of, 205; foreign banking, 223-27; International Monetary Fund, 220-23; role of national bourgeoisie, 215-19, 222; technocracy, 227-36; technology and, 243-47
Incas, 15, 16, 17, 21, 42, 43, 44
Indians, 30, 31, 32, 33, 38-50, 98, 111; Peru, 116; Veracruz, 19. *See also* specific Indians
Indigo, 91, 102, 105, 133
Indonesia, 28
Industrialization: labor force, 247-51; and market inequality, 237-43
Industrial Revolution, 173-74
Inquisition. *See* Holy Inquisition
Inter-American Committee for Agricultural Development, 96
Inter-American Development Bank (IDB), 152, 160, 228, 229-30
International Bank for Reconstruction and Development (IBRD), 228
International Coffee Agreement, 100
International Labor Organization (ILO), 282
International Monetary Fund (IMF), 7, 209, 219-23, 273, 277. *See also* World Bank
International Telephone and Telegraph (ITT), 206, 233*n*
Investments. *See* Direct foreign investments
Iron, 1, 57, 134, 135, 153-56
Isabella (Queen of Castile), 12, 16, 25

Jagan, Cheddi, 136
Jamaica, 14, 59, 66, 82
James, William, 108
Japan, 6, 11
Jesuit missions, 190
Jesus, Maria Carolina de, 281-83
Jews, 12, 18, 25, 41
Johnson, Lyndon B., 6, 78*n*, 136, 155, 195, 228, 231

Keith, Minor, 109
Kennecott Wire and Cable Company, 144, 145
Kennedy, John F., 226*n*
Kirkland, Edward, 201
Kissinger, Henry, 272
Kruel, Riograndino, 138-39

Labor: exploitation, 277; labor force, 247-57; miners, 147-53; prices and wages, 279-81; strikes, 285
Lacerda, Carlos, 231
Lane, Arthur Bliss, 111
Language: and political discourse, 266

Latin American Free Trade Area (LAFTA), 252-58
Lead, 136
Leeward Islands, 65, 66
Lenin, V.I., 205, 226
Letelier, Orlando, 272-73
Lisboa, Antonio Francisco (Aleijadinho), 57-58
List, Friedrich, 179
Loans, 227-29, 232, 234-35; railroads and, 197-200. *See also* Banking
López, Carlos Antonio, 189
López, Francisco Solano, 189, 192, 193
Louis XIV, 79

McCloy, John J., 235
McKinley, William, 71-72
McNamara, Robert, 5, 273
Magellan, Ferdinand, 14, 16
Magnetite, 137
Malaria, 50, 87
Malaya, 89
Manganese, 134, 135, 154
Mann, Thomas, 231
Mariátegui, José Carlos, 95, 140, 141
Market: cheap labor for, 275; industrialization and inequality of, 237-43; monopoly capital and, 267-68; prices and wages, 279-81
Martí, José, 69, 70
Marx, Karl, 28, 65, 180
Mayas, 17, 18, 43, 48, 50, 121
Meat industry, 1, 65, 68, 69
Médicis, Lorenzo de, 14
Melchor de Jovellanos, Gaspar, 118
Melville, Thomas, 114
Méndez Montenegro, Julio César, 112
Mercury, 32, 39, 40, 137
Mexico, 4, 13, 14, 15, 32, 38, 36-37, 41, 46, 48, 116, 208, 210, 226; agrarian reform, 120; agricultural exports, 280; cotton, 94, 95, 96; debt, 276-77; foreign capital, 218-19; importation of technology, 278; petroleum, 159-60; poverty, 282; sulphur, 136*n;* textiles, 175, 181-82
Middle East, 157
Minas Gerais (Brazil), 51, 52, 55, 56, 57, 135-36, 154, 155
Minerals: mining industry, 147-53; United States need for, 134-35, 137-38. *See also specific minerals*
Mitre, Bartolomé, 191, 192, 193
Molybdenum, 145
Montezuma, 15, 17, 18, 19
Montoneros, 182-87
Morelos, José María, 46, 116
Moscoso, Teodoro, 231

National City Bank, 108, 196
National Sugar Refining Company, 77*n*
Natural gas, 156
Netherlands. *See* Holland
New York Times, 148*n*
Nicaragua, 47, 95, 107, 110, 270
Nickel, 75, 134, 136
Nieto Arteta, Luis Eduardo, 102, 104
Niobium, 139
Nitrates, 3, 139-44, 174. *See also* guano
Nixon, Richard M., 3, 5, 229
North, John Thomas, 141, 142

OAS. *See* Organization of American States
Oil. *See* Petroleum
Onganía, Juan Carlos, 128-29
Open Veins of Latin America: aftermath of publication, 267
Opium War, 194
Organization of American States (OAS),

3, 78, 113, 114, 206, 223, 229, 230-31

Ouro Preto (Brazil), 51, 55, 60

Ovando, Alfredo, 163, 164

Palmer, Bruce, 77

Panama, 107, 108, 109, 270; debt, 277

Pan-American Coffee Bureau, 99*n*

Paraguay, 6, 42, 61, 118; cotton, 95; move for independence, 188-97; petroleum, 163

Parsons and Whittemore, 270

Patents, 244

Patiño, Antenor, 148

Patiño, Simon Ituri, 147

Patman, Wright, 243

Pearls, 11-12, 14

Pedro II, 93, 195

Pemex (Petróleos Mexicanos), 160

Peñaloza, "El Chacho," 187

Pepina y Pibernat, Juan, 85

Pepper, 12, 14

Pérez Alfonso, Juan Pablo, 269

Pérez de Holguin, Melchor, 33

Pérez Jiménez, Marcos, 169

Perón, Juan Domingo, 129, 162, 210-11, 273

Peru, 6, 20, 31, 32, 45, 269, 279; cotton, 95-96; debt, 277; guano, 139-40; Indians, 115; minerals, 136; nitrates, 139-44, 175; petroleum, 136; poverty, 282; sugar, 59, 61; textiles, 175-76

Petrobras, 161-62

Petroleos de Venezuela, 268

Petroleum, 1, 3, 96, 156-70, 270; Argentina, 136, 162; Bolivia, 163-64; Brazil, 161-62; Colombia, 160, 242; Cuba, 159; Mexico, 160-61; Middle East, 157; Paraguay, 163; Peru, 136; United States, 157-69, 217-18, 243; Uruguay, 160-61; Venezuela, 92, 136, 157, 159, 165-70

Philippines, 23, 71

Philip II, 24, 25, 26, 38

Philip III, 39

Philip IV, 27, 39

Pinochet, Augusto, 270-71, 273, 274, 285

Pizarro, Francisco, 15, 16, 19, 20, 35, 45

Plan de Ayala, 122-23

Plasmaféresis, 272

Polo, Marco, 11-12

Portugal, 15, 29, 38, 56, 61, 84, 117, 132; Methuen Treaty, 55; slave trade, 79

Potosí (Bolivia), 14, 20-22, 46, 53, 56, 60, 140, 166; coca, 47; development, 20-22; Indians, 39-40; ruin of, 31-37

Poverty: statistics, 282; urban, 250-51

Prebisch, Raú, 246, 254-55

Prices: wages and, 279-81

Priestley, J.B., 88

Protectionism. *See* Free trade and protectionism

Protestantism, 25

Puerto Rico, 59, 65, 71

Pyrochlore, 139

Quadros, Jânio, 135

Quinine, 102

Railroads, 199-202

Raleigh, Walter, 14

Reader's Digest, 105*n,* 112

Repression: endemic nature of, 283-84

Restrepo, Lleras, 99

Ribeiro, Darcy, 18, 44, 131, 279

Rockefeller, David, 232

Rockefeller, Nelson, 159, 229
Rockefeller, Peggy, 232-33
Rockefeller family: Foundation, 6; oil interests, 158, 215
Rodríguez de Campomames, Pedro, 118
Roman Catholicism, 12, 25, 30, 31; in Brazil, 53, 86; fees, 67; land ownership in Mexico, 31; Mayan religion and, 50; Potosí, 33-35
Roosevelt, Theodore, 107
Rosas, Juan Manuel de, 185-86, 191
Royal African Company, 80
Royal Dutch/Shell. *See* Shell Oil Company
Rubber, 3, 49, 61, 86, 87-91

Salt, 12, 29
Saltpeter, 139
Sandino, Augusto César, 110-11
San Salvador, 13
Santo Domingo (Dominican Republic), 59, 61, 65, 78, 83
Sanz de Santamaría, Carlos, 228
Sarmiento, Domingo Faustino, 187
Sartre, Jean-Paul, 73
Schilling, Paulo, 128
Schnerb, Robert, 198
Shell Oil Company, 157-60, 166, 268
Shipping, 260-61
Silver, 29; Amazonian, 137; Andean *altiplano,* 15; Bolivian, 14, 20-22, 32, 33, 34, 36, 39, 40, 44, 136, 145; German, 36; Mexican, 14-15, 22, 37
Slaves, 30, 31, 34, 38, 48, 52, 53-54; Central America, 107; cotton plantations, 94; revolts, 83; sugar plantations, 59, 60, 61, 66, 67, 79
Slave trade, 28; Angola-Brazil, 54; Dutch, 56, 62, 80; English, 56, 79-82, 174; French, 28; Guinea-Brazil, 54; sugar plantation, 79; United States, 202
Smith, Adam, 79, 180
Smith, Earl, 72
Smith, Walter Bedell, 113
Solano López, Francisco, 189, 192, 193, 194, 195
Somoza, Anastasio, 110-11, 270
South Sea Company, 80
Soviet Union, 75*n,* 159, 160, 209
Spain, 12, 15, 22-28, 29, 115, 132
Spices, 12, 14
Standard Oil of California, 158, 162
Standard Oil of New Jersey (Exxon), 136, 157-61, 162, 165-66, 168, 268
Standard Oil of New York (Mobil), 158
State: terrorism and, 274-75
Strikes, 285
Stroessner, Alfredo, 194, 195, 196
Sugar, 3, 29, 109; Brazil, 50, 52, 54, 56, 61-65, 130; Caribbean, 65-67; Cuba, 67-78, 176; development, 59-61; "sugar islands," 65
Sulphur, 136*n*
Sweezy, Paul, 226, 267

Taft, William H., 107
Tantalite, 137, 139
Taxes, 1, 157, 165, 168, 174, 239
Technocrats, 227-37
Technology: dependency, 277-78; foreign ownership and control, 243-47
Tenochtitlán, 19, 44
Terrorism: state and class and, 274-75; in system of repression, 283-84
Texaco, 158, 161, 166
Textiles, 175-78, 201, 239
Thorium, 137, 138
Thornton, Edward, 191, 192
Timber, 51, 68

Tin, 33, 147-52

Tires, 88

Titanium, 137

Tobacco, 54, 68, 67, 79, 91, 102

Torres, Juan José, 274

Torture, 283-84

Toussaint L'Ouverture, 66

Transport system: for commodities, 250-61

Trías, Vivian, 186

Trinidad-Tobago, 65, 174

Triple Alliance, 188, 195, 197, 200

Tupac Amaru, 44-45

Turner, John Kenneth, 121

Ubico Castañeda, Jorge, 110, 112-13, 114

Underdevelopment, 245, 285

Union Carbide, 217

United Fruit Company, 100, 106, 108-10, 206

United Nations, 3; Economic Mission for Latin America (ECLA), 93, 101, 207, 216, 251*n*, 278; Food and Agriculture Organization (FAO), 64; UNESCO, 73

United States, 4-8, 49, 261; cacao, 93; and Central America, 107-10, 113-14; CIA, 136-37; coffee, 100-101, 105, 110; cotton, 95; and Cuba, 70-75, 77; family planning, 5; foreign aid, 228-29; foreign banking, 223-27; and Haiti, 66; industrial development, 202-4; investments, 205-10, 218-19, 276; and LAFTA, 252-58; Latin American interventions, 272-73; Marine Corps, 77, 111, 123; and Mexico, 121; mineral imports, 134-38, 144-46, 149, 153-56; mineral need, 134-35, 137-38; petroleum, 157-69; protectionism, 200-4; railroads, 106; shipping, 202-3; slavery, 79; technology investment and development, 245; textiles, 202-3; westward expansion, 131-32

U.S. Steel, 91, 153

Uranium, 139

Uruguay, 6-7, 48, 128, 188, 191, 211, 230*n;* agrarian reform, 117-20; debt, 276-77; military and police budget, 271; petroleum, 160-61; repression in, 283, 284; rice, 95; wages and prices, 279

Varela, Felipe, 184

Vargas, Getulio, 99, 154, 210-13, 216*n*

Velasco Alvarado, Juan, 95, 136, 164, 220*n*, 269

Venezuela, 6, 14, 31; agrarian reform, 128; cacao, 91; imports, 268-69; Indians, 49; iron, 153-56; nationalization of oil, 268; petroleum, 91, 136, 157, 159, 165-70

Vespucci, Amerigo, 14

Videla, Jorge, 273, 275, 276

Vietnam, 6

Villa, Francisco ("Pancho"), 123

Vinhas de Queiroz, Mauricio, 216

Volkswagen: Brazilian production, 267-68, 279

Wages, 250, 251; prices and, 279-81

Walker, William, 107

Walsh, Rodolfo, 276

War of the Triple Alliance, 188-97

Washington, George, 203

Washington Post, 115

Watt, James, 81, 94

Webb, James Watson, 178

West Germany, 4, 93

West Indies, 65
Wickham, Henry, 89
Wilhelm (Kaiser), 274
Wilson, Henry Lane, 123
Wilson, Woodrow, 2
Wood, Leonard, 71
Woods, George D., 235
Working class. *See* Class; Labor
World Bank, 5-6, 221, 235-36, 239, 273. *See also* International Monetary Fund
World Coffee Information Center, 100
World Market, 237-43

Yaqui Indians, 48, 61, 121
Yucatán (Mexico), 48, 61, 121

Zander, Arnold, 136
Zapata, Emiliano, 120, 122-24
Zavala, Maza, 126
Zavaleta, René, 163
Zinc, 134, 136, 137
Zuazo, Alonso, 83
Zumbi (Indian chief), 84